CRIME AND PUNISHMENT

—— IN THE ——

RUSSIAN REVOLUTION

CRIME AND PUNISHMENT

—— IN THE ——

RUSSIAN REVOLUTION

Mob Justice and Police in Petrograd

Tsuyoshi Hasegawa

The Belknap Press of
Harvard University Press
Cambridge, Massachusetts
London, England
2017

Library of Congress Cataloging-in-Publication Data
Names: Hasegawa, Tsuyoshi, 1941– author.
Title: Crime and punishment in the Russian revolution : mob justice and police
    in Petrograd / Tsuyoshi Hasegawa.
Description: Cambridge, Massachusetts : The Belknap Press of Harvard
    University Press, 2017. | Includes bibliographical references and index.
Identifiers: LCCN 2017010883 | ISBN 9780674972063 (hardcover : alk. paper)
Subjects: LCSH: Crime—Russia (Federation)—Saint Petersburg—History—20th century. |
    Law enforcement—Russia (Federation)—Saint Petersburg—History—20th century. |
    Police—Russia (Federation)—Saint Petersburg—History—20th century. | Saint Petersburg
    (Russia)—History—Revolution, 1917–1921. | Russia (Federation)—History—Revolution,
    1917–1921.
Classification: LCC HV7015.15.Z8 H37 2017 | DDC 364.947/2109041—dc23
LC record available at https://lccn.loc.gov/2017010883

To Debbie and Kenneth

It was a terrible bequest,
Still fresh in its commemoration.
There's nothing, friends, for me to add,
You'll learn it all from my narration.
The tale I tell you will be sad.

—Pushkin, *"The Bronze Horseman"*

CONTENTS

Note on Calendar and Transliteration xi
Introduction 1
1 Prelude to Revolution 17
2 Crime on the Rise 37
3 Why Did the Crime Rate Shoot Up? 68
4 Militias Rise and Fall 109
5 An Epidemic of Mob Justice 167
6 Crime after the Bolshevik Takeover 192
7 The Bolsheviks and the Militia 228
Conclusion 260
Abbreviations 279
Notes 281
Bibliography 323
Acknowledgments 339
Index 343

NOTE ON CALENDAR AND TRANSLITERATION

Throughout the text, I use the Julian calendar. The Bolshevik regime switched from the Julian calendar to the Gregorian calendar in February 1918. When both dates are used after February 1918, I note the date according to the Julian calendar followed by the date according to the Gregorian calendar—for instance, March 1 (14), 1917.

As for Russian terms and names, I use a slightly modified version of the Library of Congress transliteration system. For names and terms familiar in English, however, I use the generally accepted form, such as Nicholas II rather than Nikolai II. Soft signs in Russian words are omitted in the text but retained in the notes.

CRIME AND PUNISHMENT

—— IN THE ——

RUSSIAN REVOLUTION

Introduction

On March 4, 1917, Russia was reborn. The February Revolution was over. Tsar Nicholas II had abdicated, bringing to a close the despised monarchy. A new provisional government was formed to replace the old regime. People from all walks of life poured into the streets of Petrograd, the capital of the empire. Giddy with happiness, total strangers greeted each other as if it were Easter—only, instead of "Christ is risen," they shouted, "Autocracy has fallen!"[1]

One year later, the Bolsheviks were in power. On the anniversary of the February Revolution, there were no celebrations in Petrograd. No demonstrations, no banners, and no speeches. Streets were deserted. Anyone out beneath the gray, oppressive sky hurried home in the silence of an especially cold and wet winter. They buried their heads in the collars of their overcoats and drew their hats over their eyes, the better to avoid seeing the world around them.[2]

How could the hopes of March 1917 have turned so quickly into bitter disillusion? The answer lies in the catastrophic social breakdown that followed the February Revolution. The Provisional Government dismantled the criminal justice system but could not adequately replace it. In Petrograd, crime spiked, begetting more, and more intensely violent, crime. Pickpockets became muggers. Robbers became murderers. People believed that merchants were taking advantage of shortages and economic decline to soak a population already suffering from rationing and deprivation. Thirsting for the order and security that political authorities could not provide, crowds turned to mob justice.

Thirsting for liquor to salve their woes, they tore the city apart in search of the wine and vodka that fueled increasingly destructive pogroms.

To understand this wrenching transformation, this book examines three issues: the breakdown of the police after the February Revolution, the consequent rise in crime, and the reaction of ordinary people. I look first at the eight months from March to October under the Provisional Government, and then at the five months under the Bolshevik regime between the October Revolution and the relocation of the state government from Petrograd to Moscow. I focus on Petrograd because it was the epicenter of the Russian Revolution, and as such, what happened there had significant impact on other regions of the empire.

This yields novel insights. Other historians have done valuable work by analyzing the failure of the Provisional Government and the Bolshevik ascent through the lenses of elite politics and social movements. These approaches prioritize the intentions and actions of politicians, intellectuals, and organized groups of articulate ideological partisans seeking to impress their visions on society. But they tend to ignore the great mass of the people, for whom grand ideas were much less important than day-to-day survival. Shifting the focus to the population enriches the narrative of the Russian Revolution and awakens us to the contingent forces that underlay the development of a Soviet state that is too often understood as a product exclusively of ideals and strategic politics.

I make two principal arguments. First, the erosion of police, rising crime, and the catastrophic breakdown of everyday life in the city after the February Revolution helped to emasculate the Provisional Government. People were forced to live in fear for their lives and property, and they reacted with sporadic explosions of mob justice, which facilitated further chaos. With the courts in disarray and the militia rendered ineffective, brute violence became the common means to settle conflicts. The bedlam in Petrograd became a defining influence on the decision making of the Provisional Government, which responded with vain attempts to centralize power in ways that defied the "centrifugal" spirit of a revolution that diffused power to the lowest rungs of society. The resulting breakdown of social order created conditions the Bolsheviks exploited.

Second, the extent and intensity of crime and social breakdown nurture a fresh understanding of the emergence of a new kind of authoritarian dictatorship under the Bolshevik regime. Violent crime and mob justice continued to rise after the Bolsheviks seized power, and the Bolsheviks were unprepared to cope. Indeed, they were largely indifferent, presuming that the establishment of their socialist utopia would bring an end to crime. But November and December brought explosive alcohol pogroms that could not be ignored. In response, the Bolsheviks turned to a variety of criminal justice methods reminiscent of those that had failed under the Provisional Government. They failed once again. The regime then turned to the Cheka, the extralegal secret police concerned with counterrevolutionary opposition, as its standard law-enforcement arm.

Thus was unrestrained violence brought upon ordinary people in the name of preserving not just social peace but also socialism and the Soviet state. This scheme would prevail for decades to come. Again, ideology and political exigency are important sources of the Soviet system, but they are accompanied by another: the contingent factor of social breakdown caused by crime and mob justice and the state's ad hoc responses to it. By attending to crime and policing under the early Bolshevik power, we can better explain how the regime created a new kind of authoritarian state. For the Soviet Union was not only protecting an obstinate power center à la traditional monarchy but was also committed to enforcing ideological conformity at the lowest level of society through extreme repression. This totalitarian approach was anti-thetical to the decentralizing aims of the revolution the Bolshe-viks inherited. It is a legacy of the daily mayhem that revolution wrought in its first year.

Historiography of the Russian Revolution

Interpretations of historical events shift in response to the con-cerns and needs of the contexts in which they are analyzed. In the case of the Russian Revolution, the resulting debates have been especially divisive, contentious, and emotionally charged because they touch on the nature of the Soviet Union itself. There is much at stake in the interpretations put forth.

Rex Wade, surveying the historiography of the Russian Revo-lution on the eve of its centennial, sees four major trends in English-language histories of the Russian Revolution.[3] Until the mid-1960s, these works were mainly concerned with political history. They emphasized political parties and their leaders and ideologies. They focused on the questions of why the Bolsheviks succeeded in seizing power and why the liberal-democratic revo-lution promoted by the Provisional Government failed.

In the 1970s and early 1980s, social history emerged as the dominant trend, significantly changing the historiographical landscape. Social historians wrote the history of the revolution from the bottom up, paying special attention to the masses, espe-cially factory workers, peasants, and soldiers. These historians challenged the prevailing liberal view that the Bolshevik revolu-tion was a coup engineered by unscrupulous activists led by Lenin, who manipulated the uneducated, ignorant masses with demagoguery. Social historians revealed that behind the Bol-shevik revolution were powerful mass movements. The masses were not ignorant, uneducated pawns of political leaders but active agents of the revolution who articulated demands and took action.[4] The October Revolution was thus a genuine revolution, not a coup, expressing the aspirations of the people. Social history continues to this day, and my study could be understood as a form of it.[5] However, as I will make clear, my book departs from earlier social history in significant ways.

Another new method emerged in the 1990s, stimulated by the era's linguistic and cultural turns among American and European historians more generally. Historians began to focus on language, symbols, and rituals. They examined "how language and symbols were developed and utilized to analyze events, shape group identities, define power relations, mark off who is 'us' and who 'them,' and help achieve political, economic, or cultural goals."[6] In the Russian context, historians closely analyzed the proliferation and use of new terms such as *burzhui* (from "bourgeoisie"), "comrades," "equality," "freedom," and "democracy." They paid attention to visual and aural symbols—banners, armbands, posters, clothing, revolutionary songs, slogans, and so on—and rituals. The linguistic and cultural turns further contributed to shifting definitions of social groups, as historians left behind rigid identifications based on "the relations of production" and adopted in their place "discursive ones." These historians became more concerned about how people "identified" themselves in relation to others.[7]

At the start of the twenty-first century, prompted by contemporary nationalism and ethnic violence, historians have begun to write "across the revolutionary divide" by placing the revolution in its global context. They often write within the more encompassing time line of 1914–1922, embracing World War I, the Russian Revolution, and the subsequent civil war. The new breed of historians sees the Russian Revolution as a transitional period between world war and civil war. They pay special attention to mobilization, nationalism, and ethnic violence and establish a comparative framework across nations participating in the turbulent years of war and revolution. The trend may be best exemplified by Russia's Great War and Revolution, an ambitious multivolume project spanning continents and employing the efforts of dozens of scholars.[8]

Soviet and Russian historians have traveled along a different trajectory. Despite the ideological straitjacket imposed on them, Soviet historians, especially the Leningrad school of historians, began publishing important scholarly works and collections of documents in the 1960s.[9] They subsequently and gingerly made contact with Western historians and discovered shared interests in the role of mass movements in the revolution. The loosening of censorship under perestroika opened up previously forbidden areas of research such as the study of non-Bolshevik socialists and the Provisional Government. Since the collapse of the Soviet Union, there has been an outpouring of scholarly activity. Russian historians are now emancipated from earlier ideological constraints and freely use methodological approaches developed by their Western counterparts. They are connecting to a vast array of émigré literature that had been closed to Soviet historians. As scholarly interest in the Russian Revolution has waned in the West, Russian historians who grew up under perestroika and in the post-Soviet era now stand at the forefront of innovative research, buttressed by troves of archival sources. This book has greatly profited from their work.

I belong to the generation of social historians who challenged the previous liberal interpretation of the Russian Revolution, and I accept the general thrust of their arguments. But social historians have too narrowly defined the task of their research agenda by rejecting the examination of nonpolitical issues. In what might be considered the manifesto of the social history of the Russian Revolution, Ronald Grigor Suny declared in 1983 that politics cannot be omitted from the social history of the revolution. This kind of history, he argued, is "more concerned with the movement and movements of social groups and classes than with patterns of fertility or mortality."[10] In a critical response, Peter Gatrell writes:

> The experiences of Russian civilians during the First World War have yet to attract systematic attention. In large measure this reflects historians' understandable preoccupation with the organization and behavior of workers and peasants during the tumultuous months of 1917. Even studies of popular attitudes and activity during the Russian revolution have tended to neglect groups that are not easily subsumed within the conventional categories of historical inquiry. The social history of the revolution has concentrated on organized social forces, whose representatives and spokesmen left behind compelling accounts of political struggle and whose actions impinged directly on the existing forms of state power. Historians have scarcely begun to step outside the world of elite politics and the revolutionary movement, or to look beyond the dynamics of labor protest and organization.[11]

Endorsing Gatrell's criticism, I ask, why not patterns of fertility and mortality? The major purpose of this book is precisely to step outside the traditional preoccupation of social historians writing about the Russian Revolution. This is not to deny the importance of politics. Quite the opposite. I aim to show how politics seeped into nonpolitical aspects of everyday life during the revolutionary period and how, in turn, these nonpolitical aspects had profound effects on political change.

Interpreting the Russian Revolution through Crime and Police

Crime and police appear unconnected with "the world of elite politics and the revolutionary movement" and have thus been largely ignored by social historians. By examining crime and police, I demonstrate how the political process penetrated into, and was in turn influenced by, a nonpolitical issue.[12] Here I will lay out some of the general contours of the crime and policing problem.

During the February Revolution, the liberals who formed the Provisional Government sought to annihilate the tsarist police. This meant sacrificing more than the existing system of law enforcement. The tsarist police had not only secured public order but also acted as the "universal administrator."[13] It was responsible for a variety of municipal government functions, including issuing all kinds of certificates and permits; performing sanitary inspections; ensuring that streets, squares, and courtyards were cleaned; and overseeing prostitutes and beggars. By eliminating the tsarist police, the Provisional Government not only cut itself off from the capital's security, but also contributed to the paralysis of city services.

A new police force was created after February, but not by the Provisional Government. It was the Petrograd city duma, the highest local authority, that established the city militia. This municipal force was responsible to society, not to the state. It would be politically neutral, run by democratically elected officers, and would govern itself at the level of Petrograd's subdistricts. But decentralization, coupled with an inherently fragile civil society weakened by rapidly intensifying social divisions, sapped the effectiveness of the city militia. It was poorly armed, badly coordinated across districts, and mostly untrained, and it lacked uniforms. Moreover, the city militia had to compete with workers' militias that sprang up in working-class districts and factories. As class conflict intensified, workers formed the armed Red Guards exclusively to protect working-class interests. The weakness of the city militia and the erosion of its authority contributed greatly to the exponential rise of crime in Petrograd.

The diffusion of power manifest in the structure and diversity of Petrograd's police organizations reflected the broad, powerful movement toward decentralization, a feature of the revolution often overlooked in the shadow of intense class divisions presumed to be the central inspiration of revolutionary politics. In Petrograd and in the provinces, decision making filtered down to the lowest-level local institutions. These bodies often ignored the Provisional Government's directives. This was an active process of resistance to central government. In Petrograd, the Provisional Government's several attempts to bring police under its control were rebuffed by workers' and city militiamen, both revealing and reinforcing the state's weakness. After assuming power, the Bolsheviks reversed the trend and reasserted central control over institutions and citizens.

The crime rate in Petrograd climbed steadily after March and then spiked frighteningly in the fall. The courts were dysfunctional, and prison security lax. Gambling, drunken disorder, narcotics trafficking, and prostitution flourished. Crime and punishment were matters of consequence in everyday life, along with other indications of breakdown: dwindling food supply, constant transportation failures, nonexistent garbage collection and street lighting, lack of running water and electricity. Epidemics erupted, filling hospitals with patients. On the eve of the October Revolution, the city was approaching a catastrophic disintegration of its social fabric.

Ordinary people reacted to this situation with anger and violence. They took the law into their own hands and subjected criminals and merchants suspected of engaging in speculation to mob justice. Frequent and brutal, mob justice bespoke the psychological state of ordinary people whose daily life was threatened by revolutionary change. Law and orderly process were replaced by naked violence.

From this point of view, it is not surprising that ordinary people were largely indifferent to the Bolshevik seizure of power. The Bolsheviks and their allies were not merely indifferent to the maintenance of public order but actively encouraged lawlessness to destroy the bourgeois system. The crumbling of the social fabric, threatened above all by crime, thus facilitated the Bolshevik takeover. But violence continued to escalate under the Bolshevik regime. It had to be tamed not only to restore order but also to maintain the Soviet state. The resulting scheme of unrestrained coercion prevailed for decades to come.

As we consider the breakdown of daily life among the ordinary people of Petrograd, it is essential to keep in mind just who the ordinary people were. They were not revolutionaries. Vladislav Aksenov introduces this crucial distinction between "revolutionary people" and "revolutionized people."[14] The former actively participated in revolutionary changes. They include not only the elite of political parties but also members of various professional and social organizations that social historians have closely analyzed. But a vast number of people, largely ignored by historians, stood outside of events. If the revolution swept through Petrograd like the river Neva that runs across its middle, then these people were leaves, branches, and debris tossed around in the currents. They did not make change; they reacted to it.

Among the revolutionized people were the upper layers of society. Some of the privileged congregated in gambling dens and other decadent circles. Many deserted the city. I also capture the concerns and frustrations of the middle class, as reflected in contemporary newspapers and journals. But, above all, I am interested in the lower rungs of society: the urban poor.[15] These were the anonymous men and women of what contemporary journalists called "the crowd" (*tolpa*). They gathered in streets, squares, and markets to commit mob justice, and they joined the alcohol pogroms. The urban poor have escaped historians' scrutiny, since they do not neatly fall into well-defined classes or social organizations based on occupational classifications. Unlike the industrial proletariat, for the most part they lacked organizational resources to channel their voices into political action. They were dismissed by the prerevolutionary and revolutionary elite alike with a mixture of disdain and fear—the ignorant, uneducated masses, bent on spontaneous outbursts of violence. The empowered Bolsheviks and Soviet historians felt similarly. These were hopelessly backward "lumpen proletariat," "dregs of society," exploited by counterrevolutionary forces to harm the interests of the proletariat and discredit the socialist state.[16]

These urban poor "did not speak": they wrote no memoirs and passed no resolutions. They were heard only through the "hegemonic" language of outside observers.[17] Yet we can capture their authentic voice. If they did not speak, they acted, and their actions were their language. As Ilya Gerasimov writes, "There is . . . reality beyond the public sphere structured by hegemonic discourses, and there are methods of analysis not constrained by the availability of 'literary texts' as primary sources."[18] Gerasimov identifies criminality as "a unique window on social practices and a particular language of self-expression and self-representation unmediated by traditional institutions."[19] Stripped of the interpretations found in newspapers, memoirs, and police reports, there are the hard facts of thefts, robberies, murders, gambling, narcotic use, and prostitution. There are the explosions of mob justice and alcohol pogroms.

What I do in the analysis of crime, mob justice, and alcohol pogroms is exactly what historian Mark Steinberg proposes: sensitive to the limitations of the sources, I engage in "the shifting dialogue between perspectives—between the rawness of described violence, interpretations by contemporaries, and a critical reading of both" to "open up the possibility of deeper interpretation."[20]

Relevance in the Contemporary World

Challenging the most recent historiographical trend placing the Russian Revolution in a continuum from World War I to the civil war, this book takes the period from March 1917 to March 1918 as a distinct "revolutionary" period. This period deserves to be studied on its own, not as a mere transitional stage from World War I to the civil war. Singling out the Russian Revolution as a distinctive period has many benefits. I focus on two. First, the Russian Revolution arises as an important case in the comparative studies of revolutions. Second, we can read the revolution as an example of how states transition away from authoritarian regimes.

In both cases, it is necessary to go beyond the specifics of the Russian Revolution and pinpoint features common to other cases of political change. We need theories that explain the Russian Revolution, but not only the Russian Revolution; we need theories common to many revolutions and cases of transition from authoritarianism. I employ two in this book: sociological theories of anomie, developed by Emile Durkheim and Robert Merton, and the theory of the failed state.

The Sociological Theory of Anomie

Emile Durkheim, one of the founders of the discipline of sociology, was concerned with the question of how societies maintain cohesion. Premodern societies, he argued, maintained cohesion by "mechanical solidarity." A single "collective consciousness," based on beliefs and sentiments common to the members of the group, directs all individuals in society. But in modern, industrial society, collective consciousness diminishes and individual differences dominate. In such a society, community forms through "organic solidarity." Organic solidarity is manifest in the high degree of interdependence brought about by the division of labor and intricate organic interdependence of population and organizations rather than collective conscious. In this context, the individual, freed from tribal boundaries, gains a degree of sovereignty and personal responsibility. But he relies on others to fulfill their own specialized tasks in order that he may be supplied with the necessities of life. Law, steeped in reason and procedure, becomes society's principal structural support, ensuring cooperation where emotional and kinship connections no longer apply. Anomie, the condition of normlessness, arises when organic solidarity breaks down.[21]

The American sociologist Robert Merton elaborated on Durkheim's theory of anomie. According to Merton, social cohesion rests on two pillars: cultural structure and social structure. The cultural structure is a set of normative values governing behavior, which is common to members of the society. The social structure consists of institutional norms, which define and regulate acceptable modes of realizing these values. When society functions well, culture and society are integrated to achieve organic solidarity. Anomie is "conceived as a breakdown in the cultural structure, occurring particularly when there is an acute disjunction between cultural norms and goals and the social structured capacities of members of the group to act in accord with them."[22]

For Durkheim and Merton, the role of the authority is paramount. The purpose of "an authority with power," Durkheim writes, is to "ensure respect for beliefs, tradition, and collective practices—namely, to defend the common consciousness from all its enemies, from within as well as without."[23] When the nominal authority loses control, solidarity crumbles and anomie reins. When this happens, the state can fail. Here the theory of anomie merges with the theory of the failed state.

The Theory of the Failed State

According to Max Weber, the state must possess a monopoly on the coercive use of force and legitimacy. The former entails "that only the state is permitted to possess the means of implementing its claim, and that only the state is capable of shutting down new sources of violence if all else fails." But the monopoly of coercive means has to be supported by legitimacy. People and nonstate agencies must accept the right of the state to exercise coercion to guarantee the rule of law. Legitimacy is therefore integrally connected with legal rule.[24]

Of political goods that the state provides, "none is as critical as the supply of security, especially human security."[25] Thus one of the state's most important tasks is "to prevent crime and any related dangers to domestic human security; and to enable citizens to resolve their disputes with the state and with their fellow inhabitants without recourse to arms or other forms of physical coercion."[26]

An important indicator of state failure is the growth of criminal violence. "As state authority weakens and fails, so lawlessness becomes more apparent," Robert Rotberg writes. "Criminal gangs take over the streets of the cities. . . . Ordinary police forces become paralyzed. Anomic behaviors become the norm."[27] Here again the theory of the failed state merges with the theory of anomie.

During the revolution, Petrograd was overwhelmed by crime and other sources of social breakdown. The failure of the state was both manifest and reinforced by its inability to establish law and order. Amid insecurity and deprivation, and inspired by revolutionary zeal for an entirely new cultural and political order celebrating pure freedom, people turned to vigilantism and self-help. The approaches of anomie and the failed state fit the Russian condition soundly. Understood this way, the Russian Revolution can serve as an important case study as we analyze other historical and contemporary political transformations.

The book begins with a brief history of the prerevolutionary situation in St. Petersburg, contextualizing what happened in 1917 when the tsar's capital took its new name. I also introduce readers to Petrograd itself—its geographic divisions and population. The next two chapters describe the sharp rise in crime after the February Revolution and examine the reasons for increasing criminality, paying special attention to political and economic crises, the breakdown of the legal order, the swelling criminal population, and the availability of weapons.

The most significant reason for the rise in crime was the failure of the revolutionary regime to create an effective police. In Chapter 4, I first describe the three types of police that emerged after the February Revolution. The Provisional Government attempted to create a centralized, state-driven police but could not overcome the powerful centrifugal force of the revolution. More effective was the city duma's attempt to create a municipal police force in the form of the city militia. But the municipal police were challenged by the workers' militia, a class-based organization designed to secure not the interests of the population as a whole but only of the working class. The formation of the city and workers' militias points to the importance of the centrifugal tendency and local self-determination.

I then analyze the competition between the city and workers' militias. Intensifying class polarization after the summer of 1917 so reduced the effectiveness of the city militia that the populace lost confidence in its ability to protect their lives and property. Workers retreated into their working-class organizations and strengthened the Red Guards to arm themselves against counter-revolution. Working-class neighborhoods proved safer than the central and southern districts, which were more reliant on the disintegrating city militia. Crime spread in these areas at a devastating pace.

The people's reaction to metastasizing crime is the topic of Chapter 5, which concentrates on mob justice. Drawing on vivid contemporary accounts, I interpret instances of mob justice as expressions of people's overall frustrations and anger at the deterioration of daily life rather than retribution for a particular crime committed. I further argue that the Bolshevik leadership exploited popular violence to justify their seizure of power.

In Chapters 6 and 7, I look at the rising intensity of crime and mob justice after the Bolshevik ascendancy, the explosion of alcohol pogroms, and how the Bolshevik regime responded, eventually injecting ideology into ordinary crime and entrusting its mitigation to the Cheka. Crime served as a stepping-stone to the creation of the Communist dictatorship, with unbridled coercive power as its centerpiece.

The book relies on contemporary news accounts, memoirs, cartoons, archival materials, and secondary writings. These are essential to establishing the factual basis of the work. But they do more than that. They help inculcate in the reader a feeling for the desperation that set in among Petrograd's residents during the year after the February Revolution. Only by sharing their fear and frustration can we understand how the daily horror of their existence had turned their initial hope and jubilation into despair, anger, and sporadic violence that eventually allowed a Leviathan state to assert itself on the broken society and fragmented population.

I. Prelude to Revolution

Winter is long and cold in St. Petersburg. The sun rises only in late morning and sets by midafternoon. Icy wind whips through the streets. Though a mighty river, the Neva freezes solid from November until March. When the ice finally breaks, the Neva roars, as if a giant were waking from its bed. Then spring comes with the smell of lilacs. From late May to early July, darkness gives way to the midnight sun, and the city glows all day long. These are some of the few constants in St. Petersburg, whose many identities—renamed Petrograd at the outbreak of World War I, then Leningrad in 1924, and St. Petersburg again in 1991—speak to its enduring significance within Russia's shifting political life. It is a place of extremes.

Unlike Paris and London, St. Petersburg is an artificial city, built for greatness.[1] On May 16, 1703, Peter the Great stood on Zaiachii Island, in the Neva, and declared, "The city will be here!"[2] It was a crazy idea. The area was uninhabited marshland, subject to periodic flooding. But Peter was determined to see his vision realized. He conscripted tens of thousands of men to drain the swamp and reinforce the ground with tens of thousands of granite boulders. Human cost did not much matter. A contemporary historian, Nikolai Karamzin, wrote, "Petersburg was founded on tears and corpses."[3]

Not just any tears and corpses, but those of the common people. Their tragedies, buried beneath glittering spires and pastel palaces, reemerged now and then in the form of revolt. This was the site of the Decembrist Uprising of 1825, when three thousand rebel troops led by aristocratic officers occupied Senate Square and denied their allegiance to the new tsar, Nicholas I. This was where terrorists assassinated Alexander II, the Tsar Liberator, in 1881. Here Father Georgii Gapon inaugurated the revolution of 1905, when he led thousands of unarmed demonstrators petitioning the tsar for better working conditions, decent wages, and universal suffrage. The tsar's soldiers responded with a hail of bullets, killing hundreds, on what became known as Bloody Sunday. And it was in Petrograd that the Russian Revolution came to a head in 1917, toppling Tsar Nicholas II in March and culminating in the Bolshevik seizure of power in October.

Before 1713, the capital had been in Moscow, but Peter wanted a break with the tradition of slumbering Muscovy. The new capital would be the window to Europe. The emperor ordered reluctant Muscovite boyars (noblemen) to shave their beards, wear Western clothes, and join him in the city bearing his name. By the end of the eighteenth century, under empresses Anna, Elizabeth, and Catherine II, the city developed into one of Europe's most beautiful, with well-organized boulevards and canals and magnificent stone buildings designed by foreign architects. When Peter died in 1725, the population was just forty thousand, but it grew rapidly, eventually benefiting from waves of industrialization and modernization. There were more than a million residents by the end of the nineteenth century, and by the middle of 1914, when Russia entered World War I, 2.1 million called it home.[4]

As the capital, center of the hereditary nobility, industrial hub, and garrison city, Petrograd was occupationally diverse and marked by massive inequality. Until 1917, the population was officially divided by estates rather than classes or occupations. According to the 1910 census, 3.8 percent of residents were members of the hereditary nobility; 3.3 percent had achieved personal nobility, which offered similar privileges that were not transferrable to later generations; 0.5 percent were clergy and 0.7 percent merchants; and, rounding out the upper class, 4.1 percent were

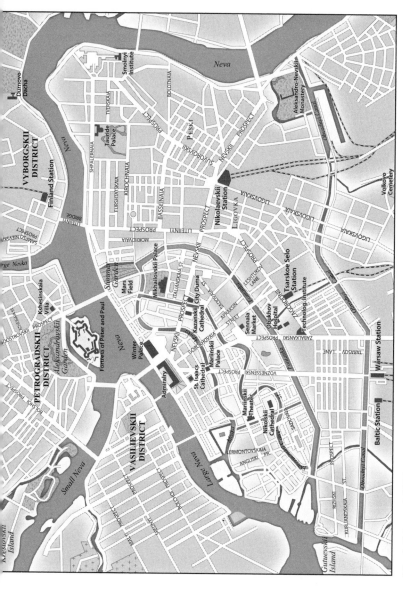

Map 1. Petrograd, 1917.

honored citizens.[5] The overwhelming majority, nearly 69 percent, were peasants. These included not only industrial workers but also artisans in all kinds of trades, cobblers, carpenters, joiners, painters, gravediggers, laundresses, bathhouse attendants, cab drivers, dvorniks (groundskeepers), domestic servants, and seasonal workers who came to the city in winter and returned to their land in the summer. The last major group, at 15.5 percent, were *meshchane:* petty bourgeoisie, including retail and wholesale tradesmen, shop owners and clerks, restaurateurs, and a wide range of *sluzhashchie* (low-level professionals) working as teachers, nurses, librarians, pharmacists, office hands, and so on.[6] Higher-ranking professionals of the bourgeoisie, such as doctors, lawyers, and professors, were counted among honored citizens. Straddling these estates was a glut of soldiers and officers, between 322,000 and 466,800 in and around Petrograd in the months before the February Revolution.[7]

Ranks and wealth did not necessarily match. It was not uncommon for bankers and industrialists to win the rank of honored citizen, which placed them below noblemen who may have been impoverished. Yet, as James Bater writes, in the period just preceding World War I, "St. Petersburg society continued to be more strongly influenced by the nobility, often profligate and sometimes penurious, a parasitic bureaucracy, and the resident military personnel than by the bankers, brokers, industrialists, and others like them, who contributed to the city's economic viability."[8] The tsarist bureaucracy dominated the central government, though the bourgeoisie had the upper hand in the city duma.

Living in St. Petersburg

Two major streets, Nevskii Prospect and Sadovaia Street, symbolized the boundaries dividing the city's privileged (*verkhi*) and its poor (*nizy*).[9] Nevskii, a 2.8-mile boulevard running from the Admiralty to Aleksandro-Nevskii Monastery through the city center, was Russia's equivalent of Regent Street in London and the Champs-Elysées in Paris. Both sides of the boulevard were lined with palaces and other stately habitats of the royalty and nobility. There were expensive shops and restaurants, as well as the banks that girded the financial power of the upper crust. Usually, between two and five o'clock in the afternoon, high-placed ladies strolled the route in fashionable dress, accompanied by their servants. Important bureaucrats, military officers in stylish uniforms, bankers, lawyers, and businessmen paraded there. Some preferred its seedier eastern end at night. The area near Nikolaevskii Railway Station, Ligovka, teemed with prostitutes and pickpockets.[10]

As a symbol of power and privilege, Nevskii was occasionally a target for protests by common people otherwise excluded from its posh surroundings. The earliest political demonstration there took place in front of Kazan Cathedral in 1876. It was immediately broken up, but not before a red flag was unfurled on Nevskii for the first time. From then on, the workers targeted Nevskii as the destination of their demonstrations. Later on, Nevskii Prospect witnessed Bloody Sunday and, during the February Revolution, a series of massive workers' demonstrations. In summer 1917, during the so-called July Days, Bolshevik-led demonstrators marched under the banner "All Power to the Soviets," only to be shot down by the Provisional Government's troops.

What Nevskii was for the privileged, Sadovaia was for the common folk. It too ran across the center of the city, cutting across Nevskii from east to west, and served as a commercial hub. Along the street were six major retail markets, of which Sennaia was the largest and most famous. Merchants sold food and wholesale goods, and shoppers frequented eateries and small workshops where artisans made clothes, boots, lamps, furniture, kitchen

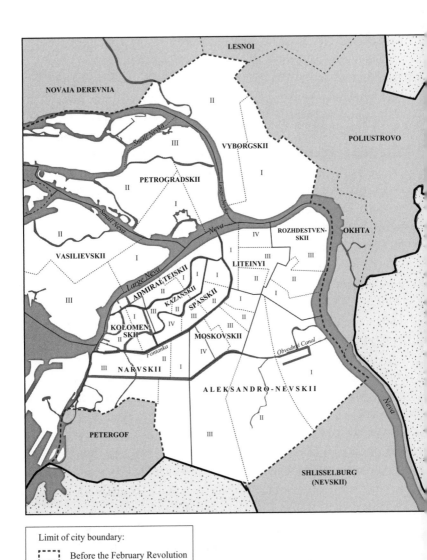

Map 2. Administrative districts of Petrograd, 1917.

utensils, and other consumer items. If a day laborer was needed, he could be found at the Nikolskii Market at the western end of Sadovaia. Many day laborers came from the countryside and gathered under separate tents according to their profession: stone layer, stove setter, gardener, carpenter, peddler, and other trades. The area bustled with poor folks shouting, cursing, spitting, and bargaining. Horse-drawn carts plied the avenue and its side streets. Panhandlers, prostitutes, and beggars mixed with common folk in taverns, soup diners, teahouses, and refreshment stalls.[11]

Beyond these segregated centers was another world, a third layer of the city. The major outlying thoroughfares—Sampsonievskii Prospect in the north, Petergofskii Tract in the south, and Shlisselburg Tract in the east—were lined with brick factory buildings and shoddy workers' apartments and shacks. At dawn and dusk, the streets of working-class districts such as Vyborgskii crowded with men and women covered in oil and dirt, on their way home or to the next shift in a factory whose smokestack never stopped spewing.

Yet, while geographic divisions were at times stark and differences of social rank were unyielding, St. Petersburg was not as rigidly segregated as the extremes of Nevskii, Sadovaia, and the working-class factory districts suggest. In fact, most districts were diverse, which contributed to the volatility of social tension during the revolutionary period.

Soviet historians, politically invested in the narrative of stratification between ordinary people and the privileged, argued, "The exploiting classes seized the better parts of the city, expelling the oppressed layers of the population to the outskirts."[12] Bater challenges this view. He finds that a range of people lived side by side throughout the city. In the center, the privileged occupied the middle floors of apartment buildings with their domestic servants, who lived in the corners of the floors. The poor rented the garrets and cellars. In the Admiralteiskii district, "there were many working-class people . . . who owed their livelihood not to the resident upper classes but to local restaurants, commercial establishments and even manufacturing enterprises." Although the First Kazanskii subdistrict was dominated by government buildings, bureaucrats, businesspeople, and professionals, the Second and the Third subdistricts saw many plebians mingled with the still dominant privileged population. More than twenty thousand itinerant workers lived in centrally located Spasskii. Factory owners lived cheek by jowl with the workers in the outlying regions that Soviet historians characterized as working-class ghettoes. "On the whole," Bater concludes, there is no basis for supposing that what had happened to the city during the decades of rapid urban industrialization had altered the customary spatial heterogeneity of classes comprising the community."[13]

A naive observer might see in such mixing an opportunity to establish ties across class lines, salving social tensions. But the effect was mostly the opposite, as poor people in central districts (Admiralteiskii, Kazanskii, Liteinyi) and central mixed districts (Spasskii, Moskovskii, Kolomenskii, and Rozhdestvenskii) found themselves surrounded by ostentatious wealth that only reminded them of the injustice of their circumstances. It was in the class-overlapping central, central-mixed, and southern districts (Narvsskii and Aleksandro-Nevskii) that housing shortages would prove most acute and violence most intense. Crime was most common near Spasskii's markets and in the areas south where petty bourgeois and unorganized artisanal workers congregated.

The Revolution Arrives

Although St. Petersburg was a diverse and heterogeneous place, social divisions were real and powerful, and the aristocracy maintained an atavistic order that clashed with the city's dynamism.

Russia under Tsar Nicholas II (r. November 1894–March 1917) was by no means a backward and stagnant country. Along with urbanization came a vibrant civil society that challenged the age-old bureaucratic autocracy. And along with industrialization came the proletariat, more dangerous because it was excluded from traditional boundaries of politics and public life. Following historian Leopold Haimson, we can isolate two polarizations that became entrenched in urban Russia before the outbreak of World War I: between the bureaucratic state (*gosudarstvo*) and educated, liberal society (*obshchestvo*); and between the privileged (*verkhi*) and the poor (*nizy*), disfranchised masses.[14] The tsar was the linchpin of an imperial order that was supposed to bring coherence and unity to an ever-changing polity.

But the intransigent Nicholas, committed to outmoded notions of autocracy and hereditary rule, could not adjust to the social change churning at the turn of the century. Inherent contradictions burst open in 1905 with Bloody Sunday and the first Russian revolution. Under pressure, Nicholas reluctantly issued the October Manifesto, which promised major political reforms. But as soon as the revolutionary crisis receded, the tsar backtracked. The Fundamental Laws, enacted in 1906, and the creation of the new quasi-legislative institutions, the State Duma and the State Council, did limit the tsar's power. But these measures did not resolve the fundamental polarizations tearing society and the political system apart. Indeed, the opposite occurred. Prime Minister Petr A. Stolypin's revised Duma election law of 1907 severely curtailed representation of the working class. Amid further industrial growth and major agrarian reforms, social tensions mounted. The workers' strike movement resumed with new intensity in April 1912, after the tsar's army massacred hundreds of workers agitating for better conditions at the Lena goldmine in northeast Siberia. Minister of Internal Affairs Aleksandr A. Makarov famously boasted, "So it was, and so it will be." In response, Duma liberals—including Alexander F. Kerenskii, the future leader of the Provisional Government—sharpened their attacks on the government. In 1913, Nicholas and Empress Alexandra celebrated the three hundredth anniversary of the Romanov dynasty with tours of St. Petersburg, Moscow, and provincial centers. But behind the facade of unity between tsar and people, the hollow celebrations of the dynasty could not hide the mounting contradictions.

In 1914, Russia entered World War I on the side of France, Britain, and Serbia against Germany and Austria. Despite initial enthusiasm, the war soon further exposed the country's political, social, and economic weaknesses. Liberals in the State Duma and beyond demanded the formation of a new government enjoying the confidence of the people. They also sought to remove the influence of "dark forces" personified by Empress Alexandra and the imperial couple's confidant, Grigorii Rasputin. The strike movement, silenced by the outbreak of war, regained momentum as urban economies deteriorated after the summer of 1915. Soldiers at the front, as well as hundreds of thousands posted in and around Petrograd, were tired of the war. Many officers secretly sympathized with the tsar's liberal critics.[15]

Amid continuing economic decline and influxes of refugees and deserters, on February 23, 1917, the working women of Vyborgskii went on strike, demanding bread. The strike spread rapidly, engulfing the entire city within two days. Strikers expanded their demands: they wanted an end to the war and the autocracy. The tsar ordered the demonstrators shot; on February 26, soldiers complied. But this triggered a soldiers' mutiny the following day. The tsar's ministers resigned, and Duma liberals formed the Provisional Committee of the State Duma (the Duma Committee) to take over the government and restore order. In the meantime, Socialist leaders established the Petrograd Soviet of Workers' and Soldiers' Deputies to represent the insurgent workers and soldiers in the capital. The contest for power between the Petrograd Soviet and the Provisional Government that emerged from the Duma Committee would become a major source of administrative tumult during the period before October.

But before that, Nicholas was determined to crush the nascent revolution. He ordered General Nikolai Iu. Ivanov's forces into Petrograd and then left his headquarters in Mogilev to join his family in Tsarskoe Selo, on the outskirts of the capital. While the troops were en route, the Duma Committee negotiated with the military high command. Duma leaders managed to convince the military brass to suspend General Ivanov's counter-revolutionary operation and accept the tsar's abdication. On March 2, Nicholas agreed to abdicate in favor of his brother, Grand Duke Mikhail Aleksandrovich. When the grand duke the next day refused to assume the throne, the monarchy officially came to an end.[16]

Crime before 1917

In St. Petersburg, the period before the revolution defied nineteenth-century European trends toward reduced urban criminality. One factor was the gradual retreat of the tsarist state, whose weakening amid industrialization and urbanization reduced capacity for policing. The Revolution of 1905–1907 also opened social spaces rife with conflict and tension.[17] Eventually, the Great War exacerbated every aspect of the social breakdown, including crime.

St. Petersburg was plagued with crime from its inception. In a city for the noble built on the backs of the poor, the hereditary rich were surrounded by hordes from the lowest rungs of society. Opportunities for criminality were everywhere, and thieves roamed in broad daylight. In order to secure public order, Peter created a powerful police system. Among the first decrees of the Governing Senate created in 1711 was an order to hang robbers where they were caught. The police also handled municipal services such as street paving, dredging wetland, garbage disposal, streetlamps, and fire brigades. The police thus became indispensable across many dimensions of social function.[18]

The modernization of industry and bureaucracy in the second half of the nineteenth century was accompanied by the modernization of crime. As a growing commercial center, St. Petersburg was an attractive site for swindling, forgery, and extortion, and emerging criminal syndicates took advantage.[19] Criminality became professionalized. Pickpockets competed to demonstrate their skill and daring. "Bear hunters" (*medvezhatniki*) broke into properties via walls and ceilings. Meanwhile, *shnifery* took a quieter approach, cracking codes and locked doors. Specialists might freelance for syndicates or, like members of the later Mafia, swear loyalty to them. These explicitly modern criminal organizations differentiated themselves from their predecessors, such as despised horse thieves, and policed themselves through codes of conduct. The cardinal rule called for absolute noncooperation with the government, especially its police. Syndicates initiated new members through a ceremony known as "coronation." They set up branches in prisons and army units. They were led by bosses—"godfathers" (*krestnyi otets*)—and developed their own patois, *fenia*. Gang members tattooed themselves to signal their allegiance. Criminality was far more sophisticated in St. Petersburg than in other large cities of the empire such as Moscow, Rostov-on-Don, and Odessa.[20]

The tsarist government attempted to respond through a modernization of its own, establishing in the 1890s a specialized investigative unit. But while the Criminal Police (*sysknaia politsiia*) was an able institution and well respected across Europe, it was insufficient. Other measures similarly could not keep up. The crime rate across the empire increased 43 percent between 1899 and 1908.[21] Murder was a steadily deepening problem. Courts heard 1,254 cases in 1880, 1,640 in 1900, and 2,244 in 1904. After the 1905–1907 revolution, the rate more than doubled to 4,857. By 1910, there were 7,531 reported killings.[22]

St. Petersburg, ever a hotbed of illegal activity, fit the national trend. The number of murder indictments at St. Petersburg Region District Court increased from 227 in 1900 to 794 in 1913. Indictments for armed robbery rose from 427 in 1900 to 1,328 in 1913. Indictment for theft, in general, increased from 2,197 in 1900 to 5,777 in 1913.[23] The crime rate was thus growing far faster than the population, which expanded from 1.4 million to 2.1 million over the same period. A. M. Nazarenko has argued that the rate of violent crime actually peaked in 1907 but also finds that lesser violations continued to mount after that date.[24]

Another important sign of the breakdown of public order amid urbanization and industrialization was the spread of juvenile crime. Petrograd's lower-class youths were ostentatious in their hooliganism. They operated in public, drinking and brawling in the streets, where anyone could see. In their early days, they were given mostly to pranks and minor property crime. They pulled bolts from benches and laughed as unsuspecting sitters spilled to the ground. Hooligans also threw rocks through shop windows and hung around markets harassing shoppers and merchants. After the 1905–1907 revolution, however, they began turning to violent robbery, rape, and murder.[25]

The war across Europe would eventually generate massive discord in Petrograd, but its effects were not immediately felt in daily problems of violent crime. Rather, the trouble at the outset was spontaneous violence associated with mobilization in the provinces. In July-August, 1914, at many assembly points in the empire, mobilized and reserve soldiers, joined by their families and villagers, rioted and attacked police, liquor stores, and food stores.

One of the largest riots took place in Barnaul in Tomsk Province, where several thousand garrison soldiers attacked government buildings, including the prison and police station. They ransacked and burned the state-run wine warehouse. The drunken mob set fire to buildings along three streets and took complete control of the city for a full day. Residents fled. Only the imperial army units brought from outside were able to restore order. Altogether 112 men were killed and 160 rioters arrested.[26] Such riots took place in forty-three provinces, resulting in more than five hundred rioters and one hundred law-enforcement agents killed and wounded.[27]

These riots, isolated events scattered across the provinces, were largely unknown thanks to government censorship. They were thus overshadowed by the putative upsurge of patriotism, as reported in the press. But the riots revealed disturbing signs of weaknesses in the tsarist regime. Police were singled out in part because they were exempt from military service. By contrast, the rioters and their families were called to sacrifice. Soldiers' wives and mothers (*soldatki*) were among the active participants. A similar hostility to the authority was clear in raids on government buildings. Attacks on liquor stores presaged one of the most chaotic aspects of the revolution to come. The military had prohibited soldiers from drinking, a tradition upon mobilization. Soldiers and townspeople considered prohibition a violation of their customary right, prompting an aggressive response.

Petrograd was spared mobilization riots, but not popular anger. In the capital city, xenophobia stoked by patriotism inspired mob violence. Jews, the historical target of Russian pogroms, were replaced by Germans. In the week after July 19, when Tsar Nicholas declared war with Germany, enthusiastic war supporters demonstrated at the British, French, and Serbian embassies to show their support for Russia's allies. On July 22, several thousand marched on the German embassy in St. Isaac's Square. On the way, they smashed the windows of stores with German names. They destroyed a German bookstore and the office of a German-language newspaper. They ransacked the embassy, throwing papers and furniture from the windows into a huge bonfire in the square. Finally, as onlookers cheered, the mob knocked down the ornamental structure atop the building. One embassy employee was killed and mutilated. The government relished public support but was frightened by such outbursts, and the Petrograd city governor, Prince Aleksandr N. Obolenskii, banned further demonstrations. Still, four more German stores were destroyed on the follow day.[28] As Joshua Sanborn argues, "The events of 1914, patriotic rallies and massive riots alike, showed the capacity and willingness of regular Russians to engage with big political issues regarding the war."[29]

Anti-German riots, experienced in Petrograd, were most violent in Moscow. The Moscow city governor, A. A. Adrianov, allowed working-class anti-German feelings to run wild. For three days in May 1915, he looked the other way as residents rampaged through private apartments and stores with German-sounding names.[30] Russians also exercised their traditional penchant for anti-Semitism, deporting Jews from the Baltic states, Poland, and, more violently, Ukraine. Military authorities in the western borderlands believed Jews were an alien element and suspected them of spying. Soldiers and Cossacks went into Jewish settlements and committed atrocious pogroms.[31] Collectively, these paroxysms of mass violence demonstrated the capacity of ordinary Russians to voice their frustrations through spontaneous outbursts, which would reach their fullest expression in Petrograd's mobs.

With the exception of the attack on the German embassy in July 1914, Petrograd was spared violent crime surrounding mobilization. In fact, in the two years after the outbreak of the war, Petrograd was one of the safest cities in Russia, although it ranked

Table 1. Crime in Petrograd, 1914–1915

Crime	Rank among cities	1914	1915
Thefts, less than 300 rubles	1	3,710	3,657
Theft, forced entry	1	1,125	1,050
Theft, more than 300 rubles	1	1,002	1,369
Swindling, extortion	1	94	153
Embezzlement	1	388	496
Horse theft	2	68	62
Unarmed robbery	1	207	60
Murder	4	14	19
Armed robbery	24	n/a	3
Attempted murder	3	n/a	11

Sources: "Gorodskiia prestupleniia za 1915 god," 941–942; "Gorodskiia prestupleniia za 1915 god— prodolzhenie," 957–958.

first in nonviolent crime such as theft, swindling, and unarmed robbery.

Several causes underlay the relative calm. One was the August 22, 1914, imperial decree prohibiting the production and sale of alcohol. The dry law was most strictly enforced in Petrograd and Moscow. The measure initially received wide popular support and contributed to reduced drunkenness and the rowdiness it caused.[32] Male conscription also reduced the number of potential criminal elements in Petrograd. At the outbreak of the war, Petrograd was placed under martial law. The city governor thus obtained the right to expel anyone deemed a threat to public safety, and police subjected known criminal gathering places to constant surveillance.[33]

The early success of wartime control measures did not last long. The effectiveness of the dry law was bound to deteriorate; if there was a will to drink, there was always a way. Illegally brewed vodka flowed on the black market. Doctors hawked alcohol prescriptions, allowing legal purchase at drugstores. The desperate drank surrogate alcohol. Cologne and varnish were popular surrogates, and pharmaceutical factories thrived on surrogate manufacture. The desperate and poor risked blindness and death as they poisoned themselves with denatured alcohol and methylated spirits. Some drank *khanzhi,* a home-brewed Chinese spirit.[34] The well-to-do could still find expensive wine, vodka, and cognac at restaurants, to which authorities turned a blind eye. Indeed, they, too, enjoyed this illicit service. Ultimately, the major effect of the dry law was to deprive the government of income from its vodka monopoly. As to consumption, "We drank, and never drank so much," was an oft-heard boast during the prohibition.[35]

As Russian troops retreated from Galicia and Poland in 1915, evacuees from the German-occupied areas they left behind inundated Petrograd. In the spring of 1915, forty to fifty thousand evacuees arrived from Galicia. In December, eighty-seven thousand came from Poland and Lithuania. The Germans opened prison gates in the occupied territories, allowing seasoned criminals to escape. Many of these, especially from Warsaw, brought their advanced techniques to Petrograd. For instance, Polish *gradushniki* introduced new burglary methods. Polish criminals were harder to catch, since they were not registered residents, and the police had no criminal files for them.[36]

Crime statistics for 1916 are unavailable due to the destruction of the tsarist police and its records during the February Revolution, but it is clear that the situation worsened. According to Dmitrii Iu. Ereshchenko, newspapers reported 1,800 cases of crime in 1915 and 2,506 in 1916.[37] Reflecting catastrophic shortages and price inflation, thefts of food products increased by 190 percent in 1917, prior to the February Revolution, compared with 1914–1915 levels. The number of thefts rose sharply as the February Revolution approached: 191 between January and August 1916 (an average of 24 per month), 244 from September to October (122 per month), and to 301 from January to February 1917 (150 per month).[38] Thefts were so frequent that newspapers created special columns—"Daily Robberies" (*Dnevnye razgromy*) and "Capital's Larcenies" (*Stolichnye khishchniki*)—to track them.[39] On November 3, 1916, a columnist, "Skitalets," lamented what he saw as a struggle of normalcy against criminality, and *Petrogradskii listok* described an "epidemic" of thievery.[40] Outrage within the middle-class newspapers bespoke the wide scope of crime, ensnaring even the highest ranks of the city. In March 1916, State Council Member and former Procurator of the Holy Synod A. D. Samarin was burgled at his apartment. The residences of the French and Japanese ambassadors and of banker V. Legran were also attacked in 1916.[41]

Crime was also growing more violent as the February Revolution approached. The murder count rose from fourteen in 1914 to thirty in 1915 and almost certainly more in the untracked year of 1916. We do know that the rate of violent robbery increased, placing more people in the path of armed men with little respect for human life. According to Ereshchenko's study of newspapers, there were fourteen violent robberies during the first five months after the outbreak of the war and thirty-four in less than two months preceding the February Revolution.[42]

One of the most celebrated robberies was the daring armed raid on Abram L. Zhivotovskii, a wealthy banker, by a gang of robbers led by Baron G. E. von Shrippen. Von Shrippen represented the "golden youths" (*zolotye molodezhi*), a decadent group of idle youths of the privileged class, bordering on the criminal world, who frequented bordellos, expensive hotels, and high-stakes gambling dens. Their ruthlessness was often described approvingly in tabloid papers.[43]

If the golden youths represented high society, hooligans were juvenile gangs of the urban poor. During the war, hooliganism took on new significance. In 1915 alone, the juvenile crime rate increased by 40 percent. Nearly all of these crimes were petty thefts. In one day in May 1915, police arrested fifty-one pick-pockets aged fifteen to seventeen; on January 30, 1916, they took in sixty-seven pickpockets between twelve and fifteen years old.[44] Wartime conditions facilitated juvenile crime. With fathers departed to the front, mothers were forced to work outside the home to support their families. Many children were left without adult supervision. Widows were often unable to fill the gaps left by husbands killed in battle, and the number of orphans multiplied. With orphanages strained beyond capacity, children were left homeless. They found new families in the form of juvenile gangs, often under the protection of adult leaders involved in the black market.[45] Hooligans claimed their own territories. The gangs fought one another, especially when they crossed boundaries; they wounded or even killed one another on the slightest provocations. Between July and December 1914, just one murder was attributed to a hooligan. That number rose to seventeen in 1915 and forty-three in 1916. There were fourteen such murders during the first two months of 1917.[46]

Criminologists also noted changes in criminal patterns. According to M. N. Gernet, between 1913 and 1916, male violent crime in the nation decreased 53 percent. In contrast, female criminal activities increased, as women were forced to support their families while their husbands and fathers were mobilized. According to D. P. Rodin, rates of serious female crimes between 1913 and 1916 experienced a 79 percent increase. Nevertheless, this should not be taken as a sign of women attaining an equal status as men in crime, since women's violent crime tended to focus on their traditional sphere: the family. A significant rise in female crime took place in infanticide, abortion, and child abandonment.[47]

Crime was exacerbated not only by popular desperation, the influx of criminal elements, and the weakness of the state, but also by the breakdown of informal structures of security. Among the most important of these were dvorniks—household employees who fulfilled the role of groundskeepers. They were traditionally valuable police informants, keeping their eyes and ears on the ins and outs of every building. During the war, however, their link to law-enforcement officials was attenuated. Many dvorniks were drafted and replaced by inexperienced newcomers. The eyes and ears, where they remained, were less reliable than before. When police inspected "nests" (*priton*) of ill repute—often cheap inns and apartments—where evacuees and poor people congregated, they often found buildings unguarded by dvorniks, or else men sleeping soundly. In some cases, dvorniks themselves were found to be involved in crime, mostly drunkenness and illegal alcohol sales.[48]

St. Petersburg's history as a criminal capital was not its destiny. At the beginning of the war, Petrograd was safer than many other large Russian cities. But even in 1914, there were signs of what was to come, and, by the summer of 1915, law and order in the capital was clearly eroding.

By that point, popular frustration with rising crime was already apparent. The first instances of mob justice, where crowds took it upon themselves to catch and punish criminals on the spot, were reported about a year after the outbreak of the war. The stage was being set for the months after the February Revolution, when the people overwhelmed the city with their anger and desolation.[49]

2. Crime on the Rise

In its April 2, 1917, issue, the popular weekly journal *Ogonek* printed an illustration depicting a new world. It shows Nevskii Prospect, and the mood is joyous. The buildings no longer bear tsarist emblems. A barefoot man with a red hat, carrying a red baton, shouts, "Rasputin was blackened like a blackberry. But I am red, like a raspberry!" That sort of talk would have earned him a prison sentence before the revolution. An agitator sells political pamphlets, also previously illegal. In the wake of the February Revolution, the city's most famous and important boulevard is no longer reserved for the privileged class. It has been democratized practically overnight.[1] See figure 1.

Despite the postrevolutionary euphoria, newspapers also reported signs of disturbing days to come. As *Petrogradskii listok* relates, late at night on March 10, a gunshot sounded on Kaznacheskaia Street in the Kazanskii District, a mostly privileged area in the city center. A crowd rushed to the scene and found a man bleeding on the snow-covered ground. Militiamen and soldiers chased after the suspects. The victim, a legal assistant called Shlosberg, was accosted on his way home by three soldiers leaving a nearby brothel. Shlosberg surrendered his valuables, including a wallet and watch, but the muggers repeatedly stabbed him even after he fell to the ground.[2] The very heart of the city, a safe area before the February Revolution, was suddenly a scene of brutal and senseless violence. Brothels were not unusual in this high-end area, but what was new were the clients: soldiers, who previously did not venture into the sacred haven of the upper classes.

Figure 1. The crowd in Nevskii Prospect after the February Revolution. *Ogonek,* no. 12, April 2, 1917, 4.

Another early example of the shifting geography, and intensity, of crime in Petrograd came on April 16. Around midnight, pedestrians on Kamenoostrovskii Prospect, in the Petrogradskii District, were shocked by cries emanating from a posh apartment. It is not that the place was usually more staid. Margarita Sezakh-Kulero, a French nightclub singer, lived in the apartment with her friend Maria Popova, and the two entertained high-society guests with wild parties. But that night, a balcony window suddenly flung open to reveal a semi-naked woman, covered in blood, screaming for help. A crowd quickly gathered at the scene and called for help. When militiamen entered the apartment, they found Kulero's servant, Olga Samoilova, lying at the entrance in a sea of blood pouring from her slashed throat. They also found Popova's dead body in the dining room, her face rendered unrecognizable by a savage beating. Kulero lay near the window with wounds on her head and both hands.

When Kulero regained consciousness, she told investigators that she and Popova had invited to their apartment two men, whom they knew as frequent visitors to the nightclub. Horrified, she recalled how the guests, one dressed as an officer and the other as an enlisted man, suddenly became violent, attacked the two women with their sabers, and killed the servant, who had rushed to the scene. The men ransacked the apartment, grabbed valuables worth 20,000–30,000 rubles, and ran away. Kulero identified one of the guests as none other than the famous Baron G. E. von Shrippen, who had pulled off a daring robbery in the guise of searching the millionaire banker Zhivotovskii's apartment in November 1916. Eventually caught and convicted for that crime, he served time in a Petrograd prison until he escaped during the February Revolution.

The papers reported the case vividly, to the public's glee and terror. Readers soaked up the scandal: the victims and assailants all belonged to a small circle of decadent pleasure-seekers far removed from their own lives.[3] Investigators found Shrippen's accomplice, Sashika Chukov, in the home of a noblewoman and close friend of Kulero and Popova's, Baroness Mengden. Not only that, but Chukov had a homosexual relationship with Shrippen, adding further salacious overtones and fanning homophobic sentiment among the populace.[4]

But for all the sensation, the story also struck an appropriately discordant note. The former hero, who had dared to rob a millionaire, turned into a brutal murderer. The savagery of the crime was particularly stunning because the victims were not limited to decadent high-class ladies. Readers could not forget the grisly death of one of their own, a defenseless servant. The incident coincided with the April crisis, triggered by foreign minister Pavel N. Miliukov's diplomatic note.[5] It is difficult to say which event, the

Kulero murder or the April crisis, generated more interest and excitement in the general public. But one can speculate that at least the readers of *Gazeta-Kopeika* were devouring the news about the Kulero murder rather than the political news.

As the months wore on, criminality became still more pervasive, and social discord was inscribed in the material of the city itself. In June, *Ogonek*'s "Petrograd These Days" column described the transformation of the Summer Garden, once an upper-class retreat lined with trees and elegant Greek marble statues. By late spring, the garden had been overtaken by crowds of gypsies, Chinese, and other minority groups. Beggars, fortunetellers, and street magicians wandered the park, hassling the guests.[6] Many statues were vandalized and lay in pieces. Hooligans and drunken soldiers used them for target practice.[7] In July, *Ogonek* cast its weary eye on Znamenskaia Square, where, before a massive statue of the reactionary Tsar Alexander III, piles of garbage lay uncollected and Muslim and Chinese women hawked their wares. The following month, *Ogonek* reported that the city's parks had become gambling dens, where workers, soldiers, and sailors staked watches, overcoats, and anything else they could lay their hands on.[8]

Baron E. N. Vrangel described how Petrograd was turning into a "dirty camp of wandering savages." Nevskii became a disorderly, dirty flea market where everything was traded. Buildings were covered with tattered announcements; people ate on the pavement, slept in the garbage, and traded whatever came into their hands. Soldiers wandered in the middle of the road with firearms, many in their underwear. Sentries sat on chairs, with cigarettes between their teeth, and chatted with women. Everybody ate sunflower seeds, and the streets were littered with their shells.[9]

Vrangel's observations and *Ogonek*'s reportage, which celebrated the democratization of Nevskii after the February Revolution only a few months before, betrayed middle-class prejudice against the lower classes taking over the city's most important boulevard. Nonetheless, it captured the drastic changes afoot. A city once kept in pristine beauty by excluding the lower strata of society was suddenly a dirty, stinking, and noisy pothole invaded by plebeians.

The city's physiological change corresponded to the deterioration of life threatened by violent crime. On October 15, ten days before the Bolshevik seizure of power, "Petrograd These Days" lamented the absence of militiamen on the streets. Thefts and robberies were committed in broad daylight.[10] In fact, the city witnessed the exponential rise of crime.

The February Revolution contributed in three fundamental ways to the mounting rise in crime. First, all prisoners incarcerated in Petrograd were freed during the insurrection. The records do not indicate how many of these were political prisoners, but we can safely assume that the vast majority were not. Second, a large number of weapons were captured by the insurgents, and many fell into the hands of criminals and hooligans. Easy access to weapons after the revolution resulted in more crime and made crime more violent.[11] Third, the tsarist police force was eliminated during the February Revolution, and the city militia that replaced it under the Provisional Government was ineffective.

Between March and October, crime induced and reinforced social breakdown, as gambling, prostitution, drug abuse, and alcoholism became rampant and, in their own way, democratized the population. But the political rivalries under dual power sapped authorities of the capacity to control crime and stem social decay. The centrifugal quality of the revolution, delegating power to the level of subdistrict commissariats, was another stumbling block. Thus two types of obstacles—structural (dual power, decentralization) and contingent (prison breaks, diffusion of weapons)—stood in the way of renewing order.

Crime during the February Revolution

In the heat of the revolution, February 23 to March 3, strikers, demonstrators, and unorganized residents, including women and youths, engaged in crimes, blurring the boundaries between political and criminal actions.[12] Undoubtedly, criminal elements in Petrograd also exploited the situation. On February 23, fourteen attacks on grocery stores were reported; on the following day, there were thirty-eight. Shop windows and doors were broken.[13] Trams were attacked and overturned. Although Soviet historians characterized such acts of violence as revolutionary, these instances were in all likelihood vandalism perpetrated by the city's teenagers or hooligans.[14] A major theft at a tobacco and clothing store in working-class Vyborgskii on the night of February 23 suggests that criminals took advantage of the diversion of police to the workers' strikes.[15]

In the early afternoon of February 27, the insurgents attacked Kresty Prison, the Women's Prison in Vyborgskii, and the House of Preliminary Detention in Liteinyi and freed all the prisoners. According to a worker who participated in the Kresty break, there was some discussion about freeing only political prisoners, but despite warning from prison authorities, the insurgents decided to let loose all twenty-four hundred people incarcerated there. Criminals and political prisoners shared a common hatred of the tsarist regime, and many political prisoners believed that criminals were also the victims of the oppressive system. The Military Prison on Nizhegorodskaia Street, the Transit Prison, and the House of the Arrested at the Aleksandro-Nevskii Monastery were also liberated. The administrators of Spasskaia Prison and the Convict Prison released their wards even before the insurgents arrived. On February 28, all the prisoners in the Lithuanian Castle were set free. Not one of them was a political prisoner. The precise number of escaped prisoners is not known, but D. Iu.

Ereshchenko estimates about twenty thousand.[16] Police precincts, the headquarters of the tsarist secret police (Okhrana), the courts of justice, and the Main Political Archives, which housed the Criminal Police's massive criminal records collection, were burned down. Escaped criminals initiated the destruction of the police records.[17]

Some escapees joined in the demonstrations. One teenage boy shouted, "I was freed from prison. Revolution! I am free! I will not steal anymore!"[18] Such repentant criminals, however, were few. Many criminals returned to their old trades. They ransacked the commissaries and cashiers' offices in their prisons, changed into civilian clothes, and proceeded to break into nearby stores. Boris Kolonitskii argues that criminals and revolutionaries easily worked together thanks to their mutual disdain for the prisons and the police, the ultimate symbols of tsarism.[19]

Insurgents seized a colossal number of weapons from regimental armories, munitions factories, and police headquarters and handed them to anyone who asked. Stinton Jones, a British journalist, wrote that everyone—including middle-class residents, young and old—was armed with rifles, revolvers, or sabers. Zigfrid Kelson, secretary of the newly created city militia wrote in his memoirs of a new style born during the February Revolution: "It was fashionable in those days to be dressed with a saber, a rifle, a revolver, a hand grenade, and a machine-gun cartridge belt hanging over the shoulders."[20] In particular, workers sought and acquired weapons—fruits of the revolution, which they considered to be one of the most important gains of the revolution. Henceforth, they jealously guarded this gain.

Armed, hungry soldiers, seasoned criminals, and hooligans roamed the streets. They began to loot and pillage stores, wine cellars, and private apartments. There was a clear danger that the insurrection would develop into total anarchy. The Military Commission organized by the Duma Committee, led by Colonel

Boris A. Engelgardt and Alexander Kerenskii, took active measures to prevent this development by gathering whatever reliable troops were available "to stop the drunken pillaging."[21]

The insurgents attacked and looted government buildings. Here again, the distinction between revolutionary acts and criminal acts was blurred. For instance, the Mariinskii Palace, the seat of the Council of Ministers and the State Council, was attacked on the night of February 27. The next day, insurgents pillaged the postal-telephone section as well as the chancellery of the State Council, from which, according to the chancellery's meticulous accounting, 41,489 rubles and 86 kopecks were stolen.[22] Police precincts and the headquarters of the Gendarme Corps on Furstatskaia Street were also pillaged and then burned. The Admiralty was spared because, at the request of Navy Minister Ivan K. Grigorovich, Chairman of the Duma Mikhail V. Rodzianko dispatched guards to the building on February 28.[23]

As February turned to March, the Military Commission was deluged with reports of attacks on liquor and wine storages. It quickly took strict measures to combat the alcohol pogroms.[24] On February 28, it established security guards in the city's known cellars and warehouses and ordered the destruction of all drinkable alcohol.[25] Some insurgents, presumably led by politically conscious workers, took preventive measures to destroy liquor stored in warehouses.[26]

A popular method of robbery in the early period of the revolution was illegal search. Insurgent soldiers and sailors, or those wearing military uniforms, broke into private homes on the pretext of searching for weapons. They then stole property and sometimes committed murders. For instance, around 10 in the morning on February 28, a group of soldiers broke into an apartment belonging to Lev Karlovich von Bock under the pretext of inspecting documents. Without waiting for von Bock to present his documents, one of the soldiers cried, "Why do we have to talk to a damn German?" and shot the man at point-blank range. After several bayonet strikes for good measure, the soldiers robbed the apartment.[27] In her memoir, Princess Ekaterina N. Sain-Wittgenstein recalled her own robbery at the hands of soldiers. They had arrived to perform an apparently legal search, but once they left, she noticed that a gold watch and other valuables were missing from her nightstand.[28]

To prevent the further erosion of public order, the Military Commission urged soldiers to return to their barracks. Duma leaders attempted to persuade officers—who, fleeing mutinies, had escaped to Tauride Palace and elsewhere—to resume leadership of their units.[29] Drawing on the few military units that maintained a modicum of discipline, the Military Commission established command posts in key areas. On March 1, Mikhail A. Karaulov, a member of the Duma Committee, issued Order No. 1, defining the criteria for carrying out arrests and searches. This order reflected both political exigency and immediate security needs: it sanctioned the arrests of "all ranks of regular and secret police and the corps of gendarmes"—which would cut down on the lingering presence of tsarist police, helping to establish the Duma Committee's revolutionary credentials—as well as "inebriates" and "burglars, arsonists, gunmen shooting in the air, and all others who are disturbing the peace in the capital." Two categories of violators were singled out: those who resisted and obstructed the forces authorized by the Duma Committee, and those who conducted searches in private apartments without special permission of the "Provisional Government." In a direct attempt to assert the Duma Committee's authority, the order demanded that only the Duma and its authorized agents had the right to issue search papers.[30]

On March 2, Karaulov issued another order, this one on the "struggle with looters." He explained that criminals released from the prisons were "disguising themselves in the lower military ranks" and "brazenly bursting into private residences, carrying out illegal searches, robbing, raping, and bringing terror." The impostors should be detained and shot in the event of resistance, Karaulov decreed. Soldiers on patrol would be required to wear white bands bearing the names of their units—an effort to identify reliable fighting men among the great mass.[31] It is not clear, however, how successfully Karaulov's order was carried out.

Combating crime was also a grave concern to the leaders of the Petrograd Soviet. The February 28 inaugural issue of *Izvestiia Petrogradskogo Soveta rabochikh deputatov* (hereafter *Izvestiia*), the Soviet's official newspaper, appealed to insurgents to "arrest hooligans who are engaging in looting and turn them over to the Commandant of Petrograd under the State Duma."[32] On March 1, *Izvestiia* appealed to "revolutionary people" to destroy liquor reserves, lest "the dregs of society . . . get drunk and begin looting and commit senseless murders, which can seriously harm the cause of the revolution."[33] The next day, *Izvestiia* called for the registration of weapons in order to get them out of the hands of hooligans and looters.[34] At this point, the Petrograd Soviet, the future rival of the Provisional Government, was still collaborating with the Duma Committee. It is also important to note that the Petrograd Soviet, representing the insurgent workers and soldiers, characterized the lower rung of society as the "dregs" of society.

Students also played a crucial role in calming the unrest. During the insurrection, attendees of Petrograd University, Military Medical School, Polytechnic Institute, Mining Institute, and Technological Institute organized volunteers to perform first aid, distribute food, and secure order. On March 1, the Military Medical School's Committee of Military-Technical Aid appealed to the insurgents to combat drunkenness, looting, and arson. Presciently, this appeal understood that the struggle against crime might lead to new crime—mob justice [*samosudy*]—and warned,

"Citizens . . . do not shoot [looters] without instructions from the patrols."[35]

To deal with common criminals and arrested policemen, the Military Commission hastily created a Lower Investigation Commission. But the commission had little impact, detaining only nineteen people in the course of its existence. Theft from former tsarist police and others deemed monarchists routinely went unpunished. Rather than handle citizen complaints, the Lower Investigation Commission often passed them on to the city governor's office for "consideration," and they remained there without any decisions.[36]

The early days of the revolutionary period presaged many of the challenges to come. The downfall of the tsar brought as much hope as uncertainty, a competition for power staged in a theater of social unrest. In just the first days, it was becoming clear that the authorities lacked the power to assert real control. We can already see how surging crime could undermine revolutionary dreams and turn the hope into disillusionment.

In later chapters, I will discuss how the people and competing authorities responded to surging criminality and social breakdown. For now, let us turn to archives and contemporary news reports to demonstrate just how bad things got in Petrograd.

Theft

Early on, officials and citizens widely believed that the increase in crime was merely a by-product of the confusion arising from the revolution. They expected crime to subside after the new political system was established under the Provisional Government. But their hopes were dashed. Ereshchenko has collected data, based on thorough archival research and newspaper accounts, showing just how intolerable the situation became.

According to Ereshchenko's findings, the incidence of theft increased ten-fold between April and the Bolshevik takeover.

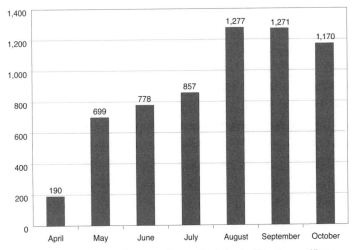

Figure 2. Thefts, April–October 1917. *Source:* Ereshchenko, "Prestupnost'," 115.

Altogether, there were 6,242 thefts in this period, an average of 891.1 per month. Between September and October 24, the average was 1,239 per month. By contrast, in 1914 there were 478.4 thefts per month, and in 1915, 506.3 per month.[37]

Ereshchenko's figures are the best available, but they underestimate the level of criminality in Petrograd. After the February Revolution, it took the city militia some time to assemble a crime-reporting system.[38] Even when the new system was in place, it was not especially reliable. Subdistrict commissariats were less than diligent in submitting daily reports to the city militia administration. For instance, in September and October, fewer than one-third of subdistrict commissariats entered reports in the administration's daily *Journal of Events.* Furthermore, many petty thefts were likely unreported. Ereshchenko relies on the journal and court records from the era, but they are incomplete.[39] Newspaper stories can therefore provide another useful marker of rising criminality.

Already in late April and early May, major thefts had become so frequent that *Petrogradskii listok* decided to restore its "Larcenies in the Capital" column. Each entry described several serious crimes and ended with a kind of ritual incantation: "And many more were also reported." On June 16, the newspaper reported more than forty complaints of thefts within a twenty-four-hour period. With a sense of alarm, the press announced that this was "unprecedented anarchy."[40] But this was just the beginning.

Between July 3 and 5, a period of political crisis known as the July Days, thieves attacked at least fifty stores and stole goods worth 3 million rubles.[41] The crime wave did not abate after the crisis was over. On July 15, there were ten reports of thefts, including six major ones in which 15,000–100,000 rubles' worth of property was stolen.[42] On August 15, property worth 5 million rubles was stolen from the Historical Museum.[43]

In the last two months leading up to the October Revolution, thievery reached new heights. Twenty thefts were registered on September 13.[44] That figure rose to 250 on October 4 and 307 on October 7. On October 14, *Petrogradskii listok* reported more than eight hundred registered thefts in the preceding forty-eight hours.[45] Spasskaia Church, Volkovo Cemetery, the Museum of Jewelry, and even the Petrograd Soviet itself were broken into. The apartment of Vera Figner, a legendary populist revolutionary, was burglarized.[46] Pickpockets flourished. Particularly dangerous areas included Nikolaevskii Railway Station and the city's crowded tramways—both the stops where people congregated and the crowded trams themselves. On April 11, just weeks after the February Revolution, *Petrogradskii listok* warned that pickpocketing had reached a "dangerous" level.[47] Of course, most petty crimes went unreported; the situation was even worse than the paper's journalists knew.

Robbery

Although thefts were a serious problem, robberies, in which victims are not only deprived of their belongings but also threatened or assaulted, presented a greater challenge due to the violence involved.

During and immediately after the February Revolution, robbery in the guise of illegal search presented a serious threat. Ereshchenko's data also show that the number of illegal searches declined after April, but this did not mean that order was restored in Petrograd. In fact, it suggests precisely the opposite: As time passed, robbers and thieves were emboldened. They learned how to get what they wanted without bothering to disguise themselves as militiamen or present fake search orders. The political crisis of the July Days saw an opportunistic return to old ways, but when the crisis was over, the number of illegal searches dwindled again.[48]

On the whole, the number of robberies steadily increased from April to October.[49] Between March and October, Ereshchenko counts an average of 20.5 robberies per month. This is a dramatic increase from 1915, which averaged 5.3 cases per month. Al-

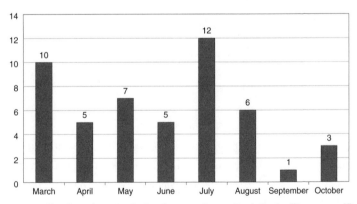

Figure 3. Illegal searches, March–October 1917. *Source:* Ereshchenko, "Prestupnost'," 120.

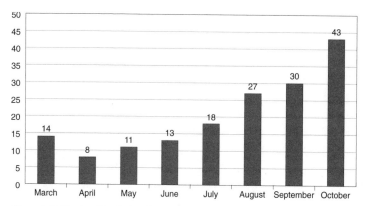

Figure 4. Robberies, March–October 1917. *Source:* Ereshchenko, "Prestupnost," 124.

though the number of robberies is probably underreported for reasons I describe above, it is safe to conclude that the incidence increased after the February Revolution, alarmingly so from September to October.

Robberies became more brazen as time passed. On July 27, about twenty soldiers in uniform arrived at the Chernigov Refrigeration Company in an official military vehicle and pulled off, with military precision, a heist worth 230,000 rubles.[50] Also in July, armed robbers attacked the building of the Governing Senate, the highest judicial authority, comparable to the Supreme Court in the United States. Between August and October, the museum of Grand Duke Mikhail Nikolaevich, the palace of Grand Duke Andrei Vladimirovich, and several churches were robbed.[51] Before the revolution, criminal syndicates had followed a code of honor in which churches were sacrosanct. It may be that, during the unrest of 1917, churches became fair game among professional criminals. More likely, though, the criminal population had expanded.

Murder

The most frightening aspect of crime in Petrograd after the February Revolution was the increase in murders. The data show that 163 murders were committed from March to October, an average of 18.1 murders a month. The murder rate, for the most part, corresponds to the trend of thefts and robberies, as the monthly breakdown shows an alarming increase for the three months before the October Revolution. The number of murders shot up in August and increased in September and October with a sharp upward curve. In fact, 65 percent of all murders took place from August to October, and the number of murders in October alone constitutes 32.5 percent of all murders committed from March to October. Compared to the murder rate in some contemporary American cities, these numbers may not seem large. But Petrograd was the site of only fifteen murders in 1914 and thirty in 1915.[52]

The Shlosberg and Kulero murder cases introduced in the beginning of this chapter were only the tip of the iceberg. Lurid news coverage of other murders both deepened and revealed the apprehension of the public. On May 18, a dead woman was found in Ekterinogofki River, her hands tied behind her back.[53] Six days

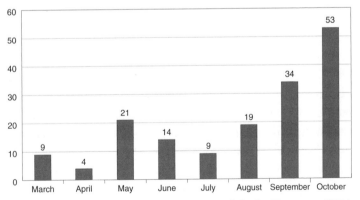

Figure 5. Murders, March–October 1917. *Source:* Ereshchenko, "Prestupnost'," 126.

later, a young Chinese woman, apparently raped, was found dead, with her eyes gouged, throat slit, and knife wounds covering her body.[54] It is likely that both murders were connected with Chinese gangs. In August, *Petrogradskii listok* reported in grisly detail the disinterment of body after body from the backyard of a psychopath.[55]

One of the most shocking cases became apparent on August 29, when a headless torso washed up on the shore of Obvodnyi Canal. A few days later, three packages containing severed legs and arms were found in different parts of the city.[56] Amid the excitement of the ongoing Kornilov Affair, the city's readers were drawn to the grisly discoveries of body parts. They proved to be parts of a wealthy Finnish trader, Arno Karlovich Seitola, who was in Petrograd on business. On August 22, he left his hotel and never returned. The hotel staff thought he had unexpectedly gone home. After hearing nothing for two weeks, on September 3, Seitola's family came to Petrograd and requested a police investigation. Detectives brought the family to the Obukhov Hospital morgue, where Seitola's brother identified the imprint of the businessman's initials on the ring finger of a right hand, from which his gold ring had evidently been removed. Further investigation demonstrated probable connections between Seitola and an organized crime family.[57] While the political crisis was unfolding at the top, the dark criminal world was operating underneath, connecting gambling, business, and murder.[58]

Another sensational case emerged in October, when a dvornik named Petrov, his wife, and three small children were brutally murdered in the same building that housed the Second Lesnoi city militia commissariat. The girls were stabbed at least fourteen times between them. Petrov must have struggled with the murderers, as his hands were covered in deep cuts. His wife's body was torn to pieces; her head was nearly severed, and both hands were cut off. Two blood-stained swords were left at the crime scene.

Rumors implicating the militia itself spread quickly, and soon more than a thousand irate residents had gathered at the militia headquarters to protest and blocked the car transporting the bodies for autopsy. The city militia administration had to call in a military unit to disperse the angry crowd.[59]

The location of the Petrov family murder was significant. Once a quiet residential suburb, Lesnoi was no longer spared. Earlier, on May 2, two deserters had broken into a house there, strangled a servant to death, beat a thirteen-year-old boy into unconsciousness, and stole money and valuables worth approximately 20,000 rubles.[60] Crime not only became more frequent and intense, but its terrain also expanded. The angry protest of the residents who surrounded the militia headquarters for several days was an expression of anger and frustration against a militia that was unable to prevent crime in their neighborhood.

Kidnapping and Rape

In June, newspapers started reporting on the disappearance of small children from streets and parks. Most victims were between four and ten years old.[61] Where they went and what happened to them remained a mystery. Though they were thought to be kidnapped, it is more likely that their mothers, unable to care for them, simply abandoned them.[62] Around the same time, the coverage of rapes also increased. Some occurred in people's apartments while they were robbed.[63] It seemed neither public nor private spaces offered any security, leaving residents with nowhere to turn. The boundary between street and home blurred.[64]

Crime and Social Breakdown

Mounting crime fostered social disintegration. It would not be an exaggeration to say that on the eve of the October Revolution, the capital of the empire was on the verge of collapse. The notion of any sort of collective life was replaced by individual self-preservation. This was expressed vividly by former tsarist Okhrana chief Konstantin I. Globachev, who had been arrested after the February Revolution and was released at the end of August:

> In the entire month of September and October, anarchy essentially ruled over Petrograd. Criminals multiplied to an unimaginable extent. Every day robberies and murders were committed not only at night, but also in broad daylight. Residents feared for the safety of their own lives. The populace, seeing that it would be impossible to expect any help from the nominally existing authority, began to organize themselves and form house guards or take other security measures in case of attacks by robbers. In every residential house, armed guards were posted each night. But this did not help, and robberies continued.[65]

Ogonek illustrated the situation in a cartoon. A couple lie in a bedroom surrounded with barbed wire, a machine gun, a revolver, and iron bars. "With 400 robberies a night, how can the citizens of Petrograd sleep?" the caption reads.[66] See figure 6. Crime bred frustration, anger, mistrust, and a yearning for escape. It was not only the propertied class that worried, but the whole population; with crime rampant, everyone understood himself or herself as a potential mark or as a bystander vulnerable to the crossfire. The effect on residents' psyches was considerable and pervasive.

Gambling

Social disintegration was manifest in widespread gambling. Before the February Revolution, gambling had been a more limited

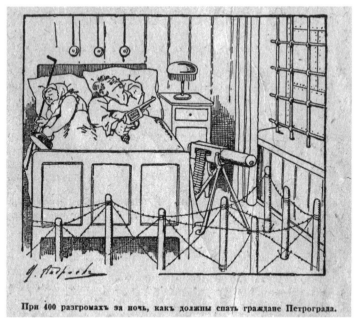

При 400 разгромахъ за ночь, какъ должны спать граждане Петрограда.

Figure 6. Citizens guarding against robbers. The cartoon's caption reads: "With 400 robberies a night, how can the citizens of Petrograd sleep?" *Ogonek,* no. 41, October 22, 1917, 17.

and covert activity. Though it remained illegal afterward, people from all walks of life gambled, sometimes openly. Women, previously excluded from gambling clubs, were welcomed. Gamblers were no longer required to show membership cards in order to access clubs, further democratizing access.[67]

Gambling flourished both in high society and among the poor. The courtyard at Obukhov Hospital in the Fourth Moskovskii Subdistrict was turned into a huge gambling den where crowds, including hospital personnel and patients, wagered away their coats, rings, watches, and what few other valuables they had.[68]

Attempts to shut down gambling operations met fierce resistance. For instance, the city militia found itself rebuffed on the night of August 4, when it attempted to break up a torch-lit gambling party of three hundred in a forest on a nobleman's estate. Among the gamblers were many criminals and deserters who did not hesitate to fire on the small cadre of militiamen and drive them away. An hour later, the gamblers repulsed another militia unit. Eventually, the militia succeeded in dispersing the crowd but made few arrests.[69]

The popularity of gambling caused a shortage of playing cards in and around Petrograd. In August, the price of a deck of cards rose to 40 rubles, more than one-third of a low-level wage earner's monthly earnings. Stores could not hold on to their inventory, and long queues formed in front of the manufacturer in the Second Kazanskii Subdistrict. On August 17, militiamen took the opportunity to inspect the identification cards of those in line and found only eight people with their papers in order. Many deserters, ex-convicts, and criminals were among the buyers, and around eighty people were arrested on the spot.[70] In the worsening food shortage, a bread line is understandable. But waiting your turn for playing cards? Few images convey in sharper relief the desperation that befell Petrograd.

The situation worsened at the end of August with the formation of new gambling groups among the privileged. An organization calling itself the Petrograd Assembly of Intellectual Workers, based in the Hotel Regina at the center of the city in the Admiralteiskii District, was nothing but a gambling den headed by infamous criminals Stanislav R. Baum and Aleksandr L. Enshtein.[71] After military authorities shut the club down on September 2, another club, called Concordia, was established with exactly the same charter as the Petrograd Assembly of Intellectual Workers.[72] The militia uncovered a similar gambling club, the Petrograd Democratic Literary-Artistic Assembly, and closed it in September. It had operated in the Café Ampir, "a notorious gathering place for swindlers, cocaine sellers, and speculators," which the murdered Finnish merchant Seitola frequented.[73]

On the eve of the October Revolution, more than seventy illegal gambling clubs had mushroomed in restaurants and cabarets, mostly in central districts. Gamblers tried to "grab everything they could, as if they had the premonition that there would soon be an end to all of this." Even high officials were known to frequent these shady locales, including Colonel G. P. Polkovnik, commander of the Petrograd Military District, and his staff; Anatolii N. Speranskii, head of the Provisional Government's security service; and Boris Savinkov, deputy minister of war under Kerenskii.[74]

In an August editorial, *Gazeta-Kopeika* noted a perverse side effect of all the gambling. Stores were refusing to sell merchandise to the usual shoppers who haggled over prices, because shopkeepers knew that gamblers could pay more. So while some entered deeper poverty, merchants hoarded goods for the gamblers who came out on top, doubling the misery of those in need. The gamblers hurt themselves and everyone else who struggled to make ends meet. "Widespread gambling is no longer a legal question," *Gazeta-Kopeika* warned. "It is a danger to the society."[75]

Drunkenness

Drunkenness in public places, quite apart from the further crimes committed by drunkards, taxed the city militia. Throughout 1917, drunkenness was the primary reason listed for detention in the commissariats. The city militia's *Journal of Events* offers the following tally for September 30 to October 4: 104 detentions for theft, 2 for injuring others, 13 for swindling, 3 for gambling, 40 for fighting, and 319 for drunkenness. Related crimes, such as the purchase and sale of spirits and alcohol surrogates and disorderly conduct, were also common.[76] The papers tended to ignore these cases, probably because drunkenness was too prevalent to be newsworthy.

It was easy for Petrograd to indulge its alcoholism. The Provisional Government continued to honor the dry law, but enforcement was ineffectual. At the same time, as a result of the dry law, the city had accumulated a massive liquor reserve during the war. Illegal underground moonshining flourished, creating a powerful second economy. From September 1916 to May 1917, the Excise Department of the Ministry of Agriculture reported 9,352 moonshining cases, more than fifteen times the number reported in 1913. Excise officials estimated that the actual number was about ten times higher.[77]

Good drinks were readily available in restaurants and clubs. Low-grade spirits and surrogates were abundant in seedier gathering places.[78] Drunkenness became such a serious problem that the First City District Soviet—which included the center-mixed districts of the Liteinyi, Rozhdestvenskii, Aleksandro-Nevskii, and Moskovskii Districts—decided to prohibit the sale of "denatured alcohol, varnish, eau-de-cologne, and other surrogates" without its permission. The Kolomenskii District Soviet accepted a proposal from Franco-Russian factory workers to close "dens of ill repute," including the bars Colombia, Maiak, and Svoboda. It is doubtful that these resolutions had much effect, though.[79]

As early as July, it appeared the zeal for drink might inspire mass criminality. The Second Kolomenskii Subdistrict militia had to call in reinforcements to suppress a riot forming at a storage facility owned by the winemaker Liubimov. Among the crowd were many soldiers, some exhorting the mob to break into the warehouse and drink everything on the spot.[80] It was another harbinger of events to come after the October Revolution.

Prostitution and Venereal Disease

The 1910 census listed 560 prostitutes in Petrograd.[81] There were surely more, however. Already in 1870s, there were 206 bordellos in St. Petersburg, with 1,528 prostitutes. These were officially registered, "ticketed" prostitutes. To prove their status, they received yellow tickets from the Medical-Police Committee under the city governor.

With the influx of population at the turn of the century, the number of prostitutes grew. Desperate for work, women became unregistered streetwalkers, doing their business in "houses of meeting" (*doma svidanii*), or what the police called "dens of debauchery." Homeowners provided them room and board in return for commissions. The Medical-Police Committee kept an eye on these prostitutes as well and issued them passports with the section for profession left blank. They thus gained the evocative and sobering nickname of "blank" (*blankovye*) prostitutes, as distinct from their ticketed colleagues. Competition between the two types of prostitutes decidedly favored the blanks, who presumably were cheaper and more readily available. By 1910, there were only thirty-two brothels with 322 prostitutes, but blank prostitutes numbered about 2,500.[82]

Some prostitutes catered to high-class clients at expensive restaurants, cabarets, and nightclubs on Nevskii, Liteinyi, and Kamenoostroskii Prospects. Aquarium, a Kamenoostrovskii restaurant, was especially prized by upscale clients. Some of the women available there spoke three foreign languages. At the lower end were more than 450 bars. Sexual transactions were conducted in most bars, which were equipped with small "service" rooms in their inner sanctums. Notorious quarters included Sennaia Square and the side streets connecting Zabalkanskii Prospect with Sadovaia.

The lowest rung of prostitutes were *gnilushchitsy* ("rotten fruit and vegetable venders"), who sold their wares along with their bodies for a bowl of soup or a glass of vodka. They congregated in the Viazemskii slums, and after the slums were torn down, they migrated to Borovaia Street, Volkovo cemetery, and bars and houses of ill repute behind Nevskii Gate.[83] The worst conditions were in night shelters, to which the most desperate prostitutes catered. It was not unusual for prostitutes to be quite young. A justice of the peace in the Fourth Spasskii Subdistrict wrote to the city governor's office on August 22 about nine prostitutes he identified operating in his building, including two eighteen-year-olds and one seventeen-year-old.[84]

The February Revolution put an end to the city governor's office and, with it, medical inspections of prostitutes. The result was a venereal disease epidemic. A casual glance at the daily newspapers shows a large number of ads devoted to the treatment of syphilis. For instance, of 101 advertisements hawking cures in the March 12 issue of *Petrogradskii listok,* 36 claimed to treat venereal diseases, and 20 focused specifically on syphilis.[85] In July, the official municipal newspaper *Vestnik gorodskogo samoupravleniia* reported that syphilis affected 2,690 out of 100,000 people. By comparison, the American Centers for Disease Control and Prevention reported a worrying uptick in the U.S. rate in 2016—to 7.5 cases per 100,000 people.[86] Prostitutes themselves demanded that medical inspection be restored, and in response, the Provisional Government created a Conference to Combat Venereal Diseases on March 20. But the effort made little difference.[87]

While medical inspections faltered, disease vectors multiplied. Critical sources included soldiers and sailors, many of whom were posted in Petrograd or arrived as deserters. In any case, their overall numbers swelled thanks to the war, and they formed long queues in front of major brothels. It was thanks to their voraciousness that some prostitutes received as many as forty-five clients a day. Unable to withstand the exploitation, prostitutes were known to surreptitiously escape from apartment and brothel windows and seek protection in subdistrict commissariats.[88]

Narcotics

Starting in the 1880s, opium, morphine, and cocaine were routinely used for medical purposes. But wartime alcohol prohibition contributed to the expansion of cocaine beyond medicine, and recreational use became fashionable in the capital in the 1910s.[89] A narcotic for the rich, cocaine was obtained under the table from drugstore clerks for two to three rubles per gram.

In general, use before the February Revolution did not extend beyond the nighttime "world of pleasure" inhabited by decadent men, their lovers, ladies of the demimonde, and the high-end prostitutes who serviced them all.[90] The February Revolution drastically changed the situation, democratizing narcotics use. Young people in soldiers' and sailors' coats, "persons without definite jobs," and low-end prostitutes bought cocaine in cafés, confectioneries, and bars. Consumption skyrocketed.[91]

Starting in the spring, newspapers took great interest in incidents involving narcotics. On March 20, papers reported a couple caught with a thousand rubles' worth of opium at Nikolaevskii Station. The man escaped, but the woman was arrested. After failing to bribe the militia for her release, she confessed and turned over information about the inner workings of the drug trade. The investigation produced locations of stashes and a list of high-society women who regularly used narcotics.[92]

Raids followed the next day.[93] One of the raids, at a small waffle café owned by a Greek named Apostolar, provides an interesting glimpse of expanding drug use. Rather than playboys and their women, this was a gathering place for society's lowest ranks. A leather bag maker was arrested there with four kilograms of cocaine, a staggering amount in any context, but most especially for a poor tradesman. An arrested soldier had ten bottles of *samogon*—illegally brewed vodka. Among the arrested were also three deserters.[94]

Particularly active in uncovering narcotics dealers was the mobile squad of the Second Moskovskii Subdistrict. The squad staked out a small teahouse with a suspicious clientele—high school and university students, soldiers, and well-dressed young women who were either privileged or high-class prostitutes. An informant revealed a room in the teahouse known as Desiatka— slang for a ten-ruble bill—where cocaine and opium were sold and used. The squad then arrested one of the dealers, Malitz Volman, and from his confession, they learned that his brother Abram Volman was the kingpin of the narcotics dealers. Abram Volman's distribution network covered not only Petrograd but also Moscow and other southern cities. The narcotics were smuggled from Germany through Sweden. Famous Petrograd swindlers such as Kostromin, Iakov Boltman, and Sergei Gebotarev worked for him. The militia soon arrested Abram Volman at Desiatka. The court gave him a paltry nine-month prison term.

Kostromin owned twenty-six furnished rental apartments where he often organized wild parties. When militiamen raided one such party, they found around forty people—including high-society women, daughters of intelligentsia, and teenage girls— engaged in a narcotic orgy. A woman lay unconscious after a six-day cocaine binge. Kostromin himself was arrested after a three-night stakeout at the Lyon inn in the notorious tenderloin district known as Peski in the First Rozhdestvenskii Subdistrict. His companions for the evening—his "personal secretary," Aleksandra Andreeva, a baroness, and a female government office worker— were also arrested. The baroness and the office worker were unconscious at the time, having overdosed on cocaine.[95]

Newspaper accounts show widespread use of narcotics in areas of the central and central-mixed districts known for vices—cheap inns, bars, and brothels. The small area between Leshtukov and Shcherbakov Lanes in the Third Moskovskii Subdistrict, in particular, was a narcotic haven. As befit the diversity of these regions, usage was not limited to any one class. Cocaine spread from the upper stratum to the middle class and even to poor tradesmen, such as the leather worker hauling four kilos in Apostolar's waffle shop. Among the arrested in the drug bust was an American singer, Black Leo, who had come to Petrograd as a cabaret singer and dancer, but soon found a more lucrative job as a narcotic dealer, adding an international flavor to the drug use.[96]

Reflecting a persistent theme in the distribution of criminality, working-class areas were mostly spared. Judging from newspaper reports and the records of the district soviets, narcotics were not a major cause of concern in working-class neighborhoods or among soldiers and the organized proletariat. For them, alcohol was the drug of choice.

After the summer, newspapers stopped reporting on cocaine. We should not infer, though, that the use of cocaine and other narcotics declined. After all, it is common today for the press to report extensively on drug scares and then turn to other topics, not because drug use has ended but because it persists beyond the point of newsworthiness. The lack of coverage in Petrograd reflects both this journalistic proclivity and the general failure of the city militia to tackle the problem. As the city militia weakened during the summer, sensational anti-trafficking efforts were in short supply. The drugs only multiplied. After the October Revolution, narcotics use was still widespread.[97]

Political Crisis and Social Breakdown

Crisis in high politics proceeded in tandem with the precipitous breakdown of social life.

During the July Days, huge numbers of Bolshevik-led demonstrators, including fully armed sailors, marched on Nevskii demanding: "All Power to the Soviets." The Provisional Government ment dispersed the demonstrators forcefully. Gun battles left as many as four hundred people dead. The Provisional Government also attempted to undermine the Bolsheviks by leaking a document purporting to show that the party was taking German money. The counteroffensive was initially successful, forcing Bolshevik leaders into retreat. Leon Trotsky, Lev Kamenev, and others were arrested, and Lenin fled into hiding in Finland.[98]

The triumph of the Provisional Government was, however, short-lived and further radicalized workers' and soldiers' organizations. Indeed, as we will see in Chapter 4, even the city militia resisted the Provisional Government's attempt to reassert central control over the police. This led to yet more erosion of police power.

In August, the government, led by Kerenskii, entered negotiations with the newly appointed army commander-in-chief, General Lavr Kornilov. The goal was to restore order in the capital. Each man was interested in using the other for his own purposes. Kerenskii was eager to exploit Kornilov's military power to suppress the Bolsheviks and their left-wing fellow travelers and to buttress his own popularity and the Provisional Government supported by the moderate socialists of the Petrograd Soviet. Kornilov, meanwhile, was intent on destroying the left in general and the Petrograd Soviet itself as the major source of disorder in Petrograd and the nation as a whole.

Having failed to reach an agreement with Kerenskii, Kornilov attempted to install himself as military dictator. On August 26, his troops marched toward Petrograd to displace the Soviet. Kerenskii and his fellow moderate socialists, panicked with the fear that the revolution was in danger, appealed to all forces to resist the putsch. Kornilov's counterrevolution was suppressed, mostly by the resistance of the workers' organizations that Kerenskii had previously suppressed. The Kornilov Affair further damaged the authority of the Provisional Government as well as the moderate socialists who had supported it.[99]

The Bolsheviks emerged as the major beneficiary of the crisis provoked by Kornilov's coup attempt. Their leaders were released from prison, and their popularity soared. They captured the majority in the Petrograd Soviet in September, and Trotsky was installed as its chairman. It was at this point that Lenin began plotting to seize power by force rather than through the Soviet. From exile in Finland and then after moving back to Petrograd, he bombarded reluctant Bolshevik leaders with strident missives arguing for a coup that would come on the night of October 24–25.[100]

This political drama played out on a stage of social upheaval. Elite competition was heightened by soaring crime; explosions of mob justice; food riots; epidemics of typhus, small pox, and scarlet fever; and paralyzed city services. Whoever was on top of the government completely lost control of the everyday life of citizens in the capital, and ordinary citizens became largely indifferent to the high political maneuvering that was unfolding.

Crime, desertion, hooliganism, prostitution, gambling, and drug abuse in Petrograd were all connected. They spread together and fed off one another, sinking the population into despair. The inability of authorities to address metastasizing problems weakened popular support for civic institutions and political parties, resulting in a vigilante mentality that would only result in more crime as mob justice swept the city.

A number of factors—prison breaks, the availability of weapons, the removal of the tsarist police—contributed to the flourishing of crime. But why were authorities powerless to respond? I have already offered the beginnings of an explanation. In the next chapter, I dig into the political, economic, and sociological foundations of criminality and the responses to it. Crime soured, reflecting and reinforcing social breakdown. The response was inept because the Provisional Government—battered by the Petrograd and district soviets and hamstrung by the powerful force of decentralization—was unable to implement a coherent, authoritative legal system respected in Petrograd and beyond.

3. Why Did the Crime Rate Shoot Up?

With crime on the rise in the earliest days of the revolution, a crackdown might have been the new government's first priority. But the preservation of law and order is challenging under even the best of circumstances, and Petrograd in 1917 was not the best of circumstances.

When the Russian people overthrew the monarchy, they did so with the expectation that its onerous system would be permanently erased. The new regime had to replace not only the police but also the legal system generally. The Provisional Government immediately wrestled with this problem, first scrapping the most offensive parts of the tsar's law and then partially revitalizing it. Separate courts—one inherited from the tsar, the other designed to represent the masses—operated alongside each other. It was a well-intended arrangement but also dysfunctional from the standpoint of justice. Parallel courts exacerbated social tension as citizens took their complaints to one or the other court according to their level of class privilege.

Seeking to preserve the humanistic essence of the revolution, the Provisional Government at first pursued lenient reforms even as crime overwhelmed Petrograd. In this we again see how crime altered the trajectory of the new Russian state, undermining the potential of the revolution by forcing authorities to respond to the needs of the day. Petrograd was coming undone amid persistent political, economic, and social chaos, and the government had to choose between faithfulness to the revolution on the one hand and the dire need for stability on the other.

The people, too, struggled to keep faith. The revolution raised expectations, and subsequent disorder trampled them. Economic decline produced shortages of food and basic necessities. Political rivalry and decentralization weakened the authorities to the point where they could not act. The result was widespread disillusionment. Petrograd's residents could not eat socialist or liberal ideals or shelter themselves under the protection of a democratic culture. They sought only to survive—a condition the Bolsheviks would eventually exploit. This may be something of a universal constant: revolution promises a great deal but seldom makes life better, at least at first.

The effects of crime in revolutionary Petrograd cannot be understood in a vacuum. To appreciate the durable impact of crime on the state, we need to account for the cataclysmic political, economic, social, legal, administrative, and psychological changes that Russia and its people underwent during the revolution. Exploring these fundamental sources of crime means turning to the factors that induced desperation, created opportunity for wrongdoing, and paralyzed the state when its intervention was most needed.

Political Instability

The Russian Revolution was a period of both roiling change and official stasis. The condition of "dual power," in which the Provisional Government could not act without the agreement of the Petrograd Soviet, mostly ensured inaction. The sclerotic government was an easy mark for growing social movements—among them the workers' movement, peasants' unrest, mutinous soldiers, and national minority separatist movements. Bolsheviks, the left wing of the Socialist Revolutionary Party, and anarchists capitalized on these social upheavals, challenging both the Provisional

Government and moderate socialist leaders in the Petrograd Soviet, who supported the government without taking power by themselves. Antiwar demonstrations provoked what became known as the April Crisis. Top ministers resigned, and the Provisional Government was forced to accept further Soviet influence by forming a power-sharing coalition with the moderate socialists. The Bolsheviks and the other radical antiwar socialists, who called themselves "internationalists," gained ground as the only parties clearly independent of the Provisional Government and its unpopular war policies. At the first All-Russian Congress of Soviets held in June 1917, Irakli Tsereteli, a Menshevik leader who joined the first coalition government as the minister of post and telegraph only to prop up the failing Provisional Government, challenged his radical opponents, stating: "There is no party willing to take power." Lenin stood up from his seat, famously challenged Tsereteli, "Yes, there is such a party." The audience laughed at this preposterously bold and seemingly unrealistic claim.

The Provisional Government lived up to its name, collapsing and reforming three times after its inception. Each government succession enjoyed less authority than its predecessor. After the July Days and the Kornilov Affair, the Provisional Government virtually lost its legitimacy entirely. In search of legitimacy beyond the Provisional Government and the Petrograd Soviet, Alexander Kerenskii sought the backing of the Moscow State Conference in August and the Council of the Republic in October by assembling representatives of various institutions and political parties as a supra body that would transcend the Provisional Government and the Petrograd Soviet before the Constituent Assembly was convened. But he only lost more ground to the ascending Bolsheviks.[1]

Needless to say, the instability of the central government was not conducive to maintaining public order. The government simply did not have the resources and sufficient time and energy to devote to the issues of crime. It is no accident, therefore, that the numbers of thefts, robberies, and murders jumped to an alarming degree after August, when the authority of the central government sank to its nadir.

Economic Crisis

Political crisis was accompanied by economic collapse, seen most acutely in the dwindling food supply, which directly affected the city's residents.[2] The February Revolution began as a bread riot, but the Provisional Government had no workable solution to this intractable issue. In an attempt to get a handle on the situation, the Provisional Government established a bread monopoly on March 29 and adopted the policy of forced grain requisition previously pursued by the tsar's last minister of agriculture. By controlling the food supply, the government hoped to keep prices down. But in July, the government received only 60 percent of the planned grain purchase; in August, only 40 percent. Without an effective monopoly, the government could not set prices. Producers were reluctant to sell. Railway transport problems, as well as the city's dwindling capacity to transport food within the city, compounded the crisis, and speculation by various organizations and individual traders took advantage of the crisis. By the beginning of October, food shortages reached catastrophic proportions. In the first ten days of October, instead of five hundred wagons of grain that the city expected to receive, only fifteen wagons were delivered. By October 14, the city had only enough bread supply to last three and a half days. The ration for bread was reduced to one pound for those engaged in physical labor and a half pound for the remaining citizens. Not only bread but also other food items became scarce. In September, the deliveries of meat were reduced to half of the expected amount, fish to 85 percent, eggs to 16 percent, and milk to 8 percent. Rations were also introduced for tea, meat, animal fat, and eggs. Consequently, food costs rose dramatically—from five to sixteen times the government price, depending on the item.[3]

Decentralization also hampered the government's ability to respond to the food shortage. In September, the city administration developed a system of bread rations, but it was forced to rely on the housing committees to issue ration cards.[4] It makes sense that the city administration did not turn to the district soviets, which competed with the municipal government. But the city administration was itself fragmented, divided in ways that mirrored the crack-up in high politics, and hampered by high personnel turnover. These weaknesses were also multiplied at the district dumas. Moreover, the district dumas had only tenuous control over their subdistrict food commissions. It was therefore easier to rely on housing committees and skip over the intermediary district dumas and subdistrict food supply commissions. This arrangement itself demonstrated the paralysis of the municipal government.

The food shortage not only induced ill health and desperation, it also directly promoted criminality. Those lacking official residency—deserters, evacuees, escaped prisoners—were denied ration cards. This created a situation where the most dangerous, crime-prone elements of society had no choice but to commit further crime to feed themselves. They stole goods and forged identification papers in order to access rations. Documentary evidence is lacking on this, but the dysfunctional food-supply mechanism must have opened great opportunities for criminal elements to engage in illegal underground theft and speculation operations. And as rations became skimpier, even legitimate cardholders turned to illegal means. Thus residents increasingly relied on street venders and markets that bucked ration rules.

Social tensions mounted in these public spaces, where people of all strata mingled.[5]

In parallel to the food-supply crisis, industrial production declined sharply. Shortages of raw materials and fuel and railway disruption continued after the February Revolution, as top priority was given to military needs. By September, metal industry production dropped to 50 percent of its February level.[6] At that point, amid acute labor disputes, productivity in Petrograd was reduced to 20 percent of the prewar level. Workers terrorized engineers, foremen, and managers, and factory committees took over the management. Some were tarred and carted off from factories in wheelbarrows. By the summer of 1917, 20 percent of Petrograd's factories and mills (568 of them) were shuttered, and 104,670 workers lost their jobs. Especially hard hit were unskilled workers. These were mostly unorganized workers who had nowhere to turn for support. To survive, they had to rely on their own means. That often meant crime.[7]

Reduced industrial production was especially acute for consumer goods. Prices of kerosene, soap, cloth, shoes, and other necessities shot up. Long queues formed in front of shoe stores and soap manufacturing factories.[8] The Provisional Government's food supply official, V. Martovskii, observed, "anyone who has had to stand for hours in a queue or run around town in a fruitless search for bread can tell you to what a state of free-floating annoyance and spite it can lead and what a fertile ground it is for pogrom agitation."[9]

Housing Crisis

Housing in Petrograd and other major Russian cities reflected stark lines of social stratification. Atop the pyramid were the owners, who lived in their own houses and apartment buildings.

Next were those with enough money to rent an apartment, whether luxurious or more modest. Less fortunate city dwellers rented a room within an apartment. The average worker might rent a corner of a room, about 2 to 2.5 square meters. Unskilled workers commonly rented a bench or cot within a corner. In many cases, more than two people or in some cases an entire family slept on a single bed.[10]

The poorest could not afford even a corner or a bench and instead lived in homeless shelters. In 1914, there were fifteen city-operated municipal night shelters and eleven privately operated night shelters in Petrograd. Altogether they could house up to eighty-two hundred people.[11] After the February Revolution, the financial difficulties of the city administration and the general economic crisis, especially the food shortages, reduced shelter capacity. This resulted in many more homeless people forced to join the ranks of those who congregated in the lawless no-man's-land on the outskirts of the city.

In contrast to the lower rungs of city dwellers, the upper and middle classes lived in three- to four-story apartment buildings; the upper middle class often had elevators and entrances guarded by doormen dressed in blue livery and embroidered caps. Visitors were closely inspected. Each floor might contain three luxurious apartments where guests would be greeted by a maid or steward.[12]

These arrangements ensured frequent contact—and conflict—between servants and their masters. Dvorniks usually lived in the basements of buildings they guarded, and they entered via separate doors. Servants and their families also used these "dark entrances" (*chernye vykhody*). Upper-middle-class apartments included communal spaces for servants, cooks, and nannies, who lived in apartment corners, basements, and attics. Revolutionary liberation deepened the tension between these haves and have-nots in close quarters. Fierce class struggle was waged not only in the streets, but also inside apartments. In August, household servants formed a union and demanded an eight-hour day, two days off each month, one month vacation per year, double pay for overtime, a month's notice before dismissal, the same food as masters, and polite treatment by their masters—including polite address.[13] In the famous Order No. 1, soldiers had issued a similar call during the February Revolution, refusing to be addressed by the familiar second-person pronoun *ty*, which had been used with serfs. Demands by the formerly downtrodden and oppressed to be treated with dignity and afforded better working conditions must have caused consternation and anger on the part of their masters, causing countless conflicts within households.

The class conflicts built into Russian housing arrangements were exacerbated by the war. In 1914, all new housing construction ceased, as resources were diverted to the war effort. At the same time, and in the years leading up to the revolution, Petrograd was flooded by new arrivals: villagers seeking work in factories ramping up output for the war and refugees seeking better lives in the imperial capital. Deserters fleeing the front lines flocked to the imperial capital rather than return to their native villages. Convicts escaping from provisional prisons also made their way to Petrograd. Deserters and criminals without proper identification had no hope of finding an apartment. Vacancies were nearly impossible to find; just 107 of the city's 200,000 apartments were available for rent in spring 1917, compared with 4,000 to 5,000 in the previous year.[14]

The severe housing shortage escalated conflict between owners and renters. At the end of April 1917, the two groups held separate meetings to air their grievances. Owners complained about the law of August 27, 1916, which imposed rent control just as the rising cost of labor and the shortage of construction materials were elevating maintenance costs. Renters complained about the lack of apartments and rents that kept going up in spite of rent-control laws. They were also getting less for their money, as basic services were significantly reduced amid the wider economic malaise and dvornik strikes that curtailed or stopped essential services.

In June 1917, the ministry of justice replaced the August 1916 law with a new one allowing building owners to raise rents by as much as 15 percent. Owners were also empowered to charge renters supplementary fees to cover basic services, including additional fees for dvorniks, waste disposal, water, and firewood.[15] The new law not only failed to solve the housing problem, but also further aggravated the conflict between landlords and tenants. Renters complained about higher rents, while owners found the new law did not do enough to defray maintenance costs.

The Cost of Living and the Decline in Real Wages

The spring after the February Revolution was a time of popular organizing. Metal factory workers were the first to be unionized. Food-industry workers, textile workers, chemical workers, and other industrial workers followed. Then came railway workers, and then printers, bakers, dvorniks, drugstore clerks, chauffeurs, bath workers, and so on. Public employees such as tram drivers, train conductors, city office workers, and postal-telegraph workers formed their own unions. Professionals—bank and credit institution workers, teachers, insurance agents—also organized. Even high school students unionized under the Petrograd Organization of High School Students, which demanded curriculum change.[16]

Unions shared three major concerns. First, they sought equality and dignity. The specifics of this demand varied depending on which union was concerned—for instance, the waiters' union wanted to abolish tipping, which it deemed degrading—but the appeal of equality and dignity was universal. Second, all unions pursued better working conditions, especially humane working hours. Third, and most important, the unions wanted better wages.

Wages for unskilled workers in February and March averaged around 2.25 rubles per day and slightly more depending on the job. These daily wages amounted to roughly 50 rubles a month. In May and June, the wages of unskilled workers increased to 5 to 6 rubles a day, around 70 rubles per month, and later, wages were raised further. Cabmen earned 50 to 140 rubles a month, but some negotiated with customers for higher fares. Dvorniks received 40 to 90 rubles in February and March, but their wages were increased to 125 rubles in May and June.[17]

Compared with unskilled workers, the wages of skilled workers rose sharply in the spring. The monthly nominal wages of factory workers increased from 70 rubles a month in the first half of 1917 to 135 rubles in the second half of the year, but real wages actually went down from 19.3 rubles in the first half to 13.8 rubles in the second half.[18] The professional classes did not fare much better. A director of a technical school received 420 rubles a month; a vice administrator of a technical school, 200 rubles; a teacher in a trade school, 91 rubles; teachers of public gymnasia, 50 to 100 rubles; clerks, 62 to 93 rubles; and doctors' assistants, 50 to 60 rubles.[19]

But nominal increases could not keep up with sharply declining real wages. Rationing and price controls could not keep food costs down. With fixed prices so low, peasants refused to sell their products to purchasing agencies, instead directing their wares to the black market. And many necessary items, especially dairy products, were not rationed or price-controlled. Even people with little money preferred haggling over relatively high prices at markets when the alternative was wasting time in long lines at stores that would accept their ration cards. Inflation spread to nonfood items as well. Rent went up. Tram fares and taxi fares rose, as did the prices of shoes and clothes. The longest queues reported in October were not to be found at bakeries but at stores selling shoes.[20]

No wonder the masses were demoralized. Preoccupied with daily survival, they grew indifferent to the abstract concerns of ideology and governance. Albert Rys Williams, an American journalist sympathetic to the revolution, overheard a worker who put the matter bluntly:

> Patience, patience, they are always counseling us. But what have they done to make us patient? Has Kerensky given us more to eat than the Czar? More words and promises—yes! But not more food. All night long we wait in lines for shoes and bread and meat, while, like fools, we write "Liberty" on our banners. The only liberty we have is the same old liberty to slave and starve.[21]

And this was the voice of the proletariat, supposedly leading the revolution. It does not require a great deal of imagination to appreciate how the unorganized and less ideologically driven lower middle classes and urban poor reacted.

Legal Breakdown

On March 3, at its first meeting, the Provisional Government decided unanimously that it alone would inherit "the entire plenitude of power that belonged to the monarch." This raised the question of the relationship between the Provisional Government and the State Duma, the legislature under the Fundamental Laws. On this question, the Provisional Government declared: "the Fundamental Laws of the Russian State must be considered invalid." Therefore, until the Constituent Assembly enacted new

Fundamental Laws, the Provisional Government was to assume not only executive power, but also legislative and judicial power. This was an extraordinary decision, tantamount to a declaration of dictatorship. The State Duma, which had been the legislative body under the Fundamental Laws and had served as the main authority during the February Revolution, was considered to be abolished.[22] Since there was no legislative institution, the Provisional Government ruled by decree.[23]

If the Provisional Government could not rely on the Fundamental Laws, whence its legitimacy? On March 2, when Kadet party leader Pavel N. Miliukov announced the formation of the Provisional Government to the insurgent representatives in Tauride Palace, someone asked, "Who elected you?" To this Miliukov answered, "It was the revolution that elected us." The problem, however, was that the Provisional Government, composed of representatives from the privileged society, lacked the support of the insurgent soldiers and workers. To secure their allegiance, the Provisional Government had to negotiate with the Petrograd Soviet for the conditions for its support. In the beginning, the moderate socialists were willing to give the Provisional Government the blessing of the Petrograd Soviet's support, but under pressure from the insurgent masses, the moderate socialist leaders retreated from this position and were prepared to give only conditional support for the government. Herein lie the origins of dual power, the unstable foundation for the Provisional Government's legitimacy.[24]

The Provisional Government was quick to realize the importance of establishing a new legal order to handle criminal, civil, military, and administrative cases. It decided that, with some exceptions, the statutes of 1864, established by Alexander II as part of his Great Reforms, would remain in force. Adherence to the 1864 statutes created two urgent needs. First, investigating former tsarist officials became a top priority. The Duma

Committee, preceding the Provisional Government, had created a Higher Investigating Commission to detain officials who were either arrested by the insurgents and brought to Tauride Palace or had turned themselves in for their own protection. Inheriting this body from the Duma Committee, on March 4 the Provisional Government created the Extraordinary Commission to investigate the transgressions of former tsarist high officials.[25] Insisting on adherence to legality, the commission was to see whether these officials had violated the law based on the 1864 statues.

Second, the new government had to bring existing statutes into line with the liberal spirit of the revolution. The Provisional Government thus took a series of measures reflecting what Leonard Schapiro calls "innocent faith in the perfectibility of man" and "detestation of violence and coercion."[26] The two ministers directly responsible for the criminal justice system, Minister of Internal Affairs Prince Georgii E. Lvov and Minister of Justice Kerenskii, were eager to establish a state based on social justice and rule of law, including a more humane penal system.[27]

To that end, on March 12, the Provisional Government abolished the death penalty and commuted all death sentences to periods of hard labor.[28] Russia became the first and only country involved in the war to abolish the death penalty in wartime. In the euphoria immediately following the February Revolution, both the bourgeois press and the socialist press hailed the move as "the most potent evidence of respect for human personality and for its right to the most valuable entity—human life," "evidence of the greatness of the popular soul and a manifestation of straightforward nobility." Vladimir D. Nabokov, a secretary of the Provisional Government, wrote on March 18 that abolition of the death penalty was "a realization of the will" of the people.[29]

A few days after capital punishment was banned, on March 17, the Provisional Government decreed amnesty for common criminals. Sentences were cut in half, and exiles were allowed to return and face a maximum of three years' imprisonment. Escapees were ordered to turn themselves in and accept reduced sentences; unsurprisingly, few accepted the offer to return to prison. Shortly after Easter, Kerenskii decreed that criminals willing to serve at the front would have their sentences vacated.[30] According to the former Okhrana chief, Konstantin I. Globachev, who had done time in Kresty, almost all criminals volunteered to go to the front. The logic, according to Globachev, was straightforward: "You think we are fools to fight in war? We will be clothed and fed, and at the first railway stop, we will disappear."[31]

The Provisional Statute on the Militia, issued on April 17, went further still, imposing strict constraints on the militia's treatment of people in detention. For instance, Article 28 stipulated that anyone arrested had to be charged within twenty-four hours or released. As a result, the majority of those apprehended in periodic raids of inns, taverns, and other seedy places where criminals congregated were back on the street the following day.[32]

In addition to the death penalty, oppressive tsarist practices such as whipping and the use of fetters, chains, and straitjackets were banned. Although these decrees were well intentioned and could be considered legitimate triumphs of human rights, Ereshchenko writes, "it is with justification possible to state that the Provisional Government's legislation on the criminal law objectively defended not the aspirations of the citizens but rather the life and action of lawbreakers."[33] Put simply, thanks to these measures, Petrograd's criminal population continued to swell.

The Provisional Government's liberal phase ended with the July Days. On July 6, it announced that it would arrest and charge with treason "those who had participated in and led the armed insurrection against the state, established by the people, as well as those who appealed to and incited others to join it." The government also ordered the Bolsheviks arrested, forcing Lenin to go underground by fleeing to Finland. Also in the crosshairs was "anyone guilty of public incitement to murder, brigandage, robbery, pogroms, and other heinous crimes, as well as to violence against any part of the population." They were "to be punished by detention in a house of correction for not more than three years, or by detention in a fortress for a period of not more than three years."[34] On July 12, exactly four months after abolition, the death penalty was restored in the armed forces.[35] The Provisional Government's attempt to centralize the militia under its control, discussed in detail in the next chapter, took place in the context of this reverse course.

The coexistence of old statutes and new inevitably led to ambiguities. These were particularly difficult to settle because the old court system was nearly paralyzed and a new one added confusion, as we will see. Under the dual power, it was also unclear who the ultimate arbiter of legal conflicts was. A comparison between two celebrated cases, the seizures of Kshesinskaia villa and Durnovo dacha, vividly shows how legal ambiguity fostered discord.

During and immediately after the February Revolution, the people's anger was directed primarily at the symbols of tsarism, including the stately homes of the imperial family and its favorites. Matilda Kshesinskaia's villa, raided and seized by insurgent soldiers on February 27, is a case in point. The owner was a famous ballerina with the Imperial Russian Theater and, at one time, Tsar Nicholas II's secret lover.[36] On March 11, the Petersburg Committee of the Bolshevik Party, having just resurfaced and resumed legal activities, moved in.[37] The villa became the Bolshevik Party's headquarters, hosting as well its military organization and the office of the party newspaper, *Soldatskaia Pravda*.[38] After Lenin returned to Russia on April 3, he spoke from the balcony to a large and excited crowd. According to the wife of the famous historian Sergei F. Platonov, who lived nearby, people gathered in front of the building constantly, arguing and fighting. Often Leninists escaped into the building for protection.[39]

Kshesinskaia appealed to the city governor, the Petrograd Soviet, and the procurator of the Petrograd Court of Justice. Finally, she sought out Kerenskii, who telephoned the distraught ballerina. He promised to protect her and gave her his private telephone number, telling her that she could call him any hour of the day or night.[40] Eventually she appealed to Kerenskii in person. The minister of justice received her politely but explained that any attempt to expel the Bolsheviks would involve bloodshed, and he was therefore reluctant to take action.[41]

Kshesinskaia eventually brought suit against the occupiers and sought restitution for property damage. The trial was held on May 5 at the court of justice in the Petrogradskii District. Lenin was among the defendants. With the infamous Bolshevik leader pit against an equally infamous darling of the tsar, the trial became a spectator event. People waited in long lines to purchase tickets. Lenin, however, did not show up.

Vladimir S. Khesin, representing Kshesinskaia, argued that personal property rights were inviolable. Mechislav Iu. Kozlovskii, defending the Bolsheviks, reminded the court that the villa had been seized amid revolution. "What legal order are we talking about," he asked, "when a revolution is going on with bullets whistling by and cannons firing?" Khesin countered, "There should be laws even in the middle of a revolution. Until new laws are established, old laws are in effect. Otherwise, there is anarchy."[42]

The judge ruled that the occupiers were to vacate within twenty days, but the suit against Lenin was dropped, supposedly because it could not be proved that he was living at the villa, but more likely because of the reluctance of the socialist leaders of the Petrograd Soviet to have a fellow leader of a socialist party put on trial. The Bolshevik Central Committee and the Petersburg Committee agreed to leave, but the Bolshevik military organization defied the order. Later, the Petersburg Committee slipped back in to continue the occupation.[43]

After the July Days, the Provisional Government expelled the Bolsheviks. But the villa was not returned to its owner. Instead a new group of soldiers, from the Bicycle Battalion, moved in. The Provisional Government was more concerned with winning the support of the Bicycle Battalion than with securing the property rights of the fallen tsar's favorite. Kshesinskaia left Petrograd to join her future husband, Grand Duke Andrei Vladimirovich, who had already escaped to Kislovodsk, in the south. The Bolshevik occupants had damaged the home, but systematic looting took place only under the occupation of the Bicycle Battalion. Khesin again brought suit, this time before both the Provisional Government and the staff of the Petrograd Military District. It was a futile effort. Neither institution had the will to expel the occupiers. Members of the Bicycle Battalion remained until the end of October, when the Red Guards took over and forcibly expelled them.[44]

Another illustrative case was the occupation of the Durnovo dacha. After the February Revolution, a group of anarchists took over the dacha belonging to the general and city duma deputy Petr P. Durnovo. These occupiers, too, established a headquarters, and soon various working-class organizations from the Vyborgskii District—such as the first subdistrict commissariat, the bakers' union, the workers' club called "Enlightenment," and administrations from local trade unions—joined them.

On June 5, a band of anarchists seized the printing press of the newspaper *Russkaia volia* to "liberate the workers' printing press from the oppression of the exploiting class" and to use it instead "for the needs of socialism." The Petrograd Soviet Executive Committee denounced it as a threat to the revolution. The anarchists responded by declaring that they would recognize no power, including the Petrograd Soviet. That same day, General Petr A. Polovtsev, commander of the Petrograd Military District, ordered everyone to leave Durnovo dacha. Two days later, workers at four factories responded by striking. Their action spread overnight to a total of twenty-eight factories.

The Durnovo incident was closely related to the Kshesinskaia villa trial and the June demonstration. On June 12, the court passed the verdict to return the villa to Kshesinskaia, but the Petrograd Military District and the workers' militia refused to carry out the order to expel the Bolsheviks from the villa, and on the evening of June 12, the Executive Committee of the Petrograd Soviet adopted a resolution to stop the execution of the evacuation.

On June 18, despite the Executive Committee's objections, the Bolsheviks staged a street demonstration demanding the removal of "capitalist ministers" from the Provisional Government. The anarchists supported this demonstration and attacked the Kresty Prison, setting free six anarchists and a Bolshevik, F. P. Khaustov, a member of the Bolshevik Party's military organization. Together with these "political" prisoners, four hundred common criminals also escaped from the prison.

The Provisional Government seized this moment and responded with a surgical operation against the anarchists. General Polovtsev, in full consultation with Minister of Justice Pavel N. Pereverzev, dispatched a Cossack regiment and an infantry battalion, with armored vehicles, to raid the dacha. Overcoming the armed resistance of the anarchists, government forces succeeded in reoccupying the dacha, detaining fifty-nine anarchists. In the process, the anarchist Sh. A. Asnin was killed, and his tattooed body was displayed for public view. Polovtsev and Pereverzev presented a photograph of Asnin to the First Soviet Congress, claiming that his tattoos were evidence of connections between the anarchists and the criminal world.[45]

Ultimately what mattered was not right but might. Thus the anarchists were expelled from the dacha, while the better organized and more numerous Bolsheviks continued to occupy the villa. Society was gradually growing accustomed to the idea that conflicts would be solved not by law but by force.

Failure of the Temporary Courts

During the February Revolution, insurgents attacked many court buildings and destroyed court records.[46] Various voluntary people's courts spontaneously sprang up at the local level to deal with criminal and civil cases.[47] The profusion of courts, not sanctioned by any higher authorities, was a source of anxiety among the Provisional Government, city duma, and legal intelligentsia, whose members feared confusion and preferred a uniform system. But the authorities were confronted with difficult problems. There was the urgency of the situation: people demanded law and order immediately, but it took time to restore old court systems and establish new ones. And there was the challenge of achieving fair representation at the court, given the animosity between ordinary people and legal experts, who came from the propertied classes.[48]

On March 3, the Provisional Government sought to assert some control over the court system by creating temporary courts (*vremennye sudy*). Each new court would be presided over by a justice of the peace and two assistant judges, one representing soldiers and the other workers.[49] The representation of the nonpropertied classes reflected more than Kerenskii's populism. Workers and soldiers had already overseen "people's courts" created spontaneously by residents during the revolution. The continued presence of soldiers' and workers' judges in the temporary courts suggests that they had gained popular legitimacy, which the Provisional Government felt bound to respect.[50]

Still, temporary courts were never intended to replace the prerevolutionary court system. The courts of justice defined by the 1864 statutes persisted alongside the temporary courts until the latter were abolished in July. Petrograd housed sixty courts of justice before the February Revolution, but only twenty-one were converted to temporary courts.[51] Of the remaining thirty-nine, some were destroyed, and others, presumably, functioned as before.

Though designed as an emergency measure to "remove misunderstandings" between insurgents and the middle and upper layers of society during the February Revolution, temporary courts became important institutions in Petrograd, handling many small cases close to people's daily lives.[52] Their jurisdiction included crimes against personal safety and property; violations of public order; violations of obligations to maintain streets, courtyards, and public places; agitation against the new regime; sale of alcoholic beverages; merchants' concealment of food; and hooliganism. Borrowing from the tsarist legal code concerning petty crimes, temporary court sentences were limited to eighteen months' imprisonment and three months' detention. In light of inflation, the maximum fine was raised to ten thousand rubles. Anyone detained without written approval from the Provisional Government or the military authorities was to be released. Court proceedings were to be open to the public and conducted orally, and courts were obligated to keep certain written records, though not of trial proceedings. Verdicts were to be decided by a majority of the three-judge panel.[53]

The temporary courts exemplified the conditions of decentralization and dual power. Though the courts were established by the Provisional Government, local nongovernmental committees were influential in their composition. Because there was no mechanism by which to choose judges from workers and soldiers, the selection was first entrusted to the Petrograd Soviet and later to district-level soviets of workers and soldiers.

Three judges rotated into each of a given court's three judicial roles. This was no trouble for the justices of the peace but proved more challenging for the workers' and soldiers' representatives. The Petrograd Soviet originally assembled sixty-four representatives, mostly socialists with legal qualifications, believing that the system would soon dissolve, and the assistant judges would return to other work. But temporary courts hung on longer than expected, and given rotations, there were not enough assistant judges to fill the benches. In March, when the temporary courts were set up, many could not be held for lack of assistant judges; workers and soldiers were reluctant to serve in tedious positions offering little pay.[54] But the district soviets soon recognized the importance of the courts and worked hard to produce appropriate delegates. By April 12, they had appointed 123 judges, leaving only three posts unfilled.[55]

It is impossible to say just who these workers' and soldiers' judges were, though a few details are available. According to V. V. Mantushkin, a justice of the peace who made the rules for the temporary courts for Kerenskii, the majority of the judges were educated and intelligent. Some served as qualified barristers in the army. Women were among those selected to represent workers.[56] Mantushkin also noted the arbitrariness of the courts, which might hand down a warning to one defendant and the maximum fine to another guilty of a similar crime. *Petrograd listok* complained of one wine dealer being improperly fined thousands of rubles for making illegal sales, while another, charged with the same crime, was fined only ten rubles. One defendant caught for public drunkenness was given a sentence of three months' imprisonment, while another was given only seven days. However, the courts were not merely capricious; Man-tushkin finds a strain of bias. In general, the courts were lenient toward thieves, but landlords and house owners were often punished with the maximum fine.[57]

Beyond their prejudiced record in adjudication of guilt and innocence, the courts operated in many other ways that profes-sional jurists found objectionable in light of legal standards. For instance, after being charged, defendants had only a few days to appear in court, making it difficult for them to find lawyers and witnesses. Fines had to be paid immediately after the verdicts were given. Those who did not have cash were escorted home under guard to fetch it. There was no right of appeal, though ver-dicts could be overturned by the minister of justice.[58]

Andrei B. Nikolaev, who has carefully examined the archives of temporary court decisions, concludes that, in most cases, the courts did not cite specific laws in making rulings or handing down sentences. When they did cite laws, they often applied them incorrectly or relied on laws irrelevant to the cases in question. Sometimes fines exceeded the maximum limits. Temporary courts also were known to decide cases over which they lacked jurisdiction. For instance, a temporary court fined two workers caught drinking in their apartment, even though no laws prohib-ited drinking in one's home.[59] Another case, reported by *Birzhevyia vedomosti,* is particularly lurid. One day in late March, a soldier came home to find his wife sleeping with her lover. He grabbed her clothes and her lover's and went out into the streets to ha-rangue the crowds in pursuit of justice. The temporary court found the wife guilty of "depraved behavior" and sentenced her to six months' confinement. The court also granted the husband permission for divorce. But the annulment of marriage was be-yond the purview of the secular courts.[60] In this case, the tem-porary court clearly overstepped its jurisdiction, but it satisfied the crowd's sense of justice. Without the temporary court, this incident may have ended in mob violence against the wife and her lover. The minister of justice often found it necessary to overturn the temporary courts.[61]

Whether or not verdicts conformed to the legal code, common people preferred to bring issues vital to their daily life to temporary courts rather than to the courts of justice. For instance, one resident sued his landlord for pulling his child's ear. The landlord, angered by this lawsuit, responded: "Go ahead and sue me, but in that case, I will kick you out of your apartment." Another sued her landlord for beating her dog. Other lawsuits involved landowners engaged in *khanzhi*—secret brewing. Still others were brought to temporary courts for "agitation against the soviet of workers and soldiers' deputies."[62]

Professional jurists were highly critical of the temporary courts. Justices of the peace found the workers' and soldiers' representatives aggravating. They rejected expert legal opinions and ruled however they saw fit.[63] Defense lawyers sometimes found themselves excluded. One of them, M. S. Ravich, wrote, "A court not based on the law is not a court. In the best case, it is possible to call it 'reprisal.'"[64] In an open letter to justices of the peace, barrister O. S. Trakhterev argued, "Nowhere in the world is there any court without appeals and cassations." He criticized not only what was missing, but also what was there: "Half-illiterate people, who know absolutely nothing about the spirit of the law, legal implication of crime, and legal consciousness [by which he must have meant familiarity of complex legal codes] serve as uncontrollable judges." The temporary courts, he concluded, needed to be abolished. "Enough!" he wrote. "The role that was assigned to the temporary court, has already played out!"[65]

In April, the city duma created a commission to improve the court system. The chairman of the commission, Senator I. M. Tiutiumov, wrote, "The present temporary court is a court of conscience, and as a court of conscience, it examines every case by its

essence without bothering . . . with [legal] formality. The temporary court does not allow either appeals or jury trials, [as it
should.]" The commission recommended establishing a review
board with representatives from the ministry of justice, the Congress of Justices of the Peace, and the Petrograd Soviet to evaluate
all decisions made by the temporary courts. But nothing came of
the recommendation.[66] The Provisional Government and the city
duma were already contemplating the abolition of the temporary
courts rather than their improvement.

Representatives of the workers and soldiers considered these
criticisms to be attacks on the rights of common people. To them,
legal niceties mattered far less than justice. They expressed their
annoyance with the minister of justice's frequent intervention in
temporary court verdicts.[67] These interventions by the minister
of justice provoked resentment among the lower classes, who
considered the temporary courts to have satisfied their sense of
justice.

Under pressure mostly from the propertied class and legal experts, the Provisional Government decided to overhaul the lower-
court system. At the city duma, as well, Mayor Iurii N. Glebov's
legal council recommended scrapping the temporary courts and
allowing the courts of justice to adjudicate minor offenses. At separate June conferences, the justices of the peace stood for restoration of the old system without the temporary courts, as assistant
judges representing workers and soldiers passed a resolution
calling for the continuation of "the current revolutionary form"
of the temporary courts.[68]

Thus, contrary to the original intention of removing misunderstandings between the propertied classes and the ordinary
citizens without property qualifications, the temporary courts
contributed to intensifying antagonism, and the Provisional
Government took the side of the propertied class. On July 9, the
Provisional Government abolished the temporary courts and

restored full jurisdiction to the old courts of justice. On July 25, newly elected justices of the peace took oaths to serve the reconstituted courts of justice, and the temporary courts shut down. The restored courts of justice began proceedings in August.[69] The defeat of the people's representation at the temporary courts became another manifestation of the Provisional Government's reverse course in response to the July Days. It is ironic that it was Kerenskii who created the temporary courts in March and then presided over their abolition.

The temporary courts lasted only five months. But in that time, they gained much popularity among the lower classes. Deprived of courts where they felt they could get a fair hearing in cases affecting their daily lives, the lower classes were left without a state-approved method to satisfy their sense of justice. After all, where could they complain if their landlord pulled their child's ear or beat their dog? Or more importantly, what should they do if they caught a pickpocket? The downfall of the temporary courts proved to be one of the essential reasons for the mob violence that erupted through Petrograd after that summer.

Sources of Disorder and Crime in Daily Life

Renters frequently sued landlords in temporary courts. Owners allegedly neglected their duty to clean buildings, stairways, courtyards, and streets and failed to repair broken walls, ceilings, faucets, stoves, toilets, and chimneys. Owners, in turn, sued renters, often in courts of justice, which were friendlier to landlords. These housing disputes created an intense battleground between the interests of property owners and those of the lower classes. A few examples provide a glimpse into these conflicts, which marked daily life in the city.

On June 27, I. A. Bausov, a landlord, sued his tenant Anna Lemeshenok, who was five weeks late paying rent for her apartment in the Narvskii District. Lemeshenok claimed she refused to pay because Bausov had ignored needed repairs. Instead, she had directed her thirty-five-ruble payment to the housing committee, which handled the repairs. This sort of activity was hardly unusual. The Narvskii District Soviet had decided to grant housing committees the right to "withhold rent in order to carry out necessary repairs in buildings and to maintain cleanliness in the courtyard and street and fulfill other sanitary and hygienic improvements to living quarters, if a house owner refuses to carry out his or her duty."[70]

But Bausov argued that there was no such housing committee in his building, that the committee was a fiction created by Lemeshenok's husband, and that Bausov himself had completed repairs the year before. The lone judge of the court of justice held in Bausov's favor. He passed the verdict to evict Lemeshenok and her family and ordered her to pay the outstanding rent.[71]

Sanitary conditions were among renters' foremost concerns, for obvious reasons. Numerous cases involving conflicts between renters and house owners are described in Nikolaev's fascinating article.[72] After the February Revolution, poor and working people felt the temporary courts, rather than the courts of justice, finally shared the sorts of concerns with which the courts of justice were uninterested, as the Lemeshenok case shows. The temporary courts were the institutions they could rely on to bring justice to these concerns. They could not have cared less about the legal niceties, and they considered the assistant judges representing workers and soldiers to be important gains of the revolution. When the temporary courts were abolished, they were left with no legal means to express their frustrations and seek justice, fostering the outbreak of mob justice.

The destruction of the old police system also undermined the role of dvorniks and doormen in crime prevention. Although not formally integrated into the police system, prerevolutionary dvorniks performed essential security functions through their close contact with the police. They represented an ambiguous gray area in the revolution. On the one hand, they had undeniable connections with the tsarist police, and yet, close to the bottom layers of the urban poor, the insurgents accepted them as their own. During the February Revolution, there was not a single instance where the insurgents attacked dvorniks, despite their known connections with the police.

After the revolution, dvorniks, like others in the lower strata of society, asserted themselves. They resented people's suspicion of their association with the former police, and they responded by organizing a union and refusing to perform security duties.[73] On May 9, amid a sharp rise in crime, City Governor Vadim A. Iurevich ordered dvorniks to fulfill their night-guard role under penalty of law. Iurevich's order was an infuriating reminder of the treatment they endured under the tsarist police. The offended dvorniks declared that they would not obey an order issued without their consultation. On May 17, Iurevich rescinded the decree, and the dvorniks agreed only to voluntary watches.[74]

The voluntary system provided little improvement in security; most of Petrograd's buildings were left unguarded, especially at night. On August 29 and again on September 16, the commander of the Petrograd Military District issued new orders to the dvorniks. Again the union opposed them and entered negotiations with the Provisional Government and city militia administration. Dvornik representatives argued that others, such as the city militia and landlords, should assume security responsibilities. They demanded that the Provisional Government take more assertive measures to expel suspicious and criminal elements, if it claimed to be serious about the city's security. The dvorniks said they wished to cooperate with the authorities but resented the city militia's hostility toward them as perceived agents of the former tsarist police.[75] The dvorniks' refusal to perform duties greatly contributed to the paralysis of essential services for people's everyday life, since in addition to guarding buildings, they also used to clear the streets and courtyards, remove garbage and human waste, and secure firewood for heating and cooking. Using the vital services they rendered for everyday life as leverage with residents, the dvorniks empowered themselves.

Leaky Prisons

Even if thieves, robbers, and murderers were caught, tried, and sent to prison, there was no guarantee they would remain securely behind bars. The February Revolution caused a serious breakdown in the security at prisons. But escapes did not end there. In fact, they were abetted by the leniency of the new government. Immediately after the February Revolution, there was euphoria about the idealized world. Aleksandr A. Zhizhilenko, freshly appointed chief of the Main Prison Administration, declared in his first order that the primary task of punishment would be to reeducate those "who had fallen to crime due to . . . personal character as well as external circumstances." It was time for "humanness" and social rejuvenation.[76] In practical terms, this meant that all the prison wardens and guards would be fired, and soldiers and officers on sick leave would be put in their place.[77] The replacement of specially trained personnel with untrained amateurs led to a serious breakdown in security. What is more, detainees were often taken to poorly secured temporary jails set up at such unsuitable sites as universities, restaurants, and movie theaters.[78]

Former Okhrana Chief Globachev described conditions at Kresty Prison, which was supposedly one of the most secure in

Petrograd. Guards, he said, often fell asleep, abandoned their posts, or put down their rifles within easy reach of prisoners. Guards would leave prisoners unsupervised in the yard. Globachev wrote that he could have escaped but chose not to only because, given his tsarist past, he felt safer behind bars than in the streets.[79]

Security became particularly lax in the summer. During the July Days, many Bolsheviks were incarcerated in Kresty, but after the Kornilov affair they were either freed or escaped, often with the aid of guards. Yet it was not just political prisoners who found their way to freedom. On August 30, 208 convicts ran away from Kresty, only 30 of them political prisoners. That same day, 150 prisoners fled the Petergofskii District Commissariat.[80] Other escapes were reported on July 2, July 27, August 2, and August 9.[81] Ereshchenko counts fifty-four reported jailbreaks between March and October.[82]

The new penal system simply did not work. Criminals did not reciprocate Lvov and Kerenskii's idealism. On the contrary, they exploited it, and crime spread rapidly.

Organized and Professional Crime

Prison escapes and returning exiles swelled the criminal population. Newspapers were filled with stories of roundups. On March 6, city militia raids detained 250 criminals who had escaped during the February Revolution.[83] A couple of days later, a militia unit and a detachment of soldiers surrounded a seedy inn called Preobrazhenskaia in Peski and detained forty-nine suspects. Many were petty thieves, but among them were ten presumably hardened criminals, sentenced by prerevolutionary courts to forced labor and exile. Those detained offered no resistance, openly declaring, "We don't care if they lock us up in jail. People will free us within a month."[84] Soon after, a March 22 raid on the cheap inn Otel, also in Peski, netted thirty more suspects, including criminals who had escaped prison during the February Revolution.[85] A group of thieves took over a hotel, Pereputie, in the notorious Ligovka District, and turned it into their headquarters. *Petrogradskii listok* described the militia's March 29 attack on the hotel as a "Fort Chabrol," a military operation.[86] Criminals even set up a base of operation at the Manege on Fontanka—the very center of the city and the location of the Pavlovskii Regiment's barracks, indicating collusion between the soldiers and the criminals. Fights broke out frequently in the nearby streets.[87] In April, *Petrogradskii listok* sounded a tone of alarm:

> If Petrograd is now being robbed and plundered, it should not surprise us, since as many as 20,000 thieves were let go from various prisons. Robbers, enjoying full civil rights, are now free to walk in the streets of Petrograd. Detectives of the Criminal Militia often encounter thieves in the streets, but there is nothing they can do. Among them there are many who had been deprived of their rights by the previous courts, but they are now scot-free, ignoring such court decisions.[88]

Newspaper articles suggest that criminals may have banded together in gangs and developed specializations. Some criminals infiltrated the militia and took advantage of its authority and information. Criminals migrating to Petrograd could establish connections easily, thanks in part to underground merchants who bought and sold stolen goods. They became important points of connection within the black-market network. Some gangs, such as the "golden youths," came from a higher social strata, which was particularly given to gambling and other illicit pleasures. This decadent layer of the privileged society formed a gray ambiguous zone bordering on the criminal world.

Making Ends Meet

The revolutionary moment not only fostered conditions conducive to criminality, but actually forced people to resort to crime. Those living hand-to-mouth amid economic decline committed crimes just to survive. Factory committees reported workers stealing necessities. For instance, at the Petrograd Cartridge Factory committee meeting on October 17, it was reported that six workers were accused of smuggling out kerosene and soap. All six confessed but claimed they could not find kerosene and soap in stores.[89]

Yet the geographic distribution of crime suggests that factory workers were not the worst off. Newspaper accounts indicate that crime was most prevalent in areas where the urban poor lived alongside the lower end of the middle class. These districts, in the south and just outside the city center (center-mixed districts), included areas of Kolomenskii, Moskovskii, Aleksandro-Nevskii, Narvskii, Rozhdestvenskii, and Spasskii. Unlike the Vyborgskii and Petergofskii Districts, dominated by the industrial proletariat working in large factories, these were home primarily to small-scale artisans, sales clerks, waiters, and others working in hospitality. Here one found slums, major markets, cheap hotels, and taverns.[90] These crime-infested areas were where mob justice was frequently committed, as we will see later.

Deserters, Soldiers, and Anarchists

Some insurgent soldiers who left their barracks during the February Revolution never returned. Instead, they joined or formed gangs. They were soon united with deserters from the front. Detached from the official institutions that enabled access to food rations, and lacking the proper documentation needed to obtain a job and a living space, these armed former soldiers turned to crime as a means of survival and an opportunity to strike it rich. Many of the estimated fifty to sixty thousand deserters living in Petrograd by July were physically and psychologically wounded, exacerbating their strife and, in some cases, contributing to their brutality.[91] Lack of military discipline compounded the problem. For instance, a certain Nikolai Osipov of the 180th Infantry Regiment was on five occasions caught deserting, returned to his unit, but came back to the capital.[92]

Gradually, criminals and deserters formed their own colonies into which not even a militiaman dared set foot.[93] When the militia did attempt raids, they met strong resistance. The deserters and soldiers-turned-criminals were not well disciplined, but they were well armed and had some training. One such operation against a criminal colony in Volkovo at the end of July resulted in a shootout lasting more than thirty minutes. All but three of the criminals escaped. In the course of at least eight of the twenty-four raids reported in July and August, militiamen were attacked by armed criminals.[94]

In May and June especially, self-proclaimed anarchists set to work "expropriating the expropriators." The Durnovo case was just one of many attempts by genuine or pseudo-anarchists to rob the privileged for supposedly ideological reasons. On April 28, eighteen people armed with revolvers and rifles ransacked the palace of Count Likhtenberg in the Second Kolomenskii Subdistrict, running off with two hundred thousand rubles' worth of valuables. Chief Arkadii A. Kirpichnikov of the Criminal Police, who personally investigated the raid, believed that these self-described anarchists were actually professional criminals.[95]

On May 7, anarchists armed with revolvers and rifles raided the apartment of a former high tsarist official in the Third Moskovskii Subdistrict and stole all his valuables. That same day, six armed anarchists attacked the home of Count Ruge in the Second

Kazanskii Subdistrict and ran away with five thousand rubles' worth of property.[96] On May 18, three men in soldiers' uniforms calling themselves anarchists and communists broke into the home of K. K. Grigoriev in the Second Kolomenskii Subdistrict and shot Grigoriev and a servant.[97] On May 21, two well-dressed men and a young woman calling themselves anarchists attacked a house in Soldatskii Lane in the Second Liteinyi Subdistrict. After seriously wounding a doorman, they ransacked the apartment and made off with all the valuables.[98]

We do not know how many of these incidents were carried out by politically committed anarchists and how many by criminals opportunistically wrapping themselves in the anarchist banner. There is much reason to doubt their ideological claims. On May 19, the militia raided a supposed anarchist headquarters in the Third Petrogradskii Subdistrict and arrested several men, including one who had participated in the raid on Grigoriev's residence. He turned out to be an ex-convict who had escaped prison during the February Revolution. Another "anarchist" captured in Petrogradskii that day was a famous armed robber named Volvonkin.[99] In at least some cases, anarchism was clearly a pretext for criminality.

This was widely appreciated at the time. A cartoon in the newspaper *Strekoza* illustrates public cynicism toward supposedly principled expropriation. A relatively harmless prerevolutionary pickpocket is juxtaposed with an armed thief wielding a banner reading "Anarchist."[100] See figure 7. This clearly illustrates the reversal of power relations. The petty criminal operated in the shadows, while the supposed anarchist claimed power, dictating terms to his submissive victim.

In another *Strekoza* cartoon dripping with sarcasm, a member of the city militia stops a thief and addresses him with the informal *ty*. The thief replies, "I ask you to address me with '*vy*' and 'comrade.'" "Why should I?" asks the militiaman. "You are

Figure 7. This cartoon captures how crime was seen to have changed. The left panel, "It was done this way before," shows a relatively benign pickpocket, while the right panel, "It's done this way now," depicts an alarming, pistol-toting anarchist. *Strekoza*, no. 24, June 1917, 8.

a crook!" The thief objects, "That's not true at all! I am an anarchist and do not recognize private property. Therefore, I am 'requisitioning' from the bourgeoisie everything that suits my fancy."[101]

A final example from *Novyi satirikon* shows a middle-class resident entering his apartment to find a robbery in progress. The resident asks meekly if the two thieves are anarchists. If so, he will give up. But if they are common thieves, he says, he will call the militia. See figure 8. The cartoon illustrates how ordinary criminals took advantage of the city militia's hesitation to get involved in political matters by presenting themselves as anarchists.

Figure 8. Titled "The Proper Tone for 1917," this cartoon shows an apartment resident interrupting a robbery. He asks whether the thieves are anarchists or simple robbers; if the former, he'll return shortly, if the latter, he'll phone the militia. *Novyi satirikon*, no. 19, June 1917, 13.

The satire in these cartoons strikes at more than false anarchists. They also take on the spread of Bolshevism, viewed as a source of class hatred against the privileged. The cartoons convey the reversal of power relations between criminals and the state, represented by a defanged militia expected to treat common people, including criminals, better than the tsarist police had. The cartoons also reflect citizens' anxiety about the sanctity of property. If anarchists could seize the Durnovo dacha and the Bolsheviks could expropriate the Kshesinskaia villa—if the imperial family, its favorites, and former tsarist officials could be robbed seemingly at will—how could a less privileged property owner feel safe?

Youth Gangs or Hooligans

Hooligans engaged in senseless, brutal violence, only to have fun. Numerous cases were reported in newspapers about hooligans attacking the outnumbered militiamen, beating them up, and disarming them.[102] If gang members were arrested, their comrades often would attack the militiamen escorting detainees, in order to free them. In some cases, hooligans shot at militiamen without any provocation.[103] Taking advantage of the political crisis of the July Days, hooligans attacked stores on Nevskii and Liteinyi Prospects. An iconic photograph from the July Days, shot by the famous photographer Karl Bulla from his studio at the corner of Sadovaia and Nevskii shows the demonstrators fleeing gunfire from government troops. Less well known is the fact that hooligans also fired at the demonstrators from rooftops.[104] To hooligans, political ideology did not matter; they gathered whenever they spotted trouble—and caused more.

As the political crisis intensified after August, and overall levels of crime rose, hooligans were emboldened. On October 11, hooligans and militia fought in the streets near the commissariat in the Second Kolomenskii Subdistrict. Eight days later, a group of hooligans seized a militiaman at his post in the Second Vyborgskii Subdistrict. They pointed a gun at his head and forced him to crawl on all fours and howl like a dog for three hours.[105] Ereshchenko finds 152 cases of beatings by hooligans from April 26 to July 1, and 252 from September 1 to October 24. Based on news reports, he calculates that the number of fights and beatings rose 3.4 times in 1917 compared with 1916.[106]

Chinese Immigrants

After the February Revolution, the Chinese ethnic question became enmeshed with the question of crime. During the war,
Russian industrialists brought Chinese laborers to Petrograd to
alleviate the labor shortage. By 1917, their number reached more
than ten thousand.[107] They were mostly unskilled and employed
on construction sites and in factories. Virtually enslaved and unable to speak the language, they were the first thrown to the streets
when layoffs hit. They formed segregated communities in the
Peski area in the Rozhdestvenskii District and along the Vindaro-
Ryvinskii Railway lines in the Third and Fourth Aleksandro-
Nevskii Subdistricts. They lived in crowded and unsanitary hovels
without toilets, water, or electricity; slept on wooden boards; and
cooked on stoves strewn about the concrete floor.[108]

Chinese communities were havens for opium smoking and
gambling. Occasional militia raids turned up many Chinese
passed out on the floor in a haze of opium smoke.[109] Organized
crime was likely responsible for the murders of five Chinese in
July and August, as gangs, so-called *khukhuzy,* fought for territo-
rial control. Recall that Chinese were suspected in the Petrov
murder case, indicating their imprint on the public psyche. As
Chinese gangs were beginning to commit crimes in Russian communities, outraged residents of Novaia Derevnia demanded their
deportation from Petrograd.[110]

After the October Revolution, police uncovered the *khukhuzy*
headquarters on Vasilievskii Island. Militia and Red Guards
raided the premises. Two gang members were killed and five arrested. During interrogation, gang members boasted that they
were 160-strong and had committed forty-seven murders and
robberies.[111]

The Breakdown of Services

During the revolutionary period, city services collapsed alongside policing. Animals starved, and in September and October, horses were often found dead on Nevskii, their foul odor filling the air.[112] Water no longer reached the upper floors of buildings. Dvorniks refused to clean gutters and take garbage to collection stations. Instead, the piles of refuse they left in courtyards and streets were exposed as soon as the snow melted in April.. Unsold fruit, vegetables, fish, and meat were thrown in the streets and left to rot. The periodic collection of human waste stopped, and cesspools overflowed with excrement. Street sweepers disappeared, and rats ran down the boulevards in broad daylight. According to an analysis by sanitation specialists, the soil of Sadovaia Street was chemically similar to a cesspool. Water sources, including the Large Neva, teemed with trash and feces.[113]

Unsurprisingly, epidemics broke out. In the summer, dysentery surpassed tuberculosis as the leading cause of death, and typhus, smallpox, and scarlet fever spread through the city. The death rate increased from 22.2 per thousand in 1916 to 25 per thousand in 1917.[114] Public baths were the major cause of epidemics. City authorities had difficulty shutting down the baths, but eventually the price for admission rose so sharply that ordinary people could no longer afford them. Body odor mingled with the stench of garbage and human waste. Trams reeked so badly in summer that a satirical journal, *Trepach*, wrote, "The smell is such that even an elephant will faint."[115]

Those looking to get around town despite squalid conditions on the roads and trams found themselves stymied by the disruption of transportation. The Transport Administration was forced to discontinue some tramlines and reduce the number of stops on others in response to shortages of electricity and usable cars. Riders faced long waits, and when a tram did finally arrive, the riders were packed in like sardines, barely able to find space to stand in the cars. Riders were restless and irritable, and endless quarrels ensued. Crowded stops and cars became favorite haunts for pickpockets.[116] Consequently, demands for horse-drawn cabs rose. Fares skyrocketed, and fare disputes often led to fights, some of which led to the death of the drivers or cabmen.

The city duma was no longer able to continue essential services due to the lack of funds. By the summer, the city's expenditure rose to 185 million rubles, while the revenue dwindled to 94 million rubles, with a deficit of 91 million rubles. There was a city duma election on August 20, the first democratic election based on universal, direct, equal, and secret voting. But the newly elected deputies debated more over whether the restoration of the death penalty was appropriate than whether to impose taxes on street venders, leaving essential city services to further deteriorate.[117]

Psychological Impacts of Revolutionary Disorder

With all of these emerging sources of crime and decay, the February Revolution was bound to have a profound and negative effect on people's minds. The old world and old masters were suddenly gone, and the oppressed became new masters. But despite apparent political empowerment, life did not improve. Instead, it worsened with each passing day. As the old ways of getting things done were disrupted, people became disoriented and confused, and soon these frustrations turned into irritation and anger. They began to associate freedom, once the watchword of a new age, with misery. "Freedom, O freedom," *Ogonek* wrote. "But why did you have to turn the . . . capital into a garbage dump?"[118] In an October cartoon entitled "What Happened to the Maiden Freedom?" *Ogonek* depicted the transformation of the goddess of freedom, born on February 27, from welcome harbinger of the future to

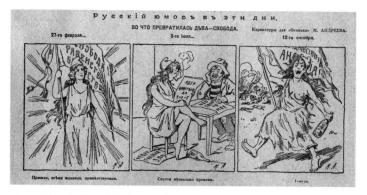

Figure 9. The decline of Maiden Freedom. She appears in full glory on February 27 (left), kills time relaxing on July 3 (center), and finally rampages drunkenly through the streets on October 12 (right). *Ogonek*, no. 41, October 22, 1917, 17.

slovenly, irrational drunkard. By October 12, the goddess, liquor in hand, marches in a blazing street among the dead. Her banner reads, "Long Live Anarchy!" See figure 9. Although this cartoon reflected *Ogonek*'s opposition to socialism, it also expressed a widely shared sentiment among city dwellers who saw freedom degenerating into chaos.[119] One cannot simply dismiss this cartoon as the biased expression of the middle class. As a worker's comment overheard by Albert Rys Williams, quoted above, indicates, this sentiment was widely shared by the working class as well.[120]

In this dismal moment, hospital admissions for mental illness increased, though one can safely assume that many more suffering people never found their way to any sort of care.[121] The psychiatrist Pavel Ia. Rozenbakh diagnosed a new mental disease, "revolutionary psychosis," whose symptoms included "susceptibility to apathy, delirium, and hallucinations closely related to current events, fear, and belligerency."[122] Withdrawal coexisted with the stuff of insanity. Newspapers reported many people with obvious mental disorders walking the streets. Suicides and divorce rates shot up.[123]

Some of the crime in Petrograd had a random quality. It was intended less to enrich its perpetrators, settle scores, or advance political agendas than to instill fear. March saw reports of black automobiles being driven madly through the streets at night, with shots being fired haphazardly from their windows. Journalists and others speculated about the culprits: former policemen, right-wing reactionaries such as the Black Hundreds, Jews, Bolsheviks. No one really knew, and the determination was left to one's political persuasion. Few of the perpetrators were caught, and the mystery continued to weigh heavily on the population.[124]

The Provisional Government failed to establish a new revolutionary legal order. On the contrary, incessant political crises eroded its authority, and the catastrophic economic crisis rent the social fabric. The city duma was broke and dysfunctional, unable to provide essential services to the citizens. Hooligans and criminals, drunken soldiers and sailors, roamed the city, brawled, and shot one another. Bystanders were easily caught up. With Petrograd breaking down, the obvious move would have been to assert police power. Instead, police power eroded alongside public services and political control.

4. Militias Rise and Fall

O f all the reasons for Petrograd's frightening increase in crime after the February Revolution, the erosion of the newly created police authority was most important. The revolutionary power attempted to replace the old tsarist police but ran aground on several major obstacles, some of them familiar by now.

First, there was the challenge of erecting a new law enforcement system amid political upheaval and economic collapse. State, municipal, party, and class organizations jockeyed for influence, undermining one another. The deepening depression made it impossible for any of them to provide effective security, leaving residents to cope on their own.

This led to further diffusion of power, just as the Provisional Government was working hard to centralize and enforce a sense of unity under the umbrella of the state. In that sense, the contingent challenges of governance added to the structural ones presented by revolutionary ideology. In the contest to build a new police authority, we see perhaps most clearly the stubbornness of organized workers' commitment to the principles of what they understood to be "democracy" and decentralization. Over the summer of 1917, workers persistently advanced these principles by maintaining the autonomy of their own militias. Occasional cooperation with the city militia aside, workers demanded independence and equated the Provisional Government's attempts to assert central control, and the official political neutrality of the municipal administration, with counterrevolution. Workers restricted their better armed and more disciplined forces to their own neighborhoods, rather than allow them to patrol a city everywhere in flames or dedicate resources to the administrative and infrastructure needs that the tsarist police had once fulfilled.

Observing the transition from the tsarist police to postrevolutionary chaos, there can be little doubt that criminality fostered conditions for state failure, which the Bolsheviks would eventually take advantage of. There were many revealing twists and turns along the way. Throughout the process, the ordinary citizens of Petrograd suffered most, setting the stage for a dreary autumn and winter in which the frustration and rage of the masses exploded in mob justice and alcohol pogroms, forcing the new Bolshevik government to finally do what its predecessors in the Provisional Government, city duma, and Petrograd Soviet could not: build a police service capable of asserting order.

The Police before the February Revolution

The police were the linchpin of the tsarist regime. They remained so even after the revolution of 1905. It was through the police administration, housed in the powerful ministry of internal affairs, that the post-1905 tsarist state controlled and established direct contact with its subjects and society at large.

The essence of the tsarist state lay in the state's power over all areas of civil society. The police served an important role in this respect, given their expansive administrative and judicial functions beyond police work.[1] State control was most complete in the capital. At the apex of the St. Petersburg police stood the city governor, who was technically subordinate to the minister of internal affairs but had the right to report directly to the tsar.[2] Under the city governor's authority were several law-enforcement outfits, of which the most relevant to this study were the precinct police (*naruzhnaia politsiia*) and the Criminal Police (*sysknaia polit-*

siia).[3] The precinct police were the core guarantors of public order and state control of subjects.

At the turn of the century, Petrograd was divided into twelve police districts and forty-seven precincts. Police inspectors and regular policemen (*gorodovye*) kept watchful eyes on the precinct level. Inspectors supervised policemen and dvorniks, as well as administrative functions such as residential record keeping, issuing announcements, and granting permits. Inspectors also made daily reports to the city governor.[4] This sort of top-down command structure would become anathema in the aftermath of the revolution, as the idea of diffusion of power took hold.

Regular policemen worked beats. They inspected and observed commercial establishments, markets, restaurants, bars, teahouses, inns, nightclubs, theaters, houses of prostitution, and homeless shelters. They did sentry duty at police boxes in strategic locations and patrolled crime-prone areas. Before the war, eight hundred police boxes were manned day and night. Police also conducted searches, detained criminals and disrupters of public order, and confiscated illegal publications.[5] They worked long hours: six hours on patrol or at outdoor posts and six hours on clerical work or guard duty per day. They were also required to take special instruction courses five times a week, after work hours.[6]

Uniformed policemen were literally the tsar's eyes and ears, "visible representatives of the tsar's authority at the ground level."[7] In 1907, St. Petersburg had 521 police inspectors and 3,897 regular police. But long hours and poor compensation made it hard to keep the ranks filled. There were 447 vacancies in 1912, 857 in 1913, and 935 in January 1914.[8] To make up for their low wages, many policemen demanded bribes in return for their protection.

Most of the regular policemen were young, unmarried men. They lived in unsanitary barracks and took their comfort from prostitutes, leading to a high incidence of venereal disease and infection.[9] They were also poorly educated. Minimally, regular police were required to be able to read and write, but even in St. Petersburg, a region of high culture, many policemen were illiterate.

Authorities attempted to combat illiteracy by instituting special preparatory school for police candidates. Prospective policemen completed a training program lasting up to a month and took an exam. Successful candidates entered the reserves and, on the recommendation of supervising officers and the city governor, might be assigned a post in the precincts. Reservists continued to take courses in reading and writing, self-defense, and the use of weapons.

After appointment to the regular police, they underwent further training in self-defense, bladed weapons, firearms, and police procedure. Inspectors underwent an additional two to three months of study covering criminal law, interrogation procedures, criminal records and reporting, and crime-scene detective work.[10] Although the tsarist government was committed to police professionalism, merit was not enough to earn promotion to the role of inspector, to say nothing of further promotions. Such opportunities were reserved for members of the Table of Ranks, the tsar's register of the nobility. Still, the tsarist government did raise the level of professionalism among inspectors and regular policemen. Many policemen may have lacked intellectual capacity, but they at least received basic training and knew how to use weapons.

Together with the regular police, the Criminal Police played a crucial role in combating crime. Throughout the nineteenth century, the rate of thefts and robberies in St. Petersburg increased at twice the rate of population growth. In response, the government created the Criminal Police in 1866. But the service was hopelessly understaffed, with only twelve permanent police investigators.[11]

This changed after the revolution of 1905–1907. In 1908, alarmed by rising crime, the Duma passed a law expanding the Criminal Police throughout the empire. Two years later, Vladimir G. Filippov, chief of the Criminal Police, launched a modernization project.[12] Criminal investigations were to collect physical evidence related to crime as well as testimonies of victims and witnesses, collect physiological and psychological profiles of those arrested or convicted, and conduct surveillance of suspected criminals and gangs.

The Criminal Police developed particular aptitude in the use of informants, who infiltrated criminal organizations and frequented establishments where criminals congregated. Dvorniks, doormen, cabdrivers, waiters, shop clerks, and pawn-shop owners were especially useful in this respect. So important were dvorniks and doormen that the Criminal Police maintained a special department to keep track of everyone in the city. Periodic reviews led to dismissals of those who had brushes with the law. Such reviews were remarkably thorough. In 1906, 13,040 of 22,237 dvorniks and doormen on file were fired, testifying to their ambiguous position between the police and the criminal world.[13] The law relied on them heavily, yet they were easily lured into criminality.

Especially important to the Criminal Police was the adoption of modern technology such as fingerprinting and photography. The service's greatest asset was its meticulous filing system, which tracked photographs, fingerprints, biological and psychological data, personal connections, arrests, and convictions. The Anthropometric Bureau, created in 1890, was responsible for maintaining these dossiers and by 1913 had produced one hundred thousand color-coded cards documenting criminals and criminal suspects.[14]

Nevertheless, the criminal police were unable to cope with the rise in crime. The tsarist regime's priority was to combat the revolutionary movement. It therefore privileged the political police over crime control. Thus in 1913, St. Petersburg had only 113 criminal investigators. In contrast, Paris had 1,200.[15]

Residents' views of the police usually depended on their social ranking. The privileged treated the police with disdain yet relied on their protection. The educated middle class resented censorship and police surveillance and especially detested informants who seemed to infiltrate every group and meeting. But like the upper class, they also enjoyed police protection. Workers, especially those involved in the workers' and revolutionary movements, hated the police. Semen Kanatchikov, a radical worker, wrote, "Even among the 'gray' workers," who were politically indifferent, "hatred of the police was so great that in their eyes the normal laws of human society did not extend to . . . the policeman in general. To beat up or even to kill a policeman was considered a great deed."[16] People's enmity was primarily directed at the gendarmes and Okhrana agents, but regular policemen and inspectors were often the targets as well.

But as Andrei B. Nikolaev shows on the basis of newly available archival materials, reactions to the police were not uniformly negative. Only a small number of police were committed supporters of the old regime; many were more critical of it. Some police even secretly helped organized workers, informing them of impending raids. Loyalty to the tsar was not an important motivation for most police, who instead chose their profession out of economic necessity or to avoid military service. This also means there was little idealism on the force. Nikolaev quotes P. K. Marchenko, of the First Kazanskii Precinct, mockingly describing his police uniform as "dog's hides." Marchenko joined the force only to avoid military service. Policing, in his opinion, was not an honest profession: one might as well have been a dog trained to please the privileged.[17]

Despite popular resentment and questionable levels of commitment on the force, the tsarist police authority was impressively effective. It had many inherent weaknesses and yet was able to maintain public order. This may have been hard to appreciate, given the many flaws of the tsarist regime. But the capacities of its police became obvious in light of conditions after the February Revolution.

The February Revolution and the Destruction
of the Tsarist Police

After the February Revolution, all that remained of the tsarist police in Petrograd were the fire brigade, the river detachment, and the mounted police.[18] Liberals and socialists agreed that the old police had to be destroyed. Insurgents stormed precinct stations, ransacked them, and often burned them to the ground. They ran off with vast quantities of weapons. Insurgents also destroyed police and court records. Extensive files—painstakingly collected by the Criminal Police, District Court, and courts of justice—were stolen, burned, or otherwise ruined. The Duma liberals, from whose ranks the Provisional Government was formed, considered the destruction of the police a revolutionary achievement.

During and even after the revolution, insurgents hunted former policemen, who disguised themselves to avoid retribution. When a policeman was caught, he was often killed on the spot or thrown into the river or canal to drown. In his memoirs, Baron N. E. Vrangel describes a raid on a police inspector's apartment in the building where he lived. Unable to find him, the crowd killed his wife and two children. Pavel Grabbe, a young military cadet, walked near the District Court and saw piles of logs. But what he thought was piles of logs turned out to be the bodies of dead policemen partially covered by snow. A young noblewoman, who worked as a nurse in the Red Cross hospital at the time, witnessed a tortured policeman with his legs attached to galloping horses being dragged through the streets. Only the lucky ones were brought to Tauride Palace for detention.[19]

Some policemen sympathized with the people and defected to the insurgents.[20] Undoubtedly, there were among the defectors men whose only interest was to avoid revolutionary reprisals. But others felt genuine allegiance to the revolution. They were dissatisfied with their jobs, poor salaries, and low social status and cast their lot with the insurgents.

As the specter of anarchy set in, the reconstruction of law and order became the revolutionary regime's most pressing concern. The new police would have profound implications for political power in postrevolutionary Russia.

State-Driven, Municipal, and Class-Based Police

Several militia organizations were formed in the scramble between March and October. They often competed, but at times they complemented one another. In the end, after the Bolshevik assumption of power, all of them ceased to exist, and police power was absorbed into the Communist dictatorship.

Historian Murray Frame has identified two major approaches to policing in nineteenth-century Europe. The first is the "well-ordered police state," in which state-controlled police maintain order and assume a wide range of administrative functions. The second model is associated with the London Metropolitan Police, established by Robert Peel in 1829. The focus of municipal police is "the interests of citizens rather than the state." Their primary function is "to protect the safety of the public rather than to carry out state-administrative tasks."[21] Two issues are involved in these approaches: first, who controls the police, the state or the municipal authority; and second, what tasks fall into the police jurisdiction, only to secure the safety of public order or to fulfill other administrative functions. The tsarist police exemplified the state-driven model. After the revolution, militias—so named to differentiate them from the prerevolutionary police—of both the state-driven and municipal variety operated side by side in Petrograd, joined by a third variety: class-based militias.

The Petrograd militia organizations originated with three sources. The first was the Duma Committee, formed by the members of the State Duma on February 27. The next day, the Duma Committee dismissed General Aleksandr P. Balk as city governor and appointed Professor Vadim A. Iurevich of the Military Medical Academy in his place. To signify a break with the past, he would be officially known as the public city governor (though the title of city governor remained more prevalent), and his task, he said, was "to insure the personal safety of citizens and of their property."[22] The Provisional Government continued to endorse Iurevich as the city governor.

Name changes aside, the new militia was designed according to the old regime's state-driven framework. The militia was to be an instrument of the central government, administratively subordinated to the city governor, who in turn reported to the minister of internal affairs. All personnel, from the chief of the militia to the rank and file, were to be appointed and paid by the state. In its structure, competencies, and goals, the state-driven militia was a faithful replica of the tsarist police.

The second source of militia organizations in Petrograd was the city itself. At an emergency meeting on the evening of February 28, the city duma created its own city militia (*gorodskaia militsiia*) "to assure the life and property of the population."[23] It appointed emissaries to each district to organize the militia. The city duma then elected one of its own members, Dimitrii A.

Kryzhanovskii, to be chief of the militia. In a sign of cross-class outreach, a Menchevik member of the Soviet Executive Committee recommended Zigfrid Kelson as the city militia's top administrator, and the city duma agreed. Looking to consolidate its authority, the city duma designated its own building on Nevskii as the city militia's central headquarters.[24]

The principles of the municipal police differed from those of the state-driven police. The city militia was to be independent of the central government. It would be controlled at the level of the city and its districts. It would serve all residents equally, regardless of class, sex, and nationality, and would be staffed by recruits from all segments of the population. Its chiefs and assistant chiefs would be elected by the residents, not appointed from above. Finally, it would be neutral in political affairs. This meant that the city militia would keep out of the mounting conflict between the Provisional Government and its opponents during the course of the revolutionary period ending in October. It was on this last point that the interests of the Provisional Government and city militia directly clashed, as the city militia refused to suppress movements against the Provisional Government.

Alongside the state and city militias was the workers' militia. The workers' militia was formed at a general session of the Petrograd Soviet on February 27.[25] One in every ten factory workers was urged to join.[26] Immediately after the general session, the Executive Committee designated headquarters for the worker's militia and appointed ten district commissars to organize the men.[27]

The goal of the workers' militia was neither to maintain order nor to secure life and property for all citizens. Rather, it was to promote the exclusive interests of the working class against its class enemies. It categorically rejected the principle of state-driven police emanating from the bourgeois Provisional Government and adamantly adhered to the principles of local autonomy and election. But this autonomy applied only to the working class; the interests of others were irrelevant to the functioning of the worker's militia. It also rejected the principle of the municipal police, since the workers' militia was intended to serve only the proletariat, not the citizenry at large. The militia was to be composed exclusively of workers.

Whether or not the militia should accept the authority of the state, one important principle was shared by all concepts of the militia: the militia should not only ensure security, but also fulfill multifarious administrative duties. The Militia Council of the Vasilievskii District, known for its radical favoritism of the workers' militia, issued an order on March 9 to G. G. Ge, the Golodai subdistrict commissar, giving him a list of the following duties in addition to maintain order: issuing identifications and certificates of residence for birth, death, marriage, divorce, free passage in the city, and the city duma; notarizing signatures; issuing permits for garbage disposal and automobile transit for repairs; issuing orders to housing authorities to repair buildings, heat apartments, ensure sanitary standards, clear streets, carry out searches with search warrants, administer registrations of building security, and carry out court orders.[28] The militia thus inherited one principle of the tsarist police, the principle of what Frame calls the "well ordered police state."

Militia Formation at the Grass Roots

Although the city and workers' militias were established from the organizational heights of the city duma and the Executive Committee of the Petrograd Soviet, the new police forces were built from below. The Executive Committee's commissars, with the exception of Aleksei V. Peshekhonov in the Petrogradskii District, played no role in the formation of the workers' militia.[29] The city duma sent emissaries to districts and selected the district head-quarters, but control devolved from there.[30]

The militias were directed primarily at the subdistrict level. This was in part a function of the revolutionary spirit: after February, power shifted from central organs to points closer to the ground.[31] In general, the lives of Petrograd's citizens revolved around subdistrict institutions. Ironically, the old regime operated in much the same way. The old police precincts, which became subdistrict commissariats after the February Revolution, provided the vital link between residents and the several authorities competing for control of them. This led to competition at the district and subdistrict levels between district dumas and soviets.

Historians have often depicted the simultaneous formation of the city and workers' militias as an outgrowth of class division between the proletariat and the bourgeoisie. But this characterization is too simplistic. Reality was more nuanced, as residents contested and negotiated principles of policing in ways that cannot be explained purely according to class interests. We can better appreciate this by examining the creation of militia organizations at the local level.

On March 1, a workers' militia formed in the First and Second Vyborgskii Subdistricts.[32] A practical response to disorder overtaking factories and neighborhoods in the absence of the tsarist police, the militia followed no central authority.[33] The First Vyborgskii Subdistrict selected V. G. Botsvadze, dispatched by the city duma, as its commissar. Headquarters were organized in Durnovo dacha, as the former precinct police headquarters had burned down.[34]

The city and workers' militias existed in tension, but they did not seek to undermine each other's legitimacy. On March 5, the Vyborgskii Soviet of Workers' and Soldiers' Deputies demanded that the chief of the city militia "officially recognize the existing workers' militia" and requested weapons and armbands.[35] The goal was independence, not exclusivity. Interestingly, the official seals of both the "Commissar of the Second Vyborgskii Subdistrict" and the "Petrograd City People's Militia" were printed on one record, indicating that the subdistrict commissariat kept open a line of communication with the city militia administration and acted in the name of the city militia. Some workers' militias operated only at factory compounds, while others fulfilled city militia functions outside the factories.[36]

At the same time, Vyborgskii workers immediately pushed Botsvadze aside, indicating the perceived importance of class purity within the militia.[37] At this point, the relationship between class-based and municipal policing was ambiguous. Although the district and subdistrict soviets accepted the authority of the city militia, they also preserved the principle of subdistrict autonomy by selecting the militiamen and the commissar themselves.[38]

In the Kolomenskii District, too, militia formation was a bottom-up affair. Subdistrict organizations initiated the process and maintained their independence. Unlike Vyborgskii, however, Kolomenskii was not a working-class district. Workers and the middle class enjoyed nearly equal clout, but here the middle class took the lead on policing by organizing two subdistrict commissariats.[39] The overarching District Militia Commission was formed on April 13, with representatives of the district duma, district soviet, the Franco-Russian Factory, and various political parties (Mensheviks, Socialist Revolutionaries, and Bolsheviks). Despite the mixed composition of the district and the diverse representation in the Militia Commission, a remarkable degree of consensus prevailed. All agreed that subdistrict autonomy, elections, and class equality were fundamental to the organization and governance of district militias.[40]

But district workers were still involved in policing. The second subdistrict's gigantic Admiralty Shipyard formed a workers' militia on March 2.[41] Sixty workers would be on active duty with another two hundred to three hundred in reserve. In addition, fifty workers were to assist the city militia, but the records of an April 8 meeting state, "The factory militia has no relations whatever with the city militia and follows the instructions of the chief of the city militia only with respect to administrative problems." Arrests and searches inside the factory could be carried out only with the permission of the factory committee.[42] The workers' militia thus created a pocket in the Kolomenskii District where the city militia had no authority.

Various Kolomenskii militias thus operated on the basis of both cooperation and autonomy, mating elements of class-based and municipal police. The workers' militia insisted on independence and refused to subordinate itself to the city militia. Its goals included the struggle against counterrevolution. But it also recognized the subdistrict commissariats and allowed the possibility of collaboration with them. The difference between the municipal and class concepts was expressed territorially, with the workers' militia claiming jurisdiction in the shipyard and its surroundings but conceding the rest to the subdistrict commissariats.

Class conflict was much sharper in the Vasilievskii District. On February 28, the city duma appointed Court of Justice judge V. V. Drozdov to be emissary to create the Vasilievskii militia. He established the First Vasilievskii Commissariat in the predominantly middle-class subdistrict.[43] Drozdov's commissariat restored order in the area along the Bolshoi Prospect and regularly dispatched patrols of ten militiamen under the leadership of one student.[44]

In the other subdistricts, however, the workers' militias took the upper hand. In the Second Vasilievskii Subdistrict, where there were many large factories, the workers' militia occupied the police station and established its commissariat there.[45] The workers' militia also controlled the third subdistrict. Workers from the Cable Factory were the major force in militia organizing in the fourth subdistrict.[46]

These workers' militias created a district-level militia council and elected a Socialist Revolutionary, Iu. A. Alekseev, its chairman. The relationship between the local militia and the central city militia was hotly debated at the Executive Committee of the District Soviet. Alekseev saw no problem with the district militia being subordinated to Kryzhanovskii's city militia, but he opposed subordination to City Governor Iurevich. The crucial question, according to Alekseev, was democratic legitimacy: Iurevich was not an elected official.[47] This debate also touched on the role of the militia. Some workers' representatives were apprehensive about a working-class organization assuming municipal tasks, such as maintaining canals and sanitation, thereby advancing bourgeois interests. Nevertheless, a majority seemed to accept that, as long as a dictatorship of the proletariat was not imminent, the workers' militia had to exist in the broader framework of civil society and thus had to accept the authority of the city militia.[48]

Nevertheless, the Vasilievskii Soviet challenged Drozdov and his middle class–dominated militia. To dislodge Drozdov's militia from the First Vasilievskii Subdistrict, the District Militia Soviet posted its own forces, composed of students, in strategic locations. The final showdown came when the District Militia Soviet called a general meeting of the first subdistrict militiamen for April 10. About three hundred people attended. Met with catcalls and parliamentary obstructions, at least twenty members of Drozdov's militia walked out of the meeting. Thereafter, Alekseev declared this meeting the founding of the First Subdistrict Commissariat.[49]

Residents of the subdistrict protested and convened a meeting of housing committee representatives on April 18 to plot a new course. The assembled decided to form a single, unified militia organization "on the elective principle."[50] Soon after, ninety-eight militiamen of Drozdov's militia held a separate meeting, demanding that the Subdistrict Militia Soviet include representatives of the housing committees, the general assembly of the militiamen, homeowners' association, cooperatives, and the district soviet. Kryzhanovskii attended this meeting and endorsed the resolution. The cleavage between the workers' militia and Drozdov's middle class–dominated militia could not be bridged, though it should be noted that both favored elections and resident representation.

In Petrogradskii District, Aleksei Peshekhonov—a member of the Popular Socialist Party, representing the right wing of the Executive Committee of the Petrograd Soviet—dominated. When he accepted the Petrograd Soviet's appointment as commissar of Petrogradskii, he also sought authority from the Duma Committee. But Miliukov refused. He was probably aware of the emerging danger of dual power and did not wish to grant any authority to the Petrograd Soviet.

After establishing his headquarters, Peshekhonov appealed to Petrogradskii residents to "maintain calm despite the developing events, to react with trust to the district commissars appointed by the new power and execute their orders, and to fulfill the obligations necessary for public service."[51] He also urged factories, mills, and social organizations to send delegates to the commissariat. Responding to the appeal, a few hundred volunteers, including intelligentsia, workers, and soldiers, assembled at the commissariat and formed a militia.[52] Peshekhonov's commissariat emerged as the most influential authority in the Petrogradskii District by absorbing some competitors and subordinating others.[53]

Although appointed by the Petrograd Soviet, Peshekhonov clearly intended to run his militia according to municipal principles, serving all citizens. Yet the commissariat found itself under continual pressure from the revolutionary masses. Its survival depended on accommodation to the mood of the crowd. When Peshekhonov refused to surrender the commissariat's weapons to a group of soldiers, they turned their guns on him. When he released the innocent people charged with counterrevolutionary activities, the crowd demanded harsh treatment. The most powerful commissar in the Petrograd District wrote in his memoirs, "All the power in essence completely rested in the hands of the crowd. The crowd held power in the form of self-government, and many undoubtedly were convinced that this was truly the people's power."[54]

There is little documentary evidence of militia formation in other districts. No record exists for the predominantly middle-class central and the central-mixed districts, nor the southern districts where the urban poor predominated. We can presume, however, that patterns from the better-documented districts held in the central areas. The middle class–oriented commissariats probably followed a path similar to Drozdov's in the First Vasilievskii Subdistrict, emerging from below and quickly establishing contact with the city militia administration via the district dumas. The militia in other districts probably followed the path of Kolomenskii.[55]

The process by which militias arose supports four conclusions. First, all of the militias, city and workers', were created as grassroots organizations responding to the urgent need to maintain public order. Second, the principles of local self-determination and election were widely shared. Third, there was division between the middle-class-dominated central districts, which favored the municipal police, and the outlying districts, where the workers' militia predominated. Fourth, this division did not preclude cooperation. There was a tacit consensus that militia organizations should be under the jurisdiction of the city militia administration.[56]

The workers' militias were characterized by an ambiguous mixture of municipal and class-based principles. They established autonomous power in the working-class subdistricts, excluding outside interference. But autonomy was not in itself a rejection of the municipal police. In fact, the workers' militia made two important concessions to the principle of municipal police. First, they accepted the authority of the city militia; maintained communications with its central administration; received financial assistance, including wages for militiamen, from the city administration, and recognized themselves as an organ of the city militia. They wore red armbands to signify their independence, but they also wore armbands with the initials of the city militia, GM, and the official seal of their subdistrict commissariats.[57] Second, though the workers' militia officially supported only working-class interests, they in fact worked to ensure the security of all citizens within their jurisdictions. All of the commissariats dominated by the workers' militia faithfully sent their daily reports to the Central Militia Administration.

The Petrograd Soviet and the Militia Question

In another sign that class politics were not predominant early in the revolutionary period, on February 28, the Soviet Executive Committee confirmed its intention to cooperate with the Duma Committee. Iurii M. Steklov, representing the Executive Committee, declared that the revolution would have "to rely not only on the workers."[58] At least for the moment, the Executive Committee believed cooperation was essential to save the revolution and that insistence on total worker self-government would doom it.

To that end, the Soviet sought to subordinate the workers' militias to the city militia. On March 2, the Executive Committee appointed two Mensheviks, V. P. Piatiev and A. V. Chernev, as liaisons to the city militia. Along with Kelson, the city militia secretary, they visited the headquarters of the workers' militia and tried to convince the men to join the city militia.[59] These emissaries attempted to bridge class divisions by enshrining both municipal and class-based policing principles in the bedrock of the city militia. Together, they wrote instructions for the militia stating, "The duty of a militiaman is to defend each and every one from all violence, offense, and arbitrariness"—an affirmation of municipal values. But these instructions also acknowledged workers' class concerns. "A militiaman must understand that he is an executive organ of the new Free Russia," they wrote, "and is obligated to combat all attempts at counterrevolution."[60]

At the level of organized policy making, the city militia's attempt to absorb the worker's militia was a success, though a Pyrrhic one. On March 5, the city militia's district commissars met with representatives of the workers' militia and approved Piatiev, Chernev, and Kelson's draft instructions. The workers' militia would be incorporated.[61] However, in an obvious concession to workers, the unified organization was renamed the People's City Militia. Unification was finalized on March 7, when the Executive Committee confirmed that the Soviet would maintain the right to appoint and control candidates for the worker's militia.[62]

But at the grassroots, subdistrict level, the decision to subordinate the workers' militia to the city militia met with vigorous opposition. On March 8, the Executive Committee of the Vyborgskii District Soviet passed a resolution refusing unification.[63] Four days later, the workers of the Cable Factory called the merger "a campaign against the workers' militia."

> This campaign, started by the bourgeois city duma, provokes in us strong protest. We maintain that, at the present moment of struggle for a democratic republic, a

struggle with the remnants of tsarism and constitutional monarchy designed by the bourgeoisie, the workers' militia must take precedence over philistine militia organizations.[64]

Ultimately, the merger was too unpopular to proceed in anything but name only. Although the workers' militia reluctantly accepted its official subordination to the city militia, it remained independent for all practical purposes and continued to police the workers' quarters of the city without city militia interference. According to V. I. Startsev's figures, roughly twenty of Petrograd's eighty-five militia commissariats were under the control of a workers' militia as of March 19.[65]

The attempt to subordinate the workers' militia to the city militia further radicalized workers. The more their independence was attacked, the more tenaciously they clung to it.

Provisional Government versus City Duma

Historians have paid attention to the tension between the city and workers' militias, which comports with the framing of the revolutionary era as a struggle between the proletariat and the bourgeoisie. But another tension characteristic of the revolutionary era, between local autonomy and central authority, also played out, further undermining the development of effective law enforcement in Petrograd. At the same time, the city governor, attached to the Provisional Government, and the city duma sparred over state-driven and municipal policing.

Kryzhanovskii and Kelson sought maximum independence from the central government. The city militia, they believed, had to transcend the interests of political parties and answer only to the residents of Petrograd themselves. Autonomy, political neutrality, and elections were therefore sacrosanct. But the Provisional Government wanted direct control over policing in Petrograd. In the course of a two-month tug of war, the city governor repeatedly attempted to secure jurisdiction of the city militia.

The city and the Provisional Government jockeyed virtually from day one. On March 1, city militia chief Kryzhanovskii issued a proclamation demanding that citizens surrender their arms to his outfit.[66] That same day, City Governor Iurevich made two decrees of his own. The first prohibited the sale of liquor, and the second asserted that only the Provisional Government and authorities it recognized could approve arrests and searches.[67] At the time, commentators understood these dueling orders for what they were: salvos in a war between centralized control and municipal self-government.[68]

On March 15, Iurevich announced unilaterally that he had taken over the city militia and that Kryzhanovskii would now serve as his deputy.[69] When the city duma protested, the ministry of internal affairs interceded. But neither Mayor Glebov nor City Governor Iurevich yielded.[70] The following day, Iurevich moved the city militia headquarters from the city duma building to the city governor's office. The city militia headquarters occupied only two small rooms on the second floor, while Iurevich monopolized the stately third floor. But while it looked like the city governor was in control, the basic conflict was unresolved, and the city militia continued to function independently. According to Kelson, down-to-earth and self-effacing Kryzhanovskii never reported to pompous Professor Iurevich and his sizable entourage. Iurevich went on issuing directives carried out by no one.[71]

With the city militia refusing to come to heel, the ministry of internal affairs tried to circumvent the city duma. On March 26, it established a Commission for Militia and Municipal Police led by two champions of centralized state power: Deputy Minister of Internal Affairs Sergei D. Urusov and Professor Vladimir V.

Sviatlovskii. The commission issued a law on April 17 declaring the old police abolished while defining the militia as the "executive organ of state power at the local level." Its financing, according to this law, would be left to the state.

At the same time, the law recognized that the militia would be administered by municipal and county councils (*zemstvos*) and allowed them to select and dismiss their local militia chiefs. Partly this was a concession to local self-government, but it also was necessitated by the abolition of governors and governors-general in the provinces. Still, the effort toward centralization under the state-driven model was undeniable. The decree bound the militia to "cooperate with the organs of the government and public authority," meaning the commissars appointed by the Provisional Government. The minister of internal affairs would be responsible for directing and reviewing militia activity, inspecting the militia, and drawing up its budget. Furthermore, the Provisional Government was empowered to temporarily suspend militia chiefs.

Reflecting a degree of inheritance from the tsar's highly concentrated bureaucracy, the new militia would have broad jurisdiction including over registrations and certifications and would maintain local infrastructure such as roads and bridges. The Provisional Government was hardly deaf to public outcry over tsarist abuses, though. As we have seen, they sought to constrain investigative powers by requiring written arrest warrants or judicial authority to hold anyone longer than twenty-four hours.[72]

The Provisional Government's militia law was to be modified for the major cities of Petrograd, Moscow, Kiev, and Odessa, affording an opportunity to witness a direct clash between the state and municipal principles. According to Kelson, two draft proposals for the big-city militia statutes were prepared, one by K. L. Bermanskii, representing the city militia, and another by the Provisional Government's commission.[73]

Challenging the Provisional Government commission's draft, the Bermanskii proposal began: "(1) The city duma belongs to the jurisdiction of the Petrograd City Public Administration; (2) The City Mayor is the overall chief of militia; (3) The city duma elects the chief of the city militia, who combines and directs activity of all militiamen of the city duma. The chief of militia is elected for three years."[74]

The Provisional Government's document uses the terms "militia chief (*nachalnik*) of districts" and "assistant militia chief of districts," but the names of these positions were crossed out by a critic of this document, who penciled in their places "district commissars" and "district assistant commissar." The term *nachalnik* was reminiscent of the tsarist police chief, and critics preferred to use "commissar" to make a clean break with the tsarist police.

The commission's draft called for elections, but only of the chief of the militia. District chiefs and militiamen were to be appointed by "the chief of the militia and the district chief" respectively, and under the supervision of the Provisional Government's commissars.[75] Bermanskii's proposal, in contrast, states, "The general supervision and guidance of the activity of the militia in the district falls to the jurisdiction of the district duma and district administration."[76]

While the commission proposed that militiamen be paid by the ministry of internal affairs, Bermanskii believed they should be paid by the city. Bermanskii's proposal disqualified former tsarist police from serving as militiamen; the commission's proposal had nothing to say about the matter. Finally, the commission wanted to institute a system of inspectors appointed by the ministry of internal affairs, who were to supervise the activities of the militia and report to the ministry.[77] Bermanskii sought to install supervisory power in four inspectors appointed by and reporting to the chief of the militia.[78]

Unsurprisingly, the city duma approved Bermanskii's draft. Less expectedly, the Provisional Government did, too. On May 18, the newly formed Provisional Government—the first coalition government, composed of liberals and moderate socialists—decided to abolish the office of the city governor. Iurevich was dismissed as city governor, and Kryzhanovskii was reinstated as city militia chief.[79] The city militia administration stayed in the city governor's building on Gorokhovaia Street rather than returning to the city duma building. Still, until the first week of the Bolshevik regime, the city governor's office lingered in the form of a commission to abolish itself.[80] The Provisional Government thus lost direct control over the police force in the capital. During the summer's political crises, it had no police to rely on except garrison troops. Whenever the Provisional Government attempted to reassert its control over the city militia, it was through the defunct city governor's office it wanted to resurrect.

It is not clear why the Provisional Government abolished the city governor's office. The formation of the coalition government may have played a role in the decision. Whatever the underlying reason, abolition was a victory for the municipal principle. The final downfall of the state-driven police model further weakened state control.

Yet in spite of overcoming the city governor, the city duma was not exactly ascendant. By May, the locus of power had already shifted to the subdistrict commissariats, to which the city duma's links were tenuous. As Kelson observed, the autonomy of the subdistrict commissariats was firmly established, "removing all power from the militia chief, reducing his role to that of a mere servant of the city administration." To Kelson, this was a necessary evil that

> grew out of the desire to remove even the slightest degree of what reminded [the people] of the organization

of the former police. It was a conscious choice to deprive the chief of all power. Frightened by the evil past of the omnipresent and omniscient police that controlled all aspects of the life of residents, they rendered the municipal police powerless. The aim to realize complete political neutrality and passivity was achieved: by law, the militia was created in such a way that it could not interfere in anything.[81]

Kelson was overstating the case. The law itself did not proscribe city militia interference in political conflicts. But this was the understanding of the city militia administrative chief officer.

From its inception, then, the city militia was undone by the very principles of local self-determination, democracy, and political neutrality on which it was founded. By resisting the Provisional Government's assertions of centralized control over the city militia, the city militia administration virtually abdicated its authority over the subdistrict commissariats.[82]

The Ineffectiveness and Criminal Infiltration of the City Militia

The city militia faced enormous difficulty recruiting patrolmen and officers. Initially, the major contingents were university and high school students and other middle-class elements, especially those experienced in law. Kelson admits that due to the lack of qualified militiamen, he had to accept even preteen boy scouts.[83]

These militiamen were often enthusiastic and, as we saw earlier, scored some victories against organized crime. But they were poorly trained and frequently lacked self-control. For instance, on one occasion in June, a militiaman allowed a dangerous recidivist to escape when he fell asleep while escorting the criminal to

Figure 10. Titled "Justifiable Panic," this cartoon points to the growing mistrust felt by the public regarding the city militia. The caption asks: "What's the matter? Why this panic?" The answer: "What, can't you see? A militiaman is inspecting his weapon." Note the armband, GM, which signifies the city militia. *Novyi satirikon,* no. 17, May 1917, 7.

court.[84] Higher authorities—the city militia administration, the chief of district militia, chiefs of subdistrict militias—were incapable of enforcing discipline. The best they could do was impose a maximum fine of twenty-five rubles, leave black marks on militiamen's records, and dismiss, but not terminate, them.[85] After a militiaman was dismissed from one subdistrict, it was common to find him a new position in another. Some militiamen did not know how to properly handle a firearm; there were reports of civilians and fellow militiamen killed in accidental shootings.[86] The press captured the popular perception of the new militia's poor firearms training. This cartoon shows citizens fleeing when a militiaman takes up a firearm. They don't know where he is going to shoot. See figure 10.

Another source of citizen distrust was criminal infiltration of the city militia. The lack of rigorous background checks and the chaos of the early revolutionary period resulted in many criminals being recruited to the force. This makes some sense, since criminals, by dint of their trade, were more familiar with laws than were ordinary citizens and were better equipped to handle weapons. They took advantage of their new positions to pursue criminal ends.

Newspapers were filled with stories of criminals in militia ranks. For instance, at the end of March, *Petrogradskii listok* reported about a certain Captain Vasiliev. This energetic man appeared at the city governor's office during the February Revolution and was appointed as its commandant of security. In this capacity, he was responsible for the safekeeping of confiscated valuables. When a woman whose jewelry had been confiscated showed up to request its return, she discovered that it had disappeared, together with Captain Vasiliev.[87]

Another famous case was that of a fellow named Menzentsev, who earned his job as chief of the mounted militia on the basis of previous service as cornet of a cavalry regiment. While Menzentsev was in Moscow ordering new horses and fodder, officers of the militia administration contacted what Menzentsev claimed was his original regiment, which found no record of him. It turned out he was not a cornet but a swindler known to the Criminal Police. Upon return to Petrograd, he was apprehended at Nikolaevskii Station.[88]

In April, a detective from the former Criminal Police recognized three militiamen at the corner of Sadovaia and Nevskii Prospect—the very center of the city. The detective immediately noticed that they were ex-convicts who had been sentenced to prison terms of fifteen to twenty years before the February Revolution. When the detective reported his findings at the nearest commissariat, it sent a patrol of militiamen to detain the men. By the time the patrol arrived, the trio had gotten word and were running away amid rifle shots.[89]

Confiscated items, including weapons, often disappeared from commissariats.[90] Sometimes they did not even make it that far, as militiamen took confiscated property directly to the black market. Militiamen robbed shops and liquor inventories, and many were detained for drunkenness.[91] On May 11, *Petrogradskii listok* printed a critical article, "Our Militia," in which it described members illegally selling spirits, taking bribes, committing thefts, handling firearms carelessly, and breaking up breadlines with a water cannon.[92]

Much of this strife might have been avoided if the city militia administration had recruited former tsarist policemen. The Provisional Government's Militia Law did not prohibit the hiring of former tsarist policemen, and many provincial cities did hire them. But the Petrograd city militia chose not to, in order to make a clean break with the tsarist police. Yet as we have seen, many tsarist policemen resented the privileged class and were thus politically acceptable to the revolutionaries. With a few exceptions, regular policemen and even inspectors were apolitical, indifferent to the regime they served. Many would have served for the city militia willingly, had they been recruited.

It is not as though the various authorities were unaware of the value of the tsarist police. Already on March 10, City Governor Iurevich released Assistant Criminal Police Chief Levikov and two other criminal detectives from prison.[93] On April 15, Iurevich announced the formation of the new Criminal Militia headed by former Criminal Police Chief Aleksandr A. Kirpichnikov, also released from prison after the February Revolution. Former investigators of the Criminal Police received 10 percent raises. The Criminal Militia operated under the auspices of the Court of Justice, the Petrograd Criminal Court, and ultimately the ministry of justice, not the ministry of internal affairs as it had before the revolution.[94]

The work of the Criminal Militia was hampered, however, partly by the stigma of being associated with the tsarist police, and partly by the shortage of resources and experienced detectives. The restoration of the Criminal Police was carried out at the initiative of the Provisional Government, not the city duma, a factor that impeded coordination between the Criminal Police and subdistrict commissariats. Most damaging was the destruction of the criminal files. It was not until August that the Criminal Militia began assembling photographs of recidivists from scratch.[95] As a result, many cases were not pursued. The Criminal Militia also was forbidden from using informants, who had been so important to the pre-revolutionary Criminal Police.[96]

The Criminal Militia did what it could, successfully investigating high-profile cases, as we saw in the Seitola murder case described in Chapter 2. But with all the obstacles in its way, it was unable to make up for the many deficits of the city militia. The refusal to recruit former tsarist patrolmen proved a serious error, undermining the capacity, credibility, and ultimately authority of the city militia.[97]

The Radicalization of the Workers' Militia

At the beginning of May, the city duma adopted a new statute designed to reduce the ranks of the city militia from twenty thousand to six thousand. Concerned about criminal infiltration of the militia, abuse of powers to search and arrest, and the glut of youngsters on the force, Kryzhanovskii ordered the subdistrict commissariats to investigate the credentials of each militiaman and purge rotten apples and youngsters. But another agenda was to reduce the number of workers' militiamen, who at this point were officially attached to the city militia. To be reappointed, a militiaman had to present a recommendation from either a recognized public organization or a political party. Deputy city militia M. G. Nashatyr explained:

> The reappointment will be carried out by a new commission, composed of two representatives of the district duma, two representatives from the district soviet of workers' and soldiers' deputies, and two representatives from the militia and district commissariats. . . . Representatives of the district soviet should be sure not to recommend any extreme elements. I can categorically declare that the Bolsheviks will be excluded from the militia.[98]

Kryzhanovskii's offensive prompted an interdistrict conference of the "people's militia" (*narodnaia militsiia*), held on May 27. There, representatives from various worker's militias accused Kryzhanovskii and the city militia of serving the "ruling classes," using reappointment "to impose from above a form of militia organization favorable to their interests." The workers protested what they saw as an effort to transform the militia into "a Western European type of police that was universally hated by all populations of the world."[99]

In response, conference attendees adopted a resolution providing for eligibility of all adults, regardless of sex, for militia service; formation of a workers' militia comprising factory workers, trade unionists, and other organized elements of the population; soldiers' eligibility to serve in the workers' militia; factory cooperation in release of workers to militia duty, as well as job and wage protection for those workers; the election of militia executive officers by militiamen themselves; and a special commission to reorganize the militia. The conference further proposed creating a new commission, consisting of representatives of workers' organizations, to replace the city militia administration.[100]

When the interdistrict conference of the workers' militia met again on June 3, it produced a new resolution demonstrating further radicalization:

> Since the militia is central to the entire working proletariat and the matter of democracy, it must be led by an organ elected on a democratic basis from below. Therefore, we resolve that we do not recognize the present Militia Soviet led by Chief Kryzhanovskii. We propose that the commission elected at the conference on May 27, 1917, assume the function of the militia administration.[101]

This conference also created a permanent executive body, the Soviet of the Petrograd People's Militia. At another meeting, on June 27, the Soviet of the Petrograd People's Militia condemned all the district dumas, except Vyborgskii's, as "counterrevolutionary and anti-democratic." It appealed instead to workers and soldiers, declaring, "A blow to the militia [is] a blow to the revolution."[102]

In considering the extremity of these measures, it is important to keep in mind that when socialists and the workers spoke of democracy, they did not mean that everyone would enjoy equal rights. They believed that the lower classes were entitled to rights from which the privileged would be excluded.[103] The location of these interdistrict militia conferences is also noteworthy from the standpoint of class division: they were held in the Durnovo dacha, which, as we have seen, was reinvented as a hub of working-class organizations and radical parties.[104] The bourgeoisie and much of the press felt differently, characterizing the dacha as a hotbed of anarchists. This characterization, in turn, instilled among the workers still greater anti-bourgeois sentiment, reinforcing class antagonism.

Amid mounting class hostility, the workers sought to cement their revolutionary gains not just by maintaining the autonomy of their militia but also by developing a separate armed group specifically to combat counterrevolution. Already by the end of April, these Red Guards, as they were known, were holding citywide conferences, indicating a high degree of organization, rapidly achieved.[105] While the workers' militia focused on maintaining public order in working-class neighborhoods, the Red Guards would sniff out class enemies. The Red Guards were well trained. Their strongly motivated membership participated in Sunday target practice on the outskirts of the city, gaining greater facility with firearms than the city militia's hapless patrolmen.

The radicalization of the workers' militia and the emergence of the Red Guards illustrate the essential political dynamics of the Russian Revolution. Politically conscious workers considered their autonomous organizations, especially the workers' militia, sacrosanct. Any attack on them was counterrevolutionary. Although the city militia administration's condemnation of the workers' militia might be seen as maintaining the principle of municipal policing, workers smelled bourgeois class interests at work. With society thoroughly divided along class lines, there was little room for class-independent claims of inclusivity.

From the standpoint of the city militia, reappointment was an abject failure, although it managed to weed out some criminal elements and youngsters. It did not greatly change the composition of the militia and did not eliminate the workers' militia, since practically all militiamen could satisfy the minimal requirement—one recommendation from a social organization or a political party. Its major effect was to further exacerbate tension between the workers' and city militias. The threat of reappointment pulled the workers' militia toward more extreme defensive positions, and the city militia, despite its political neutrality, moved further toward the Provisional Government.

The Commission to Review the City Militia

On May 28, the Provisional Government sought to reverse its earlier loss to the city duma by creating a commission to review the Petrograd city militia. Although the composition of this commission is not known, its membership was almost certainly identical to that of the ministry of internal affairs' Commission on Militia, which advocated state-driven police.

During the month of June, the review commission investigated thirty-five of the capital's subdistricts (less than a half of the total subdistricts).[106] It examined the composition of the commissariats and the militiamen, relationships between them, the effectiveness of posting duties, relationships between police and administrative duties, the city militia's effectiveness in combating crime, the registration of residents, the maintenance of order, and the relationship between the city militia and the workers' militia. Its report provides useful details about militia conditions at the subdistrict level. The report is also deeply biased in favor of state-driven policing, unfairly criticizing the powerless Kryzhanovskii for failing to impose the state's will and needlessly heaping hostility on the workers' militia.

A major source of bias is the report's obsession with "state consciousness" (*gosudarstvennost*).[107] Some political elite—liberals and moderate socialists—and commentators insisted that state interests transcended those of class and party and needed to be preserved. To that end, they wanted the state to impose its will on organizations and citizens and called for maximum state consciousness.

The report is blunt, stating, "Maintenance of public and personal security in Petrograd is so varied that, on the one hand, there exist subdistrict militias where security of person and property is guaranteed sufficiently, if not completely; but, on the other hand, there are subdistricts where the existence of the militia itself threatens the security of citizens."[108] The report divided up the subdistricts according to their performance: twelve in the city center, where the militia were most reliable and effective in maintaining order and hewed to the demands of state consciousness; twenty in the outlying workers' districts, some of which were more or less satisfactory, while others "required attention"; and three in workers' districts, where the militia itself constituted a threat to security.[109]

In the center of the city, which included the Admiralteiskii, Kazanskii, Liteinyi, Moskovskii, and Spasskii Districts and the First Aleksandro-Nevskii Subdistrict, "both the external duty of the militias and the internal work of the commissariats were carried out on the healthy basis of state consciousness and respect for individuals."[110] More than half of commissars in these districts were university educated. Assistant commissars also impressed the commission with their level of education. Senior militiamen in these districts were mostly intellectuals and possessed high "moral standards." Although lacking technical training, these senior militiamen carried out investigations with zeal. The moral quality of these subdistricts' junior militiamen was also considered high. The commission applauded them for generally shunning the radicalism of the interdistrict conference.

Perceived bright spots persisted alongside serious concerns. The commission approved of special mobile detachments of students organized to combat criminals in the Third Liteinyi and the Second and the Fourth Moskovskii Subdistricts.[111] Commissioners singled out militiamen of the First Aleksandro-Nevskii and Second Moskovskii Subdistricts, who arrested more than three thousand people in three months, for their enthusiasm. Nevertheless, the review pointed out that, even in the central subdistricts, investigations were haphazard and carried out by officers lacking technical and forensic training. There was no regular contact between these subdistricts and the Criminal Militia, indicating poor coordination.[112]

One of the most serious problems facing central subdistricts was "the extreme insufficiency of weapons." Often militiamen on posting duty were not equipped. In the Second Kazanskii subdistrict, forty-seven militiamen shared twenty revolvers.[113] The situation contrasted sharply with that of outlying districts, where workers' militia possessed weapons in abundance. The commission also emphasized that "the complete isolation of the central subdistricts from the administratively unified city militia, its chief, and its administration could be explained only by the deliberate and methodical abdication of the chief of the city militia and his administration," a damning condemnation of municipal leadership.[114]

Seven subdistricts—the Second and Fourth Aleksandro-Nevskii, First Kolomenskii, Krestovskii, First Lesnoi, First Narvskii, and Fourth Spasskii—were counted as relatively functional but a step below the central districts. Their commissars, of varied background, were less educated, and the militiamen themselves were all students, workers, and criminals, according to the report. In subdistricts where students and workers played a major role, fewer illegal searches occurred. Elsewhere, criminal elements prevailed.[115]

Compared with the central subdistricts, the militiamen in these subdistricts were less driven. Although they were better armed, they still did not have enough weapons. Few had time for target practice. Investigative and crime-prevention techniques were hit-or-miss. Methodical searches and raids practically rid the First Lesnoi Subdistrict of thieves. But the enormous Second Lesnoi Subdistrict had too few men to allow for successful investigations and patrols. Terrorized by deserters from the Bicycle

Battalion and the First Machine Gun Regiment, the city militia in Second Lesnoi was largely powerless.[116]

Another category of subdistricts was considered unreliable. This included the Third Narvskii; Third Vyborgskii;[117] First Okhta; First, Second, Third, and Fourth Petrogradskii; and First, Second, and Third Rozhdestvenskii Subdistricts. These were dominated by the workers' militia and influenced by the Red Guards. In the Third Vyborgskii, the commissariat was staffed entirely by workers, some of whom were Bolsheviks. Many militiamen were also Bolsheviks, but the subdistrict commissar testified that the militia fulfilled its obligations "accurately and undeviatingly, according to the laws and measures enacted by the Provisional Government and the city duma." The militia was well armed. The First Okhta was similar to the Third Vyborgskii. All of the First Okhta militiamen belonged to the Red Guards. Nevertheless, the report deemed the commissariat satisfactory. The Third Narvskii, Third Vyborgskii, and First Okhta recognized the chief of the city militia.[118]

All three subdistricts of the Rozhdestvenskii District looked worse. Although the commissars were mostly intellectuals, the commissariats were poorly organized. This was a serious problem given the area's large number of suspicious teahouses and taverns, which required constant observation and frequent raids. Cooperation with the military authorities was ineffective. The guards of the First Machine Gun Regiment, assigned to aid in the district, were so lax that they were suspected of assisting jailbreaks. The mere forty-five rifles afforded the militiamen were totally inadequate.[119]

In Petrogradskii, almost all militiamen were workers, except for ten soldiers and two students. Although the city militia operated in every subdistrict, the workers' militia was recognized as the official militia and received wages from the city militia administration.[120] Workers were posted along the entire Bolshoi Prospect, an area extending far beyond the workers' quarters. The workers' militia in the Petrogradskii District neither recognized the jurisdiction of the city militia nor accepted its intervention.[121]

The review commission singled out a final set of subdistricts as disastrous. These included all of Vasilievskii and the rest of Vyborgskii, where the workers' militia had complete control. In the First Vyborgskii, the subdistrict soviet elected the commissar and his assistants. Initially, there were 900 militiamen, but that number fell to 392 by the time the commission carried out its research. Either lack of funds or reappointment, against workers' militia resistance, must have resulted in the reduction. All militiamen received wages from the city militia administration. Early on, the commissariat was dominated by intellectuals, including Botsvadze. But after he was forced out, "the cultural forces disappeared." At the time of the review, the entire commissariat consisted of workers.

The militiamen staffed seventy-five posts with help from the factory militia when necessary. They were sufficiently armed, with four hundred rifles and one hundred revolvers. The subdistrict commissariat maintained contact with the chief of the city militia, reported daily events to him, and even proposed carrying out reappointments. But the loyalty of this subdistrict militia could be illustrated by its attitude toward the anarchists' occupation of the Durnovo dacha. The entire commissariat maintained neutrality.

The Second Vyborgskii Subdistrict was more disorderly than the First. Sales of surrogate spirits were widespread, along with drunkenness and gambling. Soldiers routinely interfered with the militia, and there were cases of mob justice against thieves. The commissariat only communicated with the chief of the city militia in order to obtain funds.

Of the Vyborgskii subdistricts, the second was the most radical. Headed by Bolshevik commissar N. V. Ivanov, the militia was regarded more as a revolutionary training ground than a police service. Ivanov played an important role in the interdistrict conference and resisted reappointment. But despite his resistance, he was forced to accept a substantial cut in the militia's staff after June 15. All of the militiamen were workers, some of them members of the Red Guards. Crime was a major problem in the subdistrict, and Ivanov's outfit proved powerless against it. The commissariat refused all contact with the Criminal Militia, which it considered an institution of the old regime.[122]

Vasilievskii Island also had a class-oriented militia, which occupied 132 posts—more than twice the number recommended by the district duma. Its 717 militiamen received wages from the city in addition to their regular factory pay. The district was supposed to have only thirty-one revolvers and seventy-seven rifles, but nearly all militiamen were armed with their own revolvers, which they had acquired during the February Revolution.

Relations with the city militia, which operated only in the first subdistrict, were badly strained. The soviet of the Vasilievskii workers' militia considered the city militia bourgeois and therefore dangerous. It attempted to undermine the city militia by installing in the first subdistrict a special students' militia of ninety men. Elsewhere in the district, there was essentially no contact with the city militia. Asked whether the activity of the second subdistrict militia contravened instructions from the chief of the city militia, the commissar replied that it did not "since we do not accept his instructions."[123]

In worker-dominated subdistricts, state consciousness was in short supply. Commissioners singled out the democratic selection of commissars and militiamen as particularly problematic. As the commissioners saw it, elections were responsible for the city militia administration's inability to assert discipline and state consciousness.

The report concluded, "The Petrograd City Militia is not in a position to guarantee the security of the persons and property of citizens because of the deficiencies of its present organization, the absence of law regulating its activity, and the unfitness of the majority of its militiamen." The commission recommended that the Provisional Government revamp the city militia administration, implement the militia law of April 17, and issue new rules defining the activities of militiamen and the administrative duties of commissariats.[124]

In spite of its bias and cynicism, the report is valuable because it focuses attention on the true centers of power in revolutionary Petrograd: the subdistricts. Once instituted, subdistrict militias were almost impossible to dislodge. These militias reflected the grassroots politics of their locations. In middle-class central districts, militia commissariats were controlled by the middle class. In the working-class districts of Vyborgskii and Vasilievskii, commissariats were organized by the district soviets. Where worker control was greatest, the workers' militia reigned, in defiance of the city militia.

By the time the report was released in June, relations between the city militia and the workers' militias were clearly frayed, demonstrating both the weakness of the city militia and mounting class tensions despite the city militia's formal neutrality. But ties were not completely severed, instead varying according to the politics of given subdistricts. At this stage, most of the commissariats still recognized the authority of the city militia.

The July Days and the Failure of Reform

The summer of 1917 was a turning point in Petrograd. Crime suddenly shot up, and the city militia's effectiveness and reputation rapidly declined. The erosion of the city militia's authority was part and parcel of the overall crisis—political instability, a deteriorating economy, and catastrophic social breakdown.

From the Provisional Government's point of view, the unreliability of the city militia was amply demonstrated during the July Days. True to their principle of political neutrality, the city militia stood on the sidelines rather than support the Provisional Government in suppressing Bolshevik demonstrations. In its daily *Journal of Events*, the city militia administration described no militia activities related to political events during the July Days. On July 3, only twenty-four arrests were listed, including nine for drunkenness and nine for thefts. Its entry for July 5 lists three "Important Events"—a break-in, a fire, and a public speech by a German spy.[125]

While the city militia was on the sidelines, the workers' militias and the Red Guards participated in the armed demonstrations, often considered dress rehearsals for the Bolshevik seizure of power. According to Startsev, workers' militias and Red Guards from forty-eight factories took part. Rex Wade argues, "Clearly, armed workers, as units or as individuals, did take to the streets in support of their demands. Moreover, there were no 'neutral' or wavering units, as there were among the soldiers, who could shift to support of the government and tip the balance of power."[126]

The Provisional Government sought once and for all to eliminate and disarm the workers' militia and the Red Guards. On July 3, military units loyal to the Provisional Government raided the headquarters of the Soviet of the Petrograd People's Militia. Some leaders were arrested and others went into hiding.[127] The workers, however, refused to surrender their arms. The Executive Committee of the Petrograd Soviet, supporting the Provisional Government, endorsed the surrender, but some district soviets openly defied the order, while others quietly refused to implement it.[128]

To the Provisional Government, the city militia's neutrality was a grave concern. Its inaction during the July Days amply demonstrated its indifference to the principle of state consciousness. Deputy Minister of Internal Affairs Dmitrii M. Shchepkin protested to the mayor of Petrograd that the city militia had not fulfilled its obligation to maintain order during the July Days. In some cases, Shchepkin claimed, city militiamen abandoned their posts and defied orders from the commander of the Petrograd Military District to secure government and other important buildings.[129]

Taking advantage of the setback of the Bolsheviks and the workers' militias after the July Days, the Provisional Government again attempted to impose centralized control over the militia. Immediately after the July Days, the city duma dismissed Kryzhanovskii as the head of the city militia and appointed N. V. Ivanov, a Socialist Revolutionary deputy to the city duma, its new head.[130] On July 5, Chief Ivanov issued Order No. 25, dismissing militiamen who did not fulfill their duties during the July Days.[131] Many were fired, including sixty at once in the Second Narvskii Subdistrict and everyone at the Baltic shipyard. Some workers' militia commissariats were raided, and their leaders arrested, by military units loyal to the Provisional Government. At the Second Vasilievskii Subdistrict, the commissar and ten militiamen were arrested. Similar raids were conducted at the First and Second Vyborgskii Subdistricts and the First Petrogradskii Subdistrict. These were the subdistricts that the Provisional Government's review commission had singled out as the most dangerous.[132]

Under Ivanov's leadership, and with the blessing of the moderate socialists in the Petrograd Soviet, the city militia attempted to reorganize according to the principle of state-driven police. On July 17, the Provisional Government issued a new militia law targeting both the workers' militias and the principle of municipal policing. This law rejected the elective principle and made the minister of internal affairs responsible for the appointment of all militiamen. Resurrecting the terms of the April 17 militia law, it called for the disarmament of the workers' militias. In pursuit of these reforms, Acting Minister of Internal Affairs Irakli Tsereteli, a Menshevik, also appointed his Socialist Revolutionary colleague E. F. Rogovskii as city governor, reviving the defunct office. Rogovskii reported to Tsereteli each evening "about the measures being taken to disarm Bolshevik groups." Tsereteli hoped thereby to strengthen the Provisional Government's link with the newly constituted militia.[133]

Many factory owners, who had been waiting for this moment, attempted to get rid of the workers' militias once and for all by withholding workers' pay. On July 8, managers of Osipov Leather Factory sent a letter to the Society of Manufacturers advocating the abolition of the workers' militia. Managers of Skorokhod Factory joined in the call. Simens-Schukert refused to rehire workers' militia members. The Provisional Government supported these moves, announcing that payments to workers' militias were not only unnecessary but also illegal. Some workers in the Petergofskii and Narvskii Districts decided to quit the militia and return to the factory because their managers refused to pay them while they were on militia duty.[134]

These attempts to squeeze the workers' militia failed. When Skorokhod managers announced that they would no longer honor the commitment to pay militiamen, the workers took the financial director hostage until he reneged.[135] On July 22, workers of the Franco-Russian Factory resolved that, as "counterrevolution began with efforts to disarm the revolutionary workers, the Central Executive Committee of the All-Russian Congress of Soviets should immediately countermand the Provisional Government's order to disarm the workers."[136]

Met with worker resistance, manufacturers retreated. Some factories, such as Russian Renault, gave in to workers' demand for payments while on militia duty. Others had no qualms with the worker's militia. The director of the Pipe Factory considered the workers' militia essential for factory security and discipline.[137] The Vyborgskii branch of the Society of Manufacturers "decided that disarming the workers should be the business of the military officials who decreed it and not of the factory administrations."[138] Doing so would have required a sizable and well-organized operation; neither the Provisional Government nor the military authorities had the determination and power to carry it out.

The Soviet Executive Committee's attack on the workers' militias motivated worker resentment toward the institution's moderate leadership. The grass roots countered the rightward swing between the July Days and the Kornilov Affair with deepening left-wing politics. The offensive against the workers' militia alarmed the workers and helped "strengthen their resolve to defend their armed units against efforts to disband them."[139]

Tseretelli's law also created discord between the Provisional Government and the lower echelons of the city militia, a matter to which historians have hitherto paid little attention. In response to the law, city militiamen formed a trade union.[140]

Meanwhile, district dumas protested Ivanov's order. The Rozhdestvenskii District Duma passed a resolution repealing Ivanov's order as a counterrevolutionary attempt to abolish the district-level autonomy of the city militia. The Kolomenskii District Duma adopted a similar resolution.[141] More importantly, Tseretelli's order prompted the district dumas to form an interdistrict liaison conference, which opposed the perceived attempt to suppress the people's movement and restore the old order.[142] Significantly, these resolutions were approved not just by outlying district dumas under the influence of workers' militias, but also by dumas in the central districts, which the review commission had praised for their state consciousness.

It proved impossible to dislodge the subdistrict militia power by simply issuing decrees from above. To do so—to transform the city militia into an organ of the Provisional Government—would have required a major surgical operation of which state and city authorities were, again, incapable. The city duma, in particular, depended on the district dumas and subdistrict commissariats to carry out its will and was therefore unable to defy them.

The Further Deterioration of the City Militia

Throughout the summer, the discipline of city militiamen declined precipitously. When commissars visited posts for inspection, they often found them deserted. When a commissar blew his whistle to summon militiamen, they did not show up, or they appeared reluctantly.[143] Drunkenness and black market activity among militiamen continued in spite of vocal public outrage.

A cartoon entitled "Mysterious Picture" shows a drunken militiaman escorting two other militiamen. The caption reads: "I can't figure it out. Has the drunken militiaman caught two militiamen to take to the commissariat or the two militiamen are taking the drunken militiaman?" See figure 12.

A weekly satirical journal, *Strekoza,* published a short poem lampooning the drunken police: "Nothing is sweeter to the militia / than spirits and wine requisition, / Because everyone admires it / when barrels are always flowing."[144] On July 7, *Malenkaia gazeta* wrote:

> A militiaman of the Fourth Aleksandro-Nevskii Subdistrict, Bryzgalov, became "drunk as a skunk" to the point where he passed out. He laid down flat right in the middle of the street for the night. Soon people stripped "this protector of law" of everything he had, leaving him

Figure 12. "Mysterious Picture." The caption reads: "We cannot quite figure it out. Are two militiamen taking the drunken militiaman to the commissariat? Or is the drunken militiaman taking the two militiamen?" *Novyi satirikon*, no. 20, June 1917, 27.

naked, and soundly beaten. Only his coworker saved him from becoming the victim of mob justice.[145]

Under these circumstances, it is not surprising that some residents wished for the restoration of the old tsarist police. Nikolai Vladimirovich Remizov, an artist who went by the name Re-mi, published a cartoon in *Novyi satirikon* entitled "Longing for Strong Power," which features a resident kneeling in front of the shadow of a tsarist policeman. "O, dear shadow!" the caption reads. "If only you knew how I long for you under the ray of the sun called freedom. It is too hot for me."[146]

The city militiamen expected to protect the public were often victims themselves. On August 27, a militiaman in the First Narvskii Subdistrict was attacked by a crowd demanding mob justice against his detainee, a merchant under arrest for lack of a proper permit.[147] On the same day, another militiaman was abducted by four men—three in soldiers' uniforms—disarmed, beaten, and thrown into a Krestovskii Island ditch.[148] A couple of weeks later, on September 15, an altercation at a breadline nearly turned disastrous when women waiting there started shouting profanities at a supervising militiaman, who angrily pulled his revolver. The women pounced on him. No one came to rescue the militiaman, who was beaten severely but managed to escape.[149]

Attacks on militiamen escalated in October. One incident occurred on October 2 in Golodai on Vasilievskii Island known as a gathering place for criminals, deserters, and other undesirable elements. There, a militia unit found a drunken crowd, including several deserters. The deserters attacked the head of the militia unit, a man named Kuniko, and stabbed him in the shoulder. Kuniko drew a revolver, but the crowd, shouting "Beat the *burzhui!*" surrounded, disarmed, and pummeled him. An ominous cry emerged from the mass: "Let's kill him off and throw him in River Chernyi!" Kuniko implored the crowd to take him to the commissariat. The mob assented, but while they were dragging him to the commissariat, a hooligan dealt a hard blow to Kuniko's head, breaking his skull. He was left, unconscious, at a nearby hospital.[150]

On October 10, several newspapers reported a disturbance on Tsvetochnaia Street in the Fourth Narvskii Subdistrict. A militia unit had arrested eight troublemakers among a crowd of drunken hooligans, deserters, and sailors. A sailor then fired at the militiamen, leading to a shoot-out and the sailor's arrest. At six in the evening, a crowd of sailors, workers, and hooligans gathered in front of the militia subdistrict commissariat. Some fired at the building, and a militia unit was deployed to disperse the crowd. Another sailor, who resisted the dispersal order, was arrested. Eighty people then assembled in a teahouse and decided to attack the commissariat. The militia was able to resist the attack thanks to an emergency deployment of mounted militia and Red Guards from nearby factories.[151] It is worth noting that the mounted officers—holdovers from the tsar's police—and Red Guards—whom the Provisional Government and the city militia administration wish to disband—proved more reliable than the city militia itself.

On October 23, two days before the Bolsheviks seized power, *Vechernee Vremia* reported four unrelated cases of assaults on militiamen. Hooligans attacked a militiaman in a tavern in the Third Aleksandro-Nevskii Subdistrict. At Nikolaevskii Railway Station, another group of hooligans fired at a militiaman. Drunken sailors broke into the Third Spasskii Subdistrict Commissariat. On Bolshoi Prospect in the Petrogradskii District, a crowd surrounded and ruthlessly beat a militiaman who had arrested a hooligan.[152]

Many newspapers and satirical weeklies illustrated the deepening popular disillusionment with the city militia as autumn dragged on. In an October 20 cartoon entitled "A Desperate Situation," *Petrogradskii listok* depicted a well-dressed middle-aged couple walking along a deserted Petrograd street with a knife-wielding robber in pursuit. At the corner of the street stands a militiaman wearing his armband. "We are doomed," the caption reads, "a robber behind and a militiaman ahead!" See figure 13. Another cartoon, "Caution Is Always Needed," shows a robbery victim calling out, "Help! Militiaman!" The robber responds, "For heaven's sake, don't shout! If you do, a militiaman will come and I will have to divide the loot with him." See figure 14.

The ineptitude of the city militia was always a function in part of its lack of resources, a problem that became more desperate as crime mounted over the summer. On August 6, the First Liteinyi Subdistrict commissar appealed to the chief of the city militia, citing "the extreme, urgent necessity of providing militiamen with

Figure 13. Titled "Desperate Situation," this cartoon depicts the dilemma of citizens. "It's terrible!" the caption reads. "A robber behind, and a militiaman ahead!" *Petrogradskii listok,* October 10, 1917.

revolvers for self-defense and whistles to call for help from other militiamen." On September 5, the commissar of the Third Vasilievskii Subdistrict lodged a similar complaint. On October 20, the First Lesnoi Subdistrict commissar requested fifty revolvers but was denied.[153] Even uniforms were in short supply,

Figure 14. In this cartoon, titled "Carefulness Is Always Required," the victim cries "Help! Militiaman!" The robber replies, "For heaven's sake, don't shout. If you do, a militiaman will come and I'll have to share the loot with him." *Novyi satirikon,* no. 40, November 1917, 3.

further debasing the militiamen and endangering them, as they became harder to distinguish from criminals. Eventually, city militiamen refused to patrol dangerous areas at night.[154]

Faced with this desperate situation, the militiamen's union met on September 28 to form a strike committee, affiliate themselves with the Petrograd Soviet, and demand raises, weapons, and uniforms.[155] The head of the union wrote a letter to *Petrogradskii listok,* listing the demands publicly.[156] The Criminal Militia also complained, in an August 26 letter to their chief, noting that they had not been paid for a month. They demanded a 200 percent raise, apartment allowances, and shorter working hours. They threatened mass resignations unless back wages were received immediately.[157]

On October 7, the city militiamen threatened a general strike unless their demands were met. The city duma agreed to raise junior militiamen's salaries from 175–200 rubles per month to 250. This was still a pittance, considerably less than even a low-paid artisan earned. In exchange, the administration wanted to fire a substantial number of militiamen. *Gazeta-Kopeika* predicted the strike would come, but the Bolshevik coup against the Provisional Government interrupted the negotiation before any labor action was taken.[158]

An Alternative Police Force

The city militia was never adequate, and its capacity dwindled with its numbers. From March until June, about twenty thousand men served.[159] But in May, the city passed a law restricting the force to the number not exceeding the size of the tsarist police force before the February Revolution.[160] The goal was in part to weed out criminal elements and political radicals, but the downsizing also reflected the economic crisis. According to Kelson, by June there were just four thousand militiamen, an average of sixty in each subdistrict.[161] There was no way such a small force could cope with the summer crime wave.

Rather than reinvigorate the city militia, the Provisional Government and the city administration turned first to the army. On August 22, the commander of the Petrograd Military District issued a decree allowing active-duty soldiers to assist the city and workers' militias.[162] Soldiers were hardly more reliable than militiamen, however. General Oleg P. Vasilkovskii, commander of the Petrograd Military District, described the state of the soldiers on guard duty as "lamentable" and complained that "they sit, smoke cigarettes, and leave their posts at will."[163] Still, on September 20, city militia chief Ivanov requested that the Petrograd Military

District decommission three hundred soldiers so they could be transferred to militia duty—a sign of just how desperate the city was for security.[164] On October 13, Army Minister Aleksandr I. Verkhovskii ordered a detachment to leave the front and join them. The mounted militia, in particular, received reinforcement.[165] On October 18 Colonel Georgii P. Polkovnikov, commander of the Petrograd Military District after the Kornilov Affair, ordered another four hundred soldiers to leave the front for Petrograd. By the eve of the October Revolution, three-fifths of the capital's militia posts were filled by soldiers under the command of the Petrograd Military District rather than the city militia administration.[166] At this point, commanders preferred to arm the housing committees rather than the declining city militia.[167]

Housing committees had been getting into the security business since March.[168] On March 5 and 16, they had received the city governor's sanction to police their buildings until an official militia was formed.[169] In response to dvorniks' refusal to fulfill night guard duty, a few housing committees imposed mandatory night duty on male residents and ordered entrances to buildings closed at ten in the evening.[170] By April, some housing committees expanded the duties and obligations of the residents in their buildings. For instance, in response to a series of robberies in the guise of searches in the building on Bolshoi Prospect in the Vasilievskii District, the resident committee locked all the gates and entrances to the building complex, issued resident identifications, and barred outsiders unaccompanied by authorized persons. Many other buildings in the Vasilievskii and Petrogradskii Districts were reportedly guarded by private "militiamen" from residents.[171] By the fall, housing committees, encouraged and supported by the city administration and the military, mushroomed in various parts of the city. They began organizing themselves into associations in subdistricts and districts. In September, they formed a citywide union of housing committees.

Evidence is lacking, however, on the comprehensive picture of housing committees. For instance, we do not know whether housing committees were more widespread in the central and central-mixed districts, who took the leadership, how they decided to carry out duties, and what relations they established with the city administration and the military authority. But P. Olikhov's article, "Self-Defense of the Capital," which appeared in *Petrogradskii listok* five days before the Bolsheviks' seizure of power, gives us a glimpse into the increasing role of housing committees that became widespread in the central and central-mixed districts of the city. According to Olikhov, several buildings in the First Spasskii Subdistrict as well as at least one building in the Third Kazanskii District imposed compulsory security night duties on all male residents. Several housing committees in the First Moskovskii Subdistrict formed an association and hired a cadre of armed guards to protect their buildings. In one building in the Fourth Spasskii Subdistrict, residents hired soldiers to protect them. These were all examples in the central and central mixed districts, where crime rate was high. Olikhov also revealed that the city administration, in coordination with the military authority and in consultation with the representatives of the housing committees, was drafting a general rule to sanction housing committees as official militia organizations. He predicted that soon each building in the city would be obligated to form a housing committee.[172] On October 12, the city administration formed a special committee for the security of the city under the deputy mayor, N. A. Artemiev. This committee authorized housing committees to form their own militias not only to protect their buildings, but also to patrol the streets. Their militia units were to be armed by the military and subordinated to the military authority.[173]

Through these arrangements, Petrograd residents essentially vetoed both state-driven and municipal policing. Security was filtered to the lowest imaginable level, and citizens fended for themselves. But while the housing committees received popular backing, formed a citywide union, and were armed by the military, they were no more useful than the city militia in responding to crime. What was revealed in the empowerment of housing committees was the bankruptcy of the militia system created by the Provisional Government and the city militia. Complaints recorded at the September 23 general meeting of Novaia Derevnia District housing committees spoke to the increasingly uncontrollable situation. Attendees grumbled loudly and bitterly of lawlessness. "We have to deal with such people as our conscience dictates," one disaffected person reportedly told the gathering.[174] Such talk presaged mob justice.

The Workers' Militia and the Red Guards after the July Days

The July setback sharpened workers' already acute class consciousness. But the worker's militias and the Red Guards weathered the storm. At every step of the revolutionary process, workers closed ranks and insisted on the independence of their security organizations.

The Red Guards became more entrenched and more radical after the July Days. In response to requests that the Red Guards perform regular patrols, Iustin Zhuk, an anarchist and the head of the Red Guards in the outlying Shlisselburg or Nevskii District, expressed a common sentiment: "We have nothing to sentimentalize and nothing to wait for. We must begin to beat the bourgeoisie on the head. If we work to maintain order, then the workers themselves will create fighting organizations against us."[175] Valentin Trifonov, a Bolshevik leader, rebuked Zhuk for his inflammatory statement but nevertheless called on the Red Guards to "destroy the old state order." A heavily Bolshevik-oriented five-member committee was formed at the center of the Red Guards movement.[176]

Through a combination of diffusion and elections, the Red Guards rigorously enforced revolutionary principles. Unlike the workers' militias that were originally created to maintain order, the purpose of the Red Guards was strictly armed class struggle against anticipated counterrevolution. Thirteen-man units operated at the factory or shop level. They were further organized into battalions of 480 and, from there, district detachments. At each level, commanders were elected by the guardsmen themselves. At the top of the pyramid was the Central Komendatura, comprising one representative from each district's command staff and one each from the Petrograd Soviet, the Interdistrict Conference of Soviets, and the central councils of trade unions and factory committees.[177] Organizational decisions came from the grass roots; Rex Wade notes that the process of forming Red Guards and armed workers' units took place independently of the Bolshevik leadership.[178]

If the July Days hardened the determination of the working class to protect and advance its interests, the Kornilov Affair gave it powerful impetus to further buttress the Red Guards and legitimate them as an instrument against counterrevolution. As Wade puts it, "The Kornilov Affair provided a certain feeling of relief: the dragon had reared its head, so now [workers] could get on with the long-dreaded—but also long-awaited—political and social confrontation."[179]

On August 27, the day after General Kornilov's counterrevolutionary forces began their march against Petrograd, the Central Executive Committee of Soviets formed the Committee of People's Struggle against the Counterrevolution.[180] Since the July Days, the moderate socialist leaders in the Petrograd Soviet had supported the Provisional Government in suppressing the workers' militias and curbing worker radicalism. Only when they faced Kornilov's counterrevolutionary march did the Soviet leaders reverse their policy and appeal to workers to defend the revolution. Yet, cut off from the grassroots workers' movement, the Central Executive Committee had no choice but to relegate the organization of workers' detachments to the interdistrict conference of the soviets, of which they had previously disapproved. The Soviet Executive Committee found itself toeing the fine line between relying on ground-level armed organizations and, at the same time, trying to subdue them politically.

On August 28, the interdistrict conference reconstituted the workers' militia.[181] For the first time after the July Days, the workers' militia was legitimized by association with the Soviet. It would have its own *komendatura,* consisting of three people elected by the Central Executive Committee in cooperation with the district committee of parties and the district administration. "Organization of detachments outside of this militia is not permissible," the Central Executive Committee announced. "All the weapons of the workers' force must be placed exclusively at the disposal of the komendatura, and its orders must unconditionally be obeyed." The komendatura of the workers' militia was to maintain contact with the city militia through the district soviets.[182] Through these measures, the Central Executive Committee was trying to establish its control over the workers' militia.

The Central Executive Committee also attempted to inculcate the newly reconstituted workers' militia with municipal policing principles. First, it assigned the workers' militia the task of maintaining public order, not exclusively protecting class interests. Second, it insisted that the workers' militia maintain contact with the city militia. In this way, the moderate socialists in the Executive Committee sought to arrest the workers' revolutionary zeal. Nevertheless, the Central Executive Committee's policy revealed the extent to which the workers' militia and the Red Guards had emerged as the major sources of public order. The

Central Executive Committee chose the district soviets to be the agents of contact between the workers' militia and the city militia. Furthermore, this decision was the tacit acceptance of the grim reality that in the face of the disintegration of public order, the workers' militia was a more reliable force to maintain public order even in the central and southern districts. The workers' militia was directed to patrol not just in their districts, but also in Petrograd at large.

Workers resisted the attempt by the Central Executive Committee to control workers' armed detachments. Instead, the real action took place at the lower levels of factories and subdistrict soviets. Workers created more armed detachments to defend the revolution. The Petergofskii District Soviet organized Red Guards and established what it called a "revolutionary center" with its own representatives as well as delegates from district factories and the radical wings of the political parties. A Red Guards komendatura was organized in the Fourth Narvskii subdistrict. The Vasilievskii District Soviet directed each factory to form fighting detachments.[183] In the first Kolomenskii Subdistrict, district soviet representatives attempted to dismiss the city militia commissar.[184]

As soon as Kornilov's advance was stopped, Kerenskii and the moderate socialists in the Central Executive Committee attempted to disband the workers' armed units and the Red Guards. They failed. The Interdistrict Conference of Soviets rejected this call, insisting instead on further reinforcing workers' armed units.[185] Workers' also rejected the Central Executive Committee's demand for cooperation with the city militia. When the newly created committee of the workers' militia met on September 13, a group of Red Guards persuaded the group to refuse the reorganization of the workers' militia as "a reserve force for the city militia." Over the objections of government representatives, who insisted that the fundamental task of the workers' militia should be the maintenance of order, the meeting adopted a resolution defining the workers' militia as "a workers' guard, whose task is to struggle against counterrevolution and to defend the gains of the Revolution."[186] The Red Guards and the workers' militia were merging as an exclusive instrument of working-class interests—of revolt against the bourgeois state. This caught the attention of Bolshevik leaders, who began to exploit the armed workers' movement for their advantage.

At the end of September and beginning of October, the Red Guards attempted to gather the grassroots, factory-level units into district bodies. Such organizations formed in the Vyborgskii and Narvskii-Petergofskii Districts. When the Bolsheviks captured the majority in the Petrograd Soviet in September, the Red Guards leaders found willing supporters in the new leadership. The previously underground Komendatura of the Red Guards was now incorporated under the Petrograd Soviet and moved its headquarters to Smolnyi. On October 22, under the auspices of the Petrograd Soviet, the Komendatura organized a citywide conference to merge all the Red Guards units. It adopted regulations to that end the following morning, one day before the Bolsheviks seized power. The Red Guards were not always well organized and well disciplined, but they served the Bolsheviks reliably during the coup.[187]

The struggle for power at the subdistrict level after the February Revolution reveals much about the changing politics of Petrograd and the new Russian state. While the Provisional Government promoted centralization, both the city and workers' militias went their own ways, following distinct principles of, on the one hand, formally apolitical municipal authority and, on the other, avidly politicized class consciousness. The immediate need for security, and the ideological contest roiling the city, overshadowed top-down directives from the Provisional Government, the city governor's office, the city duma, and even the Petrograd Soviet.

But neither the city nor the workers' militias were successful in stemming the rising tide of crime. The situation was worsened by the conflict between the Provisional Government and the city duma and between the city militia administration and its militiamen. But structural factors were also to blame. The city duma had created the city militia as a municipal police force, but it quickly realized that this idealistic project was unworkable thanks to intensifying class division. Principles of local administration, election, and political neutrality contributed to the erosion of the city militia, and after the July Days, the city militia administration was forced to embrace the state-driven model. The collapse of the municipal police demonstrated the inability of the bourgeoisie to sustain a civil society. As the city militia weakened in the summer and fall of 1917, the workers' militia and the Red Guards emerged as the strongest police power.

Both the Provisional Government and the city duma had lost legitimacy in the eyes of city dwellers. Unable to rely on higher authorities to protect their lives and property, they were left with housing committees and fellow factory workers. The road to mob justice was wide open.

5. An Epidemic of Mob Justice

The day after the February Revolution, a popular newspaper, *Malenkaia gazeta,* printed the following in bold print on its front page: "Rus', you are free! / When the tsar is above the people, there is autocracy / When the tsar is among the people, there is constitutional government / When the people are above their own government, they are free."[1] To the Russian people, freedom meant life totally without restraint, without even constitutional rule. This, in the eyes of many, was the meaning of freedom.

As revolutionary dreams grew more remote, the people of Petrograd turned to vigilantism. They still took seriously *Malenkaia gazeta'*s call for power to the people. Competing would-be authorities could bicker all they wanted. Political movements could cover the town in leaflets. Intellectuals could scoff or sympathize as their ideological proclivities demanded. For ordinary people, what mattered was not law or theoretical abstraction but the hard stuff of living without food and basic security, and they would deal with their challenges as they saw fit.

As the crowd came to appreciate its own vulnerability, it turned to mob justice—*samosudy,* literally self-administered justice or a court of one's own. It was the ultimate symbol of February's hopes dashed. Only three months after its stirring headline, *Malenkaia gazeta* published a perceptive commentary by Dalekii Drug ("distant friend"), who lamented, "Instead of *narodovlastie* we have *samovlastie.*" Instead of power to the people, power to the self.[2]

Mob violence mollified the crowd psychologically, yet it also contributed to the disorder that so frustrated the great mass of people. Those living in relatively functional contemporary societies may have difficulty relating to these conditions. Imagine if every couple of days, for months on end, groups of hundreds and sometimes thousands paraded through your hometown with the bloodied, unconscious husk of a recently beaten man. What if that parade ended with the man drowning as spectators laughed and hurled stones at his writhing body?

This scene and similar ones played out in Petrograd dozens of times in 1917, saturating the atmosphere with terror. Fear bred rage, which resulted in more violence and thus more fear and more rage. Drawing on the work of the era's sociologists, including Emile Durkheim and Gustave Le Bon, we can develop a picture of the crowd venting its disappointments and pressing its will against the surrounding collapse of society. Yet these efforts only led to more disappointment and collapse. Officials could not break the vicious cycle, alienating the people from politics and setting the stage for Lenin's October coup. By then, the people of Petrograd were consumed by the daily struggle for survival in an essentially failed state. As a result, they largely ignored the Bolshevik takeover.

Mob Justice Rising

Mob justice had occurred sporadically in urban centers prior to the February Revolution. Mobilization riots in 1914 and Moscow's 1915 anti-German pogrom are cases in point. But the mob justice committed during the Revolution was unique in three respects: it was universal, touching urban and rural areas alike;[3] it was frequent, repeatedly reinforcing popular frustration at the conditions of daily life; and it was extraordinarily brutal.[4] May was a turning point.[5] On May 13, *Petrogradskii listok* reported three cases of mob justice from the previous day, marking "a new stage."[6] After that date, so many cases filled the newspapers that, on June 20, *Gazeta-Kopeika* was compelled to debut a new column, "Today's Mob Justice."[7]

Based on newspaper accounts and archival materials, D. Iu. Ereshchenko has documented eighty-five instances of mob justice between March 1917 and the October Revolution. Using similar sources, I find six additional cases.[8] Small statistical discrepancies aside, there is no doubt that the incidence of mob justice steadily rose during this period. Ereshchenko's data show roughly one incident every three days from May to July, increasing to more than one every other day between August and October 24, the day before the Bolshevik coup.[9]

The sudden increase in mob justice paralleled the jump in crime and the abolition of the temporary courts. There is good reason to believe that these factors—lawlessness and the inability to control it—drove public outrage. I collected eighty-six cases with known targets, of whom fifty-two were suspected criminals. Twenty-two of the suspected criminals were petty thieves and pickpockets, seventeen were armed robbers who inflicted no bodily injuries, ten were armed robbers who inflicted injuries,

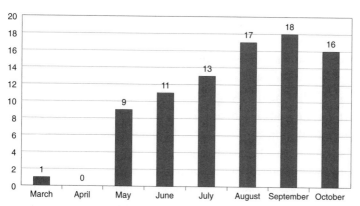

Figure 15. Incidents of mob justice, March–October 1917. *Source:* Ereshchenko, "Prestupnost'," 171.

two were murderers, and one was a rapist. Other victims included twelve militiamen, nine merchants, nine political opponents, two bystanders, and two hospital personnel. Thus for the most part, mob justice was meted out against either noncriminals or in response to minor trespasses. Rarely could the punishment be said to have fit the crime.

Almost all cases of mob justice against militiamen were committed after August, suggesting that people were fed up with the militias' ineptitude in enforcing law and order. Seven of the nine attacks on merchants had anti-Semitic overtones. Mob justice against merchants peaked in July and August. There was only one case in October. But there were four food riots in August and six in September. Most political disputes resulting in mob justice took place after the July Days.

Tackling Thieves and Robbers

One of the most frightening aspects of mob justice was the cruelty of the crowd toward petty criminals. A few sample incidents demonstrate the wantonness born of mass frustration.

At dawn on May 27, 1917, three burglars were found hiding in an apartment on Srednaia Podiacheskaia Street in the Fourth Spasskii Subdistrict. News of the break-in spread quickly, and a crowd soon surrounded the house. The crowd exploded when it learned that the subdistrict commissariat had been notified, and yet nothing had been done. "Why only stare at them? Drag them out into the streets! Let's settle the matter without the militia," someone shouted, according to a newspaper report. After dragging the men outside, the crowd beat them "persistently" (*uporno*) and "cruelly" (*zhestoko*). When the city militia arrived, two of the burglars were unconscious. With difficulty, militiamen separated the angry crowd from its victims.[10]

July 9 saw two incidents of mob justice. On Nevskii Prospect, tram passengers caught three pickpockets in their car. They brought the men to the commissariat but, along the way, beat them to death in broad daylight. Elsewhere, on Zagorodnyi Prospect, a crowd beat up a burglar and hung on his chest a placard reading, simply, "Thief."[11]

On August 19, a mob caught a particularly unlucky burglar. Rather than turn him over to the city militia, the group decided to hold their own trial on the spot. After all, as one of the mob declared, "The people's court is the most just and quickest. Thieves will escape from the militia. We must not allow this to happen." The people's court moved swiftly indeed, in minutes convicting the thief and sentencing him to death. The mob then began to punch him and beat him with rocks and the heels of their shoes. The city militia finally arrived and demanded that the crowd turn over the thief. It responded by hurling rocks at the militiamen, injuring one in the head. The militia did manage to take custody of the thief, but attempts to arrest the rabble-rousers failed. The injured militiaman and thief were brought to the Obukhov Hospital, the latter in hopeless condition.[12]

On October 14, a gentleman wearing a military cap with an engineering insignia entered a store on the second floor of Apraksin Market, in the Second Spasskii Subdistrict. Accompanying him were an elegantly dressed woman in her twenties and a young man in a soldier's uniform. They stole an array of goods but were caught as they tried to escape. A shopper shouted loudly from the stairs to people outside, "Let's punish these criminals who are making profits by stealing all over Petrograd!"

Within ten minutes, a crowd of hundreds gathered outside the Apraksin Market, blocking trams and horse-drawn cabs in the street. Nearby stores locked their doors. The subdistrict commissar immediately dispatched the militia, but the crowd demanded that the criminals be turned over to them. A detachment of soldiers was also sent to protect the nearby State Bank. The crowd met the soldiers with hostility, shouting, "You are just like militia. You are protecting criminals!" Soldiers who had joined the mob threatened to disarm the on-duty soldiers if they refused to let the crowd have its way.

The crowd surged toward the store, broke in, and dragged the man in the military cap outside. The elegantly dressed lady sought refuge in a telephone box. The deputy commissar brandished his revolver in an attempt to protect her but was attacked by a young man in a soldiers' uniform wielding a saber. Amid the confusion, the crowd grabbed the woman from the telephone box and pulled her into the street. A man in an officer's uniform shouted, "Don't stand on ceremony," produced a revolver, fired two shots, and killed the shoplifter in the military cap. A few minutes later, another man in the crowd shot the woman to death.

The third thief hid in the store until the mounted militia captured him and escorted him to the subdistrict commissariat. Thousands of people gathered at the commissariat, demanding that the criminal be handed over. The militia discreetly transferred him to another subdistrict commissariat. When the criminal did not appear, the crowd moved on, smashing store windows.[13]

Such was the frenzy of the mob only ten days before the October Revolution. These cases were by no means exceptional. Indeed, the process became routine. On October 17, *Petrogradskii listok* reported matter-of-factly, "Yesterday there were three cases of mob justice against thieves. Thieves were almost beaten to death in all these instances."[14] By October, mob justice was so common that even the breathless, sensationalist tabloid press had seemingly grown bored of it.

Though gruesome and draconian, mob justice did not stem the crime rate. On the contrary, it contributed to escalating lawlessness and violence. In response, petty criminals armed themselves, leading to further carnage. *Petrogradskii listok* reprinted a letter allegedly sent by criminals to a paper, *Iuzhnyi krai*. This letter was an ultimatum to the public:

> We will kill anyone we encounter in dark corners. This is our only revenge against mob justice. Breaking into a house, we will not simply steal but will kill everybody, even babies in the cradle. We will end our bloody reprisal only when mob justice is stopped.[15]

It was as if another class struggle was being waged—not between the proletariat and the bourgeoisie but between the criminals and straight society.

Merchants as Victims

Rationing caused dramatic increases in food prices throughout Petrograd. With the distribution system unable to meet demand, street merchants mushroomed. Disagreements over fair prices and accusations of speculation and thievery were daily occurrences. At times, these conflicts degenerated into mob justice.

On August 2, the Third Spasskii Subdistrict Commissariat learned that a crowd was gathering in front of Bekker's stockroom in Sennaia Square, where they suspected a large quantity of soap was being hoarded. Deputy Commissar Sharikov and several militiamen rushed to the scene. After inspection, Bekker's inventory turned out to be perfectly legal, and Sharikov arranged for the soap to be sold to the people outside. But a price dispute led to further consternation. By coincidence, another merchant arrived, carrying leather goods in two carts. The crowd stopped the carts and attempted to confiscate the goods. Sharikov inspected the leather merchant's papers, as well. These, too, were in order, and Sharikov declared the confiscation illegal.

Angered, the crowd of "women, children, workers, and soldiers" surrounded Sharikov and beat him. The poorly armed militiamen were unable to rescue their deputy chief. Voices rang out: "Kill him, kill him!" "Throw him into the canal and drown him!" But more moderate elements prevailed. They decided to tie Sharikov to the cart and bring him to the Executive Committee of the Petrograd Soviet. A segment of the crowd broke off and marched through the streets with their prisoner, beating him along the way. When they arrived at the Executive Committee's offices, Sharikov was barely conscious. His body was covered in bruises and cuts and was drenched in blood. He was taken to the hospital in critical condition.

Back in Sennaia Square, the crowd attacked a Jewish merchant named Brikker, who had spoken out against the mob justice against Sharikov. Amid shouts of "Beat the Jew!" the crowd decided to throw Brikker into the Fontanka River. Beaten and bloodied, Brikker escaped to the Third Spasskii Commissariat. The crowd chased him down, broke into the Commissariat building, and attempted to drag militiamen out. With a few warning shots, the militia dispersed the crowd. The remainder of the Sennaia Square mob then caught a Jewish boy working at a slaughterhouse, tied him to a cart, and hung on him a sign reading "Marauder" and "Exploiter." As they did with Sharikov, the crowd dragged the boy through the streets, beating him along the way.

At this point, thousands had assembled, stalling trams on Sadovaia Street and breaking their windows. From one of the tramcars, a young man tried to restrain the crowd, calling out, "This kind of violence violates the spirit of the revolution and threatens the residents." The crowd responded with shouts: "He must be a Jewish speculator. Beat him!" They rushed into the tram and savaged the young man. He was unconscious when the militia came to his rescue.[16]

A few weeks later, on September 7, Apraksin Market was the site of another incident of anti-Semitic mob violence.[17] As elsewhere, perceived hoarding set off the crowd. In this case, some shoppers found a large quantity of dumplings hidden at the bottom of a merchant's cart. Immediately, a crowd of several hundred surrounded him. Shouts of "Beat the Jew!" rang out, and the crowd followed, subjecting the merchant to a severe thrashing. It took fifty mounted militiamen and a detachment of soldiers to suppress the riot.[18]

Attacks on merchants reflected not just anti-Semitic sentiment but also the hunger of Petrograd's urban poor. The eve of the October Revolution witnessed sporadic food riots, some in response to venders who refused to sell goods, instead holding out for higher bidders. Crowds attacked the Petrogradskii District Food Supply headquarters at Srednyi Prospect on September 13. The next day, a crowd demanded that a store in the Second Vasilievskii District sell all its cooking oil. When the store's financial officer refused, the crowd attacked. But militiamen appeared in time and took him to the commissariat for his protection.[19] A week later, a crowd a thousand strong boarded a ship transporting cooking oil while it docked at Obvodnyi Canal and filled their containers.[20] That same day, the Petrograd City Food Supply store in the First Moskovskii Subdistrict was pillaged by shoppers left empty-handed at the store's closing. Militiamen rushed to the scene, but the angry crowd pounced and disarmed them. Only the arrival of a mounted militia unit quelled the food riot.[21]

Targeting Political Opponents

Even early in the Revolution, partisan divisions occasionally resulted in fights. For instance, after Bolsheviks took over Kshesinskaia villa, their supporters outside often escaped into the building in order to avoid violent crowds of political opponents who gathered there. Political conflict intensified after the July Days, leading to more and bloodier confrontations.

On July 6, a man made a speech calling for the Petrograd Soviet to arm itself. Angry soldiers subjected him to mob justice. One of the soldiers cut his head with saber. By the time the ambulance arrived, he had already lost consciousness, and when it arrived at the Obukhov Hospital, he was dead.[22] This incident was likely connected with the conflict of the July Days, when pro-Provisional Government soldiers were angered by a pro-Bolshevik orator.

On August 12, a political discussion on the corner of Gorstkina Street in the Third Spasskii Subdistrict turned bloody. A group of about fifty people gathered to discuss the war and the Moscow State Conference that Alexander Kerenskii had called. One orator in a soldier's uniform spoke against the war and criticized the conference. Responding to him, a man in civilian clothes, a supporter of the Provisional Government, spoke in favor of the conference. The two men came to blows, and the civilian injured the soldier. The soldier called him "a spy and a traitor" and asked others to help him. The crowd surrounded the civilian and began beating him. The crowd then dragged him through the streets and pushed him into the Fontanka. The victim swam across the river, but someone in a crowd gathered on the opposite bank pulled a revolver and killed him. Militiamen observed the entire incident but made no effort to intervene.[23]

Immediately after the July Days, Bolsheviks were the primary victims of politically motivated mob justice. But the tables turned in August. Civil discourse had become impossible, and political debates often incited the rage of the crowd.

Medical Personnel Attacked

On the morning of September 14, a mentally ill patient escaped a psychiatric institution in the Third Rozhdestvenskii Subdistrict. Claiming that doctors and nurses had beaten him, he called to the people around him for help. A crowd marched to the institution, demanding an explanation. The deputy of the institution attempted to calm the crowd but succeeded only in stoking its wrath. As the mob descended on him, a nurse intern came to his rescue, but she, too, was beaten.[24] Similarly, on October 11, soldiers raided a hospital they suspected of malpractice after one of their comrades died following an operation. Believing that he had been murdered, they subjected the hospital workers to mob justice.[25]

We have no way of knowing if the psychiatric patient's claim was true or if the soldier's operation was botched by the doctor. In a more functional society, such complaints would be investigated by an appropriate authority. But the temporary court that once handled these cases had been abolished, and the crowd was eager to take its place. With no authority to resolve civil disputes, might would make right.

The Perpetrators of Mob Justice

Newspapers often referred to participants in mob justice as I do here: *tolpa,* "the crowd." Beyond this, those involved were *neizvetnye*—"unknown." But while the individuals who formed the crowd will likely remain anonymous forever, descriptions from the time period enable prudent speculation about which social groups took part. We know that although most participants were predominantly men, women also actively joined mob justice, especially against merchants who were suspected of exploiting residents in need of food and household goods.[26]

There is reason to believe the crowd mostly comprised the urban poor, rather than organized workers and soldiers or more privileged members of society. Language is revealing on this point. Among the many changes brought by the revolution, one was a flowering of new terminology. When, at the beginning of March, City Militia Chief Dmitrii A. Kryzhanovskii addressed militiamen as "gentlemen" (*gospada*), workers' militiamen chafed. "There are no gentlemen here," they replied.[27] Instead, "comrades" (*tovarishchi*) was the popular term of address among the vanguard of the revolution—and only them. Thus, shortly after the February Revolution, when Grand Duke Nikolai Mikhailovich addressed a militiaman as "comrade," the militiaman indignantly replied, "I am not your comrade."[28] At the same time, according to Boris Kolonitskii, "comrade" was reserved for politically conscious workers and soldiers and did not penetrate deeply the lower strata of urban dwellers.[29] Politically conscious factory workers distinguished themselves from "these dark masses" by their language and dress, which emphasized their "culturedness."[30] Tanja Penter notes hostility between lumpen proletariat and organized workers in Odessa;[31] Petrograd featured similar antagonism. The word "comrade" rarely appears in newspaper accounts of the rhetorical heat that warmed up Petrograd's mobs, suggesting that organized workers were a minor presence in instances of mob justice.

One word that does show up often in contemporary accounts is *burzhui,* derived from "bourgeois." This term denoted anyone outside of the lower classes. At scenes of mob justice, dissenting voices, counseling caution and moderation, were frequently drowned out by shouts of "Beat the *burzhui!*"[32] Unlike "comrade," *burzhui* was very much in the lexicon of the urban poor.[33]

Middle-class identifiers, by contrast, are absent from the accounts. The actions of the crowd also make clear that participants had little interest in middle-class institutions. Hence, in one of the examples given earlier, the mob dragged a militiaman to the Petrograd Soviet, not the Provisional Government or the city duma. And as we have seen, economic hardship at times inspired the mob's anger, indicating that those involved were probably not well-off.

We might therefore reasonably speculate that the crowd was poor and mostly hostile to the privileged layers of society, although it is possible that some people Daniel Orlovsky identifies as "lower-middle strata" occasionally joined in. But in spite of their lower-class bona fides, the crowd probably was not politically organized or attuned to social movements.

Who were the urban poor? According to the 1910 census, Petrograd was home to 234,000 industrial workers, 77,000 *sluzhashchie* (lower-middle-class professionals and service workers), 52,000 transport workers, 25,000 waiters and cooks, 41,000 city employees, 58,000 artisans, and 260,000 household servants and butlers.[34] Orlovsky includes among the *sluzhashchie* sales clerks, cashiers, bookkeepers, and pharmacy employees; post, telegraph, and railway employees; mid-level business managers, municipal and other public-sector employees, paramedical personnel, teachers, and low-ranking technicians.[35] Some in the lower-middle strata were members of trade unions.

Those I define as the urban poor were situated below this lower-middle tier. Among others, they include artisans, low-end hospitality staff, street peddlers, cab drivers, dvorniks, household servants, and unskilled laborers, mostly nonunionized. They were certainly a part of the "laboring masses" but were also distinct from the industrial proletariat. In addition to permanent and semipermanent residents, undocumented seasonal workers and unskilled workers seeking employment joined the ranks of the urban poor. To this we must add an army of the unemployed. The

nonorganized urban poor outnumbered the better-organized industrial workers by more than two to one, yet the urban poor have
largely eluded historians' analysis.

For want of precise terminology, historians occasionally
lump some of what I call the urban poor into the category of
meshchane—"petty bourgeoisie." But this term is not applicable.
Nor is "lumpen proletariat." These terms do not capture the heterogeneity and amorphousness of the urban poor. Social mobility
and porous geographic boundaries ensured both movement and
proximity between the urban poor and the lower-middle class.
Some people classified as industrial workers likely had more af-
finity for the urban poor. Statistics taken from the factory census
for 1917 indicate that in the Narvskii, Aleksandro-Nevskii, and
Moskovskii Districts, many factories were tiny, employing fewer
than twenty workers.[36] These workers more closely resembled artisans than they did the industrial proletariat toiling in gigantic
Vyborgskii and Petergofskii factories. Their outlook may have
been more like that of the urban poor who were their neighbors.

The geographic breakdown of mob justice from May to October indicates that mob justice was especially common near
markets, especially Apraksin, Sennaia, and Aleksandrovskii Markets, in the Third Spasskii Subdistrict.[37] It is safe to assume that
the shoppers there were poor folks seeking daily necessities and
servants of the middle and upper classes. Parts of these districts
that were home to large contingents of the urban poor also experienced frequent mob justice. These districts also had particularly
high crime rates. Rozhdestvenskii included the rough neighborhood of Peski. Aleksandro-Nevskii and the Fourth Moskovskii
Subdistrict included the notorious crime-infested area of Ligovka,
near Nikolaevskii Railway Station.

Few cases of mob justice were reported in the city center: none
in Admiralteiskii or the First Spasskii and First Vasilievskii Subdistricts. There were three cases in Kazanskii, two of them in the

less-privileged Third Subdistrict, near Kolomenskii. One instance in the First Petrogradskii Subdistrict, at Sytnoi Market, was similar to those at Spasskii markets. Mob justice was also rare in the working-class districts such as Vyborgskii and Petergofskii.[38]

Thus, while direct evidence is hard to come by, we can be fairly confident that the urban poor were particularly well represented in the crowd. Both journalistic accounts and the geographic distribution of mob justice point to this conclusion.

The Participation of Soldiers and Hooligans

Soldiers, too, were major participants in mob justice. They lived side by side with the urban poor and mingled with them in the streets and markets. Soldiers intensified the violence associated with mob justice. When they felt their group interests threatened, they responded in gruesome fashion, as the next two cases illustrate.

Around noon on July 8, a car approached People's House near Aleksandrovskii Park in Petrogradskii, where the soldiers of the 178th Infantry Regiment were quartered. As the car passed in front of People's House, the passengers began shooting at the soldiers, who immediately fired at them. The driver attempted to get away at full speed, but angry soldiers blocked the car's path. Soldiers pulled the passengers from the stopped car and literally tore them limb from limb. When city militiamen arrived at the scene, they collected the heads, hands, and feet that were strewn about and delivered them to the hospital.[39]

On the morning of August 15, near Semenov Bridge on the Fontanka, a hooligan approached a soldier selling cigarettes and selected a pack. When the soldier demanded payment, the hooligan threatened him with a dagger. When the soldier sought help from his comrades in the barracks, the hooligan responded by burying his dagger in the soldier's chest and abdomen. Another soldier rushed to help his bleeding comrade, and the hooligan knocked him down with the butt end of the dagger.

Soldiers then poured out of the barracks and caught the hooligan. They decided to finish him off then and there and threw him into the Fontanka. The hooligan turned out to be a good swimmer, though. The soldiers sat in the "box seats" on the riverbank, caught him, and dragged him out of the water. They beat him with oars and sticks and then cut him to pieces.[40] The term "box seats" is interesting, indicating that some instances of mob justice became a spectator event, a kind of theater.

Mob justice was thus another arena of criminality in which soldiers actively participated. They were positioned on both sides of the social divide. Now and then they guarded people and property from lawlessness and violence; now and then they contributed to those worsening problems.

Like soldiers, hooligans were especially trigger-happy. They often joined in mob justice, presumably not to punish criminals but for the excitement. They threw rocks at drowning victims in the rivers and canals, and they were often the first ones to shoot.

Lawyers and Journalists Speak Out

Opposition to mob justice was palpable across political lines. On October 8, the Petrograd Association of Barristers adopted a resolution declaring the epidemic of mob justice to be the greatest threat facing the city. The resolution demanded respect for the law and called for the establishment of a politically independent justice system akin to the tsarist courts destroyed by the revolution.[41]

Journalists were also attuned to incidents of street justice and reported them in newspapers of every political stripe. They did not merely relay events but also sounded alarms, warning that mob justice—and, more generally, disrespect for the rule of law—posed a grave danger to the creation of a genuine civil society.

On October 20, in the conservative *Vechernee vremia,* a commentator known as P. R. decried the frightening criminal infestation of Lesnoi. The once-placid suburb was now beset by murderers and thieves, some acting in broad daylight. When burglars broke into houses in the middle of the night, residents knew to feign sleep for fear of otherwise being killed. P. R. isolated the resulting psychological decay among residents:

> "What is the militia doing?" The sad answer is: the militiamen themselves are committing robbery. To walk in front of the commissariat is as dangerous as walking alone in the forest. Therefore, the bitterness against the militia is extraordinary in Lesnoi. . . . And those whom the militia cannot defend turn to crime. This is the foundation on which the angry and monstrous cruelty of mob justice is based. In fact, the powerlessness of the militia changes the defenseless citizens into criminals, since this psychology transforms people into merciless ugly crowds who commit mob justice.
>
> Every place in the streets of Lesnoi is connected with horrible memories. There is the place where a murder took place; here is the place a robbery was committed. This house was robbed. As the darkness sets in, unhappy residents lock their doors, and tremble with the slightest noise.
>
> In order to feel this fear, come to Lesnoi, and walk in the streets. You see a man in a leather jacket, another in a soldier's overcoat, or a Chinese with rugs—you look at them, and instinctively and against your will, you are afraid of them. You watch their every move, wondering

if they are going to grab their revolver or their dagger and go after you. You cannot help asking the question: Is he a robber or not? Perhaps, his black jacket is what he stole when he killed someone yesterday.

This is not a persecution complex. This is the feeling of deep fright that accompanies the complete loss of trust in other people. This feeling appears in Lesnoi in its clearest form, but it is spreading throughout Petrograd.[42]

Such concerns were shared on the left. In an October edition of the left-wing newspaper *Novaia zhizn'*, Maxim Gorky, then a left-wing intellectual, wrote:

All the dark instincts of the crowd, irritated by the ruin of their life, lies, and dirty politics, will burst out and begin to befoul [everything], poisoning all with malice, hatred, and vengeance. People, unable to destroy their own beastly stupidity, will kill each other. Unorganized crowds will come out and wander in the street, barely understanding what they want, and, from behind this crowd, adventurers, thieves, professional murderers "will begin to write the history of the Russian Revolution."[43]

Crowd Psychology

How could everyday people commit the kinds of atrocities traced here? Examples of mob justice abound in history, as we know from the savagery of lynching in America and anti-Semitic pogroms throughout Europe. We may not have to look far back in history, as we have seen the horrifying murder of Farkhunda Malizada, a twenty-seven-year-old Afghan woman wrongly accused of burning the Quran in March 2015, a death graphically captured on video.[44] It is useful, therefore, to expand our horizon for a moment and review the work of two turn-of-the-century French sociologists, Emile Durkheim and Gustave Le Bon, who observed the emergence of the masses in European society.[45]

Durkheim argued that primitive society, as he understood it, cohered through mechanical solidarity, while organic solidarity served as the glue of advanced industrial society. Mechanical solidarity is so called because it is enforced—through repressive rules and kinship ties founded in emotional connection. Here, a strong sense of collective consciousness transcends individual interests. Organic solidarity, by contrast, is not secured through collective consciousness but rather by the high degree of interdependence brought about by the division of labor and the reliance of organizations and residents on one another.

But the mechanical does not simply evolve into the organic and thereby fade away. The two kinds of solidarity might coexist. In an advanced capitalist society, organic solidarity predominates, but an element of mechanical solidarity persists. It follows that when organic solidarity atrophies, mechanical solidarity asserts itself.[46] Arguably, this is what happened in Petrograd in 1917. The epidemic of mob justice can be interpreted as the reversal of the modernizing process—a regression from what Durkheim called "organic solidarity" to "mechanical solidarity," a process that Moshe Lewin calls "primitization."[47]

When the collective consciousness binding a community is weakened, Durkheim writes, "We should react vigorously against the cause of what threatens with such a lowering of the consciousness . . . so as to maintain our consciousness in its entirety." He goes on:

> When some cherished belief of ours is at stake we do not
> allow, and cannot allow, violence to be done to it with
> impunity. Any assault upon it provokes an emotional

reaction of a more or less violent nature, which is turned
upon the assailant. We lose our temper, wax indignant
against it, inveigh against it, and the sentiments stirred
up in this way cannot fail to be translated into action.[48]

In conditions of mechanical solidarity, punishment is "passionate
reaction," performed "for the sake of punishing." Punishment,
often excessive, does not so much redress a wrong or correct mis-
behavior as recover solidarity.[49]

Durkheim points out the importance of "unanimity" in meting
out punishment and the role that emotion plays in achieving
it. He asserts that "in large gatherings of people an emotion can
assume . . . violence" and further that "since the sentiments that
crime offends within a single society are the most universally collective ones of all, . . . they cannot possibly brook any opposition."
These sentiments need "a more violent form of satisfaction" in
order to "recover . . . vitality."[50]

These passages perceptively describe the dynamics of mob justice. Anyone seen as violating the crowd's sense of justice not
only transgresses individuals' understanding of the moral right
but also ostracizes himself from the community. The infraction
must be met by the community as a whole, and its desire for redress will not be satisfied by anything less than extreme brutality.
The crowd gathers, holds a "people's court," unanimously passes
a sentence far outstripping that demanded by the crime, and
thereby silences any dissent challenging the solidarity it has con-
structed through collective emotion.

Durkheim's analysis suggests that mob justice sought to recap-
ture the empowerment promised by the revolution, though by
other means. The February Revolution offered dignity on the
basis of civic freedom and escape from class-based oppression.
But, overwhelmed by insecurity and economic desperation, the
crowd found itself still helpless and powerless and attempted to

correct that state through mechanical solidarity. The crowd sought not retribution against specific crimes but against the failure of the new society to keep them safe enough to enjoy the liberty they were falsely assured. In a way, by restoring a sense of solidarity, mob justice fleetingly empowered the helpless to manage the vicissitudes of their daily existence.

While Durkheim largely turned his attention to society in the abstract, Gustave Le Bon, a social psychologist, focused on one of its concrete manifestations. In *The Crowd: A Study of the Popular Mind* (1895),[51] he argues that this new phenomenon was a normal outgrowth of industrial society—with significant implications:

> Whoever be the individuals that compose it, however like or unlike be their mode of life, their occupations, their character, or their intelligence, the fact that they have been transformed into a group puts them in possession of a sort of collective mind which makes them feel, think, and act in a manner quite different from that in which each individual of them would feel, think, and act were he in a state of isolation.[52]

Under these circumstances, personal intellect recedes, "the heterogeneous is swamped by the homogeneous, and the unconscious qualities obtain the upper hand."[53]

On Le Bon's reading, crowds are marked by four characteristics: anonymity, contagion, suggestibility, and unanimity. Individuals are submerged in crowds and thereby become anonymous. Being anonymous, the members of a crowd are less disposed to restraint and responsibility. This augments opportunities for contagion: "In a crowd every sentiment and act is contagious, and contagious to such a degree that an individual readily sacrifices his personal interest to the collective interest." Such sacrifice is contrary to people's nature, something "of which a man is scarcely capable except when he makes part of a crowd."[54] Le Bon also noticed that crowds are easily swayed, willing to undertake the "accomplishment of certain acts with irresistible impetuosity." Finally, crowds behave unanimously because dissenting voices are drowned out and attacked.

> We see, then, that the disappearance of the conscious personality, the predominance of the unconscious personality, the turning by means of suggestion and contagion of feelings and ideas in an identical direction, the tendency to immediately transform the suggested ideas into acts; these, we see, are the principal characteristics of the individual forming part of a group. He is no longer himself, but has become an automaton who has ceased to be guided by his will.[55]

Crowds not only subsume individuals but also lend them a sense of empowerment. "In crowds the foolish, ignorant, and envious persons are freed from the sense of their insignificance and powerlessness, and are possessed instead by the notion of brutal and temporary but immense strength."[56]

Le Bon may well have been describing Petrograd's descent into mob justice. Anonymity reinforced the passions of the crowd and supplied the medium of contagion. The crowd silenced dissent. Liberated by anonymity and empowered by consensus, the crowd indulged in cruelties its members would never have countenanced otherwise. As soon as their victims were sacrificed, they silently dispersed.

While Durkheim suggests that crowd behavior reflected a recourse to primitive community, Le Bon sees the crowd as a phenomenon of its own time. It could happen only in an industrial society where individuals, freed from the traditional collective consciousness that had bound the members, became atomized.

Le Bon may have the upper hand in interpretation. It is true that in some respects mob justice replicated practices in villages left behind in the age of mechanical solidarity. Villagers routinely gathered in traditional courts to convict and execute horse thieves, arsonists, and suspected witches.[57] Many in Petrograd had moved from rural areas for work, and one might reasonably speculate that, with modern legal systems failing, the urban crowd was applying the only other system of justice it knew. The term *samosudy*, with its invocation of a court of one's own, speaks to continuity between village collective violence and urban mob justice.

However, urban dwellers did not share bonds and common interests in the way of peasants residing in self-contained communes. The members of the crowd did not know each other. They gathered by happenstance, united not by community but by their collective sense of injury. Mob justice in Petrograd is therefore fundamentally different from village justice. It does not hark back but instead looks forward to collective violence in mass society.

The Bolsheviks Take Advantage

Before the Bolsheviks seized power, Lenin paid scant attention to crime and the breakdown of public order. He was interested in the sufferings of the "laboring masses" only in an abstract sense. The details did not concern him. He wanted to overturn the foundations of that suffering yet had little understanding of, and did not care much about, the specifics and therefore what might be done in practical terms to alleviate it. All that mattered was eradicating the bourgeois order—especially the army, police, and bureaucracy, three principal instruments of proletarian oppression. This alone was the realization of a free, just, and livable society.

Some Bolsheviks were more attuned to the facts on the ground. As mob violence spread across the empire in the fall, political opponents blamed the Bolsheviks and their fellow travelers for fanning rabid class hatred, pitting the poor against society as a whole. Most Bolsheviks in the provinces responded by arguing that mob violence signaled the despair of the poor, who were angered by the government's inability to remedy the economic situation. Predicting the Bolshevik reaction to the alcohol pogroms under their regime, these Bolsheviks also blamed counterrevolutionary reactionaries for instigating riots in order to discredit revolutionary forces. On the whole, however, provincial Bolsheviks did not approve of mob violence, and in some cases tried to circumvent it, although they opposed deployment of the army for crowd control.[58]

Lenin ignored these provincial views. After returning to Petrograd in April, all his attention and energy were focused exclusively on seizing power, and mob violence was no obstacle to that goal. In fact, it seemed to further it. A student of Carl von Clausewitz, Lenin inverted the Prussian general's famous dictum, turning politics into an extension of war. Lenin believed that politics, like war, is a zero-sum game, and thus the enemy's loss would be the revolutionaries' gain, and vice versa. He therefore rejected any action that might strengthen the bourgeois order, even if it could have made life more tolerable for the poor. That is why he and fellow Bolsheviks in Petrograd were hostile to demands that the workers' militias and the Red Guards set aside struggle against counterrevolution in order to maintain law and order. The more the bourgeoisie were weakened by popular violence, the better the Bolsheviks' chances of taking over the state.

In an article published in September, "The Russian Revolution and the Civil War," Lenin celebrated episodes of mob violence as "spontaneous movements" revealing the people's discontent and their demands for socialist revolution.[59] He would continue to equate mob violence with political expression as he rallied the party toward armed insurrection. Lenin was thus not merely indifferent to mob violence; rather, he welcomed social breakdown into a state of anomie, which created favorable conditions for the Bolsheviks' seizure of power.

That moment, in October, is also described as a revolution. But it differs drastically from what preceded it in February. The February Revolution was shot through with a democratic spirit, as members of every social stratum celebrated the end of autocracy. The October Revolution, by contrast, took place amid apathy. The population had tired of revolutionary change. Crime and social decay had left them indifferent to politics, which seemed to have no effect on their daily strife. They were still poor, starving, and beset by lawbreaking that officials were powerless to stop. Naked force, not legitimate government, was the arbiter of any conflict. Under these conditions, the majority took little notice of the Bolsheviks' usurpation of power.[60]

On the day the Provisional Government was overthrown, the stores and restaurants were open, the trams ran, and the cinemas were crowded. The momentous event that "shook the world" was almost unnoticed by the contemporaries.[61]

6. Crime after the Bolshevik Takeover

The Bolsheviks rode a crime wave to power, so it should perhaps not be surprising that they were initially unmoved by criminality in Petrograd. Busy sinking the foundation of the socialist utopia, the dreamers of the early Soviet state paid little heed to the deprivation of those they claimed to represent. The misery of life under the pall of constant violence and theft did not register until it threatened the legitimacy of the nascent regime.

That time came thanks to the alcohol pogroms, which escalated dramatically during the first few months of Bolshevik authority. Looters broke into shops, breweries, distilleries, and customs houses; the private cellars of restaurants, the wealthy, and civic organizations; and even churches and the Winter Palace itself. Liquor fueled the anger of the crowd, which fought any and all to protect the stolen bounty. Fires and gun battles caused emergency personnel to work hard around the clock for days on end.

In the past, historians have brushed aside the alcohol pogroms as epiphenomena. They were supposedly of no significance to the unfolding political drama of the revolution.[1] But this is a misleading view that gives undue primacy to the role of ideology and elite politics in driving historical outcomes. As I show in the next chapter, the intensity of the alcohol pogroms and other forms of mob violence offered a wakeup call, significantly affecting the Bolsheviks' attitude toward crime and police in particular, and governance in general. The destructiveness of the crowd strengthened Soviet authorities' conviction that police power must be under strict, centralized control and that crime should be addressed coercively.

It is essential to place oneself on the scene in Petrograd in late 1917 and early 1918 to appreciate the sheer horror the new regime faced. Hundreds died in the alcohol pogroms, millions of rubles' worth of property was stolen, and many of the city's cultural treasures were brought to ruin. The people, through the chaos they sowed, forced the young regime's hand, inadvertently provoking the establishment of a new kind of police state that rejected the liberalizing and centrifugal aims of the revolution that helped bring the Bolsheviks to power.

The Bolshevik Ascent

The Bolsheviks seized power through the Petrograd Military Revolutionary Committee (Petrogradskii Voenno-revoliutsionnyi komitet, or VRK), which was formally attached to the Petrograd Soviet but under de facto Bolshevik control. The Second Congress of the All-Russian Soviets of Workers' and Soldiers' Deputies was to meet on October 25, but anti-Bolsheviks walked out in protest. On October 25–26, Bolshevik-led forces stormed the Winter Palace and arrested the ministers of the Provisional Government. Alexander Kerenskii fled the capital in disguise. On the 25th, the congress opened without anti-Bolshevik delegates. The next day, the Bolsheviks established a government, the Council of People's Commissars, or Sovnarkom, to replace the Provisional Government. The All-Russian Soviets would be the legislative branch. Without the anti-Bolshevik parties, the legislature was mostly a rubber stamp for the Sovnarkom, dominated by Vladimir Lenin, and Russia was effectively ruled by the Sovnarkom's decrees. Until December 7, when it was disbanded, the VRK was the instrument that implemented those decrees. The VRK had at its disposal the Red Guards, the workers' militias, and loyal troops officially subordinated to the commander of the Petrograd Military District.

The Bolshevik power was in shaky shape, challenged not only by anti-Bolshevik forces, but also by the strikes staged by the railway workers' union, Vikzhel, which called for the establishment of a broader socialist government. The Bolshevik leadership was split over this, leading to resignations of some leaders from the government.[2]

Pitted against the Bolshevik government were anti-Bolshevik deputies who had walked out of the Congress. These deputies hoped to replace the Bolshevik power via elections for a new Constituent Assembly. Thus, the elections for the Constituent Assembly loomed as the first significant event to test the legitimacy of the Bolshevik power. This ballot—the first statewide democratic elections in Russia and also the last until 1989—were held in mid-November. Nationally, the Socialist Revolutionaries— including Right SRs, who opposed the Bolsheviks, and Left SRs, who supported them—received 41.4 percent of the votes cast. Bolsheviks received 24.0 percent, Mensheviks 2.6 percent, and the Kadets 4.7 percent. The SRs won 370–380 of the Constituent Assembly's 715 seats, Bolsheviks 168–175, Left SRs 39–40, Mensheviks and Kadets 17 each. Combined, the Bolsheviks and Left SRs had only 30 percent of the seats.[3] As Rex Wade writes, according to these results, "the Bolsheviks would be an influential minority, but a minority nonetheless, and therefore presumably would have to relinquish government power."[4]

Petrograd, the capital of the first socialist revolution, looked different from the rest of the nation. There, the Bolsheviks won a plurality, gaining 45 percent of the votes and capturing six seats to the Constituent Assembly. The Kadets finished second with 26.2 percent, good for four seats. SRs placed third with 17 percent of the vote and just two seats. While the Bolsheviks won majorities in the outskirts (Vyborgskii, Vasilievskii, Narvskii, Lesnoi, Nevskii, Petergofskii, Novoe Derevnia, Okhta, and Poliustrovo), the Kadets won majorities in the center and the center-mixed districts (Admiralteiskii, Aleksandro-Nevskii, Kazanskii, Liteinyi, Moskovskii, Rozhdestvenskii, and Spasskii). The Bolsheviks won pluralities, but not majorities, in the Kolomenskii and Petrogradskii Districts.[5]

The election returns in Petrograd show two important facts. First, the city was polarized between the center, where the Kadets had the strongest influence, and the outlying districts, where the Bolsheviks predominated. Second, although the Bolsheviks gained more votes than any other party, they were still in the minority in the city as a whole. If revolutionary values of decentralization prevailed, each district where the Kadets gained a majority could have formed an autonomous government with its district dumas and subdistrict commissariats in opposition to the Bolsheviks. It is therefore no wonder that the Bolsheviks considered the Kadets the most serious threat to their power. Their influence in the capital city mattered more than their unpopularity on the national scale.[6]

Thus, despite Petrograd's plurality vote for the Bolsheviks in the Constituent Assembly, it was clear that the party had not consolidated power in the all-important capital and therefore nationally. On November 28, the Sovnarkom began that consolidation, issuing a decree outlawing the Kadets as "enemies of the people." Bolshevik detachments and the Red Guards arrested Kadet leaders, including two delegates to the Constituent Assembly.[7]

Eventually, the Bolsheviks would have to decide what to do with the Constituent Assembly, whether they would allow it to be convened, and what they would do when it met. When the Constituent Assembly was summoned on January 5–6, as it is well known, the Bolsheviks closed it by force.[8]

But one of the immediate tasks for the Bolsheviks from the end of November to the beginning of January with regard to the problem of power was how to deal with another challenge: the city duma. Headed by elected SR mayor G. I. Shreider, the city duma could still stake the strongest claim to legitimate government in Petrograd, being the only institution that was based on the four-tail (universal, direct, equal, and secret voting) democratic election in August until the election for the Constituent Assembly. On October 24, one day before the Bolsheviks seized power, the city duma created the Committee of Public Safety in order to "protect citizens' life and and property, to take measures against violence, pogroms, and robberies, and to assist the wounded and sick." Between the fall of the Provisional Government and the convocation of the Constituent Assembly, the city duma presented itself as the only legitimate institution, and denounced the Bolshevik coup as the illegal usurpation of power, not based on popular will. The Committee of Public Safety reaffirmed the city militia's allegiance to the city duma and provided militiamen with five thousand new armbands with the insignia of the City Militia of the Committee of Public Safety.[9]

Crime under the Bolsheviks

The Bolsheviks were anxious to smash everything connected with the old order. But possessing no specific solutions to any of the crises besetting Russia in 1917, their approach to crime in Petrograd only made life worse. Under Bolshevik authority, the quantity and intensity of violent crimes outpaced the previously unprecedented levels of the post-February period. Describing the further collapse of city life in the months after the October Revolution, Meriel Buchanan, daughter of the British ambassador, wrote, "One might have imagined oneself in a City of the Dead."[10]

The first few weeks after the October revolution were remarkably calm. On the 27th, *Izvestiia* reported of the previous day, "No violence was perpetrated on peaceful citizens. On the contrary, the number of usual criminal acts has been seriously reduced."[11] Albert Rys Williams, an American journalist sympathetic to the Bolshevik power, was boldly optimistic: "The first fruits of the revolution are law and order," he wrote. "Never was Petrograd safer than after passing into the hands of the masses."[12]

He spoke too soon. By the middle of November, the crime rate had shot up again. The week of November 7 through 13 saw eight petty thefts, eight robberies, three unauthorized raids on gambling clubs, and four attacks on wine cellars.[13] There are no accurate crime data available for this period, but newspapers reported 31 robberies in October, 41 in November, 94 in December, 94 in January, 137 in February, and 101 in March. The actual rate of robberies was most likely much higher, as was criminality on the whole. As the incidence of serious crime and mob justice increased, newspapers no longer had space to report lesser crimes such as pickpocketing and other nonviolent petty theft.[14]

Not only did the incidence of robbery rise steadily after the October Revolution, but the crimes also became more elaborate. Many robberies were now committed by large groups, with most participants dressed as soldiers or sailors. There is no way of knowing whether the robbers were actually soldiers or sailors, but they were always armed and often behaved more violently than their pre-October counterparts. Their bounties also grew by orders of magnitude. And they often prepared getaway cars. There were still lone wolves out to steal small amounts on the spur of the moment, but their crimes were probably too numerous and commonplace to be newsworthy. As crime became more common, more brutal, and more sensational, so too did the mob justice carried out in response. And not only was mob justice itself a crime, but it also served to protect organized crime by depriving police of potential sources of inside information. They could not, after all, question a lynched wrongdoer.

On February 4 (17), 1918, N. Shebuev wrote in *Petrogradskii golos*:

> The impudence of robbers is growing every day. . . . Even before a money carrier, having withdrawn a large sum from the State Bank, reached the exit, a car approached, and a group of robbers jumped out. The robbers surrounded him, took all the money—760,000 rubles—and drove away. At eight o'clock in the evening at Papern, a shop on Nevskii, robbers thoroughly searched the entire premise without any pretense of hurrying up. . . . They drove off with their loot, while people watched with amazement, their mouths agape. On Monday, not far from Tuchkov Bridge, a merchant family held a huge wedding. When the party reached its climax, a gang of robbers arrived suddenly, shouting, "Hands up!" The guests turned over everything they had: gold watches, fur coats, and all. Then, in no rush, the robbers asked for food and ate a meal before driving away.[15]

The next month a keen observer using the name "M. R—g," wrote a commentary entitled "Criminal Petrograd" on the basis of a conversation with an anonymous criminal investigator. Some claims are embellished, but the article nonetheless provides a succinct encapsulation of the situation in Petrograd. M. R—g recognized that crime, already at catastrophic levels before October, had grown since: one could not step outside without witnessing murders and armed robberies, the author declared. Nine in ten robberies ended in murder. All law-enforcement officials could do was encourage residents to "Protect yourself on your own" because "no one is in a position to help you in any way." The most violent criminals had access to abundant cars and machine guns, while criminal investigators had just a few cars and no gasoline with which to fill them. Looters could rely on fleets of motorcycles and trucks, but the Criminal Militia received no support from the government.

The most successful way to pull off a robbery, M. R—g continued, was to conduct illegal searches for weapons. A thief could illegally gain entrance to a building by presenting fraudulent search orders, fabricated or stolen from legal authorities. The Criminal Militia would learn about such crimes only from newspapers. M. R—g conservatively put the number of thieves in Petrograd at about forty thousand.

Although criminal syndicates were a serious problem, any two or three people could band together and successfully execute a robbery if they had access to a car and a half-decent Nagant rifle, which was mass-produced for the Russian army. On a good night, even a small cadre of armed thieves could steal fifteen to seventy-five thousand rubles. Robbers were typically young; many older and more experienced thieves abandoned their trade for fear of mob justice. Instead, they turned to the black market, where they dealt in stolen goods. The new blood, M. R—g explained, learned old tricks from the retired veterans they interacted with underground.[16]

Newspaper reports support much of M. R—g's analysis. For example, raids of clubs, restaurants, stores, and private apartments, sometimes by robbers posing as law enforcement, were rampant. With the collapse of the previous police regime, multiple agencies now issued search orders. They were loosely controlled and lacked coordination, inviting and simplifying forgery. Moreover, restaurants and private clubs were tempting targets thanks to their illegal alcohol sales and openness to wealthy gamblers. There was good loot to be found, and in substantial quantity. Robbers also felt they could use fake papers to steal from the private residences of the wealthy with relative impunity. They knew that the new regime was not sympathetic to the complaints or concerns of the rich—the exploiting class. Not that every large-scale robbery was draped in Robin Hood–style justifications. On January 16, 1918, seven armed men with false papers stole forty thousand rubles' worth of valuables from the Bolshevik seat of government at Smolnyi.[17]

One notable case of large-scale robbery using illegal papers came on November 21, when a group of well-armed, uniformed men raided the "literary-artists" club Rampa. They announced themselves as VRK commissars and presented VRK orders to close down the club. After blocking all the exits, they instructed the two hundred panicked guests not to move. They proceeded to search everyone for money and weapons. With raised hands, the gamblers meekly complied. Some women tried to hide purses and jewelry under tables and behind curtains, to no avail. The supposed commissars left the club with heaps of money and valuables. A manager attempted to contact the VRK but received no response.[18]

Another illustrative case took place on December 16. It started out much like the Rampa experience. At three o'clock in the morning, ten robbers armed with rifles and a bomb raided another supposed literary-artists club in the Second Liteinyi Subdistrict. They, too, blocked the exits and proceeded to confiscate money and valuables from about fifty gamblers. But only nine of the robbers left; one stayed behind with the bomb and was discovered in the kitchen. When the Criminal Militia arrived, the young thief peacefully surrendered. Angry gamblers attacked him, but the militia was able to retrieve him, preventing mob justice.

Interrogation revealed that the young robber was a teahouse waiter who had been persuaded by his hooligan friends to join the "expropriation" of the club in order to "teach the exploiting bourgeoisie a lesson." The gang provided the waiter with the explosive and a revolver. A chauffeur was paid eighty-five rubles to drive a getaway car but claimed he had no knowledge of the robbery. A few days after the arrest, five more members of the gang were arrested at a teahouse on Suvorov Prospect. Eventually, the whole group was apprehended. Most turned out to be unemployed.[19]

These episodes demonstrate some consistent dimensions of robbery under the Bolshevik power and validate many of M. R— g's claims. First, they reveal the prevalence and targeting of high-stakes gambling dens after the October Revolution. Since gambling was illegal, victims could not claim restitution of their lost money and property. And the VRK had renewed bans on gambling, which may have left gamblers disposed to behave when lawmen ostensibly presented themselves.[20] Second, these examples indicate that serious crimes were perpetrated by organized groups, especially unemployed youths. As M. R—g wrote, anyone with weapons and a car could form a gang. We also see how the class hatred propagated by anarchists and Bolsheviks justified theft. Finally, the second of these episodes speaks to the perilous unintended consequences of mob justice. If the dispossessed gamblers had had their way with the young waiter turned thug, there would have been no investigation, and the hooligan gang most likely would have gotten off scot-free.

The increase in muggings also demonstrates the mounting level of violence M. R—g isolated. If stealthy pickpockets attracted less press attention, it was largely because of the greater concern presented by robbers approaching their victims at gunpoint, sometimes in broad daylight. Muggings occurred on the streets and in trams. Gangs on four wheels would drive up next to pedestrians, rob them, and depart at speed. Victims of street robberies often ended up dead. On January 12, Sergei Karnovich Valua, a famous actor attached to the Imperial Aleksandr Theater, was fatally attacked by six soldiers on the Fontanka embankment near Nevskii Prospect. An officer with Valua at the time could do nothing to help him; his weapon had been confiscated.[21] Five days later, Professor Rozenbakh, a noted neurologist, was murdered by muggers in front of his house near the Summer Garden in the First Admiralteiskii Subdistrict.[22] In tsarist days, this fashionable area had been the safest in the city.

Rozenbakh was killed a day after one of the most brazen crimes of the early Bolshevik period. On January 16, the Italian ambassador, Marquis del Torreta, was traveling to his embassy by sleigh when he was stopped by three men in a car under the pretext of searching for weapons. The muggers grabbed his briefcase, a gold cigar case, a moneybag, a gold tiepin, and his fur coat and boots and drove away, leaving the ambassador half naked and trembling in the icy streets. The poor ambassador had to walk back to his apartment barefoot. The attackers turned out to be Red Guards.[23] That same day, the Dutch ambassador was mugged on Mokhovaia Street, in the First Liteinyi Subdistrict. Thieves entered his car and stole a briefcase and wallet containing two thousand rubles.[24] Foreign diplomats had never been attacked before the October Revolution.[25]

Bolshevik officials were not immune to mugging, demonstrating the opportunism at the heart of criminals' claims of expropriating the expropriators: urban warfare, not class warfare, was afoot. Two of the most shocking victims were the head of the Petrograd Cheka, Moisei S. Uritskii, and Commissar of Justice Petr I. Stuchka. On the night of February 7 (20), a group of muggers robbed them of their boots, overcoats, waistcoats, and jackets. Uritskii and Stuchka identified themselves, but the muggers did not mind stealing from officials of the Soviet government.[26] On February 9 (22), three officials of the commissariat of justice were robbed at gunpoint in their horse-drawn cab while carrying a large sum of money to pay employees.[27] On March 8, four armed men stole more than a million rubles from a commissariat of education money carrier, prompting complaints from the Petrograd Cheka about the "unacceptable carelessness with which various Soviet institutions transport large sums of money."[28] On March 23 (April 4), Elena Stasova, a secretary of the Central Committee of the Communist Party—the new name for the Bolsheviks—was robbed of eight thousand rubles by three armed men.[29]

After the October Revolution, major firms and institutions also came under greater threat from organized crime. On January 10, ten armed sailors broke into one of the warehouses of the Customs' Office on Gutuevskii Island, seizing a large quantity of goods. More attacks followed over the next two days. Thirty armed men perpetrated another robbery on the island on February 8 (21), loading cars with stolen furs.[30]

On the night of January 28, a band of more than fifty thieves in soldiers' and sailors' overcoats attacked the cashier's office of the Northern Stock Society. The intruders must have known that 1.5 million rubles were being delivered that day. They overcame the resistance of the company's Red Guards, broke into the office, and tried to crack open a huge iron safe where the money was kept. Unable to breach the safe with their rudimentary tools, they decided to carry it to a getaway car, but the safe was too heavy. After struggling for hours, they gave up, leaving four Red Guards dead and several others wounded at the scene.[31]

On February 4 (17), eight armed men in soldiers' uniforms proved more successful when they broke into the apartment of a Swedish citizen named Labgard, who owned a store on Nevskii. They robbed him of 1.2 million rubles.[32] One wonders why such a large sum was in the apartment. It appears that some people considered it safer to hide cash in their homes or carry it with them than keep it in a bank, suggesting that the normal banking system had ceased functioning.[33]

Robbers often engaged in armed confrontations with militia and Red Guards.[34] An unusual incident on February 6 (19) demonstrates the chaos that spilled over into daily life: a funeral procession turned into a shootout. This episode originated with a robbery at a factory near Moscow Gate, where a gang stole a million rubles. Red Guards arrived at the scene and exchanged gunfire with the robbers. A number of Red Guards were wounded, and at least one robber was killed. Later, Red Guards discovered the dead man was a Catholic and traced the church where his funeral was to be held. When his funeral procession approached Zagorodnyi Prospect, the Red Guards, who had taken up position there, began firing randomly at the mourners. They ran in all directions in panic and confusion. A priest and cantor were among those shot. Soldiers of the Semenovskii Regiment, stationed nearby, heard the gunshots, rushed to the scene, and arrested everyone near the canal, including the wounded priest. Thanks to the testimony of two Catholic soldiers, who regularly attended services at the priest's church, he was released immediately and survived. The cantor, however, did not.[35]

Along with the incidence of robbery, the number of murders climbed after the Bolshevik takeover. No systematic data are available, but based on newspaper reports, I count 8 murders in November, 16 in December, 25 in January, 42 in February, and 27 in March—a total of 118. The rate remained consistent in June through December 1918, which saw 168 murders.[36] My count is probably low, given the many missing days for which newspapers were not available to me. Even so, the number of murders is very high. There were only 14 murders in Petrograd in 1914 and 30 in 1915. There were 90 murders under the Provisional Government, from March to October 1917—a high number but still better than that of the year following the Bolshevik assumption of power.[37]

Easy access to weapons aggravated the murder rate. Family quarrels, conflicts among friends, and disputes between merchants and customers more readily resulted in tragedy. In December, a militiaman, A. Kachevskii, shot his wife and her lover amid an illicit tryst. On January 3 at Sennaia Square, a soldier shot a comrade who refused to sell him a loaf of bread at the desired price. It is doubtful that, under better social conditions, a petty squabble such as this would have resulted in a cold-blooded killing.[38]

For the most part, however, murders were associated with robberies. The list of such cases is long. There were the cases of Valua and Rozenbakh as well as those of less distinguished individuals. For instance, on March 20 (April 2), at the corner of Sadovaia Street and Bankovskii Lane, five young men mugged a money carrier for the tobacco firm Bogdanov. When the money carrier called for help, the robbers shot him in the head, killing him instantly.[39]

The most famous murder of the period was politically motivated. On the night of January 6, two Kadet leaders, Andrei I. Shingarev and Fedor F. Kokoshkin, were killed at Mariinskii Hospital. A doctor by profession, Shingarev was the minister of agriculture in the first Provisional Government as well as leader of the city duma's Committee of Public Safety. A conscientious liberal, Shingarev fiercely opposed both the tsarist regime and the Bolshevik usurpation of power. Bolsheviks considered him a formidable adversary. Kokoshkin was a respected constitutional scholar and a Kadet member of the Constituent Assembly. The Bolsheviks arrested both men and incarcerated them in the Fortress of Peter and Paul. They were then transferred to the hospital for the treatment of illnesses, only to be brutally murdered by a band of radical sailors and anarchists, assisted by the guards on duty.

The Bolshevik regime, initially shaken, established an investigating commission on Lenin's order and detained a number of sailors connected with the killings. But the main suspects escaped. Although the commissar of naval affairs, Pavel E. Dybenko, ordered their capture, the Bolsheviks proved reluctant to pursue the case. For one thing, they were loath to provoke sailors on whose loyalty the regime depended. More important, though, the most influential Bolshevik leaders, Lenin and Felix Dzerzhinskii, came to view the murdered men as counterrevolutionaries and therefore expendable.[40] Maxim Gorky commented, "Shingarev and Kokoshkin, innocent and honest people, lie dead, but our authorities lack both the strength and conscience to bring their murderers to trial."[41]

Mob Justice

After the October Revolution, the frequency and intensity of mob justice escalated significantly. Six cases were reported in November, eleven in December, fourteen in January, twenty-one in February, and two in March.[42]

The first case of mob justice after the October Revolution took place on Tram No. 3 near Sennaia Market in late November. A young man, suspected of having stolen a wallet from a passenger, was pulled off the tram. A crowd gathered, beat him, and threw him semiconscious into the Fontanka. Someone in the crowd, who apparently felt sorry for him, dragged him out of the river and brought him to Obukkhov Hospital.[43] This Good Samaritan was lucky that he was not subjected to mob justice as well.

The bloodlust of the crowd produced terrible injustice. On December 9, a middle-aged woman waiting for her tram at Neva Gate noticed that her wallet was missing. Convinced it had been stolen, she blamed a teenager standing at the tram stop. The crowd surrounded him but could not find the wallet. They beat him up anyway. Red Guards arrived, but rather than quell the violence, they joined the crowd and helped throw the teenager into the icy Neva. He attempted to swim to shore, but one of the Red Guards shot him before he reached the riverbank. The crowd then searched the woman and discovered that her wallet had fallen behind the lining of her overcoat. The angry crowd then threw her into the river as well. What happened to the woman is not known, but the crowd silently dispersed.[44]

The brutality of the mobs was extraordinary, as several drunken men in the Second Narvskii Subdistrict learned on December 21. That night, in their apartment, they got into an argument with a woman—likely a prostitute—attacked her, and tried to steal her jewelry. In the process, they smashed her head, killing her. Simultaneously, a thirteen-year-old girl happened to enter the apartment. The men attacked her, too. At the sound of her shrieks, building residents rushed to the scene. The Red Guards and the City Militia were summoned, and the murderers arrested. While the Red Guards escorted the murderers to the commissariat, a crowd formed and demanded that the men be executed on the spot. They grabbed the murderers and began to beat them. They then dragged two of them to a fence, made them stand with their backs to the crowd, and shot them. The crowd beat the other two with sticks and the heels of their shoes and trampled them. One of the victim's hands was torn right off. Finally someone, perhaps out of pity, shot them both.[45]

In December, a man named Liubakhanskii killed a fellow guard named Churbanov. To hide his crime, he cut the body into twenty-nine pieces and dropped the body parts from the American Bridge into the Obvodnyi Canal. He was arrested by the militia and put into the commissariat jail. On January 3, 1918, he was escorted out of the Third Aleksandro-Nevskii Subdistrict commissariat to the Revolutionary People's Court. A crowd gathered. One of them had a placard saying: "Citizens! Look at this monster. He killed and cut a man into 29 pieces. Let's hand down a people's sentence." The crowd shouted: "Death to the murderer!" In view of the stormy atmosphere of the crowd, the Red Guards decided to return to the commissariat without taking him to the

Revolutionary People's Court. In the meantime, a huge crowd of more than one hundred people had gathered at the commissariat. They held a meeting and decided to try the murderer with mob justice. The Red Guards went out and asked the crowd to calm down. The crowd responded: "Death! Death!" Suddenly, the crowd broke the door open and dragged Liubakhanskii out. Surrounded by the angry crowd, he walked, with his hat in his hand, and begged: "Have mercy on me." "Death! Death!" responded the crowd. In front of a small red warehouse, he was stripped of his overcoat, coat, and shoes. Liubakhanskii was forced to stand facing the crowd without a blindfold. Not thirty steps from him stood six men with rifles. Uneven volleys were fired. Liubakhanskii, stood for a few second and then slowly fell on the snow. But he was still alive. Again volleys were fired. Still he moaned, and his body twitched. One of the executioners approached and shot the murderer in the head with his revolver, finally killing him.[46]

Not all of the victims of mob justice during the early Bolshevik period were robbers and murderers. On January 16, a man in a soldiers' uniform was subjected to mob justice for perceived price gouging. He was selling bread for five rubles per pound at the corner of Gorokhovaia Street and the Fontanka in the Third Spasskii Subdistrict when a crowd gathered demanding that he lower the price to three rubles. He refused, and the crowd threw him into the Fontanka. The merchant tried desperately to reach the shore, but the crowd pelted him with rocks and ice until he drowned.[47]

As before the October Revolution, mob justice attracted considerable criticism. In a December essay for *Vechernii Chas* entitled "The Bloodthirsty Public," the journalist O. Tomskii condemned the crowd as more frightening than the crimes to which they responded. The revolution, he argued, had cheapened the value of human life. Under tsarism the death penalty troubled many people, even when applied to serious criminals.

Yet now it was considered perfectly justifiable, even obligatory, "for stealing a wallet with three rubles in it or failing to pay for laundry."

Tomskii recalled a scene on a tram in which the passengers almost uniformly agreed that all criminals had to be executed in order to spare the public. When a gentleman in an overcoat and a fur hat, apparently a member of the intelligentsia, reproached the passengers for their zealousness, a soldier glared at him and demanded, "So, you are saying that we must forgive?" The man agreed that punishment might be necessary but argued, "We should not impose the death penalty on all criminals." Angry riders shouted in response, "We have to get rid of the bad grass from the field!" and "A rotten apple will spoil the whole barrel!" The experience left Tomskii in fear of his neighbors. "You can feel that these people will not hesitate to deprive a man of what is most precious and valuable—his life—for even trifling reasons," Tomskii wrote. "Their faces lit up with excitement. Their eyes glittered with malice and open, unvarnished hatred."[48]

A February 3 (16) *Novaia Petrogradskaia gazeta* article credited to "An Eyewitness" followed a similar line. The author noted the excitement of ordinary citizens who threw a robber into the Fontanka, underscoring the significance of mob justice as a spectacle for ordinary people to witness. There were reportedly many women in the crowd, including a group of giggling schoolgirls. The crowd stared at the victim in the river and quietly asked themselves, "Is he going to drown?" The author was stunned to find that the victim did not beg for mercy and speculated that he knew any cries would only provoke the crowd further. He swam desperately toward the piling of the bridge. The eyewitness wrote:

> The crowd that filled both banks of the river quietly and attentively watched the robber struggle for his life. A boy threw a piece of ice at the victim, saying, "Don't let him

get to the piling." No one stopped the boy. What struck me most was the eerie silence of the crowd.

In ancient Rome they pushed the criminals off of the Tarpeian Rock. In twentieth-century Petrograd, we have the Fontanka instead. The cruelty of the crowd in Petrograd is, however, equal to that of the Roman mobs.[49]

Another interesting observer wrote under the name Monte Cristo. On January 19, Monte Cristo described a scene of mob justice in *Petrogradskaia vecherniaia pochta.* More significant than the account was Monte Cristo's case for a new approach to criminal justice. Monte Cristo rejected the Bolshevik system, which equated crime with political counterrevolution and therefore enabled excessive punishment while leaving crowds with largely a free hand. Monte Cristo argued that crime was politically neutral and, therefore, that the criminal justice system should transcend class and political interests.[50]

Left-wing intellectuals, such as Gorky, did not exempt the Bolsheviks from criticism for mob justice under their watch. Gorky devoted many of his "Untimely Thoughts" columns in *Novaia zhizn* to the brutality of mob justice and criticized the Soviet government for its failure to establish a legitimate criminal justice system. On December 21, he wrote, "Having abolished the old courts in the name of the proletariat, their lordships, the People's Commissars, have strengthened the consciousness of the 'street,' its right to 'mob trials'—a bestial right."[51]

Mob justice eventually emerged as a serious concern of the regime as well. *Izvestiia,* a government paper, wrote in February, "Mob justice is a blemish on the revolution. It shames its honor. Do not mete out punishment against anyone without trials."[52] *Krasnaia gazeta,* a Communist Party organ, accepted that the revolution had to punish its enemies but argued that the crowd's violence had no place in revolutionary justice. The paper lamented especially cruel punishments, such as quartering and boiling to death, which were reported in some provincial towns. Enemies of the revolution deserved to be punished only by methods befitting the new enlightened state.[53]

On February 16 (March 1), Commissar of Justice Isaak Z. Shteinberg decreed mob justice "counterrevolutionary." From then on, anyone caught committing mob justice would be sent not to the Bolsheviks' newly established criminal court but to another novel establishment in Russian criminal justice: the Tribunal for the Struggle against Counterrevolution.[54] After months of swelling violence, there would be only two instances of mob justice in March.

Anarchist Crime

Before seizing power, and during the early days of their regime, Bolsheviks often set aside their ideological disagreements with anarchists and collaborated toward common ends. Iosif S. Bleikhman, Efim Z. Iarchuk, Vladimir S. Shatov, and other anarchists joined the VRK, and anarchists worked alongside Bolsheviks to overthrow the Provisional Government. Leading anarchists such as Iustin P. Zhuk and Anatolii G. Zhelezniakov participated in the storming of the Winter Palace. And it was Zhelezniakov, as chief of the guard at Tauride Palace, who carried out the Bolsheviks' order to disperse the Constituent Assembly on January 6, 1918.[55] As Lenin noted of the anarchists in 1921, he "sometimes succeeded in reaching agreement with them about aims" if not "as regards principles."[56]

Thus cooperation between the two groups was purely opportunistic. When in power, the Bolsheviks came to regard anarchism as a threat and sought to undermine their erstwhile partners. One of the leading figures in the crackdown was Lenin's personal secretary, Vladimir Bonch-Bruevich. Lenin's trusted aide and Dzerzhinskii's rival sounded the alarm in an article, "Horror in the Revolution," describing the anarchist sailors of the ship *Respublika* of the Second Guard Marine, who allegedly arrested officers and executed some without trial. Lenin ordered Bonch-Bruevich to investigate and punish as necessary. Bonch-Bruevich tried the anarchist sailors in an impromptu revolutionary court and directed other sailors to deliver the surviving arrested officers to Smolnyi.

The sailors ignored the order, instead stashing the officers in a hiding place where the sailors proceeded to drink and carouse with prostitutes. After their orgy, they brought two of the officers outside and executed them. The remaining officer was kidnapped and driven around the city, as the anarchist sailors extorted ransom money from his acquaintances. Eventually, Bonch-Bruevich, with the help of Bolshevik sympathizers in the Marines, managed to rescue the officer and bring him to Smolnyi. But the anarchist sailors threatened to attack Smolnyi to retrieve him. With the help of loyal detachments and the Red Guards, Bonch-Bruevich captured the anarchist sailors' barracks and disarmed them.[57]

Burevestnik, the organ of the Petrograd Federation of Anarchists, openly called the anarchists to join the alcohol pogroms, and many anarchists were more than willing to respond to this call.[58] When Bonch-Bruevich's Cheka arrested a self-proclaimed anarchist-criminal, Dalskii, the anarchists sent an ultimatum, threatening to attack the Soviet government.[59] The anarchists often appropriated private houses and possessions. For instance, a group of anarchists seized a house on Stremiannaia Street in the First Moskovskii Subdistrict and looted all the apartments in this house. When Bonch-Bruevich's Cheka detachment arrested them, they had in their possession many valuables they had "expropriated."[60]

Another striking example of the new Bolshevik-anarchist relationship came in February on Vasilievskii Island. A group of anarchists seized a villa belonging to Baron Gintsburg and refused to vacate despite a categorical injunction from the Petrograd Soviet. The authorities eventually dislodged the anarchists with force and discovered that they had stolen jewelry, rugs, furniture, paintings, mirrors, and other items.[61] The case is notable as a kind of mirror image of the Durnovo dacha occupation in June 1917. Back then the Bolsheviks supported the anarchists, who resisted the Provisional Government's order to expel the occupiers. Now, with the Bolsheviks in power, the tables were turned.[62]

The Bolsheviks feared the anarchists not only because they were ideological opponents but also because they were influential and thoroughly armed. Well capitalized thanks to their "expropriations," the self-proclaimed anarchists obtained weapons and bomb-making expertise. They fortified themselves by turning seized buildings into armed camps. When the anarchists held a conference at a former women's college in the First Moskovskii Subdistrict, they showed up fully armed.[63] They also had many followers in the armed forces and even among the Red Guards. The Bolsheviks had to tread carefully to curb their excesses and eliminate their destabilizing influence without completely alienating them. This explains why the Bolsheviks were reluctant to pursue the Shingarev and Kokoshkin murder case.

On January 30, the Petrograd Soviet banned the anarchist newspaper *Burevestnik*.[64] The Soviet also strictly prohibited anarchists' seizures of private homes and instructed the district soviets to take resolute measures against groups that defied the new government.[65] It was a hypocritical measure. The Bolsheviks themselves confiscated properties belonging to the privileged class, which they used as offices and for the resettlement of proletarian families.[66] Expropriating the expropriators was all well and good, but only when sanctioned by the Bolshevik regime.

Alcohol Pogroms

More than any other sources of social breakdown in Petrograd, alcohol pogroms jolted the Bolshevik regime.[67] According to the city duma's data, there were 570 wine and vodka cellars and warehouses in the city, worth 30 million rubles at prerevolutionary prices.[68] The regime was loath to destroy the inventory because it could derive revenue from the liquor, in spite of official prohibition. Beer and wine sales continued in stores.[69] Given weak security and Russians' legendary drinking habits, these locations were easy targets.

As noted earlier, alcohol pogroms did not materialize suddenly after the October Revolution. Similar incidents were widespread during mobilization in July–August 1914.[70] Ordinary people considered drinking their right and prohibition a repressive measure. Igor V. Narsky and Yulia Y. Khmelevskaya write:

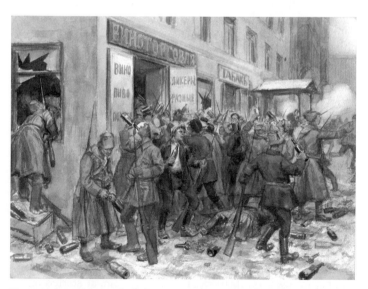

Figure 16. Ivan Alekseevich Vladimirov, *Revolutionary Workmen and Soldiers Robbing a Wine-Store* (Petrograd, January 1919). Ivan Alekseevich Vladimirov Paintings, Box 1, Painting 15. Hoover Institution, Library & Archives, Stanford University.

> The behavioral and verbal character of the emotional displays of those who participated in the alcohol riots suggests that they perceived free access to "the goods," hidden from them by the state and "bourgeoisie" during the three years of war and prohibition, as a well-earned holiday, compensation for the privations and sacrifices they had endured. . . . The looting of alcohol reserves . . . combined a display of physicality and sociality, elements of ritual and revolt.[71]

Thus the alcohol pogroms can be interpreted as ordinary people's celebration of the final liberation from the oppressive practice of prohibition. But the Petrograd alcohol pogroms in November–December 1918 and again at the end of January 1918 were notable for their ferocity and duration, and they took place in the capital itself, the "cradle of the proletarian revolution."[72]

Initially, the Bolshevik regime was blissfully indifferent to the danger of alcohol pogroms. It was not the Bolsheviks but the city duma's Committee of Public Safety that first attempted to destroy liquor reserves in order to eliminate the object of potential attacks. On October 26, one day after the Bolshevik assumption of power, the city duma empowered the district dumas to close bars, teahouses, and dining halls that were selling liquor illegally.[73] The Admiralteiskii Committee of Public Safety, fearing that a mob would attack the wine cellars of the Winter Palace, asked that guards be posted there. The Central Committee of People's Sobriety, through the city duma, proposed that all reserves of wine and vodka be destroyed.[74]

Violent alcohol pogroms began on the night of November 4–5, with attacks on the wine cellar of Grand Duchess Ksenia Aleksandrovna, in the First Admiralteiskii Subdistrict. It started when Soviet Executive Committee chauffeurs broke in. The uninvited guests partied drunkenly and wildly, attracting others outside.

Red Guards dispatched to suppress the disorder instead joined in. More than twenty-five hundred bottles of expensive wine were consumed, pilfered, or destroyed, and the cellar itself was ruined.[75]

At this point, the Bolshevik government took notice. On November 7, Commissar of Education Anatolii Lunacharskii, also a Bolshevik deputy of the city duma, who was responsible for cultural treasures damaged during the storming of the Winter Palace, proposed shipping all the wine from the Winter Palace to the Kronstadt Fortress on an island about twenty miles west of Petrograd. This way, he hoped to protect the palace's remaining treasures from the mob.[76] But protecting the home of the fallen tsar was not a high priority for the VRK, which, in any case, was strained by pressing duties. Lunacharskii's proposal went unheeded. The VRK also ignored a November 8 city duma decision to destroy the city's liquor reserves, reflecting a bitter rivalry between the two organizations, as discussed in the next chapter.[77] The VRK did remove guards caught snatching bottles of wine from the palace cellar or drinking while on duty. The VRK removed the Preobrazhenskii soldiers and replaced them with what it thought to be more reliable soldiers from the Pavlovskii Regiment, but that was all.[78]

In the days thereafter, drunken orgies elevated tensions across the city. On November 13, a band of soldiers at a rail station busted up a wagon loaded with spirits and started drinking directly from the tank. Railway workers attempted to stop them, but the soldiers fired at them and chased them away. That same day, a huge pogrom took place at Durdina, a brewery on Obvodnyi Canal. Soldiers of the Fourth Railway Battalion, who were sent to guard the brewery, could not resist the temptation to do the opposite. They broke open the refrigerated storage and slugged what they could find. Soon a few hundred people had gathered at the gate with buckets, flasks, and bottles. Drunken soldiers welcomed them into the courtyard, where the parched masses binged freely. Beer was poured straight from barrels, guns were fired into the air, and the sodden lay passed out on the ground. Eventually, the VRK dispatched the Petrogradskii Regiment to shut the party down.[79]

On the night of November 23, Lunacharskii's fears were realized. Crowds, interspersed with men in soldiers' and sailors' uniforms, breached the security barrier surrounding the Winter Palace and raided the wine cellars. The guards put up little resistance, and soon joined in. Thousands of bottles of fine wine were opened and consumed, stolen, and smashed. The cellars filled with a sea of wine. People dipped their mugs, buckets, and even boots into the wine and slurped it up.

Word of wine pouring into the Neva spread around town. More people swarmed to the palace from all directions. Soldiers arrived in trucks and drove away with cases upon cases of wine. Desperate drinkers got down on all fours and licked the snow, stained vivid red and yellow from the bottles shattered all about. Women and children sold bottles to passersby who preferred not to join the mob directly. The sociologist Pitirim Sorokin, who witnessed this second storming of the Winter Palace, wrote:

> Broken bottles littered the square; cries, shrieks, groans, obscenities, filled the clear morning. Many of those who entered the cellars could not get out, owing to the press of those who madly pushed forward to get in. The cellars swam in wine from broken casks and bottles and many men were actually drowned in the flood of it.

Firefighters at last washed the wine into the sewers and the Neva, and the area surrounding the Winter Palace was cordoned off.[80]

The VRK was finally convinced that liquor reserves were hazardous to public safety and order. By November 29, it had decided to destroy all the liquor in the city.[81] But the attempt to force sobriety on the people of Petrograd did not go as planned. Soldiers tasked with liquor disposal saved bottles to drink themselves or to sell. When it became clear that the government was targeting a given wine cellar, mobs would break in and make off with most of its contents before authorities arrived. The destruction order merely induced further drunken mob behavior.

Within a few days, the pattern had been set. On December 1, soldiers and sailors raided a cellar belonging to the Raul restaurant in the Second Admiralteiskii Subdistrict and carried away thousands of bottles of wine. Crowds rushed in to salvage whatever had been spilled on the cellar floor, and gunshots were heard until ten in the morning. People lay dead or wounded. The usually busy streets were empty of people and cabs. That same day, soldiers and sailors attacked the wine cellar belonging to Prince Oldenburg on Kirpichnyi Lane in the First Admiralteiskii Subdistrict and destroyed many bottles and barrels of rare Portuguese Madeira wine.

In the Second Liteinyi Subdistrict, other soldiers and sailors joined by civilian "volunteers" raided the Chereponnikov liquor store under supposed VRK orders. The group shot the necks off of bottles, the quicker to open them, and drank them down on the spot. Inebriates poured into the streets; area residents barricaded themselves inside their apartments. Gunfire rang out all night and into the morning, scattering panicked shoppers waiting in bread lines. Soldiers were found selling cognac for ten rubles a bottle.[82] Meriel Buchanan witnessed a drunk soldier swaying toward a burning building and brandishing his pistol at passersby. "A little further along another soldier lay face down in the snow, an empty bottle still clutched in one hand," she wrote. "Two little boys stood nervously at a distance, and a third, more courageous, tried to loosen the fist-clasped fingers from the bottle, to see perhaps whether there were a few drops left."[83]

Also on December 1, when sailors and Red Guards arrived at the Ivan Ion vodka distillery in the First Aleksandro-Nevskii Sub-district with VRK orders to destroy stored barrels, enormous crowds swarmed from all directions, broke into the cellar, and began drinking right on the spot. Outnumbered, the sailors and the Red Guards requested army reinforcements. At four in the afternoon the next day, a truck carrying soldiers and Red Guards arrived at the scene. They fired machine guns into the air to disperse the drunken crowds. Inside they found soldiers, Red Guards, hooligans, and others lying passed out in the cellar.[84] "Last night Petrograd was under the complete control of drunkards," *Gazeta dlia vsekh* reported. The drunken orgies spread to the Liteinyi District, where five people were killed and twenty wounded. Most of the casualties were soldiers. In addition, the cellars of five restaurants, including the famous Vienna, were attacked.[85] Every time a cellar was destroyed, a crowd rushed in to drink and pilfer bottles to sell. Through the city center, armed, drunken people staggered and lay in the streets.[86]

On December 2 and 3, the pogrom also expanded to Vasilievskii Island. A military unit sent by the VRK arrived at a liquor warehouse called Tomin, but instead of guarding the warehouse, they began a drinking binge. Soon a swarm of hooligans joined them. Above the warehouse, where the Lyon Credit Bank had its offices, workers fought off the drunken intruders. In the meantime, a new wave arrived and began tussling with the first occupiers, who refused to share their loot. Newcomers denounced the occupiers as "counterrevolutionaries" and "enemies of the people." Angered by this name-calling, the earlier occupiers grabbed a young man from the new group and tried him via a hastily assembled people's court. Its verdict was, predictably, the death sentence; he was shot and killed on the spot. At some point, the building was set ablaze. The fire, fueled by the ample liquor stores, engulfed the warehouse and bank office immediately. Drunkards poured onto Malyi Prospect, shooting aimlessly. A stray bullet killed a woman walking with a baby.[87]

Another band of robbers on Vasilievskii Island broke into the wine cellar on Ninth Lane and engaged in a shootout with hooligans who came to share in the loot. An armored car was brought in to suppress the drunken orgy, but the shootout continued until two in the morning.[88]

Even Vyborgskii, the hotbed of working-class organization where Red Guards in particular were disciplined, succumbed. In the first days of December, gunshots were heard on Vyborgskaia Embankment, then along Sampsonievskii Prospect. Wine cellars were attacked, but mostly by hooligans rather than workers and soldiers.[89]

The next several days brought unbridled chaos. According to Bonch-Bruevich, on the night of December 4–5, police recorded 69 alcohol pogroms and 611 reports of related crimes.[90] The most serious was an attack on Petrova, a vodka distillery in the Third Moskovskii Subdistrict. At seven in the evening, a group of soldiers broke into the basement and started bingeing. By nine o'clock, gunshots were heard. The VRK sent a Red Guards detachment with machine guns, but the drunken soldiers shot back, driving the Red Guards away. News spread fast, and swarms of soldiers and residents rushed to the scene to buy vodka at the cheap price of two rubles a bottle. The drunken orgy continued through the night. At five in the morning, fires started burning throughout the building. The city's full complement of fire engines was called in, but the drunken crowds shot at the firefighters, killing and wounding many.[91]

Journalist O. Tomskii wrote an eloquent commentary on the scene at Petrova. Amid the flying bullets and broken glass, he witnessed a soldier, drunk out of his mind and bleeding from an open wound, crawl through the snow on gnarled fingers toward a bottle of vodka. In a raspy voice he muttered, "Comrade, give me a drop before I die." Another soldier heard his plea, gave him a half-empty bottle, and asked, "What will you trade for it?" The dying man offered an orange, but the final agony overcame him before he could finish the vodka. Such scenes were repeated over and over again at the alcohol pogroms. The people's passion for the bottle was so strong that they were indifferent even to death. To them, freedom was drinking—even if it meant dying on all fours with bullets whizzing overhead.[92]

Tomskii reported an even grizzlier sight at the Miuller distillery in the First Kazanskii Subdistrict. There, a crowd guzzled vodka from an iron tank until something unexpected stopped them. Submerged in the tank were the corpses of two men who had arrived earlier, dived into the tank, and drowned in the sea of vodka. If only Lenin and Trotsky had seen one of alcohol pogroms, Tomskii sighed. "Would they then have reflected on the tragic consequences of their actions?"[93]

Other pogroms occurred at the wine cellar belonging to Count Shuvalov in the First Moskovskii Subdistrict, the cellar belonging to Prince Gagarin, the Shitta winery in the First Vasilievskii Subdistrict, the Hotel Evropeiskaia, and the Bavaria brewery on Petrovskii Island.[94] The city militia was nowhere to be found, and its replacements were of little more use. Latvian sharpshooters called to quell a pogrom in the Fourth Spasskii Subdistrict joined in the looting.[95] Altogether, twenty people were killed in the pogroms of early December.[96]

In a December 6 speech at the Petrograd Soviet session, Bonch-Bruevich warned, "The revolution is in danger of literally being drowned in vodka and wine."[97] Asked by a reporter about how the Bolshevik government was dealing with the alcohol pogroms, Lunacharskii did not seem optimistic. "The whole of Petrograd is drunk," he replied.[98]

The Extraordinary Commission to Combat Pogroms

On December 7, the Petrograd Soviet established the Extraordinary Commission (Cheka) to Combat Pogroms, installed Bonch-Bruevich as its head, and set up its headquarters at Smolnyi.[99] Bonch-Bruevich placed the city under martial law and prohibited public gatherings. Any attack on liquor warehouses and stores, or on apartments, would be punished severely, he said. He put armored cars on patrol.[100] He also ordered dvorniks and doormen to fulfill night duties, as Vadim A. Iurevich and Georgii. P. Polkovnikov had under the Provisional Government. As before, this order immediately provoked the Union of Dvorniks and Doormen to declare a strike, which began on December 3. The strike lasted three days, leaving all the buildings without night guardsmen.[101] Later, the Sovnarkom issued a decree ordering all hooligans arrested, sent to the Fortress of Peter and Paul, and tried at the Military Revolutionary Court. More than two thousand were rounded up.[102] At long last, the highest authority of the Bolshevik regime was frightened enough to undertake serious measures against pogroms. But as the French journalist Gabriel Domergue observed, "It was too late."[103]

The pogroms reached their apex between December 7 and 9. The December 7 issue of *Gazeta dlia vsekh,* which recorded the most detailed chronicle of the alcohol pogroms, listed nine attacks on wine and vodka cellars. Each followed the familiar pattern: crowds gathered, broke into the cellars, pillaged, and binged. The military and the Red Guards sent by Bonch-Bruevich's Extraordinary Commission exchanged gunfire with the drunken looters but could not suppress them.[104]

The attack on Petrova was still under way on December 7. A military detachment sent by the VRK chased the crowd away with machine-gun fire. Some looters drowned, and others burned to death in the basement fire.[105] At Bekman, a vodka factory in Kolomenskii, shootouts took many more lives. Military units surrounded the premises and waited until looters had passed out before taking action.[106]

The fiercest battle occurred on December 8, between looters and Red Guards at the winery near Tuchkov Bridge on Vasilievskii Island. The looters, mostly soldiers, erected a snow fortress within the winery. From their tactical positions, the looters repulsed wave after wave of Red Guards. The soldiers inside took turns drinking and shooting every ten minutes. When the Red Guards finally broke through, the looters jumped into a ditch to escape, their pockets filled with clanking bottles. *Gazeta dlia vsekh* marveled that the soldiers had apparently learned something useful from their military experience.[107]

That same day, the apartment wine cellar belonging to the restaurateur M. P. Nosov in the Third Spasskii Subdistrict was attacked in spite of militia protection. The two guards were easily overcome by a group of suspicious men in soldiers' and sailors' uniforms. After the guards were disarmed, more than thirty additional armed men arrived, shooting in all directions. One group robbed Nosov's apartment, and the other broke into his wine cellar. They also broke into a cellar owned by the French military attaché, Captain Bugeauld, and emptied it of ten thousand rubles' worth of liquor.[108]

On December 10, the Keller, Bekman, and Petrova distilleries were still under attack. Gunfire was incessant throughout the city. Crowds attacked the Vasilievskii Island wine cellars belonging to Eliseev, owner of the most famous grocery store on Nevskii Prospect, and the Imperial Economic Society in Ligovka. Armored cars patrolled the city, and fire brigades were out in force. Many more deaths were reported.[109]

After December 10, the incidence of alcohol pogroms declined. The reason was simple: most of the city's major liquor storages had been raided. But there were still some attacks, resembling a mopping-up operation. The Raul wine cellar was attacked in Ligovka. Fire brigades had worked for several days to destroy the massive reserves there but did not manage to get rid of it all, and a special guard unit was placed on one of remaining cellars. Rumors had it that the remaining wine was reserved for the Bolshevik leaders, and the guards deserted the position in disgust. A new guard troop also refused to protect the wine for the Bolsheviks.[110] The last pogrom of the wave that began in November came on December 12, when armed men attacked Sokolov's wine cellar in the Fourth Aleksandro-Nevskii Subdistrict.[111] Between December 14 and 23, the newspapers contained no reports of alcohol pogroms.

But on December 23, another huge pogrom took place. Forty-three sailors and soldiers from the Keksgolm Regiment attacked the wine cellar of the Imperial Yacht Club in the First Admiralteiskii Subdistrict. The looters entrenched themselves in the cellar and barred all others from entering. At the gate of the building, they sold wine for as little as three rubles and as much as a hundred rubles per bottle. The Red Guards and troops were sent in, killing one looter and wounding several others. According to the Extraordinary Military Commissar, Georgii I. Blagonravov, the remaining looters were arrested and sent to the Fortress of Peter and Paul.[112] On the same night, a wine cellar belonging to Princess Bobrinskaia in the Second Admiralteiskii Subdistrict was attacked. Looters drank or stole at least seven hundred expensive bottles of wine.[113]

The Petrograd Soviet responded by again instituting martial law and decreeing that any attempt at pogroms would be countered with merciless machine-gun fire—and without warning.[114] The last pogrom of the second wave took place on New Year's Eve, when a group of soldiers raided a wine cellar at Sadovaia Street.[115]

Relative calm endured until late January when two attacks occurred on wine cellars at hotels.[116] On January 21 armed looters attacked Stal's wine cellar in the First Admiralteiskii Subdistrict.[117] In the Fourth Spasskii Subdistrict, three hundred armed soldiers raided a wine cellar belong to the firm, Express. After a two-hour party in the cellar, the band of drunken soldiers pillaged stores along Voznesenkii Prospect from Sadovaia to St. Isaac Square. Red Guards eventually shot at and dispersed the looters.[118] On the same night, looters raided the wine cellar of Voznesenskaia Church, which contained bottles reserved for the Eucharist. A priest pleaded with the men, appealing to their respect for the sacred, but they merely showered him with obscenities and shot him without warning. Latvian sharpshooters and fire brigades were called in. The next day, the looters returned. This time, an armored car was sent to chase them away. At least 10 people were shot dead during the melee.[119] On January 24, 31 liquor stores were attacked, and 120 people died in resulting shootouts. Crowds again raided the Bekman distillery, causing 4 deaths and 20 injuries.[120]

One of the largest pogroms, on January 29–30, was also the last. It began when a Red Guards shift arrived for duty at the customs hangar on Gutuevskii Island but found the preceding shift unwilling to leave. The two groups of Red Guards began to fight, and rogue Red Guards who stationed themselves in the hangar's wine warehouse began firing machine guns, repulsing the loyal Red Guards unit. At seven in the evening, another Red Guards unit was sent in. But the rogues, now thoroughly drunk, beat them back. Two hours later, Smolnyi decided to send two companies of Latvian sharpshooters, but by this time the pogrom had spread across the island. Hooligans snuck into the hangar and pillaged it. Eventually, the ferocious Latvian sharpshooters drove out the drunken crowds. But at two in the morning, a new group of hooligans arrived and set fire to the hangar. In spite of the danger, the crowd swelled and continued its drunken orgy. Ten fire brigade units were called to prevent the blaze engulfing the entire island. Only at six in the morning did a third team of Red Guards manage to expel the drunks. Forty people lost their lives.[121]

It is not clear precisely why the assault on the customs hangar brought an end to the pogroms. The government's harsh measures played a part, but the historian Vadim I. Musaev argues that the exhaustion of the city's liquor reserves was the key factor. There was simply nothing left to drink.

The detailed news reports lead to some clear conclusions about the character of the pogroms. For one thing, we know that soldiers were the prime movers. Recognizing the unreliability of the army, the government preferred to fight back with Red Guards, but they often joined in the disorder they were sent to suppress. The Latvian sharpshooters were not entirely trustworthy either, but they turned out to be the most dependable source of law enforcement. They were not always available, though, as their skill and professionalism placed them in high demand.

Other major groups of participants were hooligans and plain drunks—everyday people looking for a fix. Judging from the locations of the pogroms, it appears that the urban poor in the central-mixed and southern districts contributed heavily to the violence, as they often traveled to wine cellars in the center of the city. Alcohol pogroms were comparatively rare in working-class districts. There is notable overlap here with participation in mob justice, with the exception of women. Although women played an active role in some mob justice cases, especially against merchants, few were involved in the pogroms. Those who were involved mostly sold bottles in the streets rather than drinking in the cellars.

Not only can we be confident about the perpetrators of the pogroms, but we also can be fairly sure of their motives. Bolshevik leaders claimed looters were organized by enemies of the revolution, an interpretation of events that became standard in Soviet historical writings.[122] But there is no reason to believe the pogroms were anything other than spontaneous, undirected, and disorganized. No planning was necessary; the city teemed with eager drinkers.

The Bolshevik view was a conspiracy theory based on tautological reasoning. Officials recognized that the alcohol pogroms damaged the socialist state but claimed that poor people therefore could not be responsible: never would they undermine the institutions that stood for their interests. Hence the Kadets and reactionary monarchist Black Hundreds, hoping to topple the socialist government, must have been the power behind the lumpen proletariat. But as contemporary newspaper writers such as Tomskii, Homo Novus, and F. Sologub argued, the Bolsheviks had a shallow and false understanding of the urban poor—their views, interests, and motivations.[123] The new government exploited the supposed nobility and revolutionary fervor of the "laboring masses" for its own convenience. After all, it was on those ordinary people that the Bolshevik ax would soon fall.

7. The Bolsheviks and the Militia

I n any revolution the struggle for power will involve a struggle for control over the means of coercion," Mary McAuley writes in *Bread and Justice*, her magisterial volume on early Soviet social policy. "Thus violence is written in from the start."

> Curbing the "centrifugal logic" of the revolution has to be one of the first tasks of those claiming authority and this entails establishing control over the armed antagonists, including those who may be supporters. In Petrograd the very vitality of the revolution exacerbated the situation. The attempts, at the grass roots, to dispense with the police, with the old court system, and the civil service, within the context of a deepening economic crisis, led to growing social disorder, both aggravated by unchecked armed intervention and, in turn, encouraging it even further. The struggle for political power and control over the use of force extended from one with political opponents to a battle with crime; measures were adopted to fight on different fronts at once and boundaries became blurred.[1]

This statement captures the essence of the formation of the Bolshevik power in Petrograd. Leaving other aspects of Bolshevik policy to McAuley's definitive work, in this chapter I examine how the Bolshevik regime engaged in that "battle with crime" and how the contingencies of that battle, more than any ideological commitment, engendered a state of dictatorship.

With respect to law, Lenin was an instrumentalist. As he saw it, law had no normative function. Rather than express transcendent values, it was just the "means to a political end." The tsar's laws and the Provisional Government's laws and all their legal institutions served the interests of the ruling class, so the task of the socialist state was to replace them with new ones serving the proletariat. Ultimately, when a classless society was established, law and its formal structure would become unnecessary and disappear.[2] In the socialist future that Lenin envisioned, security would be provided by "merging the police force, the army and the bureaucracy with the entire armed people."[3]

Among Bolsheviks, faith in a people's militia was widespread and deeply held. But as the poet Vladimir Mayakovsky wrote, "The love boat has crashed into the everyday." Once they seized power, the Bolsheviks had no idea how to act on their creed. Their ideology did not prepare them for the infestation of crime in the capital, for the violence from below that they had helped to unleash. They responded with ad hoc measures, albeit governed by political motivations. With each step they took, the noose of coercion and central control tightened.

The Red Guards versus the City Militia

As we have seen, the most serious initial threat to Bolshevik power in Petrograd was the city duma, which claimed the sole legitimate power in Petrograd based on the popular election. It created the Committee of Public Safety, which demanded the sole allegiance of the city militia and sought to control the police power. Immediately after the Bolshevik seizure of power, the Committee of Public Safety appealed to the district dumas to form the district committees of public safety inviting representatives of "revolutionary and democratic organizations." The Committee of Public

Safety further instructed the local committees and the city militia to destroy liquor storages, ban the sale of spirits, guard the wine reserves in the Winter Palace, and organize housing committees to provide security. Housing committees in turn were to obligate men between the ages of fifteen and fifty-five to fulfill night-guard duty, ensure building entrances were closed, and issue identification cards to residents.[4]

Anxious to smash the bourgeois city militia, the VRK issued a decree on October 25 abolishing its commissariats. Instead, the city militia would be under the jurisdiction of the district soviets.[5] On October 28, Aleksei I. Rykov, commissar of internal affairs, issued a decree establishing the workers' militia as the sole police power for the maintenance of order.[6] But undoing the city militia was not an easy task, since the entrenched principle of local self-determination empowered subdistrict commissariats, especially in the central districts. The city militia remained loyal to Militia Chief Ivanov, who, on October 27, directed city militia organizations "to defy the orders of the VRK and the Soviet power, remain at their posts, refuse to submit themselves to the representatives of the VRK, and maintain control of the commissariats unless physical force was exercised."[7]

A major clash seemed imminent, but the Bolsheviks pragmatically decided to bide their time. They understood that subdistricts would work hard to maintain autonomy. More urgently, the city militia was the only organization that could combat crime in some districts, especially the central and the central-mixed. The regime still lacked reliable police power beyond a few loyal Red Guards and military units.

What emerged was a complex mixture of police organizations serving different masters: the city militia and the housing committees under the city duma's Committee of Public Safety, and the Red Guards, workers' militias, and military under the VRK. In some cases, district soviets attempted to take over their local commissariats but withdrew when they met resistance from the city militia.[8] In others, the VRK successfully dismissed city militia commissars but was forced to reinstate them under pressure from the city militia.[9] In still others, the Red Guards and the city militia patrolled together, even if they did not share control of the commissariats themselves.[10] And in perhaps the most convoluted hybrids, representatives of the city militia and the VRK operated commissariats together.[11]

Even in the working-class districts, the city and workers' militias sometimes cooperated. At a November 2 meeting of militiamen in the Second Vyborgskii Subdistrict, the Bolshevik G. V. Arkhipkin recognized the competition between the VRK and the remnant of the Provisional Government represented by the city militia under Ivanov. But his concerns were not ideological: "The Vyborgskii District Soviet will not require the militiamen's active demonstration of support [for the new power]," he announced, "but only demand that they stay at their posts and defend the citizens from pogroms, violence, robberies, and murders."[12] Even in Petrograd's proletarian heart, representatives of the nascent Soviet regime were careful not to "bolshevize" the militia immediately.

Indeed, not only were Bolshevik-leaning districts willing to cooperate with the city militia, but, maintaining the idealism of the revolution, they prized their independence from the central Bolshevik power. On November 6, the city militiamen of the Third Vasilievskii Subdistrict, which the Provisional Government's review commission had identified in June as the subdistrict most influenced by working-class radicalism, passed the following resolution in response to the VRK's order to disband the city militia:

> The city militia must always remain neutral and independent of the political upheaval that is taking place. It

can work in complete agreement with the Revolutionary Committee in the matter of securing residents' property and safety. Therefore, we consider it necessary to request that the Vasilievskii District Soviet of Workers' and Soldiers' Deputies dismiss the new commissar, restoring the administration of the commissariat to [previous] Commissar E. N. Goldberg. This is the only way to restore the activity of the commissariat that has been violated, and this resolution is supported by the majority of the commissariat.[13]

The VRK's high-handed decree provoked resentment from the subdistrict commissariat, just as the Provisional Government's attempt to abolish subdistrict autonomy had in July 1917. The militiamen of the First Admiralteiskii Subdistrict adopted a similar resolution on November 8.[14] Neither resolution could properly be interpreted as mere reflections of bourgeois hostility to the Bolshevik regime. These subdistricts were not concerned with class politics but with the protection of municipal principles: subdistrict autonomy, elections, and political neutrality.

Yet these principles would doom the city militia. Subdistrict autonomy deprived the city militia of organizational coherence. Neutrality proved impossible—even suicidal—in the face of a revolutionary power determined to annihilate, root and branch, any organization that deviated from its political line. Neither the city duma nor the city militia administration could provide the leadership the city militia needed; both had been enervated precisely by the principle of subdistrict autonomy. As soon as the Bolshevik regime began suppressing the city duma's Committee of Public Safety as a counterrevolutionary organization, the destruction of the city militia was inevitable.

The Decapitation of the City Duma

While the Bolshevik regime was careful not to destroy the city militia immediately, it quickly set to work toppling its leadership—the city militia administration—and the source of its legitimacy: the city duma itself. In his appeal to "all members of the Central Committee and the working class of Russia," Lenin characterized the city duma as "the good-for-nothing Kornilov supporters, sons of capitalists and landlords" and supporters of the uprising of "military cadets."[15] On November 1, the VRK ordered the Red Guards to search Chief Ivanov's office and arrest and bring him to the investigation commission in Smolnyi.[16] The Red Guards seized the city militia administration and closed it down. On November 17 the VRK moved the city militia administration from Gorokhovaia Street to a building at the corner of Sadovaia and Voznesenskii Prospect, where neither essential equipment nor telephones were available. But the staff maintained allegiance to the city duma. Mayor G. I. Shreider declared, "We still have a militia that is ready to serve us."[17]

The operation against the city militia administration was part of a larger operation against the city duma. It is important to note that these actions took place amid the excitement for the elections for the Constituent Assembly that began in Petrograd on November 12. On November 15, the Sovnarkom discussed how to deal with the city duma. On the following day, it issued two decrees both penned by Lenin. The first was the decree to dissolve the city duma. It alleged that the duma, whose deputies had been elected before the Kornilov's counterrevolution, no longer expressed the will of the people, as demonstrated in the elections to the Constituent Assembly. It had lost the people's trust and "continued to exploit its formal rights for counterrevolutionary actions against the will of the workers, soldiers, and peasants . . . for sabotage and destruction of public work."[18]

The second decree announced a new city duma election, which was to take place on November 26. Those who did not recognize the decree of dissolution of the city duma and those who engaged in illegal use of city property—for instance, continued use of typewriters and papers—were to be disqualified to run for the new duma.[19] This virtually disqualified a majority of the deputies, who did not recognize the Bolshevik seizure of power. Then on the night of November 18, troops acting on VRK orders arrested the leaders of the city duma, including Shreider, Vladimir Nabokov (Kadet), MaksimVinaver (Kadet), and others. This high-handed action provoked unanimous protest of non-Bolshevik deputies. The VRK was forced to release all the prisoners.[20] Mayor Shreider, released from detention, defiantly appealed to the populace to defend the city duma as the only legitimate authority in the city. But the city militia was too weak and fragmented to dislodge the Red Guards. Two days later, sailors and Red Guards unceremoniously occupied the city duma building and forced the remaining deputies to evacuate the premise.[21]

The Kadets, Right SRs, and Mensheviks were disqualified to run for the new city duma, and appealed to the citizens to boycott the elections. Many district duma deputies followed their leaders and organized meetings to denounce the Bolshevik decree of dissolution. Representatives of many housing committees joined these meetings. The Bolsheviks approached the election with utmost care, mobilizing the district soviets for election campaigns, and effectively eliminating the potential opposition from the list of candidates. With a few exceptions, only Bolsheviks and Left SRs were on the ballots. The elections took place on November 27–28 without disruptions, but only 396,000 residents voted. This means only 31 percent of eligible voters voted for the city duma election, and 58 percent of those who had participated in the Constituent Assembly did not vote for the city duma election. Most importantly, the residents in the central and central-mixed districts virtually boycotted the city duma election. The result of the election was a "land-slide" victory for the Bolsheviks, who "won" 188 seats and allowed 10 to go to the Left SRs, fore-shadowing decades of sham Communist elections to follow.[22] Thus, the city duma, the only legitimate institution with popular mandates, which offered a powerful challenge to the usurpers of power and which still served as the only organization to provide essential services to the city's residents, was strangled to death by the threat of bayonets.

The dissolution of the city duma was in a sense a dress re-hearsal for the dissolution of the Constituent Assembly that was to come eight weeks later. Observing that no serious protests and demonstrations occurred after the surgical operation against the city duma, the Bolsheviks must have felt confident that they would be able to carry out another surgical operation, this time against more formidable opponents in the forthcoming Constit-uent Assembly.

On November 30, the first newly elected city duma had its first session, and elected Mikhail I. Kalinin as the new mayor. On the following day, Kalinin and another Bolshevik representative, Dmitrii Z. Manuilskii, met with the representatives of the now defunct old city duma: its chairman, A. M. Argutinskii-Dolgorukov (SR), and a duma deputy, S. D. Shchupak-Vladimirov (Men-shevik). Both declared that they would not recognize either the Sovnarkom or the new city duma. Kalinin unceremoniously an-swered: "Neither the Sovnarkom nor the city duma needed your approval."[23]

The Debate over the City Militia

While the Bolsheviks were dismantling the city duma, they dis-cussed what to do with the city militia. The party was split over the future of the institution. The radical Bolsheviks, represented by the politician and military commander Vladimir A. Antonov-Ovseenko and Red Guards chief Valentin Trifonov, were faithful to Lenin's idea of universal militia duty and proposed abolishing the city militia as soon as possible. More cautious were Felix Dzerzhinskii and VRK member V. A. Avanesov, who advocated retaining the city militia to combat crime. "It is not necessary to liquidate it," Avanesov argued, "but to reorganize it."[24] To the extent that the city militia might restore a semblance of order, it was useful to the Bolshevik regime. Militiamen were also defecting to the Bolshevik side. At a Union of Militiamen conference in mid-November, six thousand members acknowledged the authority of the VRK. Only six hundred remained loyal to the city duma.[25] This may reflect less a shift in opinion than a concession to practical necessity: the city duma, which paid city militia salaries, was being taken over by the Bolsheviks. It was better not to bite the hand that fed them. In any case, the city militia was coming to heel.

The Bolsheviks took both positions—abolition and reform—to heart. On November 19, the VRK passed a resolution directing all the district soviets to appoint commissars where they had not already done so and to dismiss all the militiamen who had not assented to the Soviet power. This meant the city militia would persist, albeit under total Bolshevik control. But this was only a temporary measure. At this time, the VRK created the Commission to Liquidate the Old Militia and Organize Security for the City of Petrograd. Dzerzhinskii, having apparently switched his position, was a member of the commission.[26]

Under the auspices of the liquidation commission, Trifonov proposed replacing the city militia with a proletarian militia supervised by Red Guards, who remained subordinated to the district soviets. This system therefore involved a curious combination of municipal and class-based policing: universal workers' militia duty alongside district autonomy. In other words, even radical proponents of Leninist orthodoxy respected the centrifugal character of the revolution. However, Trifonov's proposal was never implemented.[27]

In December, abolition began in earnest. On December 2, the liquidation commission ordered local soviets to dismiss any militiamen who could not procure two recommendations from factory committees, trade unions, or military units.[28] This reappointment process, reminiscent of Dimitrii A. Kryzhanovskii's attempt in June, was intended to filter out any militiamen still loyal to the city and district dumas. Two days later, the VRK acknowledged "the decision of the Petrograd Soviet and the commissariat of internal affairs" to close down the city militia entirely. Between December 9 and 12, the Red Guards occupied district duma buildings and shuttered them. In the meantime, the new subdistrict commissars appointed by the liquidation commission reviewed the militiamen's credentials.[29] Finally, on December 30, the Petrograd Soviet adopted a resolution to abolish the old city militia by January 30, 1918, though the city duma would provide money to compensate the fired militiamen.[30] Despite their long-held goal of immediately abolishing the city militia, it took the Bolsheviks more than three months to accomplish this goal.

Notably, just as the Bolsheviks were working hardest to wipe out the city militia, criminality and alcohol pogroms were peaking. Bolshevik leaders were therefore partially responsible for the uptick in robberies and popular violence, as they were systematically undermining an institution vital to mitigating disorder.

The Bolshevik Response to the Alcohol Pogroms

The Bolshevik regime was initially indifferent to the danger of alcohol pogroms. Only after the attack on the Winter Palace wine cellar was the VRK finally convinced of the danger. But even then, the Bolshevik leadership was indecisive. On the one hand, the Sovnarkom appointed I. F. Bydzan as the Commissar for the Struggle with Drunkenness, with the responsibility of destroying liquor reserves.[31] The VRK also passed a resolution to try alcohol dealers and anyone found drunk in public before the Military Revolutionary Court it had hastily created. Finally, the VRK prohibited further alcohol manufacturing and obligated owners of storage facilities to register their existing inventories.[32] On the other hand, the VRK instructed the district soviets, Red Guards, and district commissariats not to destroy any alcohol.[33] Apparently, the Bolsheviks were still interested in protecting this economic resource.

Bydzan ignored the VRK's contradictory order. On November 27 and 28, he set out to destroy the reserves with the assistance of a detachment of Baltic sailors brought from Helsingfors.[34] In an ironic, if predictable, twist, Bydzan himself proved beneath reproach. When confiscated liquor was found in his apartment, the VRK impounded the contraband and brought the erstwhile white knight before its Investigation Commission.[35] On December 1, with alcohol pogroms spreading all over the city, the VRK replaced Bydzan with Ivan V. Balashev.

On December 3, the Petrograd Soviet created a competing organ, the Extraordinary Military Commissariat in the City of Petrograd, and appointed Georgii I. Blagonravov, commandant of the Fortress of Peter and Paul, as its head. Blagonravov was to destroy all wine cellars, "get rid of" hooligans and "counterrevolutionary bands," and arrest and disarm looters.[36] The resulting jurisdictional dispute between the VRK and the Petrograd Soviet led to a compromise in which Balashev would lead the effort against alcohol pogroms and Blagonravov would serve as his deputy. As we have seen, however, it was the Extraordinary Commission to Combat Pogroms, created by the Petrograd Soviet on

December 5 and headed by Vladimir Bonch-Bruevich, Lenin's trusted personal secretary, a noted ethnographer specializing in the study of sectarians, and the brother of General Mikhail D. Bonch-Bruevich.[37] With the establishment of this commission, the Bolsheviks were finally paying serious attention to the alcohol-fueled discord. Bonch-Bruevich placed the city under a state of siege and prohibited public gatherings. He declared that any attempts to break into facilities housing alcohol—liquor storages, warehouses, stores, and apartments—would be punished severely. He was not satisfied with dispatching only Red Guards and army detachments to trouble spots, and deployed armored cars to patrol the city.[38] The Sovnarkom issued a decree ordering the arrest of all the hooligans in the city. They were to be sent to the Fortress of Peter and Paul and tried at the Military Revolutionary Court. More than two thousand hooligans were rounded up.[39]

This newfound concern for law and order was reflected in the Extraordinary Commission's introduction of Bolshevik ideology into crime control. As Lenin put it, "The bourgeoisie goes for the most sinister crimes, bribing the dregs of society and unleashing these elements, inducing them to get drunk for pogroms."[40] Bonch-Bruevich and Blagonravov shared that view, characterizing the alcohol pogroms as a conspiracy engineered by counterrevolutionary elements, led by the Kadets and the Black Hundreds. Bonch-Bruevich further contended that the attacks were connected with the dvornik strikes, similarly intended to subvert the Revolution. Before October, the Bolsheviks had characterized the riots as expressions of popular dissatisfaction, but once in power and faced with the alcohol pogroms, they dismissed the people they had once encouraged. No longer the noble laboring masses to be salvaged and liberated, they were the "dregs," willing tools of counterrevolution. The unproven equation of pogroms with counterrevolution licensed harsh punishment.[41]

On January 28, the regime held a joint conference of the Petrograd Soviet, district soviets, and the military administration to discuss security measures in the city. Bonch-Bruevich acknowledged that crime threatened not only the citizens' safety, but also the legitimacy of the regime itself, an important admission that historians thus far have not taken seriously. Having at last recognized the gravity of the situation, the regime issued an ultimatum: criminals could either leave the city within twenty-four hours or forswear lawbreaking. Alexander Kerenskii and Prince G. E. Lvov had tried a similar strategy in the immediate aftermath of the February Revolution, with one significant difference: the enforcement mechanism. Bonch-Bruevich served notice that, after the twenty-four-hour grace period, all criminals, without regard to the severity of their actions, would be shot at the scene of their crimes.[42] This call for summary justice, reminiscent of Peter the Great's decree in 1711, was codified in Order No. 1 of the Extraordinary Staff of the Petrograd Military District, issued on February 9 (22), which stated:

(1) The Petrograd Military District is placed in a state of siege.

(2) All persons who are engaged in thievery, robbery, assaults, burglaries, expropriations, and other criminal acts shall be shot by detachments of the revolutionary army on the spot;

(3) Private individuals, organizations, and institutions that do not have permission must immediately surrender all bombs, hand grenades, shells, and explosive materials to the district soviets of the workers', soldiers', and peasants' deputies;

(4) District soviets shall collect these weapons at the storage in the Vyborg District, and those who do not

surrender explosives within forty-eight hours shall be placed outside the law.[43]

This was not empty posturing. Red Guards were unleashed in the streets, where they shot criminals on sight, before the crowd could act. Newspapers reported that the bodies of the dead were strewn everywhere. They resulting sharp decline in crime did not go unnoticed.[44] *Vecherniaia zvezda* reported on February 22 (March 7):

> Only two weeks ago, tens of armed raids and robberies were committed. All attacks were conducted with the knowledge that they would not be punished. The robbers raided banks, post offices, money carriers, and apartments not only at night but also in broad daylight, in full view of thousands of witnesses. Within one week (from February 10 to 17), the total sum of stolen properties and money amounted to more than 10 million rubles. The homicides at the time of the robberies numbered more than thirty, and an equal number were wounded. The reduction in crime can be explained by the strict measures taken against robbers. Based on the decision of the Extraordinary Commission, criminals were shot on the spot. Since the decree was issued, more than a hundred criminals were punished in this way.[45]

"The ardor of our Rocamboles and Rinaldo Rinaldinis has greatly cooled," the paper added, referring to two literary anti-heroes popular across nineteenth-century Europe and Russia.

It is true that the incidence of mob justice and alcohol pogroms dropped considerably, but *Vecherniaia zvezda*'s analysis was not entirely accurate. Robberies and murders only declined temporarily, as we have seen. Undoubtedly, though, this draconian measure did help to alleviate the problem of mob justice. With Red Guards mowing down criminals in the streets, the mob had fewer potential victims.

It is not clear how long the state of siege and other emergency measures persisted. Most likely they remained in force for the life of Bonch-Bruevich's Cheka, which was disbanded at the beginning of March.

The Bolshevik Municipal Administration

It was not just liquor that was exhausted in the first few months after the Bolshevik takeover, but also the people themselves. Beyond problems associated with crime, urban life in Petrograd had been deteriorating for a full year. Having seized municipal administration from the city duma, the Bolsheviks were taking charge of a wide range of services that had succumbed, in part with their help, to dysfunction.

The new Bolshevik mayor, Mikhail I. Kalinin, and his staff had to deal with food distribution, garbage collection, public health, transportation, resident registration, marriage and death certificates, the operation of night shelters and orphanages, the provision of electricity and water, snow removal, firefighting, and the licensure of street merchants, cabdrivers, and beggars—all as the city's revenues rapidly declined and professional experts had either deserted or were fired.[46] These tasks were far beyond the capabilities of the Bolshevik administration. Consequently, city life, already precarious, declined even further.

Food and fuel shortages were especially pressing. Residents scrounged and bartered. With food being requisitioned by the state, a flourishing cadre of "bagmen" (*meshochiki*) transported food and goods illegally. By November, as the long, dark winter was setting in, the electricity supply was already intermittent and living quarters were limited to a six hours' supply per day. In December and January, the supply was further reduced to three hours—for the lucky ones. In some parts of the city, electricity was cut off altogether. Residents were forced to use candles and kerosene lamps, causing skyrocketing kerosene prices. The city's fifteen thousand street lamps, once a proud symbol of its beauty and modernity, were turned off.[47] Foreign visitors noted that the lively Petrograd they remembered had become a dark, eerie ghost town.[48]

During the winter of 1917–1918, the city's central heating system stopped functioning. With temperatures well below freezing, people resorted to *burzhuika*—simple iron stoves with bent chimneys. As fuel was in short supply, residents used whatever firewood they could find. When none was available—thanks in part to the dvornik strike, which meant there would be no firewood delivery—they burned their furniture, walls, ceilings, floorboards, and books. Pipes froze, and residents had to carry water home from the rivers.[49]

The first snow fell in the city on November 9 and quickly melted. But it snowed hard throughout December, covering streets, squares, and bridges in heavy piles. Just as the tsarist city governor ordered homeowners to remove snow from their frontage, the Soviet government made snow removal obligatory for homeowners and fined scofflaws anywhere from one to five thousand rubles—a stiff penalty. When this was not enough, the regime obligated every citizen. With housing committees doling out assignments, intellectuals and the bourgeoisie were given especially tough jobs. The new masters of the working class were eager to see the former exploiting class try its hand at manual labor.[50] It was not compassion, but a deeply felt sense of revenge that drove the passion of the revolution.

At the same time, the already-strained transport system broke down further. Due to electricity shortages, trams operated intermittently and irregularly. Any cars running were jam-packed. The transport of goods was paralyzed for lack of horses. There was no hay with which to feed them, and many starved. Others were slaughtered for food. Warning of food poisoning and epidemics, newspaper advertisements and flyers around town admonished residents not to eat rotten horsemeat off the streets.[51] Owning dogs was a luxury and was taxed as such. With their owners hungry and unable to pay, countless dogs ended up in peoples' stomachs.[52]

Throughout the unlit streets, covered in ice and snow, unsmiling people shuffled silently in ill-fitting clothes and tattered boots. Many could afford nothing better, but even those who could refrained. They feared wearing anything fashionable or even functional, lest they be robbed or singled out as bourgeois enemies.[53] Styles changed. Gone were frock coats, fur hats, bowler hats, neckties, and cuffs, symbols of the hated bourgeoisie. Now people wore soldiers' overcoats, leather jackets, and the sorts of caps popular among the working class. Formerly aristocratic ladies hawked their possessions in the streets. Some, desperate, slid into prostitution.[54]

The same pattern held with respect to public health. Crisis had set in before October, but the real catastrophe began after the Bolsheviks took over. The water supply to most apartment buildings stopped. Filth and dust accumulated in the stairways and streets. Garbage piled up in streets and courtyards. Food and vegetables were sold without any sanitary inspections. Soap was scarce, and due to the power shortage, bathhouses and laundries closed. Everything and everyone in the city was unwashed; every place and person reeked. Historians often forget, but the revolution was accompanied by stench and foul odors.

In defiance of the Bolshevik regime, some doctors and nurses refused to work, further degrading public health. As professionals, medical staff were treated by the Bolsheviks with suspicion, and a good number working for the municipal health commissions were fired.[55] There were 2,000 doctors in the city in 1914, but by 1921, only 920 remained. The precise change in number between October 1917 and March 1918 is, unfortunately, not known. Unsurprisingly, Petrograd experienced waves of epidemics. The first was typhus. In February 1918, 413 patients were hospitalized for typhus, and in March, 896.[56] In the spring, small pox hit; 15,581 cases were registered in May. The worst came in summer, when cholera broke out.[57]

It is no wonder, then, that the first anniversary of the February Revolution went uncelebrated in Petrograd.[58] People were consumed with the hardship of daily survival, indifferent to politics and grand ideas. Few had the energy to observe the date, much less the inclination.

The Emergence of the Bolshevik Police State

Against this background of extreme social decay, and in light of the apparent success of harsh measures in stemming mob justice and alcohol pogroms, the Bolsheviks began instituting a new criminal justice system. Two days after Bonch-Bruevich's Extraordinary Commission to Combat Pogroms was created, the VRK was disbanded. On that day, another extraordinary commission was created almost surreptitiously: the Cheka, the secret police headed by Felix Dzerzhinskii.[59] Officially the All-Russian Extraordinary Commission to Combat Counterrevolution and Sabotage, Dzerzhinskii's Cheka handled political crime.[60]

Initially, Dzerzhinskii's Cheka was to be subordinated to the All-Russian Executive Committee of the Soviets, its task limited to investigation. But it was soon shunted over to the Sovnarkom, headed by Lenin, under the jurisdiction of the people's commissariat of internal affairs. In the Sovnarkom, Dzerzhinskii struggled with the commissar of justice, Left SR Iakov Shteinberg. While

Shteinberg wanted the Cheka constrained by law, Dzerzhin-skii abhorred any institutional and legal limitations. He had a powerful ally in Lenin. Inevitably, Dzerzhinskii got his way, and the Cheka acquired extralegal status. Encumbered by neither law nor oversight and equipped with its own armed units, the Cheka arrested, imprisoned, and executed anyone it deemed a counterrevolutionary saboteur.[61]

Another arena in which the Bolsheviks moved to gain control was housing committees. After the October Revolution, some housing committees expanded their activities in view of the absence of effective organizations to secure public order. In working-class Vyborgskii, the committees accommodated Bol-shevik control and officially subordinated themselves to the VRK. But middle-class areas in the central and center-mixed districts were less sanguine. In any case, the Bolsheviks were de-termined to deprive all of the housing committees of power and categorically refused to arm them.[62] When representatives of central district housing committees asked the VRK to release weapons to them, their request was denied, contributing to rising crime and alcohol pogroms that struck these areas especially hard.[63] After the Petrograd Soviet abolished the city militia, the task of the housing committees was limited to the security of the houses themselves, acquisition of firewood, distribution of food-ration cards, and allocation of apartments. External security, over which the committees had tried to assert control, was transferred completely to the Red Guards.[64] Self-administration was stran-gled by top-down hierarchy.

Housing-committee leadership gradually shifted to the Bol-sheviks and their supporters, who were strongly backed by the district soviets. Middle-class elements were isolated and gradually squeezed out. The new leaders discharged their various duties, such as reassigning apartments, in ways that privileged lower-class residents and penalized the bourgeoisie. Here, too, the decentralization process was being reversed. Along with the city militia, housing committees lost their autonomy to district soviets under the thumb of the Bolshevik Party. It was called "democratic centralism," but only the second half of that concept was reflected in reality. Democracy was a fig leaf.

The Survival of the Criminal Militia

Like the Provisional Government before it, the Bolshevik regime chose not to abolish the Criminal Militia. Instead, that police force was reorganized as the VRK's criminal investigation division (*otdel*). Initially, there had been tension, as the VRK occupied the Criminal Militia headquarters on October 29 but found the detectives unwilling to work for the new regime. The tension between the Criminal Militia and the Bolshevik regime continued for a few months. But as the crime rate rose, the Petrograd Soviet decided to restore the Criminal Militia. In November, the detectives demanded raises and assurances of their political neutrality— they refused to investigate cases that were political in nature.[65] With crime out of control, the Petrograd Soviet agreed, and in December, A. A. Kirpichnikov was reinstated as chief of the Criminal Police. Kirpichnikov had previously been the top investigator within the tsarist police and under the Provisional Government, making for a career reminiscent of that of Joseph Fouché, who served as a minister of police under the French monarchy, revolutionary regimes, and finally Napoleon.

The Bolshevik government did not, however, completely shake off its suspicion of the Criminal Militia. Direct evidence is hard to come by, but events suggest division among radical and moderate Bolsheviks, with the former advocating abolition of the Criminal Militia and the latter inclined to preserve it in light of the crime problem. On January 5, the Sovnarkom issued a decree closing down the Criminal Militia. In response, delegates from the Criminal Militia petitioned Commissar of Justice Shteinberg. They demanded that the detectives be kept on, but again on the condition that they not be involved in political cases. They told Shteinberg that if their demands were not met by January 15, they would strike, leaving residents unprotected. Radical Bolsheviks, having already resolved to shutter the Criminal Militia, would have gladly seen the inspectors walk off the job. But Shteinberg promised to meet their demands and asked them to continue working.[66] The alternative would have been further mayhem.

The Criminal Militia survived. By maintaining a tenuous thread of continuity between the tsarist and Bolshevik regimes, it demonstrated the importance of professionalism even in a period saturated with ideology. But it faced many familiar difficulties. Its headquarters was constantly on the move. It lacked forensic equipment and access to informants, and its records had been destroyed. The Bolshevik power did not fund it sufficiently. Above all, it suffered the stigma of the tsarist police, which only heightened the Bolsheviks' suspicions toward its insistence on political neutrality. In some respects, that neutrality made the Criminal Militia increasingly irrelevant. As the Civil War began in earnest and more common crimes were deemed counterrevolutionary, there was less for the Criminal Militia to do. It ceded a good part of its jurisdiction to the Cheka.[67]

The Establishment of a New Court System

The old judicial system based on the 1864 code of laws, inherited by the Provisional Government, was not dismantled overnight.[68] The district court—presided over by the justices of the peace, the Court of Justice, and the Governing Senate as the highest judicial authority—continued to function. For instance, ten days after the

October Revolution, and to the consternation and indignation of Bolshevik leaders, the procurator of the Petrograd Court of Justice ordered the release of former tsarist Minister of Internal Affairs Nikolai A. Maklakov.[69]

This system was destined to be challenged. Mocking the liberals who insisted on the rule of law, Lenin wrote in July 1917, "A court is an organ of state power. Liberals sometimes forget that. It is a sin for a Marxist to forget it."[70] In March 1918, looking back on the Bolshevik experience right after the October Revolution, he wrote that the "unconditional duty of the proletarian revolution was not to reform the court system . . . but to demolish it completely, to sweep the entire old court and its apparatus from its foundation. This essential task of the October Revolution was accomplished."[71]

Lenin's narrative, however, leaves out a number of complications. The Bolsheviks wanted to wipe the slate clean and institute a new centralized system, but they could not ignore the spontaneity of the masses, which moved to create a new legal system from below. Some Bolsheviks, especially at the local level, may have agreed with this effort. They genuinely believed that the establishment of people's courts was one of the gains realized by the October Revolution, and that they were restoring the temporary courts lost to the poor by their abolition by the Provisional Government and the city duma. The result was a temporary system much like the predecessor instituted after the February Revolution.

The subdistrict soviets took the initiative, establishing people's courts in their areas. The first people's court created was in the Vyborgskii district, in which Lesnoi and Novaia Derevnia were included. In this district, five branches were established. Each had five judges, one representative each from the district soviet, district administration, district council of housing committees, district bureau of trade unions, and the factory committees.[72] To assist the people's courts, the VRK established its Investigating Commission.[73] The next districts to establish people's courts were the Petergofskii District and then the Porokhovskii, Petrogradskii, and Spasskii Districts.[74] We do not know much about other districts.

The district soviets asked experienced justices of the peace to assist, but nearly all legal experts boycotted the courts, leaving them in the hands of workers who were poorly versed in law. Usually, two spoke against the defendant and two in his or her defense. Like the temporary courts before them, the people's courts were marked by the active participation of the working class and dealt with a variety of cases close to the lives of ordinary people. They heard cases about drunken militiamen discharging weapons into the air, juvenile delinquency, and illegal alcohol sales. Usually, the courts were lenient toward those arrested for drunkenness, but stricter with restaurant and bar owners who illegally sold liquor or hosted gambling.[75]

The temporary and people's courts had similar shortcomings. No records were kept, sentences were based on dubious legal foundations, and decisions were often arbitrary. The new courts could hardly keep up with the rash of cases. Both the middle class and the urban poor were likely shut out of positions of authority, since appointments were made by district soviets. And the leniency of the people's courts toward drunks, those tearing the city apart in pogroms, must have provoked the public's displeasure. No wonder, then, that residents, especially those in the central, central-mixed, and southern districts excluded from representation, continued to choose mob justice over the people's courts. As McAuley puts it, "The wave of crime, lawlessness, and the absence of a police force created an environment in which the courts could be but puny instruments of justice."[76]

The Bolshevik government recognized that it could not afford to leave the execution of law to the people's courts, just as it could not maintain the old court system. It did not take long for the ax to fall. On November 22, the Sovnarkom issued a Decree on the Court, eliminating the old judicial system and establishing a new one in its place. The district courts, courts of justice, Governing Senate, army and naval courts, and commercial courts were abolished all at once. The new courts would be overseen not by justices of the peace but by justices elected by local soviets. This system would handle civil cases in which restitution could not exceed three thousand rubles and criminal cases in which sentences could not exceed two years. All decisions would be final, with no right to appeal. Judicial investigations, procuratorial inspections, barristers, and private attorneys were also abolished.[77] William Pomeranz distills the result: "The most dynamic part of the Russian legal system—the institutions responsible for forging a national legal consciousness—were summarily swept away."[78]

The decree did not, however, invalidate the 1864 legal code. The regime promised that a new code would be established later, but in the meantime, courts would take a hybrid approach.[79] Judges were "to be guided in making decisions and passing sentences according to the laws of the overthrown government only to the extent that these have not been annulled by the Revolution." The Provisional Government adopted a similar policy after the February Revolution, with one important difference. Under the Bolshevik system, verdicts were not to "contradict the revolutionary conscience and revolutionary sense of legality."[80] This caveat planted the seeds of future Soviet arbitrariness. Before it took its last breath, the Governing Senate, clearly seeing this danger, accused the Bolshevik leadership of "undermining the very foundations of the state structure and depriving the population of the last vestige of legal protection of their personal and property right."[81]

On February 15, 1918, the All-Russian Executive Committee of Soviets and the Sovnarkom issued a second Decree on the

Court, which created the district people's courts that were to preside over the cases that exceeded the jurisdiction of the lower people's courts, streamlining the court system, quite similar to the pre-October system. In April 1918, the Petrograd District People's Court was organized with the participation of professional jurists: two judges from the abolished District Courts, former secretaries of courts of justice, judicial investigators, and some professional barristers.[82] This was not the restoration of the old court system, however. The jury system, the appeals procedures, the bar system, and the role of the Governing Senate as the ultimate judicial authority were abolished by the first Decree on the Court. This was, therefore, tantamount to absorbing the entire judicial authority within the ministry of justice.

The Decree on the Court had another important provision: the establishment of a Revolutionary Tribunal overseeing political crimes and speculation in goods, which was seen as counterrevolutionary, and serious crimes that exceeded the jurisdiction of local courts. These political crimes would be beyond the jurisdiction of the people's courts, demonstrating the will of the state to restrain local spontaneity and assert central control over crimes challenging its own legitimacy. The Revolutionary Tribunal was to be presided over by a chair and six judges appointed by the provincial or city soviets. Reflecting the vertiginous pace of change after the October Revolution, on December 21, Commissar of Justice Shteinberg issued a supplementary instruction invoking the November 22 caveat, in the process solidifying the Bolshevik leadership's preference for revolutionary consciousness and central control over centrifugal spontaneity and self-determination: "The Revolutionary Tribunal shall be guided by the circumstances of the case and the dictates of revolutionary conscience," he declared.[83]

Following the Decree on the Court in November, the Red Guards got busy closing the courts of justice. Altogether, the city was home to sixty courts of justice in October, but by December 6 only twenty-six remained. In one case, a detachment of Red Guards entered a court while it was in session, closed it down, kicked everyone out of the room, and posted a security guard to prevent reentry.[84] This paralleled the Bolsheviks' attempt to destroy the city duma and eliminate the city militia. The party was surgically removing remnants of the old institutions one by one.

To Lenin's disappointment, however, the Revolutionary Tribunal was mild in handing out verdicts.[85] In the first place, it could not impose the death penalty. At its first session after the Bolshevik assumption of power, while Lenin was absent, the Congress of the Soviets abolished capital punishment. Eliminating the death penalty had been an achievement of the February Revolution, later undermined by Kerenskii. The Congress of Soviets wished to overturn Kerenskii in order to proclaim its first humanitarian act. But Lenin reportedly was furious, shouting, "How can you have a revolution without firing squads? . . . What other means of repression do you have?"[86]

Though it was careful in applying draconian penalties against political enemies, the Bolsheviks had already moved ahead with death penalties against criminals and looters via the emergency measures, which established provisions for summary justice. The contradiction would have to be resolved. It soon would be, in favor of maximum punishment for criminals and political enemies alike.

The Revolutionary Tribunal's reluctance to pass harsh verdicts did not please Lenin, Trotskii, and other leaders who were itching to pull the trigger against the "enemies of the people." To fulfill their wish, they surreptitiously restored the death penalty on June 16, 1918. The Commissar of Justice, P. I. Stuchka, who replaced Shteinberg, had adamantly opposed the death penalty during his brief tenure of office. He introduced the "Resolution" on the verdict of the Revolutionary Tribunal, which stipulated:

"Revolutionary Tribunals are not bound by any rules in the choice of measures against the counterrevolutionary." The death penalty was slipped into the law without specifically mentioning the term itself. When the Bolsheviks first administered the death sentence, the Deputy Prosecutor, N. V. Krylenko, explained that the victim had been condemned not "to death" but "to be shot."[87] It took three more months beyond the period this book covers to restore the death penalty, though by the use of casuistry. Once this barrier was crossed in 1920, however, the death penalty was added openly to the Bolshevik law.[88] By then the civil war had been raging for two years.

The Red Guards Falter

With the old city militia abolished, the new militia yet to be created, and military units generally unreliable, Petograd was left with a dangerous vacuum of police power. The Red Guards, operating at the district and subdistrict levels, were called on to fill it.[89] As the tasks assigned to the Red Guards expanded, however, the dependable among them thinned out. The most conscientious were sent to the front for expeditionary missions, especially food requisition, and were later mobilized into the regime's new Red Army.[90] There are no accurate statistics concerning the number of Red Guards operating in the capital, but drawing on records of Red Guards recruitment from major factories, the Soviet historian Anton Fraiman puts the figure at twenty-two thousand in November 1917, plus seven to eight thousand reserves. Fraiman estimates that, by February 1918, the number of active Red Guards was reduced to sixteen to seventeen thousand.[91]

We cannot assume that the Red Guards were always loyal supporters of the Bolshevik regime. As mentioned in Chapter 6, rogue Red Guards were involved in a shootout at Gutuevskii Island. Some participated in alcohol pogroms and street muggings. The Italian ambassador was most likely mugged by Red Guards. V. Tikhomirov, an official of the people's commissariat of internal affairs, claimed that the Red Guards fulfilled their political functions "with utmost reluctance"—a scathing rebuke. There were serious conflicts between the district soviets and the Red Guards organizations. Manifesting anarchist tendencies, some Red Guard organizations declared themselves self-governing, free of interference from even the district soviets and the Petrograd Soviet.[92] Clearly, the Red Guards could not substitute for the abolished city militia. The regime still needed a new police system.

Centralized Police

The Bolshevik leadership's responses to mass violence and insecurity during its first months in power follow a consistent pattern. Whenever a crisis emerged, the regime reacted hastily and in an ad hoc manner. Whatever long-range vision Bolshevik leaders possessed left little imprint on its choices. The Sovnarkom, commissariat of internal affairs, commissariat of justice, VRK, All-Russian Executive Committee of the Soviets, and Petrograd Military District, along with Bonch-Bruevich's and Drerzhinskii's Chekas, issued contradictory decrees and fostered organizational confusion. Jurisdictions overlapped, and chains of command were poorly defined. It was often unclear who had the right to arrest, imprison, and punish and on what legal basis.

Circumstances began changing after March 10–11, when the Bolsheviks moved the capital from Petrograd to Moscow. Petrograd was demoted to the second city, detached from the seat of government. At that point, the Bolsheviks began to streamline the often-contradictory and overlapping militia organizations in Petrograd. Bonch-Bruevich's Cheka was terminated. On

March 28, the Petrograd Soviet granted exclusive jurisdiction for security to the new regional commissariat of internal affairs, which operated at the district level through its Committee of Revolutionary Security.[93] It also decided that the new militia would not draw universally from the citizenry but instead have permanent employees, a move toward professionalization under a single police power.[94] It was a tacit recognition of the failure of Lenin's utopian vision of a people's militia.

Although the period after March is beyond the scope of this book, it is helpful to get a glimpse of what came next, to see the direction that policing took after the Bolsheviks asserted centralized control. In July 1918, the Petrograd Soviet reorganized the Committee of Revolutionary Security and renamed it the Komendatura of Revolutionary Security. Police authority was vested in the Central Komendatura, to which the fourteen district and forty-nine subdistrict komendaturas were subordinated. Civil affairs were detached from the militia and transferred to the local soviets. The Central Komendatura was in turn subordinated to the commissariat of internal affairs of petrograd province, of which the city was the major component. By the middle of 1918, the city had six to seven thousand professional militiamen under the Central Komendatura.[95]

Finally, on August 18, the Soviet government adopted the Law of the Soviet Militia, which streamlined militia organizations nationwide. The centralization of the Soviet police force was thus completed. In this process, the principle of local self-government was jettisoned, and all police forces were made to follow the top-down, state-driven model. As Murray Frame argues, this law was a replica of the Provisional Government's April 17 militia law.[96]

The establishment of a permanent, salaried Soviet militia was a far cry from Lenin's idea of universal armed militias. Nevertheless, this militia was not entirely to return to the tsarist notion of state-driven police. Unlike the tsarist police, the Soviet militia was highly ideological. It excluded all who were "inimically disposed or even neutral towards the Soviet power." This was important, the commissariat of internal affairs stressed, lest militiamen wrongly protect the rights of all citizens regardless of class. In its journal, the commissariat declared, "The first responsibility of the Soviet Militia is the protection of the rights of the working class and the poorest peasantry." Excluded from protection were the former exploiting classes.[97]

Thus centralization triumphed over local self-determination in police organization as it had in political administration. A detailed discussion of police exploits, which did not begin until April, is beyond the scope of this book. But as historian Vadim Musaev describes, the newly created police authority was also ineffective, setting the stage for the Cheka's politicization of ordinary crime.[98]

The Cheka Takes on the Crime Problem

On February 21, 1918, after the Brest-Litovsk peace negotiations were broken off and the Germans began advancing toward Russia, Lenin issued a draft decree, "The Socialist Fatherland in Danger." This decree singled out categories of people—including ordinary criminals such as speculators, burglars, and hooligans—to be executed by the Cheka on the spot. In other words, the Cheka would no longer be combating only counterrevolutionaries and saboteurs, but also common criminals—and with the harshest possible means.[99] Put another way, common criminals were now considered counterrevolutionaries.

Interpreting this decision, Richard Pipes writes, "Lenin included summary justice for ordinary criminals . . . in order to gain support for the decree from the population, which was sick of crime, but his target was his political opponents, called 'counterrevolutionary agitators.'" In other words, Pipes sees the inclusion of common crime merely as a tactical move, a sweetener to induce the popular acceptance of a detested state institution of terror.[100] For purposes of crime control, however, the inclusion of ordinary crime was not a mere bargaining chip. Rather, it was the central purpose of the decree, the last resort when all other efforts to build a functional socialist police had failed. The only remaining option was to apply naked, brutal violence against criminals, and the only available institution to carry this out was the Cheka. The decree effectively made permanent the draconian emergency measures of February 9.

In June 1918, Dzerzhinskii explained what he saw as the Cheka's twin missions: "to fight the enemies of Soviet authority and of the new way of life." These enemies included "both our political opponents and *all bandits, thieves, speculators, and other criminals who undermine the foundations of the socialist order.*"[101] Common criminals were "socially dangerous" and therefore subject to extrajudicial sanctions.[102] The Cheka set to work. The first victims of the Cheka's summary justice were a notorious blackmailer and bandit, Prince Eboli, and his mistress, on February 24, 1918. Four days later, two more bandits were shot. Until July 6, the beginning of the Red Terror, the Cheka spared political adversaries, executing criminals only.[103]

The Cheka's powers were not limited to summary justice. As its role expanded, it acquired the right to try, imprison, and exile anyone it deemed counterrevolutionary. It also gained the right to run the prison system as well as penal colonies, the forerunners of the Gulag.[104] With the Cheka, the Bolsheviks had finally found the answer to the question of crime.

The Bolshevik policy toward the police and the court system evolved as the regime struggled to find solutions to the reality it faced. The policy did not emerge wholesale from an ideological blueprint. It was a contingent process, as the new regime balanced its political goals and power needs with the practical task of restoring order. The Bolsheviks tried many approaches, all of which failed until it turned to the Cheka. But even failed attempts had consequences. They all served as steps toward the final destruction of one of the central tenets of the Russian Revolution from February to October: the decentralization of power. The result of these steps was less a successful law-enforcement system than a centralized one, comprising trained, professional militiamen, subordinated to the state.

A similar process played out in the courts. At first, the Bolsheviks experimented with ground-level people's courts. But the new system could not cope with the vast quantity of civil and criminal cases. The Bolsheviks responded by absorbing the court within the executive. Again centralization was the name of the game.

Ultimately, the solution to disorder was not centralization but repression. Even as the Bolsheviks abandoned revolutionary values via centralization, they claimed the revolution as their ideological heart, to be protected by a Cheka empowered to fight ordinary crime configured as counterrevolutionary. Crime needed to be eradicated by any means—not just because it threatened public order but also because it threatened the socialist state.[105] Crime would be met with a machine of terror unencumbered by law or institutional oversight. The disorder of the revolutionary period thus served as an important stepping-stone for the Bolsheviks toward establishing the first totalitarian state.

Conclusion

When we examine the Russian Revolution through the lens of crime, a new picture of the period emerges. After the February Revolution, Petrograd experienced catastrophic social breakdown, resulting in a state of anomie. Under the Provisional Government, the state proved unable to exercise its monopoly over coercive power to enforce the law. It failed to establish an effective legal order through the court system, police, and prisons, and it could not provide essential social services. As society lost cohesion and class antagonisms deepened, the Provisional Government lost its legitimacy. The state was failing in large part because life was simply unbearable for so many citizens. Whatever their politics, whatever their hopes, they needed security and basic services that the state could not provide. The result was a vicious cycle in which social breakdown produced mob violence, which produced further social breakdown.

The Bolsheviks seized power in October 1917, exploiting the process of social breakdown, which they had encouraged. Their naive utopian goal of creating a new society on the ashes of the old soon ran aground. Under the Bolshevik power, social disintegration accelerated. The regime was not only threatened by political opponents, but also by the catastrophic breakdown of public order. Each stopgap measure failed. Eventually, the Bolshevik regime had no choice but to entrust the task of combating ordinary crime to the extralegal instrument of the brutally coercive secret police.

The Erosion of Police Power and Its Consequences

The tsarist police force was the lynchpin of government control over its subjects. It performed a range of tasks in addition to maintaining order in localities, especially in the capital city. The February Revolution destroyed the tsarist police, but it failed to create a new police force capable of ensuring the security of the citizens. Criminals who had been locked up in prisons were released during the revolution, and thanks to the Provisional Government's lenient laws, they filtered back into society with their unscrupulous skills as pickpockets, burglars, robbers, and murderers. Soon deserters and hooligans joined them, swelling the criminal population in Petrograd. Access to weapons released during the revolution also made crime staggeringly violent. Criminal acts of all sorts—thefts, robberies, murders, gambling, narcotics trafficking—skyrocketed, especially after the summer of 1917, coinciding with the erosion of political stability and the intensifying economic crisis.

The Provisional Government attempted to assert control by reconstituting the state-driven police through the city governor's office. But the tsarist police force, which had provided the vital link between the central government and its subjects, was annihilated, and the city governor's office was abolished. With this connection severed, the Provisional Government was cut off from the citizens. Its attempt to recreate a centralized police ended in failure.

The city duma created a city militia based on the model of Western municipal police forces, following three principles: elections, local self-government, and political neutrality. As society became more polarized and class conflict escalated, it became impossible to maintain a force that served all citizens equally. After the summer, the city administration leaned toward the state-driven model. But this move provoked resentment among the city militiamen, who were entrenched in the subdistricts. At this point, the authority of the city militia seriously eroded. Citizens lost all trust in the city militia's ability to protect their lives and property.

The third form of police power that emerged from the February Revolution was class-based. Workers created their own militias to operate in working-class districts. Composed exclusively of workers, the primary purpose of these groups was to protect and advance the interests of the working class. It was from the workers' militias that the more class-conscious Red Guards were drawn. As class polarization intensified, the workers' militias asserted their control over working-class districts. On the eve of the October Revolution, working-class neighborhoods, protected by the workers' militias and Red Guards, were safer than the central, center-mixed, and southern districts, where the city militia was the only police authority.

Both the city and workers' militias were created from below, as spontaneous movements arising from subdistricts and factories looking to maintain law and order. Thus the process of creating militia organizations reflected an important aspect of the Russian Revolution: the centrifugal diffusion of power and self-determination at the ground level. The efforts by the Provisional Government and the city duma to impose centralization were strenuously opposed not only by the workers' militia, but also by the subdistrict city militia as well.

The Urban Poor and Mob Justice

But behind these worsening changes that made people's lives nearly unbearable, more fundamental changes were taking place in people's values and society's institutions. With the destruction of the old regime, cultural values and social institutions underwent profound change. What was accepted in the old regime was turned upside down. New values based on equality and freedom were supposed to replace the old ways, but various groups could not agree on what exactly constituted those new cultural values. After the revolution, lower-class folks in shabby clothes promenaded on Nevskii Prospect and invaded formerly exclusive parks. Low-ranking soldiers crammed onto tramcars and insisted on riding for free. New language reflected new social relations. The hierarchical structure that ensured social cohesion under the old regime was supposedly destroyed, but in reality it lingered on. Interpretation of the law became ambiguous, and the new court system functioned poorly. The erosion of police power deprived the nominal authority of its capacity to enforce the law, and the law lost legitimacy. Naked coercion became the only means to settle conflict.

The deterioration of urban life hit the urban poor especially hard. The shortage of necessities, above all food, and skyrocketing prices forced them to scrounge for their survival. Standing in long queues for bread and other necessities, traveling long distances to and from the markets, and haggling over prices became daily routines. Unlike the industrial workers, most of the urban poor did not belong to unions. When the temporary courts were abolished, they lost their lone outlet for voicing frustrations and complaints. Pent-up anger welled inside them.

Thieves, robbers, and merchants perceived as profiting from their misery served as scapegoats. When criminals were caught in the streets or markets, crowds assembled and subjected them to mob justice. Disputes over the prices of goods could result in mob justice against merchants. But mob justice was not merely retribution for a specific transgression. It was the crowd's revenge, the outpouring of frustrations over lives worsening by the day. It symbolized the fleeting empowerment of the urban poor and reflected their psychological brutalization. It also affirmed the "primitization" of society, whereby individualism and rationality gave way to mechanical solidarity, as defined by Emile Durkheim.

Crime and the Police under the Bolshevik Power

The Bolsheviks came to power thanks in part to the social breakdown. Upon assuming power, they had no idea how to maintain public order beyond their naive plan to smash the standing army, police, and bureaucracy and replace them with a militia based on universal service. Meanwhile, crime spread rapidly and widely and became exponentially more violent. Accordingly, mob justice escalated in incidence and violence.

Bolshevik policy contributed to this trend. To establish a monopoly on power, the Bolsheviks attempted to systematically destroy their rival organizations. They first decapitated the city duma and eventually abolished the city militia. But this left the Bolsheviks with limited power to handle crime. This weakness led to the unprecedented explosion of alcohol pogroms in November and December. The extent and violence of the pogroms took the Bolsheviks by surprise. At one point, the head of the Extraordinary Commission to Combat Pogroms, Vladimir Bonch-Bruevich, declared that the revolution was being drowned in a sea of liquor.

If mob justice was one form of popular violence, then the alcohol pogroms represented another. Paraphrasing Alexander Pushkin, Fedor Sologub characterized these alcohol pogroms as a "senseless and merciless" form of traditional Russian revolt (*bunt*).[1] Although the alcohol pogroms have not been treated seriously by historians and have been dismissed in most cases as a small episode, I would argue that the popular violence that exploded in the form of alcohol pogroms was an integral part of the Russian Revolution. The potential for a spontaneous explosion of violence always lay within the large layers of the unorganized, alienated urban poor.

The alcohol pogroms inspired a new Bolshevik policy toward crime. No longer did the Bolsheviks entertain the idealistic and unrealistic plan to create a universally conscripted militia. Instead, they began in earnest the process of creating a highly centralized, state-driven police power. But their ad hoc measures were not successful in stemming the rising tide of crime. Eventually, they had no choice but to entrust the task of combating crime to the Cheka, the secret police created to combat counterrevolution. Common crime was now characterized as a political act. The Cheka, unencumbered by legal restrictions and possessed of strong military force, was endowed with the right to arrest, try, imprison, execute, and deport criminals to forced labor camps.

The Bolsheviks' approach to crime represented a reversal of the centrifugal movement that had transferred power outward and downward to the lowest levels of society. The principle of local self-determination had been firmly entrenched between March and October 1917. By imposing the highly centralized state-driven police, the Bolsheviks put an end to local initiative. The Bolsheviks' centralized police force was not, however, an exact restoration of the tsar's. Under tsarism, there was a clear distinction between the political and criminal police. Under the Bolshevik regime, this distinction was eliminated. Crime became a counterrevolutionary act threatening the Soviet state. Crime thus served as a stepping-stone toward the creation of the pervasive instrument of terror that became an integral part of the Communist dictatorship.

The Importance of Social Stability

In recent years, we have witnessed many authoritarian regimes toppled. Why is the move to liberal democracy thereafter so difficult? My study of crime and police offers one explanation. It suggests that, in the course of revolution and regime change, the maintenance of social stability is a crucial test of the new order. Furthermore, any postauthoritarian regime has to confront the impossibility of immediately remedying the accumulated economic, social, and political ills that led to the previous regime's overthrow.

The case of the Russian Revolution can help us understand why such transitions are so challenging. To see why, we should consider two broader theoretical frameworks that encompass the revolution and enable comparison to other transitional circumstances. The first is the theory of anomie as introduced by Emile Durkheim and elaborated by Robert Merton. The second is the theory of the failed state.

"The crisis consists precisely in the fact that the old is dying and the new cannot be born," Antonio Gramsci wrote. "In this interregnum a great variety of morbid symptoms appear."[2] The period of the Russian Revolution was precisely such an interregnum. The symptoms were gruesome indeed, and the public response was anomie.

As Durkheim saw it, anomie, the condition of normlessness, arises when organic solidarity fails. Recall that Durkheim viewed organic solidarity as the source of cohesion in modern, industrial society. Such societies replace "collective consciousness," based on beliefs and sentiments held in common, with division of labor and a high degree of social differentiation. But if individual differences dominate, how does a modern society achieve cohesion? Durkheim postulated that in a modern society "extensive and prolonged contacts between various groups emerge to achieve a degree of organic solidarity." Occupation-based intermediary associations "foster individual autonomy and dignity" and at the same time "provide a nonexclusive moral environment capable of advancing social cooperation, greater social justice, and the extension of social rights." Individualism is "a social product, like all moralities and all religions. The individual receives from society even the moral beliefs which deify him."[3]

When "the division of labor fails to produce sufficiently effective contacts between its members and adequate regulations of social relationships," anomie arises, and with it deviant behaviors.[4] Elaborating on Durkheim's observation, Sebastian De Grazia writes, "Anomie is the disintegrated state of a society that possesses no body of common values or morals which effectively govern conduct." De Grazia's definition fits perfectly the conditions of the Russian Revolution.[5]

Crime and punishment lie at the core of Durkheim's analysis. According to Durkheim, "Crime is deviant conduct that violates prevailing norms and offends the conscience of the upright, provoking them to passionately felt punitive reactions that are authoritatively enforced by the form of law." To him, "the central function of punishment is not to control crime, but to sustain and enhance solidarity."[6] The job of "an authority with power" is to "ensure respect for beliefs, tradition, and collective practices—namely to defend the common consciousness from all its enemies, from within as well as without."[7] When the authority recedes, society is left without legal means to enforce its norms. A passion for punishment—for the maintenance of solidarity—remains, but it can only be fulfilled by the people themselves. Thus anomie produces a dangerous feedback loop. Lawlessness breeds terror, which provokes the far greater terror of mass violence, as the crowd seeks to reassert the cherished norms threatened by the very state of terror they cannot help reinforcing.

Merton parses these ideas further. In his account, social cohesion is founded on two pillars: cultural structure and social structure. The cultural structure is "a set of normative values governing behavior which is common to members of a designated society or group." The social structure "consists of institutional norms which define and regulate the acceptable mode of reaching these values." When society functions well, cultural and social structure are integrated, producing organic solidarity.[8]

Like Durkheim, Merton sees crime in sociological terms. Aberrant behavior is "a symptom of dissociation between culturally prescribed aspirations and socially structured avenues for realizing these aspirations." Too much aberrant behavior makes for social instability and, ultimately, anomie "conceived as a breakdown in the cultural structure, occurring particularly when there is an acute disjunction between cultural norms and goals and the socially structured capabilities of members of the group to act in accord with them."[9]

One might argue that organic solidarity never existed or that it was greatly weakened before the revolution, per Leopold Haimson's theory of two polarizations. But I would argue that a modicum of solidarity existed even as the end of the monarchy approached. Tsarist Russia was not a lawless society. The court system functioned, and, more generally, the empire cohered in spite of its diversity. The semi-parliamentary system, though flawed in many respects, persisted. The police managed to maintain public order.

This organic solidarity was swept away by the revolution. The old hierarchical system of estates—and associated values, customs, and language—was dislodged in favor of new values of equality and freedom.[10] But these were always contested. In the resulting cultural confusion, the distinction between what was acceptable and what was unacceptable became blurred.

If culture became normless, then social structure lost the capacity to enforce institutional norms. The law became ambiguous, the court system malfunctioned, the police were ineffective, and violence became the most effective means to settle disputes. In other words, the two pillars that make society functional and integrated were broken, creating a state of anomie.

Historians have amply covered competition among diverse ideological orientations and political cultures. What I have tried to examine is how the mass of the people responded to the anomie fostered in part by that competition. Here, Durkheim's analysis is especially valuable because it takes seriously the psychology of the crowd under a state of anomie.

Durkheim sees a deeper meaning in the collective action of the crowd. It may look irrational, yet mob justice is not "personal vengeance." It is punishment and therefore "vengeance for something sacred which we vaguely feel is more or less outside and above us."[11]

> It would indeed be mistaken to believe that vengeance is mere wanton cruelty. It may very possibly constitute by itself an automatic, purposeless reaction, an emotional and senseless impulse, and an unreasoned compulsion to destroy. But in fact, what tends to destroy was a threat to us. Therefore in reality it constitutes a veritable act of defense, albeit instinctive and unreflecting. We wreak vengeance only upon what has done us harm, and what has done us harm is always dangerous. The instinct for revenge is, after all, merely a heightened instinct of self-preservation in the face of danger. . . . It strikes somewhat at random, a prey to the unseeing forces that urge it on, and with nothing to curb its accesses of rage.[12]

These passages insightfully describe the meaning and dynamics of mob justice. But at best, mob justice empowered the people of Petrograd fleetingly. The momentary solidarity it produced dissolved quickly, with each of the aggrieved reverting to his or her atomized state. Mob justice, like the criminal acts inspiring it, therefore served as another source of anomie.

Russia as a Failed State

The theory of the failed state is urgently needed in today's world. As the political scientist Jean-Germain Gros puts it, "If the main existential threat to life, liberty, and the pursuit of happiness in the twentieth century was the all-powerful state (Leviathan), in the twenty-first century the primary menace is the all-powerless, or failed, state."[13]

Max Weber defines the state as "a political organization that wields exclusive coercive power over a large area and group of people, which power it uses to tax, maintain internal order, make war, peacefully engage other states (i.e., practice diplomacy), deliver social services, and protect property rights."[14] This exclusive access to coercive power, a monopoly on the legitimate use of violence, means "that only the state is permitted to possess the means of implementing its claim, and that only the state is capable of shutting down new sources of violence if all else fails." In other words, "no force, no state."[15]

If the monopoly over coercive power is one of the essential qualities of the state, legitimacy is another, since people and non-state agencies have to accept the right of the state to exercise coercion to guarantee the law. Legitimacy is integrally connected with legal rule. As Andreas Anter explains, "State rule is 'rule by virtue of legality,' by virtue of belief in the validity of legal *statute* and the appropriate juridical 'competence' founded upon rationally devised rules."[16] Weber summarizes the function of the state as follows:

> The basic functions of the "state" are: the enactment of law (legislative function); the protection of personal safety and public order (police); the protection of vested rights (administration of justice); the cultivation of hygienic, educational, social-welfare, and other cultural in-

terests (the various branches of administration); and, last but not least, the organized armed protection against outside attack (military administration). These basic functions are either totally lacking under primitive conditions, or they lack any form of rational order. They are performed, instead, by amorphous ad hoc groups or they are distributed among a variety of groups such as the household, the kinship group, the neighborhood associations, the rural commune, and completely voluntary associations formed for some specific purpose. Furthermore, private association enters domains of action which we are used to regard exclusively as the sphere of political associations.[17]

Here Weber's distinction between primitive conditions and modern rational order merges with Durkheim's distinction between mechanical and organic solidarity.

Of the political goods that the state provides, "none is as critical as the supply of security, especially human security."[18] In addition to protecting the territory from outside invasion, one of the most important tasks that the state is expected to perform is "to prevent crime and any related dangers to domestic human security; and to enable citizens to resolve their disputes with the state and with their fellow inhabitants without recourse to arms or other forms of physical coercion."[19]

The Russian state that emerged after the February Revolution failed to meet these criteria. Under dual power, no one body enjoyed a monopoly on the legitimate use of force. Nor did either the Provisional Government or the Petrograd Soviet enjoy legitimacy. Corporate groups within these institutions refused to subordinate themselves to the law. What Weber describes as primitive conditions corresponded to the situation in Petrograd during the Russian Revolution.

Rampant criminal violence is an important indicator of state failure. "As state authority weakens and fails," Robert Rotberg writes, "so lawlessness becomes more apparent. Criminal gangs take over the streets of the cities. Arms and drug trafficking become more common. Ordinary police forces become paralyzed. Anomic behaviors become the norm."[20] Such was the case in Petrograd, where citizens responded to police ineptitude by forming housing committees and contracting with soldiers to secure their buildings and neighborhoods. In the working-class districts, it was not the official police, but the nongovernment forces of the workers' militias and Red Guards that maintained public order. Where effective private policing was not available—that is, everywhere outside working-class neighborhoods—citizens' frustrations exploded in mob violence.

The Bolsheviks inherited the quickly failing state. Witnessing the acceleration of the disintegration of the state, however, they reasserted the monopoly of coercive power, reversed the decentralized centrifugal forces into central control, integrated the police power into the newly created Cheka, and established a one-party dictatorship by eliminating political opponents. The Bolsheviks thus wrested control over the means of coercion, but they never pursued the other quality that Weber cited as essential to the state: legitimacy. In revolutionary terms, that would have required democracy and diffusion of power. These were sacrificed so that order might be restored.

Psychological Sources of Violence

Popular violence in Russia predates the revolution. Mark Steinberg interprets street violence under the tsar as an expression against "the oppressive and aggressive world—a world of 'daily humiliations.'"[21] But while violence may at one time have been a form of resistance, after the revolution, it became something else.

One must recognize the fundamental differences of criminal violence between the prerevolutionary period and the revolutionary period. In the first place, crime during the revolution was qualitatively more violent and quantitatively exponentially more numerous. If the episodes of street violence that Steinberg talks about were knife-wielding fights, bar brawls, and sex crimes, then they were outshone in the revolutionary period by gun toting, brazen robberies, and cold-blooded murders. There was also a shift in power relations between criminals and the law-enforcement agencies. After the oppressive regime was overthrown and freedom and equality were, at least in theory, the major fruits of the February Revolution, why did crime shoot up, if crime was a form of resistance? We must look to other explanations, such as those provided by Durkheim and Merton. Violent crime, mob justice, and alcohol pogroms were reactions to anomie.

The carnage of World War I also contributed to the brutalization of people's psychology. Those most powerfully affected were the soldiers themselves. As Joshua Sanborn writes, military training in any army aims to "desensitize" soldiers to acts of violence through strict hierarchical discipline, emphasis on the techniques of killing (aim four meters above your target from four hundred meters away), and the placement of killing in a larger symbolic context (for the fatherland).[22] On battlefields, soldiers witnessed the results of atrocities: corpses lying on the ground and mutilated body parts scattered around. Fedor Stepun asked, "In the name of God, tell me, is it really possible to see all of this and not go out of your mind?" Then he answered his own question: "Yes, in fact. It turns out that it is possible and not only is it possible not to go out of your mind, but much more, it is possible to eat, drink, and sleep on the very same day, and possible even not to dream about it afterwards."[23] It is hardly surprising that, if the battleground was normal, soldiers had trouble functioning normally in civilian life.

This psychological brutalization happened at an unprecedented scale. It affected all countries engaged in the war. The collective violence throughout Europe in this era must be understood in this context. In the case of Russia, the rigid hierarchy between officers and soldiers, and the exceptional brutality of training characterized by hazing, likely made the situation even worse.[24]

Soldiers and deserters brought their distorted mind-set home. S. S. Ostroumov, a noted Soviet criminologist, wrote, "During the war years, the value of human life has fallen to the lowest degree. The mass murders on the battlefields make many people 'accustomed' to similar affairs, and thus crimes against life are raised to the maximum."[25] Psychiatrist E. K. Krasnuchkin wrote, "In the psyche of each participant in the war, removed from their hearth, tossed about from place to place, gladly preserving their life by ending the life of another, . . . living in constant danger, protecting themselves not only with weapons, but also with lies and deception, . . . primitive instincts must naturally be aroused."[26] A similar process of psychological brutalization affected evacuees, many of whom witnessed mass killing, pillage, and rape and were left either traumatized or desensitized.

It is less clear, however, just how the war affected the minds of civilians. But as we have seen, they experienced other sources of psychological change. Freedom was, in a sense, the culprit. On March 5, the day after the February revolution ended, *Malenkaia gazeta* declared, "Freedom occurs when the people are above their own government."[27] At a glance, many lovers of freedom will share this sentiment. But well-adjusted citizens in free states tend to recognize that their societies are more liberal than libertarian—

that freedom is not complete but instead comes with reasonably justified limits. As the Scottish Enlightenment philosopher Adam Ferguson put it, "Liberty or Freedom is not, as the origin of the name may seem to imply, an exemption from all restraints, but rather the most effectual applications of every just restraint to all members of a free society whether they be magistrates or subjects."[28] Likewise, Durkheim wrote, "Liberty is the fruit of regulation."[29]

The residents of Petrograd may not have understood this. Their zeal for the greatest possible diffusion of power, and their attempts to overturn all existing forms of social restraint, are in some ways understandable. But the change they demanded was truly vertiginous. Mob justice, after all, exemplified what the urban poor interpreted as their freedom. This was the "people's court"—their will, unconstrained. Mob justice also reflected their anger at the realization that freedom was, for practical purposes, being denied as a result of crime, economic collapse, and the breakdown of social services. Their pent-up rage found its outlet. To paraphrase Frantz Fanon, "Violence was under their skin."

Alcohol pogroms were another important example of freedom gone awry. Among soldiers and the urban poor, many associated freedom above all with freedom to drink. Since 1914, they had lived under prohibition. It was inevitable that once the security surrounding the accumulated alcohol stores grew lax, the masses would grasp what they felt was rightfully theirs.

Durkheim was remarkably prescient in recognizing how an anomic society might attempt to restore solidarity. In the essay "Two Laws of Penal Evolution," he noted that the intensity of punishment is greater in absolute governments. These governments "become invested with a kind of religiosity," he wrote. "Where absolute government exists, political offenses are seen as sacrilegious and are violently repressed, and all offenses tend to become political and are seen as attacks on the sovereign power."[30] This is precisely how the Bolsheviks responded to social breakdown. They not only deployed extreme coercion but also declared all crime counterrevolutionary, merging state violence with the quasi-religious ideology of communism.

The Significance of Violence

What is the significance of the violence committed during the Russian Revolution? I would argue that it played a crucial role. The violence committed by criminals as well as the urban poor in the form of mob justice greatly contributed to the disintegration of society, laying the groundwork for the Bolshevik seizure of power. Contrary to Bolshevik expectations, however, criminal violence and mob justice continued to escalate, and the explosion of the alcohol pogroms pushed Russia further into the state of anomie. Noting the nexus between war and revolution, Peter Holoquist argues that "only in the aftermath of 1917 did violence become a regular and constitutive feature of *everyday political life*."[31] It would be more accurate to say that violence became a regular and constitutive feature of *everyday life,* period. Eventually, the Bolsheviks used unprecedented coercion to suppress crime, but by characterizing ordinary crime as counterrevolutionary, and relegating the task of combating crime to the Cheka, they imposed their own hegemonic power over the citizenry.

History does not allow us to test counterfactuals. We cannot know if a less violent revolution would have resulted in a less violent postrevolutionary state. We do know that Bolshevik ideology envisioned utopian popular self-rule, with citizens responsible for their own safety and that of others. We know that, when they first took power, the Bolsheviks believed that security would arise naturally from the realization of their ideological goals, with no need of police or courts or prisons. And we know that nothing like this occurred. There could hardly be a more eloquent expression of the role of ordinary people in shaping political change. Much of what the Bolsheviks stood for was swept away as they responded to public rage. It was not so much tsarists and capitalists who, by dint of counterrevolution, undermined the free and equal socialist peace. It was instead everyday people, unorganized citizens with no politics to speak of but with frustration in their hearts.

To say that the Soviet police state was a product of events rather than intention is not to pass any sort of judgment on Bolshevik aims but rather to recognize an abiding dilemma of governance. As Gros writes, "States abate violence when they effectively monopolize its means, but this capacity also enables states to visit untold violence on those they do not like, including the innocent."[32] Having endured unprecedented state violence in the twentieth century, humanity is now confronted with the products of a more anarchic world: ethnic violence, civil wars, mass displacement, and terrorism. We are left still to fill gaps between, on the one hand, the absent or failed state and, on the other, the Leviathan.

ABBREVIATIONS

Newspapers

BV:	*Birzhevyia vedomosti*
Ekho:	*Ekho*
GD:	*Gazeta drug*
GDV:	*Gazeta dlia vsekh*
GK:	*Gazeta-Kopeika*
IZ:	*Izvestiia Petrogradskogo Soveta rabochikh i soldatskikh deputatov*
Iz KPZh:	*Izvestiia Komiteta Petrogradskikh zhurnalistov*
KG:	*Krasnaia gazeta*
MG:	*Malen'kaia gazeta*
NPG:	*Novaia Petrogradskaia gazeta*
NV:	*Novoe vremia*
NVCh:	*Novyi vechernyi chas*
NVek:	*Nash vek*
NZh:	*Novaia zhizn'*
PEkho:	*Petrogradskoe ekho*
PG:	*Petrogradskaia gazeta*
PGol:	*Petrogradskii golos*
PL:	*Petrogradskii listok*
Prv:	*Pravda*
Pt:	*Pieter*
PVes:	*Petrogradskii vestnik*
PVP:	*Petrogradskaia vecherniaia pochta*
PZh:	*Petrogradskaia zhizn'*
Rch	*Rech'*
VCh:	*Vechernii chas*

Vech:	*Vecher*
VGS:	*Vestnik gorodskogo samoupravleniia*
VN:	*Vechernyia novosti*
VO:	*Vechernie ogni*
VPoch:	*Vecherniaia pochta*
VSlo:	*Vechernee slovo*
VV:	*Vechernee vremia*
VVed:	*Vechernyia vedomosti*
VZvez:	*Vecherniaia zvezda*
VZvon:	*Vechernii zvon*

Document Collections

Dekrety Sovietskoi vlasti:
Dikrety Sovetskoi vlasti o Petrograde, 25 oktiabria (7 noiabria) 1917 g.–29 dekabria 1918 g. (Leningrad: Lenizdat, 1986).

Petrogradskii sovet:
Petrogradskii sovet rabochikhi i soldatskikh deputatov v 1917 godu: protokoly, stenogrammy i otchety, rezoliutsii, postanovleniia obshchikh sobranii, sobranii sektsii, zasedanii, Ispolnitel'nogo komiteta i fraktsii 17 fevralia–15 oktiabria 1917 goda, vol. 1 *(17 fevralia–31 marta 1917 goda)* (Leningrad: Nauka, 1991).

PVRK:
Petrogradskii Voenno-Revoliutsionnyi Komitet: Dokumenty i materialy, 3 vols. (Moscow: Nauka, 1966).

RSP:
Raionnye sovety Petrograda v 1917 godu: Protokoly, rezoliutsii, postanovlenia obshchikh sobranii zasedanii ispolnitel'nykh komitetov, 3 vols. (Leningrad: Nauka, 1964–1966).

Revoliutsionnoe dvizhenie:
Velikaia Oktiabr'skaia Sotsialisticheskaia Revoliutsiia: Dokumenty i materialy, 6 vols. (Moscow, 1957–1959), vol. 1, *Revoliutsionnoe dvizhenie v Rossii posle sverzheniia samoderzhaviia* (Moscow, 1957).

NOTES

Introduction

1   Kolonitskii, *Simvoly vlasti i bor'ba za vlasti*, 57–87.
2   *VSlo*, 3 / 23 / 18 (4 / 3 / 18). For abbreviations for newspaper titles, see the "Abbreviations" section at the end of this book. Newspaper dates follow the month / day / year format. This reference, therefore, is *Vechernee slovo*, March 23 (old style) and April 3 (new style), 1918. For an explanation of the use of calendars, see "Note on Calendar and Transliteration" in the front matter.
3   For the most recent comprehensive review of historiography on the Russian Revolution, see Wade, "Revolution at One Hundred." Outside the Soviet Union / Russia, historians writing in English have stood at the forefront of the study of the Russian Revolution. This is not to deny the importance of other historians, especially in France, Germany, Israel, and Japan. A survey of historiography, though interesting and important, is beyond the scope of this book. I would like to add, however, that my initial work followed the historiographical trend of Japanese historians in the 1960s. I would be remiss if I failed to acknowledge scholarly debts to Japanese historians.
4   The list of these monographs is too numerous to be cited here. For more details, see Wade, *Russian Revolution*; Wade, "Revolution at One Hundred"; and Acton, Cherniaev, and Rosenberg, *Critical Companion to the Russian Revolution*.
5   Historians began to explore the revolution in the provinces, following the tradition of social history. For individual monographs and articles, see Wade, "Revolution at One Hundred," 30–33.
6   Wade, "Revolution at One Hundred," 19. The most important work for this approach is Figes and Kolonitskii, *Interpreting the Russian Revolution*.
7   Smith, "Russian Workers and the Politics of Social Identity," 1.
8   This trend was ushered in by Peter Holquist's pioneering book, *Making War, Forging Revolution* (Cambridge, MA: Harvard University Press, 2002). At the time of this writing, five books have now been published in the Russia's Great War and Revolution series: vol. 1, *Russia's Culture in War and Revolution* (books 1 and 2); vol. 2, *The Empire and Nationalism at War;* and vol. 3, *Russia's Home Front in War and Revolution* (books 1 and 2).

9   This is not the place for a comprehensive review of Soviet historiography of the Russian Revolution. I should note, however, the importance of active publication efforts in the 1920s before the historical profession fell victim to Stalinist ideological conformity. My description here is limited only to the period after the 1960s, when historians in the Soviet Union began to produce serious works shaking off strict ideological shackles.

10   Suny, "Toward a Social History of the October Revolution," 34. Suny revised his view in his 1994 article under the influence of the linguistic turn. He stated: "No longer can social categories and identities be taken as given as fairly stable or as expressing clear and objective interests emanating from their essential nature." Suny, "Revision and Retreat in the Historiography of 1917," 182.

11   Gatrell, *Whole Empire Walking*, 2.

12   I first proposed the need to study crime and police in an article and a book published in Japanese in the 1980s: "Hanzai, keisatsu, samosūdo" and *Roshia kakumeika petorogurādo no shimin seikatsu*. In English, I published "Crime, Police, and Mob Justice in Petrograd during the Russian Revolution of 1917," "Crime and Police in Revolutionary Petrograd," and "Gosudarstvennost', obshchestvennost' and klassovost'." I also published two articles in Russian in 1994 and 2001. While I was the first and the only scholar who examined the Russian Revolution from the point of view of crime and police in the 1980s and 1990s, my call to examine the Russian Revolution from this perspective has been answered in three recent works by Russian historians: Musaev, "Byt gorozhan"; Musaev, *Prestupnost'*; and Ereshchenko, "Prestupnost'."

13   Weissman, "Regular Police in Tsarist Russia," 56.

14   Aksenov, "Povsednevnaia zhizn' Petrograda i Moskvy," 29.

15   Sarah Badcock uses "ordinary people" as opposed to the elite, eschewing "lower class," *narod* (people), or *trudiashchiesia* (working people). See Badcock, *Politics and the People in Revolutionary Russia*, 5.

16   See also the insightful analysis of the urban poor in St. Petersburg in Steinberg, "Blood in the Air;" Gerasimov, "Subalterns Speak Out"; Petersen, "'Not Intended for the Rich.'" In analyzing spontaneous riots at the end of 1917 and at the beginning of 1918, V. V. Kanishchev characterizes the main participants in riots as marginalized *meshchane* [petty bourgeoisie]. But *meshchane* excludes vast masses of people in the service sector and artisans in small workshops. See Kanishchev, *Russkii bunt*, 134–135.

17   Gayatri Chakravorty Spivak, "Scattered Speculations on the Subaltern and the Popular," in *Postcolonial Studies* 8, no. 4 (2005): 475–476, quoted in Gerasimov, "Subalterns Speak Out," 52. I am using the language developed by historians of postcolonial studies or subaltern studies, although I am reluctant to categorize the urban poor as subalterns.

18   Gerasimov, "Subalterns Speak Out," 52, 53.

19   Gerasimov, "Subalterns Speak Out," 54.

20   Steinberg, "Blood in the Air," 99–100.

21   Clinard, "Theoretical Implications of Anomie and Deviant Behavior," 3–9.

22   Merton, *Social Theory and Social Structure*, 186–193.

23 Durkheim, *Division of Labor,* 66.
24 Anter, *Max Weber's Theory of the Modern State,* 26, 33, 58.
25 Rotberg, "Failed States, Collapsed States, Weak States," 3.
26 Rotberg, "Failed States, Collapsed States, Weak States," 3.
27 Rotberg, "Failed States, Collapsed States, Weak States," 6.

1. Prelude to Revolution

1 Munro, *Most Intentional City.* For a history of St. Petersburg, see Lincoln, *Sunlight at Midnight.* For its cultural history, see Volkov, *St. Petersburg.* For its architecture, see Shvidkovsky, *St. Petersburg.*
2 Volkov, *St. Petersburg,* 6.
3 Quoted in Volkov, *St. Petersburg,* 11.
4 See "Naselenie," *Sankt-Peterburg, Petrograd, Leningrad,* 417; Bater, *St. Petersburg,* 310–311; *Petrograd po perepisi 15 dekabria 1910 goda,* Issue 1, 39. According to this census, the exact number in Petrograd was 1,905,589 in 1910. According to Z. G. Frenkel', the population of Petrograd at the end of 1913 was 2,073,600, and by the end of 1914, it grew to 2,132,900, but in the middle of 1914, prior to the war, it was 2,103,000. Frenkel', *Petrograd perioda voiny i revoliutsii,* 10, 12.
5 Honored citizens were those who were recognized by the government as contributing to society but were not recognized as members of the nobility. They were, however, ranked above merchants. Merchants were only those members who belonged to guilds. Thus a vast majority of those who engaged in trade were excluded.
6 Orlovsky, "Lower Middle Strata in 1917," 529–530; Orlovsky, "Lower Middle Strata in Revolutionary Russia," 248–268.
7 Wildman, *End of the Russian Imperial Army,* 124. According to Wildman, the number of soldiers in Petrograd was 180,200, and 151,900 were in the suburbs. According to Martynov and Shliapnikov, the number of soldiers in Petrograd was approximately 160,000. Martynov, *Tsarskaia armiia v fevral'skom perevorote,* 58; Shliapnikov, *Semnadtsatyi god,* 1:160. According to Kochakov, it was 271,000. Kochakov, "Petrograd v gody pervoi mirovoi voiny i fevral'skoi burzhuazno-demokraticheskoi revoliutsii," 61. This figure is based on the data of the commissary section of the army and inflated, since it included servicemen in administrative units. According to the data given by the Military Commission of the State Duma, it was 170,000. According to the materials in the Extraordinary Investigation Commission of the Provisional Government, there were 180,000 soldiers as of February 1, 1917. See Burdzhalov, *Vtoraia russkaia revoliutsiia,* 96–97. There were 69,800 in Tsarskoe Selo, 70,300 in Petergof, Oranienbaum, and Strel'na; 33,900 in Krasnoe Selo; and 21,700 in Gatchina.
8 Bater, *St. Petersburg,* 370. Also see Kruze and Kutsentov, "Naselenie Peterburga," 138–139.
9 A major thoroughfare was called a "prospect," distinguished from an ordinary street (*ulitsa*), which was further distinguished from a smaller lane (*pereulok*).

10 Almedingen, *My St. Petersburg*, 111. For St. Petersburg before the war, also see Almedingen, *Tomorrow Will Come;* Williams, *Russia of the Russians;* Dobson, *St. Petersburg.*

11 Iukhneva, *Etnicheskii sostav i etnosotsial'naia struktura naseleniia Peterburga*, 122–123.

12 Kruze and Kutsentov, "Naselenie Peterburga," 110–111.

13 Bater, *St. Petersburg*, 373–377.

14 Haimson, "Problem of Social Stability in Urban Russia"; Haimson, "Problem of Political and Social Stability."

15 See Hasegawa, *February Revolution: Petrograd, 1917*, and its revised edition, *February Revolution: The End of the Tsarist Regime and the Birth of Dual Power*, chaps. 1–11.

16 Hasegawa, "Duma Committee, the Provisional Government."

17 The safest major capital in Europe was Berlin, a city of more than two million, where the convictions for murders from 1900 to 1914 were between 0 and 13. Blackbourn, *Long Nineteenth Century*, 373. The convictions for murders in London were somewhere between three and five per 100,000. Manual Eisner, "Long-Term Historical Trends in Violent Crime," 87.

18 Konstantinov, *Banditskii Peterburg-98*, 10–11; "Politsiia," *Entsiklopedicheskii solvar'* (Blokgauz-Efron) 24:328; *S.-Peterburgskaia stolichnaia politsiia i gradonachal'stvo: Kratkii istoricheskii ocherk* (St. Petersburg: Tovarishchestvo R. Golike i A. Bul'borg, 1903), 1–52.

19 For notorious swindlers such as Son'ka-Zolotaia Ruchka (Son'ka Golden Hand), Anna Zilbershtein (Aniutka-Ved'ma), and Ol'ga Zeldovna Shtein, see Konstantinov, *Banditskii Peterburg-98*, 26–38. Also see Sidorov, "Voina pervaia," 1.

20 Kostiukovskii, "Istoriia"; Volkov, *Violent Entrepreneurs*, 56, 60. For horse thieves, see Konstantinov, *Banditskii Peterburg-98*, 39–40.

21 In the empire as a whole, taking the number for 1899 as the base, the number of crimes rose to 120 percent in 1905, 127 percent in 1906, 142 percent in 1907, and 143 percent in 1908, indicating a 43 percent increase in 1908 compared with 1899. E. N. Tarnovskii, "Dvizhenie prestupnosti v Rossiiskoi imperii za 1899–1908 gody," *Zhurnal ministerstva iusitsii*, no. 9, 1909, 60, quoted in Nazarenko, *MVD*, 34.

22 McReynolds, *Murder Most Russian*, 20. According to Ostroumov, the number of murders indicted to district courts increased to 110 percent in 1906 (taking 1899 as the base), 93 percent in 1907, and 91 percent in 1908. The number of murders rose from 30,942 in 1909, to 31,113 in 1910, 32,500 in 1911, 33,879 in 1912, and 34,438 in 1913, an increase of 12 percent compared with 1909. Ostroumov, *Prestupnost' i ee prichiny v dorevoliutsionnoi Rossii*, 67, 69.

23 Neuberger, *Hooliganism*, 289. The St. Petersburg District Court covers an area beyond the city of St. Petersburg. Therefore, these numbers should not be mistaken for the crime numbers within the city of St. Petersburg.

24 Nazarenko, *MVD*, 36.

25 See Neuberger, *Hooliganism*. For prerevolutionary street crime, see Steinberg, "Blood in the Air," 97–119. Also see Ostroumov, *Prestupnost'*, 86–90.

26 Sanborn, "Mobilization of 1914," 277; Kanishchev, *Russkii bunt*, 42.

27 Kanishchev, *Russkii bunt*, 37. See also Sanborn, "Mobilization of 1914," 275–279; Sanborn, *Drafting the Russian Nation*, 30–31. The most detailed descriptions of all these riots are given by Kanishchev, *Russkii bunt*, 36–43. Riots were repeated in the mobilization of 1915 as well, though they were not widespread and were smaller than those in 1914. Kanishchev, *Russkii bunt*, 44–46.

28 *BV*, 7 / 23 / 14; Kanishchev, *Russkii bunt*, 43; Lohr, *Nationalizing the Russian Empire*, 13–14.

29 Sanborn, *Drafting the Russian Nation*, 31.

30 Lohr, *Nationalizing the Russian Empire*, 31–36, 45–46.

31 For this, see Gatrell, *Whole Empire Walking*; Sanborn, *Drafting the Russian Nation*; and especially Lohr, *Nationalizing the Russian Empire*, 145–148.

32 Chagadaeva, "Sukhoi zakon i chernyi rynok"; see the same article in Politiko, http://politiko.ua/blogpost75564; also see Pashkov, "Antialkogol'naia kampaniia."

33 Ereshchenko, "Prestupnost'," 41–42; Berman, "P'ianstvo i prestupnost'." Criminologists were divided about the causes of the general decline in crime for the first one and a half years after the war. While E. N. Tarnovskii attributes it to the prohibition and patriotism, M. N. Gernet and D. P. Rodin believe that the decline of the male population due to mobilization and the poor criminal records accounted for the decline of crime. See Kowalsky, "Transforming Society," 346–348.

34 Chagadaeva, "Sukhoi zakon i chernyi rynok."

35 Narsky and Khmelevskaya, "Alcohol in Russia," 398–401. According to Narsky and Khmelevskaya, during the war the sale of alcohol in pharmaceutical establishments grew ten- to twentyfold. Compared with 600 cases reported in 1913, the cases of moonshine increased to 1,825 in the second half of 1914, and 5,707 in 1915. For alcohol and its impact on society, see George Snow, "Perceptions of the Link between Alcoholism and Crime in Pre-Revolutionary Russia," *Criminal Justice History* 8 (1987): 37–51; Laura L. Phillips, *Bolsheviks and the Bottle: Drink and Worker Culture in St. Petersburg, 1900–1929* (DeKalb: Northern Illinois University Press, 2000); and Kat Transchel, *Under the Influence: Working Class Drinking, Temperance, and Cultural Revolution in Russia, 1895–1932* (Pittsburg: University of Pittsburgh Press, 2006).

36 Ereshchenko, "Prestupnost'," 43–48.

37 Ereshchenko, "Prestupnost'," 60.

38 Ereshchenko, "Prestupnost'," 65.

39 Ereshchenko, "Prestupnost'," 60–61.

40 *GK*, 11 / 3 / 16; *PL*, 10 / 13 / 16.

41 Ereshchenko, "Prestupnost'," 63–64.

42 Ereshchenko, "Prestupnost'," 74.

43 Ereshchenko, "Prestupnost'," 72–74. Abram L'vovich Zhivotovskii was a board member of the Russian-Asian Bank. As for von Shrippen's raid of Zhivotovskii's apartment, see *GK*, 11 / 4 / 16; 11 / 16 / 16; 11 / 20 / 16.

44 Ereshchenko, "Prestupnost'," 75–76.

45 Ereshchenko, "Prestupnost'," 76. In 1916, the police arrested a gang of thieves, led by a peasant woman from Samara, Aleksandra Iakovlevna Kukoleva, known

as Auntie Sasha, and her seventeen-year-old son, Nikolai Kukolev, and six underage children. This gang specialized in break-ins, committing more than forty-two burglaries. Ereshchenko, "Prestupnost'," 77. According to Ostroumov, from 1911 to 1915, 55 percent of imprisoned children younger than seventeen years old were orphans, semi-orphans, or illegitimate children. Ostroumov, *Prestupnost'*, 87.

46 Ereshchenko, "Prestupnost'," 80, 82.

47 M. N. Gernet, *Prestupnost' i samoubiistvo vo vremia voiny i posle nee* (Moscow: Izdatel'stvo TsSU SSR, 1927), 141; D. P. Rodin, "Statistika prestupnosti vo vremia i posle Evropeiskoi voiny v raznykh stranakh," *Problemy prestupnosti*, no. 1 (1926): 176; both quoted in Kowalsky, "Transforming Society," 352–353.

48 Ereshchenko, "Prestupnost'," 86–87.

49 Ereshchenko, "Prestupnost'," 92–93.

2. Crime on the Rise

1 *Ogonek* (no. 12, April 2, 1917, 14), was a weekly illustrated magazine, started in 1899 by S. M. Propper, as the literary-artistic supplement of *Birzhevyia vedomosti*, a daily newspaper aimed at a middle-class readership. From 1902, it became an independent illustrated journal with a circulation of 120,000. http://www.nounb.sci-nnov.ru/vExp/33.php (accessed June 20, 2016).

2 *PL*, 3/11/17. The three main newspapers I draw on are *Petrogradskii listok* (*PL*), *Petrogradskaia gazeta* (*PG*), and *Gazeta-Kopeika* (*GK*). According to Louise McReynolds, *PL* tended to be more sensational than *PG*. The first two represented a moderate-liberal position amenable to a middle-class readership. In 1916, *PL*'s circulation was 128,500, and *PG*'s was 50,000. *GK*, which aimed at the working class, had a circulation of 220,000 in 1913. McReynolds, *The News under Russia's Old Regime*, chaps. 3, 6, and 10; for the circulations, see 297. Neuberger, *Hooliganism*, 15–22. In addition, I occasionally cite *Birzhevyia vedomosti* (*BV*), aimed at middle-class readership with a 1916 circulation of 57,000, and the more conservative, often anti-Semitic, *Novoe vremia* (*NV*) and its evening paper, *Vechernee vremia* (*VV*). In 1916, *Novoe vremia*'s circulation totaled 76,000.

3 *PL*, 4/17/17, 4/18/17, 4/20/17; *GK*, 4/18/17; *PG*, 4/18/17. Von Schrippen's raid in Zhivotovskii's apartment was reported in *GK*, 11/4/16, 11/16/16, 11/20/16. This murder case is famous enough to be mentioned in Aleksandr Solzhenitsyn, *Krasnoe Koleso* (Paris: YMCA Press, 1991), 2:400.

4 *PL*, 5/22/17.

5 For the April crisis, see Wade, *Russian Revolution*, 83–84.

6 *Ogonek*, no. 24, June 25, 1917, 376.

7 In other gardens and parks, as well, many statues, including the statue of Heracles in the Alexander Garden, were toppled by hooligans and soldiers. Aksenov, "Povsednevnaia zhizn'," 92.

8 *Ogonek*, no. 26, July 7, 1917, 410–411; *Ogonek*, no. 32, August 20, 1917, 508.

9 Vrangel', *Vospominaniia ot krespostnogo prava do bol'shevikov*, 366. Also see Nikolai Punin's observation on street scenes in Nevskii in the September 1 entry

in his diary. Punin noted all walks of life mingling in Nevskii, "all these 'bourgeois,' the unrestrained soldiers in yellow boots, the innumerable merchants who set up shop right on the sidewalk, the prostitutes and brokers." He observed, "There isn't a social class or line of work that would refuse to be involved in speculations. You see some petty lieutenants whispering their propositions and prices to an impoverished Jew, you see ladies in white fur caps scribbling numbers and addresses into little address books under the diction of some kind of insufferable swindler, boys loiter near a group of people at the entrance to a café, dandies stroll along the street, prostitutes laugh and tug at the sleeves of men, and the men, who were, with an elegant gesture, sizing them up like horseflesh with a chuck under the chin, . . . satisfying themselves and becoming aroused . . . there it is, the revolutionary Nevsky Prospect; the capital of a great people in a time of troubles." Punin, *Diaries of Nikolai Punin,* 53–54.

10 *Ogonek,* no. 32, October 15, 1917, 683.

11 Hasegawa, *February Revolution* (1981), 287–288.

12 Kolonitskii, *Simvoly vlasti,* 20–21.

13 Ereshchenko, "Prestupnost'," 96–97.

14 Ereshchenko, "Prestupnost'," 94; Aksenov, "Militsiia," 3. For the Soviet interpretation, see Leiberov, *Na shturm samoderzhaviia,* 143.

15 For other thefts in the Rozhdestvenskii District and the Petrogradskii District, see Ereshchenko, "Prestupnost'," 97–98.

16 Ereshchenko, "Prestupnost'," 100–103; Nikolaev, *Revoliutsiia i vlast',* 513–514.

17 Aksenov, "Militsiia," 3; Jones, *Russia in Revolution,* 108–109; Nikolaev, "Vremennye sudy v Petrograde," 4–9. The majority of the destroyed courts of justice were located in the outskirts of the city; many courts survived the revolutionary destruction at the center. Challenging the prevailing view that it was the criminals who took the initiative of attacking the courts of justice to destroy the criminal records, Nikolaev argues that it was rather the insurgent soldiers and sailors who were the main culprits. The insurgents were interested in destroying the Okhrana files, but unable to distinguish between the Okhrana files and criminal files, they destroyed both.

18 Nikolaev, *Revoliutsiia i vlast',* 514; Ereshchenko, "Prestupnost'," 101; Kolonitskii, *Simvoly vlasti,* 32.

19 Kolonitskii, *Simvoly vlasti,* 32–33.

20 Jones, *Russia in Revolution,* 119; Kel'son, "Militsiia fevral'skoi revoliutsii," Pt 1: 164; Aksenov, "Militsiia," 4.

21 Nikolaev, *Revoliutsiia i vlast',* 515–516.

22 Nikolaev, *Revoliutsiia i vlast',* 516–517.

23 Nikolaev, *Revoliutsiia i vlast',* 517–518.

24 Attacks on wine cellars and vodka storages were reported at numerous places in the city, mostly in the central districts. The report indicated many soldiers and crowds were intoxicated. Nikolaev, *Revoliutsiia i vlast',* 518–519.

25 Nikolaev, *Revoliutsiia i vlast',* 519–520.

26 For instance, the wine cellar of the Arsenal was destroyed by the insurgents, and a group of insurgent workers dumped five barrels of spirits into Obvodnyi Canal

at the corner of Ligovskii Prospect and Obvodnyi Canal. Ereshchenko, "Prestupnost'," 140.

27 Nikolaev, *Revoliutsiia i vlast'*, 520.

28 Sain-Wittgenstein, *Dnevnik*, 81–82; Nikolaev, *Revoliutsiia i vlast'*, 520.

29 Nikolaev, *Revoliutsiia i vlast'*, 521.

30 TsGA SPb, f. 131, op. 1, d. 2, l. 2; M. Karaulov, "Prikaz po gorodu Petrograda," *Iz KPZh*, 3/4/17; also see Nikolaev, *Revoliutsiia i vlast'*, 522; Browder and Kerensky, *Russian Provisional Government*, 1:61–62. The reference to the "Provisional Government" is strange, since the Provisional Government was not formed until March 2. Either Karaulov considered the Duma Committee to be a provisional government when he issued the order, or he changed the body of the authorizing agency—either the Duma Committee or the Military Commission—to the Provisional Government when the order was printed on March 4.

31 *Iz KPZh*, 3/3/17; Nikolaev, *Revoliutsiia i vlast'*, 523; Browder and Kerensky, *Russian Provisional Government*, 1:62.

32 "Ne dopuskaite grabezhei," *IZ*, 2/28/17.

33 "Osteregaites' p'ianstva," *IZ*, 3/1/17.

34 "Registratsiia oruzhiia / revoliutsionnyi Petrograd," *IZ*, 3/2/17; Nikolaev, *Revoliutsiia i vlast'*, 526.

35 "K naseleniiu," *Iz KPZh*, 3/1/17; Nikolaev, *Revoliutsiia i vlast'*, 525.

36 Ereshchenko, "Prestupnost'," 142.

37 Ereshchenko, "Prestupnost'," 112. These statistics are by no means complete, since these numbers represented the data on only six days (April), thirty days (May), twenty-five days (June), twenty-one days (July), twenty-one days (August), thirty days (September), and twenty-five days (October).

38 The city militia inherited the tsarist police's reporting system. Each subdistrict commissariat, like each precinct of the tsarist police, reported each day to the city militia headquarters, which in turn assembled the reports in its *Journal of Events.*

39 Court records are from the Petrograd Trial Chamber (*Petrogradskaia sudebnaia palata*) and the courts of justice, which I did not use.

40 *PL*, 4/27/17, 4/29/17, 5/10/17, 5/17/17, 5/18/17, 5/19/17, 5/21/17, 6/8/17, 6/9/17, 6/17/17. "Stolichnye khishchniki" first appeared in *Petrogradskii listok* on April 26. According to *Petrogradskaia gazeta*, the number of reported thefts and robberies on June 15 was sixty. *PG*, 6/16/17.

41 *GK*, 7/6/17, 7/11/17.

42 *PL*, 7/16/17; *PG*, 7/16/17.

43 *PL*, 8/17/17; *GK*, 8/15/17.

44 For thefts in September, see *GK*, 9/2/17, 9/6/17, 9/7/17; *PL*, 9/12/17, 9/14/17.

45 *PL*, 10/1/17, 10/14/17, 10/18/17; *GK*, 10/3/17, 10/4/17, 10/8/17.

46 *PL*, 9/12/17, 9/14/17, 9/17/17, 9/19/17, 9/20/17; *GK*, 10/4/17, 10/12/17. For the theft in Vera Figner's apartment, see *PL*, 10/6/17.

47 *PL*, 4/11/17; Ereshchenko, "Prestupnost'," 116.

48 Ereshchenko, "Prestupnost'," 124–125.

49 Ereshchenko, "Prestupnost'," 125.

50 *PL*, 7/28/17.

51 Ereshchenko, "Prestupnost'," 125. For robberies that took place in October in the Admiralteiskii District, see TsGA SPb, f. 131, op. 1, d. 41, ll, 5–6ob, 7–8ob, 17–18ob. They are not included in Ereshchenko's sources, which indicate that Ereshchenko's meticulous searches in archival sources miss some.

52 Murder statistics reported in *Ves' Peterburg* are as follows:

Year	St. Petersburg	Suburbs	Monthly Average
1896	117	10	10.6
1899	127	17	10.8
1900	178	11	15.8
1902	156	16	14.3
1903	206	24	19.2

These figures were given to the author by Joan Neuberger.

53 *PL*, 5/19/17.

54 *PL*, 5/25/17. How the newspaper concluded that this was a rape victim was not indicated. But it reveals that *PL* either sensationalized the event, expressed the fear of widespread rapes, or stoked the fear of crime committed by Chinese.

55 *PL*, 8/12/17, 8/13/17.

56 *PL*, 8/29/17.

57 *BV*, 9/6/17.

58 The Seitola case also revealed that the Criminal Militia were pursuing detective work professionally and efficiently despite the difficulties faced during the revolution.

59 *PL*, 10/2/17, 10/4/17; *VV*, 10/4/17; *GK*, 10/5/17, 10/6/17.

60 *PL*, 5/3/17.

61 Aksenov, "Povsednevnaia zhizn'," 54–55.

62 Kowalsky, "Transforming Society," 353.

63 Aksenov, "Povsednevnaia zhizn'," 53–54.

64 Aksenov, "Povsednevnaia zhizn'," 107–110, 116–118, 121–123.

65 K. I. Globachev, "Pravda russkoi revoliutsii: vospominaniia byvshego nachal'nika Petrogradskogo okhrannogo otdeleniia," Bakhmeteff Archives, 131–132.

66 *Ogonek*, no. 41, October 22, 1917, 17.

67 *PL*, 4/16/17.

68 *GK*, 6/14/17.

69 *GK*, 8/5/17.

70 Some came from Dvinsk and Revel, and all the playing cards they had with them were confiscated. Among them was a Jew who had twelve hundred decks of cards. *PL*, 8/18/17, 8/19/17. Singling out a Jew here seems to indicate the paper's anti-Jewish leaning.

71 GARF, f. 5141, op. 1, d. 35, ll, 10, 10ob, 11, 12, 12ob, 13; GARF, f. 5141, op. 1, d. 15, ll, 4a, 4b, 4v, 4g, 4d, 4zh, 4e, 4z; GARF, f. 5141, op. 1, d. 15, ll, 8, 8ob.

72 GARF, f. 5124, op. 1, d. 35, ll. 24, 26, 26ob, 29, 29ob, 30, 34ob, 35, 35ob, 36, 36ob, 37, 37ob, 38, 38ob, 39, 39ob. It is important to note that this order to shut down

the gambling club came from the military authority, not from the militia, indicating that by then the Petrograd Military District assumed direct responsibility for the security of Petrograd. On this, see Chapter 4.

73 GARF, f. 5141, op. 1, d. 35, 54ob; TsGA SPb, f. 31, op. 1, d. 250, ll. 12–12ob.

74 Kel'son, "Padenie vremennogo pravitel'stva," 200. Boris Savinkov was a former Socialist Revolutionary terrorist who turned into a right-wing SR leader supporting the war. He became a confidant of Kerenskii and was appointed as the deputy minister of war. He was instrumental in introducing Kornilov to Kerenskii, and he played an important role in the negotiations between them during the Kornilov Affair. When Kornilov initiated the offensive against the capital, he appointed Savinkov as the military governor of Petrograd. When Kerenskii refused to support Kornilov, Savinkov resigned from the Provisional Government.

75 *GK,* 8/8/17.

76 TsGA SPb, f. 131, op. 1, d. 3, l. 61. In the First Vyborgskii Subdistrict alone, fifty-four cases of detention due to drunkenness were reported from October 1 to October 25; see TsGA SPb, f. 131, op. 1, d. 61, ll. 1–48.

77 Narsky and Khmelevskaya, "Alcohol in Russia," 399.

78 Ereshchenko, "Prestupnost'," 139.

79 *RSP,* 1:200–201, 349. For the reaction of other district soviets to drunkenness, see *RSP,* 2:158, 179 (Petergofskii District Soviet); 3:47 (Petrogradskii District Soviet); 270, 323 (interdistrict conference of district soviets).

80 *GK,* 7/4/17.

81 *Perepis' 1910 goda,* no. 2. The largest contingents were in the Spasskii District (109), followed by the Narvskii District (103), the Moskovskii District (74), the Petrogradskii District (74), and the Rozhdestvenskii District (71).

82 Lebina and Shkarovskii, *Prostitutsiia v Peterburge,* 23, 37.

83 Lebina and Shkarovskii, *Prostitutsiia v Peterburge,* 32.

84 TsGIA SPb, f. 569, op. 12, d. 1519, ll. 6–7. This report was sent to the city governor's office, which was supposed to have been closed down, but as this report shows, this office was in some ways still functioning. (More on this in Chapter 4.)

85 *PL,* 3/12/17.

86 *VGS,* 7/2/17. "Syphilis and Gonorrhea Rates Have Risen Sharply in US, CDC Says," https://www.statnews.com/2016/10/19/sexually-transmitted-diseases-stds-rates (accessed 12/21/16).

87 Aksenov, "Povsednevnaia zhizn'," 102.

88 Aksenov, "Povsednevnaia zhizn'," 103–104. In the 1920s the journal, *Rabochii put',* published a series of valuable information about prostitutes' use of alcohol and narcotics, their social origins, and lengths of service. See Visloukh, "Prostitutsiia i narkomaniia," 320; Visloukh, "Prostitutsiia i alkogolizm," 324; Ol'ginskii, "Prostitutsiia i zhilishchnyi vopros," 210; and Sanchov, "Prostitutsiia, kak ona est'," 125–126.

89 Also, the war contributed to the spread of morphine use among the medical professions—doctors, nurses, and medical workers, especially in the military. See Vasilyev, "War, Revolution, and Drugs," 415–425. Another important ele-

ment related to narcotics use is opium among Chinese immigrants. For opium use among the Chinese, see Chapter 3.

90 Shkarovskii, "Sem' imen 'koshki'," 467; Visloukh, "Prostitutsiia i narkomaniia," 318–321; Vasilyev, "War, Revolution, and Drugs," 420–421.

91 Shkarovskii, "Sem' imen 'koshki'," 467–468.

92 *GK,* 3 / 21 / 17.

93 *PG,* 3 / 23 / 17; *PL,* 3 / 22 / 17; *GK,* 3 / 22 / 17.

94 *PL,* 3 / 22 / 17.

95 *PL,* 5 / 4 / 17, 6 / 17 / 17; "Unichtozhenie pritona," *VV,* 5 / 4 / 17; "Aristokraticheskii priton," *VV,* 5 / 13 / 17. It is interesting to note that the baroness's name was not given in the newspaper.

96 *PL,* 6 / 17 / 17.

97 Shkarovskii, "Sem' imen 'koshki'," 468. Shkarovskii argues that by 1919 the cocaine was sold in teahouses, public dining halls, communal hotels, and night lodgings all over the city, and a network of narcotics dens emerged in the Nevskii, Spasskii, Liteinyi, and Moskovskii Districts, especially near Nikolaevskii and Tsarskoe Selo railway stations.

98 For the July Days, see Wade, *Russian Revolution,* 181–186; Rabinowitch, *Prelude to Revolution,* 135–205.

99 For the Kornilov Affair, see Wade, *Russian Revolution,* 194–205.

100 See Wade, *Russian Revolution,* 206–239. For more details, see Rabinowitch, *Bolsheviks Come to Power.*

3. Why Did the Crime Rate Shoot Up?

1 For the political history of the Russian Revolution, see Wade, *Russian Revolution.*

2 For economic conditions during the Russian Revolution, see Volobuev, *Ekonomicheskaia politika.*

3 Kruchkovskaia, *Tsentral'naia gorodskaia duma,* 62–63. According to Kruchkovskaia, the city administration had in its possession only 4 automobiles and 120 horse-drawn carts to deliver food from railway depots to distribution centers. For the food supply crisis, see Lih, *Bread and Authority in Russia;* Kitanina, *Voina, khleb i revoliutsiia,* 340–346; Davydov, *Nelegal'noe snabzhenie Rossiiskogo naseleniia i vlast.*

4 Aksenov, "Povsednevnaia zhizn'," 112–113.

5 Aksenov, "Povsednevnaia zhizn'," 113.

6 Volobuev, *Ekonomicheskaia politika,* 185.

7 Ereshchenko, "Prestupnost'," 112–113. According to *PL,* the number of unemployed reached eighty thousand by June. *PL,* 6 / 18 / 17. William Rosenberg argues that in view of the unprecedented economic and social crisis caused by scarcity, the collapse of finance and economic exchange, and the "multiple dimensions of loss," it is hard to see "how the dual Provisional Government and Soviet regime could have fully understood, much less successfully managed the real and anticipated problems of scarcity, financial collapse, social dislocation

and loss which continued to fuel the violent path to catastrophe." William G. Rosenberg, " 'Beyond the Great Story' of War and Revolution," paper presented at the International Colloquium, Epokha voin i revoliutsii (1914–1922), St. Petersburg, June 9–11, 2016, 31.

8   Kruchkovskaia, *Tsentral'naia gorodskaia duma,* 66.

9   Quoted in Lih, *Bread and Authority in Russia,* 75.

10   Aksenov, "Povsednevnaia zhizn'," 113–115. It is helpful to understand that *dom* (house) denotes an entire residential building. Therefore, a *domovyi komitet*—a housing committee—is not a committee that was organized by residents who owned single-dwelling houses, but rather a committee of the building.

11   Frenkel', *Petrograd perioda voiny i revoliutsii,* 65–66; Aksenov, "Povsednevnaia zhizn'," 114–115. Those who used these facilities were artisans (*remeslenniki*) (30 percent), unskilled laborers (34 percent), unemployed, handicapped, and beggars. For the most part, half of these unfortunate people were kicked out of corners, and one-third were permanent residents of night shelters. Only 20 percent constituted those who sought shelters for the night.

12   Aksenov, "Povsednevnaia zhizn'," 115–116. For rental housing, see "Rental Apartment House," in *The History of St. Petersburg-Petrograd 1830–1918: Guide* (St. Petersburg: State Museum of the History of St. Petersbvurg, 2006), 64–71, which includes many photographs and illustrations in color.

13   *GK,* 8/3/17.

14   *PL,* 4/27/17.

15   *GK,* 8/8/17, 8/10/17; "Khronika gorodskoi zhizni," *Gorodskoe delo,* no. 17–18: 406; Aksenov, "Povsednevnaia zhizn'," 119–120.

16   Aksenov, "Povsednevnaia zhizn'," 151–156. For the union of domestic servants, see Rendle, *Defenders of the Motherland,* 70–71. By 1912, 30 percent of all working women were employed in service. Rendle, *Defenders of the Motherland,* 70. For the demands of household servants and chauffeurs and the inconveniences that the eight-hour working day caused, see Jones, *Russia in Revolution,* 247–250. On forming unions, see *PL,* 3/6/17 (servants), 3/22/17 (dvorniks), 4/15/17 (bath workers), 4/5/17 (cooks), 4/17/17 (waiters), 4/26/17 (pharmacists). According to *Petrogradskii listok,* even thieves had a union, called the Knights of Knives and Screwdrivers. At their founding conference, a seasoned thief complained that he was pickpocketed. *PL,* 5/3/17.

17   Aksenov, "Povsednevnaia zhizn'," 132–134. Aksenov's figures are based on the information given at the Labor Exchange, which served as an unemployment office.

18   Aksenov, "Povsednevnaia zhizn'," 136.

19   Aksenov, "Povsednevnaia zhizn'," 136–138.

20   *Russkie vedomosti,* 10/6/17, quoted in Aksenov, "Povsednevnaia zhizn'," 145.

21   Williams, *Through the Russian Revolution,* 90.

22   For this, see Hasegawa, *February Revolution* (2017), chap. 29; see the document in Strozhev, "Fevral'skaia revoliutsiia 1917 goda," 143–144; Nikolaev, *Revoliutsiia i vlast',* 562–563. In fact, without waiting for the Constituent Assembly, the Provisional Government changed the system of local administration by abolishing the governors and granting the local self-governments, called *zemstvos,* to govern provinces and counties (*uezdy*) under the commissars appointed by the

Provisional Government. Browder and Kerensky, *Russian Provisional Government*, 1:243. Furthermore, on September 1, Kerenskii declared that Russia was a republic, before the convocation of the Constituent Assembly. Browder and Kerensky, *Russian Provisional Government*, 3:1657–1658.

23 The tradition of enacting laws by decree was inherited from the tsarist regime. This was also passed over to the Bolshevik regime. See Pomeranz, "Provisional Government and the Law-Based State."

24 Hasegawa, "Duma Committee, the Provisional Government."

25 The Extraordinary Commission of Inquiry, created on March 4, was headed by N. K. Murav'ev. It did not complete its work before the October Revolution, but its inquiry was published in seven volumes, *Padenie tsarskogo rezhima,* between 1924 and 1927. See Gertsenzon, ed., *Istoriia,* 22–26, Tagantsev, "Iz moikh vospominanii," 247. On the Muraviev Commission's work, see William Pomeranz's unpublished paper, "Investigating the Russian Revolution in Real Time: The Role of Special Legal Tribunals during the Provisional Government," paper presented at the workshop, Russia's Failed Democratic Revolution, February–October 1917: A Centennial Reappraisal on the Russian Revolution, Chicago, August 27–30, 2015.

26 Schapiro, "Political Thought of the First Russian Provisional Government," 113.

27 Fedor F. Kokoshkin, Chairman of the Provisional Government's Juridical Conference, which advised it on all legislation, stated: "Our conception of a state regime is based on three principles—the principle of the inviolability of civil liberty and civil equality, the principle of the guarantee of complete rule by popular will, and the principle of realizing the bases of social justice." Browder and Kerensky, *Russian Provisional Government,* 2:1200. Quoting Kokoshkin, White argues that the Provisional Government's commitment to create a liberal state based on the rule of law was genuine, and implies that Schapiro's harsh indictment must be understood in the broader objectives of the Provisional Government. White, "Civil Rights," 295–297.

28 Browder and Kerensky, *Russian Provisional Government,* 1:200.

29 *Rch,* 3/18/17, quoted in Browder and Kerensky, *Russian Provisional Government,* 1:203. For the various editorial comments, see pages 199–204. Vladimir Dmitrievich Nabokov should not be confused with his son, Vladimir V. Nabokov, the famous writer.

30 *PL,* 3/18/17.

31 K. I. Globachev, "Pravda russkoi revoliutsii," Bakhmeteff Archives, 117–118.

32 Browder and Kerensky, *Russian Provisional Government,* 1:220.

33 Ereshchenko, "Prestupnost'," 162. For the law prohibiting brutal prison practices, see Browder and Kerensky, *Russian Provisional Government,* 1:204. To review the criminal law in light of the new revolutionary situation, the Provisional Government created within the justice ministry a review commission, headed by Vasilii A. Maklakov, a Kadet. But this commission did not produce any results. Tagantsev, "Iz moikh vospominanii," 249.

34 Browder and Kerensky, *Russian Provisional Government,* 3:1358.

35 Browder and Kerensky, *Russian Provisional Government,* 2:982–984; Gertsenzon, *Istoriia,* 38–40.

36 Kschessinska, *Dancing in Petersburg,* 164–165. Similarly, Countess Kleinmikhel's house was confiscated by the insurgents and she was arrested. When she was released three days later, she found her house partly looted and destroyed. The house was turned into a revolutionary club by the soldiers and other insurgents, where she was allowed to use only two rooms for herself and several more for her servants. Brown, *Doomsday 1917,* 62–65.

37 The Bolshevik Party did not accept the change in the name of the capital to Petrograd, considering that the change reflected the tsarist regime's xenophobia, and continued to call its organization the Petersburg Committee.

38 Kulegin, *Delo ob osobniake,* 3–4.

39 Kulegin, *Delo ob osobniake,* 4.

40 Kschessinska, *Dancing in Petersburg,* 168. At the end of March, the procurator of the court of justice asked the chief of the city militia about Kshesinskaia. TsGA SPb, f. 1695, op. 2, d. 430, l. 50.

41 Kschessinska, *Dancing in Petersburg,* 168.

42 Kulegin, *Delo ob osobniake,* 8.

43 For more on the debate within the Bolshevik Party as to how to respond to this verdict, see Kulegin, *Delo ob osobniake,* 9.

44 After the October Revolution, the villa was used by various institutions. In 1957, the government decided to transfer the Museum of the October Revolution there. The museum was renamed the Museum of the Political History of Russia in 1991.

45 See Rabinowitch, *Prelude to Revolution,* 64–65; Boll, *Petrograd Armed Workers' Movement,* 146–152; Nikitin, *Rokovye gody,* Part 3, 5–18. Pavel Pereverzev (SR) replaced Kerenskii as minister of justice, and Kerenskii assumed the post of minister of war and navy, vacated by Aleksandr I. Guchkov. The commissar of the Second Kolomenskii Subdistrict, Moisei M. Kharitonov, a Bolshevik, refused to fulfill Pereverzev's order to expel the anarchists, claiming that he only obeyed the order of the Petrograd Soviet. Musaev, *Prestupnost',* 31–32. Kharitonov was one of Lenin's fellow comrades who returned to Russia in the famous sealed train from Zurich.

46 For the destruction of court records and court properties, see various reports from justices of the peace in various districts: TsGIA SPb f. 520, op. 1, d. 554, ll. 2–11. All the court records—criminal, civil, and Okhrana (state political police)—were destroyed, some completely and others partially, but the latter cases were exceptions.

47 For more details of these people's courts, see Nikolaev, "Vremennye sudy," 11–13.

48 A justice of the peace presided over the court of justice, created as a part of the judicial reform of 1864 under Alexander II, which adjudicated minor criminal cases whose sentences did not exceed one year of prison and a 500-ruble fine. Justices of the peace were elected for a three-year term by residents older than twenty-five years of age, who met two requirements: education (higher than high school) and property qualifications. A list of candidates for justices of the peace was prepared by the local marshal of the nobility or the mayor of a city and approved by the governor or city governor. Elected justices of the peace had to be

confirmed by the Senate. In 1889, under Alexander III, justices of the peace at the county level were abolished except in several major cities. "Mirovye sud'i v Rossii," in Lebedeva, ed., *Nastol'naia kniga mirovogo sud'i*; "Mirovye sud'i," *Entsiklopedicheskii slovar'* (St. Petersburg: Brokgaus-Efron, 1896), 37:427–432. From this it is clear that justices of the peace represented property classes.

49 TsGIA SPb, f. 258, op. 27, d. 170, l. 52; TsGA SPb. f. 258, op. 27, d. 170 l. 52; Browder and Kerensky, *Russian Provisional Government,* 1:192. Nikolaev, "Vremennye sudy," 14.

50 Nikolaev, "Vremennye sudy," 13–14.

51 Nikolaev, "Vremennye sudy," 23.

52 For the Temporary Court, see Mantushkin, "Vremennye sudy," 184–192. For the Statutes of the Temporary Court, see Mantushkin, "Vremennye sudy," 190–192; Gertsenzon, *Istoriia,* 26–27; TsGA SPb, f. 520, op. 1, d. 556, ll. 17–17ob. For a reaction to the temporary courts, see *PL,* 8/8/17.

53 TsGIA SPb, f. 520, op. 1, d. 556, ll, 17–17ob. Also, see Nikolaev, "Vremennye sudy," 14–17; Gertsenzon, *Istoriia,* 26–27.

54 Nikolaev, "Vremennye sudy," 19–23. The ministry of justice of the Provisional Government and the city duma argued over how to pay for service at the temporary courts. This conflict was resolved only on September 23, when the ministry of justice retroactively agreed to pay ten rubles a day for the presiding judge and five rubles a day for each assistant judge. Nikolaev, "Vremennye sudy," 19.

55 Nikolaev, "Vremennye sudy," 22.

56 Nikolaev, "Vremennye sudy," 22–23.

57 *PL,* 8/8/17; Mantushkin, "Vremennye sudy," 189. For specific cases against landlords resulting in heavy fines and prison terms far beyond what the old laws had allowed, see Nikolaev, "Vremennye sudy," 28–29, 30.

58 *PL,* 8/8/17.

59 Nikolaev, "Vremennye sudy," 28–29.

60 *BV,* 3/29/17, quoted in Nikolaev, "Vremennye sudy," 30.

61 Nikolaev, "Vremennye sudy," 24–27, 28–29.

62 Nikolaev, "Domovladel'tsy pered Vremennym sudom," 144.

63 Nikolaev, "Vremennye sudy," 31–32.

64 Quoted in Gertsenzon, *Istoriia,* p. 27. According to White, the temporary courts were strongly disliked by the Provisional Government's liberal jurists. White, "Civil Rights," 305.

65 O. S. Trakhterev, "Stolichnym mirovym sud'iam. Otkrytoe pis'mo," *NV,* 4/14/17, quoted in Nikolaev, "Vremennye sudy," 33.

66 Nikolaev, "Vremennye sudy," 33.

67 Nikolaev, "Vremennye sudy," 34–35. For instance, the sentence of nine-month imprisonment given on March 28 by the 21st Temporary Court (Spasskii District) to Ensign A. E. Naumov of the automobile regiment for swindling was overturned by Minister of Justice Kerenskii in April. Kerenskii remanded the case to the Military Court, which had jurisdiction over the matter. Another sentence by the temporary court of a six-thousand-ruble fine and/or six months' imprisonment against a house owner was overturned by the minister of justice

for the misapplication of the law regulating the responsibility of owners. Nikolaev, "Vremennye sudy," 28.

68 Nikolaev, "Vremennye sudy," 28.

69 Nikolaev, "Vremennye sudy," 33–36; *PL*, 8/8/17.

70 Nikolaev, "Domovladel'tsy pered Vremennym sudom," 142.

71 Nikolaev, "Domovladel'tsy pered Vremennym sudom," 142. It is not clear if Lemeshenok was renting the apartment in her name or if her husband also lived in the same apartment.

72 Numerous other complaints were lodged against house owners for failing to maintain sanitary conditions. For this violation and other infractions, the temporary courts imposed stiff penalties on house owners in excess of that allowed by the criminal code. Some cases were overturned by the minister of justice. See Nikolaev, "Domovladel'tsy pered Vremennym sudom."

73 *PL*, 5/22/27.

74 *PL*, 5/9/17, 5/16/17, 5/17/17.

75 TsGIA SPb, f. 569, op. 21, d. 41, ll. 1–3.

76 Gertsenzon, *Istoriia*, 31–32; Ereshchenko, "Prestupnost'," 163; Cherniaev, "Gibel' dumskoi monarkhii," 658.

77 Browder and Kerensky, *Russian Provisional Government*, 1:205–206.

78 In addition to the prisons, the list included temporary jails at the higher educational institutions (Technological Institute, Mining Institute, Historical-Philological Institute), a movie theater, a restaurant, and a bar. See TsGIA SPb, f. 520, op. 1, d 556, ll, 28, 33. One can imagine the consternation of professors and students when they witnessed their lecture halls and laboratories turned into jails.

79 Globachev, "Pravda russkoi revoliutsii," Bakhmeteff Archives, 124.

80 *GK*, 8/31/17; *PL*, 8/31/17.

81 *PL*, 7/2/17, 8/1/17; *GK*, 7/27/17.

82 Ereshchenko, "Prestupnost'," 165.

83 *PL*, 3/7/17.

84 *PL*, 3/10/17; *VV*, 3/9/17.

85 *PL*, 3/22/17. Similar raids and arrests of criminals were also reported in the Vasil'evskii District, where criminals congregated in Gavanskoe Field. *PL*, 3/16/17.

86 *PL*, 3/23/17, 3/30/17.

87 *PL*, 4/24/17, 5/17/17; Ereshchenko, "Prestupnost'," 118.

88 *PL*, 4/24/17.

89 *Fabrichno-zavodskie komitety* (1982), 261–262; Ereshchenko, "Prestupnost'," 117–118.

90 Ereshchenko's data do not reveal how the thefts were distributed among the various districts. He divides the cases only into two categories: the outskirts (1,734 cases, 59.8 percent) and the central districts (1,167 cases, 40.2 percent). Ereshchenko, "Prestupnost'," 116–117. I presume that Ereshchenko adopted the division used by the former tsarist police between the four central districts (the Admiralteiskii, Kazanskii, Spasskii, and Moskovskii Districts) and the rest of the districts.

91 *PL*, 7 / 23 / 17.

92 Ereshchenko, "Prestupnost'," 156.

93 Hasegawa, "Crime, Police, and Mob Justice," 251; Ereshchenko, "Prestupnost'," 119. Such colonies existed around the Olympia amusement park on Zabalkan-skii Prospect, Village Volkovo in the Fourth Aleksandro-Nevskii Subdistrict, Galernaia Gavan', Gavanskoe Field, and Golodai, all on Vasil'evskii Island, the bars Vena (Vienna) in Neva Gate and Shanteller in Ozerki, the area called Simentsy, a large area between Obvodnyi Canal and Zagorodny Prospect, the area near the Nikolaevskii Railway Station known as Ligovka, Peski in the Rozhdestvenkii District, and Gutuevskii Island.

94 *PL*, 7 / 26 / 17, 7 / 27 / 17, 7 / 29 / 17, 7 / 30 / 17, 8 / 24 / 17; *GK*, 8 / 5 / 17, 8 / 8 / 17, 8 / 20 / 17.

95 *PL*, 4 / 29 / 17, 5 / 2 / 17; Golder, *War, Revolution, and Peace in Russia*, 67.

96 *PL*, 5 / 7 / 17.

97 *PL*, 5 / 19 / 17.

98 *PL*, 5 / 21 / 17.

99 *PL*, 5 / 20 / 17.

100 *Strekoza*, no. 24, June 1917, 8.

101 *Strekoza*, no. 30, 1917, 5

102 For numerous examples, based on newspapers and archival materials, see Eresh-chenko, "Prestupnost'," 132–133.

103 Ereshchenko, "Prestupnost'," 133–134.

104 Ereshchenko, "Prestupnost'," 134.

105 *PL*, 10 / 19 / 17, *GK*, 10 / 19 / 17.

106 Ereshchenko, "Prestupnost'," 138.

107 See Siegelbaum, "Another Yellow Peril?" 307–330; *VGS*, 7 / 4 / 17, 8 / 5 / 17.

108 For the living conditions in such hovels, see *PL*, 5 / 5 / 17; Aksenov, "Povsednevnaia zhizn'," 115.

109 *PL*, 4 / 25 / 17; *PG*, 7 / 26 / 17; Ereshchenko, "Prestupnost'," 128–129.

110 *PL*, 9 / 23 / 17; see also *Fabrichno-zavodskie komitety*, 56; *VGS*, 8 / 5 / 17.

111 *PG*, 11 / 17 / 17.

112 *PL*, 9 / 27 / 17, 9 / 28 / 17, 9 / 30 / 17.

113 Aksenov, "Povsednevnaia zhizn'," 91–95.

114 Aksenov, "Povsednevnaia zhizn'," 97–98. It became worse during the Civil War: 43 (1918) and 80 (1919) per thousand.

115 *Trepach*, no. 20, 1917, 9, quoted in Aksenov, "Povsednevnaia zhizn'," 95.

116 For the crisis of transport, see "Khronika gorodskoi zhizni," no. 8: 339. For the crisis of water supply and accumulation of wastes, "Khronika gorodskoi zhizni," no. 9–10: 375–376. For the crisis of heating, "Khronika gorodskoi zhizni," no. 9–10: 405.

117 Mil'chik, "Petrogradskaia tsentral'naia gorodskaia duma," 192–197. For the breakdown of voting in districts, see Kruchkovskaia, *Tsentral'naia gorodskaia duma*, 126–127. By June the city required 16 million rubles for the militia, 4.2 million for the fire departments, and in excess of 14 million for city hospitals with the total expenditure rising to 92.8 million. "Khronika gorodskoi zhizni," no. 8: 339.

118 *Ogonek*, no. 23, June 1917, 363, quoted in Aksenov, "Povsednevnaia zhizn'," 93.

119 *Ogonek,* no. 41, October 22, 1917, 17.

120 Williams, *Through the Russian Revolution,* 90.

121 The number admitted to the hospital for mental illness increased from less than one person a month in prerevolutionary days to fifty people a month after the February Revolution. Aksenov, "Povsednevnaia zhizn'," 42.

122 *BV,* evening edition, 5 / 18 / 17, quoted in Aksenov, "Povsednevnaia zhizn'," 43. Professor Rozenbakh was killed near the Mars Field in November. See Chapter 6.

123 Aksenov, "Povsednevnaia zhizn'," 43–44. For suicides and divorces, see Aksenov, "Povsednevnaia zhizn'," 48–52.

124 Aksenov, "Povsednevnaia zhizn'," 44.

4. Militias Rise and Fall

1 According to Robert Abbott, a summary of police work published in 1856 ran for some four hundred pages. Abbott, "Police Reform in Russia," 5. For various administrative tasks that fell into the jurisdiction of the police, see Nazarenko, "MVD," 6.

2 Nazarenko, "MVD," 19.

3 Other police included police reserves; mounted police (*konno-politseiskaia strazha*); factory police; river police (*rechnaia politsiia*); fire brigade (*pozharnaia komanda*), and first aid stations. Nazarenko, "MVD," 20; see also *S.- Peterburgskaia stolichnaia politsiia i gradonachal'stvo: Kratkii istoricheskii ocherk* (St. Petersburg: Tovarishchestvo R. Golike i A. Vil'borg, 1903).

4 "Politsiia," *Entsiklopedicheskii slovar'* (St. Petersburg: Brokgauz-Efron, 1898), 24:331–336; "Gradonachal'nik," *Entsiklopedicheskii slovar',* 18:492; "Gradonachal'nik," *Novyi entsiklopedicheskii slovar'* (St. Petersburg: Brokgauz-Efron, n.d.), 14:663; "politsiia," *Sankt-Peterburg, Petrograd, Leningrad* (Leningrad: Nauchnaia izdatel'stvo Bol'shaia Rossiiskaia Entsiklopediia, 1992), 503; "Gradonachal'stvo," *Sankt-Peterburg, Petrograd, Leningrad,* 165; "Okolotochnyi nadziratel'," *Entsiklopledicheskii slovar'* (St. Petersburg: Brokgaus-Efron, 1892), 42:828. Nazarenko, "MVD," 26–27.

5 Nazarenko, "MVD," 27–28.

6 Nazarenko, "MVD," 22–23, 26–27.

7 Abbott, "Police Reform in Russia," 8.

8 Nazarenko, "MVD," 28–29. In addition, police reserves existed to assist regular police. The reserve policemen were in charge of the registration of cabs and automobiles, and control of dvorniks. In 1907, police reserves numbered 60 inspectors and 264 reservists. Nazarenko, "MVD," 33–34.

9 Nazarenko, "MVD," 48.

10 Nazarenko, "MVD," 60–62, 63–65.

11 "Sysknaia politsiia Rossiskoi imperii," Istoricheskii forum, http://forum.mozohin .ru/index.php?topic=578.0 (accessed July 5, 2016); "Sysknaia politsiia v Rossii vo vtoroi polovine XIX v.," http/lawthesis.com/sysknaya-politsiya-v-rossii-vo vtoroy polovine-hih-nachale-hh-v (accessed July 5, 2016).

12 Nazarenko, "MVD," 6–7. For Filippov, see Nazarenko, "MVD," 37–38. Filippov's mobile detachment captured 2,572 criminals, including 493 recidivists of thefts and 420 hooligans. In 1908, the number of captured criminals rose to 3,488.

13 Nazarenko, "MVD," 39, 41. In 1907, St. Petersburg had 45 clubs, 42 entertainment establishments, 38 houses of prostitution, 85 hitching stations, and 108 inns.

14 Nazarenko, "MVD," 39–40. For more on the introduction of modern methods of criminal investigation under Filippov and its cultural significance, see McReynolds, *Murder Most Russian,* 149–159.

15 Ereshchenko, "Prestupnost'," 89–90; Nazarenko, "MVD," 6–7, 39.

16 Zelnik, trans., *Radical Worker in Tsarist Russia,* 96. In 1906 to 1907, sixty-four St. Petersburg policemen were killed and forty-nine wounded.

17 Nikolaev, "Nastroeniia i politicheskie vzgliady petrogradskikh politseiskikh," 1–39.

18 The mounted police was maintained through the city governor.

19 Vrangel', *Vospominaniia,* 354–356; Grabbe, *Windows on the River Neva,* 135; Isaakova Memoirs, Bakhmeteff Archives, 151. According to Vrangel', during the raid one floor polisher was mistakenly caught while hiding under the bed, but he was later released. One chimney sweep was shot in the room and killed. Another "disguised" police officer was caught near Znamenskaia Square, but he was a peasant who had come to visit his brother.

20 Nikolaev, " 'Pod krasnym flagom,' " 41–49.

21 Frame, "Militsiia vo vremia Russkoi revoliutsii 1917 goda," 110–111.

22 *Iz KPZh,* 2 / 28 / 17; Hasegawa, "Formation of the Militia," 305.

23 Burdzhalov, *Vtoraia russkaia revoliutsiia,* 272; *Rch,* 3 / 5 / 17; Hasegawa, "Formation of the Militia," 306.

24 Kel'son, "Militsiia fevral'skoi revoliutsii," Pt 1: 162–163. For more detail of the formation of militia organizations during the February Revolution, see Hasegawa, "Formation of the Militia," 306–307; Wade, *Red Guards and Workers' Militias,* 36–57.

25 The motion to create the militia was made by a Menshevik, M. A. Brounshtein. According to Sukhanov, some wanted to add the function of combating the remaining forces of tsarism. But Sukhanov reminded the audience that the Duma Committee already had the Military Commission for this purpose, and he urged other deputies not to confuse the tasks. The general session adopted the original motion. N. N. Sukhanov, *Zapiski o revoliutsiii,* 7 vols. (Berlin: 1922–1923), 1:132.

26 *Petrogadskii sovet,* 22; Sukhanov, *Zapiski o revoliutsii,* 1:132; Hasegawa, "Formation of the Militia," 304–305; Wade, *Red Guards and Workers' Militias,* 40–42.

27 Shliapnikov, *Semnadtsatyi god,* 1:154; Hasegawa, "Formation of the Militia," 305; Wade, *Red Guards and Workers' Militias,* 41–42, 54–55. These ten gathering points were in the industrial regions: Vyborgskii, Petrogradskii, Vasilevskii, Rozhdestvenskii, Moskovskii, Nevskii, and Narvskii Districts. These designations, avoiding the central districts, indicate that the Executive Committee did not have the notion of creating an all-city militia organization.

28 GARF, f. 5141. op. 1, d. 2, l. 23. Lenskii suggested that some of the duties should be transferred to other municipal units, but recognized for the moment the need to fulfill the duties that the militia inherited from the old police, and listed fifteen such duties that more or less corresponded to the administrative duties given to Ge. Lenskii, "Gorodskaia militsiia, ee organizatsiia i kompetent-siia," 273.

29 For instance, Aleksandr Shliapnikov, a Bolshevik leader appointed as the commissar for the Vyborgskii District, was totally preoccupied with the work of the Bolshevik Party and the Executive Committee of the Petrograd Soviet and spent absolutely no time on the organization of a militia. Shliapnikov, *Semnadtsatyi god*, 1:154; Wade, *Red Guards and Workers' Militias*, 41; Hasegawa, "Formation of the Militia," 305. Only seven district headquarters were designated, but there is no evidence to indicate that workers paid any attention to these gathering places.

30 These emissaries included V. G. Botzvadze, a flamboyant commissar in the Vyborgskii District; A. V. Peshekhonov in the Petrogradskii District, N. P. Zelenko in the Aleksandro-Nevskii District; V. V. Drozdov in the Vasilievskii District; M. N. Benua in the Kolomenskii District; and N. A. Oppel' in the Moskovskii District. The decision to send emissaries to various districts has been known from Kel'son's memoirs. But Kel'son gives the names of only select districts and emissaries. An archival document contains a list of gathering places in each district and the names of the emissaries dispatched to various districts. TsGA SPb, f. 131, op. 1. d. 3, l. 57.

31 The only exception was the Petrogradskii District, where Peshekhonov's leadership was responsible for creating a district commissariat.

32 Startsev, *Ocherki*, 44. The formation of a militia in the Aivaz and Old Parviainen factories was reported in *IZ*, 3 / 2 / 17.

33 Rex Wade, based on Kel'son's memoirs, emphasized the role played by Botzvadze. It is difficult to ascertain, however, how much influence he exerted in the formation of the Vyborgskii District's militia organizations. His name appears in the archival materials, indicating that he did play a certain role, perhaps in uniting all these amorphous workers' militias into a subdistrict unit, and yet, once the militia was formed, it was the workers' themselves who controlled these organizations.

34 Startsev, *Ocherki*, 43–44; Kel'son, "Militsiia fevral'skoi revoliutsii," Pt 1: 175.

35 GARF, f. 5141, op. 1, d. 37, l. 2. This request was signed by the commissar of the Vyborgskii District, whose handwriting I cannot decipher, but it is clear that it is not Botzvadze.

36 GARF, f. 5141, op. 1, d. 37, ll. 13, 14.

37 In May, Botzvadze, as the commissar of the Second Vyborgskii Subdistrict reported a murder case to the chief of the city militia. TsGA SPb, f. 1675, op. 2, d. 430, ll. 215–215ob. Botzvadze's name reappeared in 1918 as commissar of the Liteinyi District, this time with his faithful police dog, Dick. He appears to have eased out of the Vyborgskii District but continued to work in the militia organizations in the Liteinyi District, a more middle-class-dominated neighborhood, as a Bolshevik commissar. See *PGol*, 2 / 17 / 18. Botzvadze is one of the colorful

characters who emerged after the February Revolution. He continued to serve in the Bolshevik regime, but his subsequent fate is not known.

38 For more details about the formation of the Vyborgskii Subdistrct commissariats, see Hasegawa, "Crime and Police in Revolutionary Petrograd," 12–13.

39 See Hasegawa, "Crime and Police in Revolutionary Petrograd," 13–14. GARF, f. 5141, op. 1, d. 1, l. 13. Since the Second Baltic Marines had their barracks near Kriuchkov Canal, it is almost certain that it was the Marine units that were recruited for patrol duty. GARF, f. 5141, op. 1, d. 1, l. 14; GARF, f. 5141, op. 1, d. 37, l. 30.

40 GARF f. 5141, op. 1, d. 10, l. 19, 19ob.

41 GARF f. 5141, op. 1, d. 10, l. 31.

42 GARF f. 5141, op. 1, d. 10, ll. 24–28.

43 *IZ*, 3 / 1 / 17; Startsev, *Ocherki,* 43; *RSP,* 1:365.

44 *IZ*, 3 / 3 / 17.

45 Startsev, *Ocherki,* 45.

46 *Revoliutsionnoe dvizhenie,* 455–456.

47 *RSP,* 1:83–84, 365.

48 *RSP,* 1:83–84.

49 TsGA SPb, f. 131, op. 1, d. 2, ll. 66, 66ob.

50 GARF, f. 5141, op. 1, d. 1, l. 15; GARF, f. 5141, op. 1, d. 2, l. 11.

51 *IZ*, 3 / 1 / 17, 3 / 2 / 17.

52 Peshekhonov, "Pervyia nedeli," 271. V. M. Shakh, a Menshevik and Peshekhonov's assistant, was entrusted with organizing the militia force. Peshekhonov was interested in creating a militia from all layers of society, but Shakh sought a more a class-oriented militia. Nonetheless, in the end Peshekhonov was satisfied with the "high moral level" of the militiamen assembled by Shakh. Peshekhonov, "Pervyia nedeli," 289; Wade, *Red Guards and Workers' Militias,* 52–53.

53 Peshekhonov, "Pervyia nedeli," 304–305.

54 Peshekhonov, "Pervyia nedeli," 288–289, 295, 299.

55 For scattered evidence of the formation of militia organizations in other districts, see Wade, *Red Guards and Workers' Militias,* 55–56.

56 For the complete list of the subdistricts, their locations, and the names of the subdistrict commissars, see TsGA SPb, f. 1695, op. 2, d. 430, ll. 55–57.

57 Startsev, *Ocherki,* 49–50.

58 *Petrogradskii sovet,* 1:26; Zlokazov, *Petrogradskii Sovet rabochikh i soldatskikh deputatov,* 53.

59 Kel'son, "Militsiia fevral'skoi revoliutsii," Pt 1: 167; *Petrogradskii sovet,* 202; Startsev, *Ocherki,* 47–48.

60 Kel'son, "Militsiia fevral'skoi revoliutsiia," Pt 1: 167.

61 Kel'son, "Militsiia fevral'skoi revoliutsiia," Pt 1: 168; Startsev, *Ocherki,* 48.

62 *Petrogradskii sovet,* 177.

63 *RSP,* 1:124.

64 *Revoliutsionnoe dvizhenie,* 488. The deep dissatisfaction with the merger was also expressed in the meeting of the Executive Committee of the Vasilevskii District Soviet on March 26, although the overwhelming majority of the committee favored the subordination of the workers' militia to the city militia. *RSP,* 1:83–84.

65 Startsev, *Ocherki,* 52. According to Startsev, workers' militiamen also numbered at least half of the twenty thousand total militiamen in the nominally unified city militia. The number seems extremely high, but it must include all members of the workers' militias who served as city militiamen by taking turns.

66 *PL,* 3 / 5 / 17; *IZ,* 3 / 4 / 17.

67 *PG,* 3 / 5 / 17.

68 *PL,* 3 / 15 / 17.

69 *PG,* 3 / 16 / 17.

70 *PL,* 3 / 16 / 17; "Khronika gorodskoi zhizni," no. 7: 283.

71 Kel'son, "Militsiia fevral'skoi revoliutsii," Pt 2: 152.

72 For the law on the militia of April 17, see Browder and Kerensky, *Russian Provisional Government,* 1:218–221. Musaev cites the archival source on this law: TsGA SPb, f. 131, op. 1, d. 1, ll. 22–23, 26. Musaev, *Prestupnost',* 15; Frame, "Militsiia vo vremia Russkoi revoliutsii 1917 goda," 113–114, based on *Sobranii uzakonenii i rasporiazhenii pravitel'stva,* May 3, 1917, 837–843. For the composition of the commission, see "Khronika gorodskoi zhizni," no. 7: 286. For more details about the qualifications of militia chiefs and their assistants with regard to education and length of military service, payment of militiamen, and the system of inspection, see "Khronika gorodskoi zhizni," no. 8: 335.

73 The archives contain two undated documents, the first entitled "Temporary Statute [*polozhenie*] of Organization and Composition of Petrograd City Militia." GARF, f. 406, op. 2, d. 20, ll. 1–4 and TsGA SPb, f. 131, d. 2, ll. 41–47. *Petrogradskii listok* also introduces the city duma's version, which it claims the city duma had adopted at a special session. *PL,* 4 / 4 / 17. The second document is entitled "Temporary Statute of Organization and Composition of the Militia of the Cities of Petrograd, Moscow, Kiev, and Odessa." GARF, f. 406, op. 2, d. 20, l. 1; TsGA SPb, f. 131, op. 1, d. 2, ll. 41, 97.

74 GARF, f. 406, op. 2, d. 20, l. 1; TsGA SPb, f. 131, op. 1, d. 2, l. 97.

75 TsGA SPb, f. 131, op. 1, d. 2, l. 41; TsGA SPb, f. 131, op. 1, d. 2, l. 97.

76 GARF, f. 406, op. 2, d. 20, l. 1ob.

77 GARF, f. 406, op. 2, d. 20, ll. 46–47.

78 GARF, f. 406, op. 2, d. 20, l. 1ob. See also Musaev, *Prestupnost',* 16–17.

79 *PL,* 5 / 18 / 17.

80 On May 20, the city governor's office issued a new regulation on handing out weapons. TsGA SPb, f. 569, op. 20, d. 313, ll. 6–6ob.

81 Kel'son, "Militsiia fevral'skoi revoliutsii," Pt 2: 162.

82 For Lenskii's criticism of Kel'son's notion of municipal police, see Lenskii, "Gorodskaia militsiia, ee organizatsiia i kompetentsiia," 269.

83 Kel'son, "Militsiia fevral'skoi revoliutsii," Pt. 1: 163; Aksenov, "Militsiia," 42.

84 *GK,* 6 / 23 / 17; Ereshchenko, "Prestupnost'," 145.

85 Aksenov, "Militsiia," 45. Under the tsarist regime, criminal records were entered into passports, which became known as "wolf's passports."

86 *NZh,* 6 / 30 / 17; *PG,* 4 / 6 / 17; Ereshchenko, "Prestupnost'," 145.

87 *PL,* 3 / 21 / 17.

88 *PL,* 5 / 19 / 17. This episode also indicated that the city militia inherited the tsarist mounted police.

89 *BV,* 4/16/17. Similar cases were reported also in; *BV* (evening), 5/25/17; *Rch,* 4/11/17, 5/10/17, 5/13/17, 5/25/17; *GK,* 7/20/17; *NZh,* 5/25/17, 8/5/17; *PL,* 5/11/17, 6/11/17. Also see Peshekhonov, "Pervyia nedeli," 447; Ereshchenko, "Prestupnost'," 146.

90 Ershchenko, "Prestupnost'," 146.

91 Ereshchenko, "Prestupnost'," 147–148.

92 *PL,* 5/11/17.

93 *PL,* 3/10/17.

94 *Za 8 let,* 51–52; *PL,* 4/1/17; TsGA SPb, f. 74, op. 1, d. 6, l. 37; TsGA SPb f. 74, op. 1, d. 11, l. 31. The former statute of the Criminal Police was abolished only on July 11, and the new statute was adopted on the same day. The chief of the Criminal Militia received five hundred rubles per month; assistant chief, four hundred rubles; inspectors, three hundred rubles. TsGA SPb, f. 74, op. 1, d. 6, l. 7.

95 *Za 8 let,* 55.

96 Musaev, *Prestupnost',* 18–19.

97 Like the Criminal Police, the Mounted Police was also restored. Although documentary evidence is lacking, there were numerous references in newspapers about dispatching the mounted police to troubled spots. In fact, the mounted police were more reliable than the regular city militia detachments. Similarly, the River Police, the Fire Brigade, and the First Aid continued to function, although which jurisdictional control they entered after the February Revolution is not clear. The tsarist police was not entirely destroyed by the February Revolution, indicating its resilience.

98 *PG,* 6/15/17.

99 TsGA SPb, f. 131, op. 1, d. 5, l. 1. Also see Wade, *Red Guards and Workers' Militias,* 110–111.

100 TsGA SPb, f. 131, op. 1, d. 5, l. 2. Also see Wade, *Red Guards and Workers' Militias,* 110–111.

101 TsGA SPb, f. 131, op. 1, d. 5, l. 3.

102 Startsev, *Ocherki,* 87.

103 In this sense, the term had the same connotation as "the third estate," as used by Abbé Sieyès used in his celebrated pamphlet, "What Is the Third Estate" in 1789. Sieyès identified only the third estate as the "nation" and excluded the first and the second estates outside the body politic.

104 A veteran anarchist, Petr Kropotkin visited the Durnovo dacha and was appalled by the convergence of the anarchists-communists and common criminals. Cherniaev, "Anarchists," 223.

105 Wade, *Red Guards and Workers' Militias,* 84–99.

106 GARF, f. 5141, op. 1, d. 8, ll. 40–78.

107 For more details on this report, see Tsuyoshi Hasegawa, "Crime and Police in Revolutionary Petrograd," 18–26.

108 GARF, f. 5141, op. l, d. 8, ll. 40–41.

109 GARF, f. 5141, op. l, d. 8, ll. 40–41.

110 GARF, f. 5141, op. l, d. 8, l. 41.

111 As discussed in Chapter 2, the Second Moskovskii Subdistrict mobile detachment had scored a spectacular success in uncovering a large narcotic ring. *PL,*

5 / 4 / 17. Also see the activities of the mobile detachments in the Second Kolomenskii Subdistrict, which was created on April 1. GARF, f. 5141, op. 1, d. 10, ll, 1, 2, 2ob, 3, 4, 5.

112 GARF, f. 5141, op. 1, d. 8, ll. 49–50.

113 GARF, f. 5141, op. 1, d. 8, l. 49.

114 GARF, f. 5141, op. 1, d. 8, l. 53.

115 GARF, f. 5141, op. 1, d. 8, ll. 54–56. When the commission referred to "workers," it should be noted that these were not industrial proletariat, since large factories did not exist in these subdistricts.

116 GARF, f. 5141, op. 1, d. 8, ll. 57–59.

117 This must refer to the Poliustrovo District, as, officially, there was no Third Vyborgskii Subdistrict.

118 GARF, f. 5141, op. 1, d. 8, ll. 59–60.

119 GARF, f. 5141, op. 1, d. 8, l. 63.

120 GARF, f. 5141, op. 1, d. 8, l. 64.

121 GARF, f. 5141, op. 1, d. 8, l. 65.

122 GARF, f. 5141, op. 1, d. 8, l. 69.

123 GARF, f. 5141, op. 1, d. 8, ll. 70–71.

124 GARF, f. 5141, op. l, d. 8, l. 76.

125 GARF, f. 5141, op. 1, d. 38, ll. 17, 19.

126 Startsev, *Ocherki,* 88–89; Wade, *Red Guards and Workers' Militias,* 120.

127 Wade, *Red Guards and Workers' Militias,* 128.

128 Wade, *Red Guards and Workers' Militias,* 122–123.

129 *PG,* 7 / 7 / 17.

130 *PG,* 7 / 8 / 17; *GK,* 7 / 8 / 17.

131 GARF, f. 5141, op. 1, d. 18, l. 163.

132 Wade, *Red Guards and Workers' Militias,* 123. See the review commission's report above.

133 Tseretelli, *Vospominaniia o fevral'skoi revoliutsii,* 2:362; Wade, *Red Guards and Workers' Militias,* 124.

134 Wade, *Red Guards and Workers' Militias,* 124–125.

135 Wade, *Red Guards and Workers' Militias,* 125–126.

136 Wade, *Red Guards and Workers' Militias,* 126.

137 Wade, *Red Guards and Workers' Militias,* 126–127.

138 Quoted in Wade, *Red Guards and Workers' Militias,* 126.

139 Wade, *Red Guards and Workers' Militias,* 128.

140 *GK,* 7 / 25 / 17.

141 *VGS,* 7 / 29 / 17, 8 / 2 / 17.

142 *VGS,* 8 / 8 / 17.

143 Aksenov, "Militsiia," 10–11.

144 *Trepach,* no. 23, 1917, 3, quoted in Aksenov, "Militsiia v gorodskie sloi, 46.

145 *MG,* 7 / 7 / 17, quoted in Aksenov, "Militsiia v gorodskoi sloi," 46.

146 N. Re-Mi, "Toska o tverdoi vlast," *Novyi satirikon,* no. 18, May 1917, 1.

147 *PL,* 8 / 27 / 17.

148 *PL,* 8 / 27 / 17.

149 *GK,* 9 / 15 / 17.

150   *PL*, 10 / 3 / 17; *GK*, 10 / 3 / 17.
151   *PL*, 10 / 10 / 17; *GK*, 10 / 10 / 17; *VV*, 10 / 10 / 17. On the same day, it was reported that the Vasilievskii District Militia Commissariat was attacked by a crowd that was angered by the news that a militiaman had himself committed a murder. Someone in the crowd called for burning down the building. The militia fired a shot at the crowd, seriously wounding one person. *VV*, 10 / 10 / 17.
152   *VV*, 10 / 23 / 17.
153   Musaev, *Prestupnost'*, 42; TsGA SPb, f. 131, op. 1, d. 2, l. 165.
154   Ereshchenko, "Prestupnost'," 150.
155   *GK*, 9 / 28 / 17.
156   *PL*, 9 / 29 / 17.
157   *GK*, 8 / 26 / 27; TsGA SPb, f. 74, op. 1, d. 1a., ll. 15, 16, 98–98ob. The petition for higher wages was also approved at the meeting of 160 Criminal Militia investigators on October 4, 1917. See TsGA SPb, f. 74, op. 1, d. 11, ll. 14–14ob, 15–15ob.
158   *GK*, 10 / 13 / 17.
159   Ereshchenko, "Prestupnost'," 145; Kel'son, "Padenie Vremennogo Pravitel'stva," 195; Startsev, *Ocherki*, 68.
160   Ereshchenko, "Prestupnost'," 151. Ereshchenko lists the number of tsarist police at 10,958, but this seems too high unless it includes branches other than the regular police.
161   Kel'son, "Padenie Vremennogo Pravitel'stva," 195–196; Ereshchenko, "Prestupnost'," 151.
162   Startsev, *Ocherki*, 93; Musaev, *Prestupnost'*, 38.
163   Musaev, *Prestupnost'*, 44–45. General Oleg Petrovich Vasil'kovskii was the commander of the Petrograd Military District from July 19 to August 28, that is, after the July Days until the Kornilov Affair.
164   TsGA SPb, f. 131. op. 1, d. 2, l. 151.
165   *VV*, 10 / 13 / 17.
166   TsGA SPb, f. 131, op. 1, d. 2, l. 167. Colonel Polkovnikov was appointed as commander of the Petrograd Military District in September after the Kornilov Affair. His predecessor, General Kouskii sided with Kornilov, but Polkovnikov supported the Provisional Government.
167   On October 20, the military commanders refused to give weapons to the Lesnoi District and Okhta District militias. TsGA SPb, f. 131. op. 1, d. 2, ll. 165, 176.
168   Ereshchenko, "Prestupnost'," 166.
169   *BV*, 3 / 16 / 17; *PG*, 3 / 5 / 17.
170   *VV*, 3 / 9 / 17.
171   *PL*, 4 / 28 / 17.
172   P. Olikhov, "Samookhrana stolitsy," *PL*, 10 / 19 / 17.
173   *GK*, 10 / 12 / 17.
174   Quoted in Ereshchenko, "Prestupnost'," 170.
175   Quoted in Startsev, *Ocherki*, 239–240.
176   Wade, *Red Guards and Workers' Militias,* 129–130. The piaterka consisted of Valentin Trifonov, his brother Evgenii, Vladimir Pavlov, A. Kokrev, and Iustin Zhuk. The first four were Bolsheviks, and Zhuk was an anarchist. A sixth

member, A. A. Iurkin, also a Bolshevik, soon joined. Wade, *Red Guards and Workers' Militias,* 130.

177 Wade, *Red Guards and Workers' Militias,* 131–132. Wade does not explain the obvious contradiction between the elective principle of the guardsmen and the need to keep them under the Bolshevik-dominated piaterka. It is important to note that although the aim of the "Workers' Guards" was to "struggle against counterrevolution," the guards were to "undertake safeguarding the streets and buildings in times of trouble with permission of the Central Komendatura." Wade, *Red Guards and Workers' Militias,* 132.

178 Wade, *Red Guards and Workers' Militias,* 136.

179 Wade, *Red Guards and Workers' Militias,* 137.

180 The Central Executive Committee was the highest executive leadership of the All-Russian Soviets. Its members were elected in June, and dominated by moderate socialists.

181 *RSP,* 3: 293.

182 *RSP,* 3: 295–296.

183 Wade, *Red Guards and Workers' Militias,* 134–135.

184 TsGA SPb, f. 131, op. 1, d. 2, ll. 156–156ob.

185 Wade, *Red Guards and Workers' Militias,* 138.

186 Wade, *Red Guards and Workers' Militias,* 145.

187 Wade, *Red Guards and Workers' Militias,* 148–155. For the role of the Red Guards in the Bolshevik seizure of power, see pages 195–207.

5. An Epidemic of Mob Justice

1 *MG,* 3 / 5 / 17.

2 Dalekii Drug, "Smertnaia kazn' 'iavochnym poriadkom,'" *MG,* 6 / 27 / 17.

3 These cities and rural areas include Baku, Ekaterinodar, Kiev, Saratov, Ekaterinoslav, Yalta, Arkhangel'sk, Vladikavkaz, Rostov-in-Don, Novocherkassk, Perm', Kislovodsk, Odessa, Krasnoiarsk, Blagoveshchensk, Khar'kov, Kherson, and also some villages. See GARF, f. 1791, op. 6, d., 44, 45, 46. The Militia Affairs of the ministry of internal affairs did not have detailed data on mob justice reported from local militia organizations and had to rely on newspaper clippings. This itself demonstrates the breakdown of information regarding militia affairs as well as the Provisional Government's failure to have a firm grip on police matters in the empire.

4 Strangely, this unique feature of the Russian Revolution has not received historians' full analysis, although Orlando Figes refers to some instances. Figes, *A People's Tragedy.*

5 As far as I can tell, the first incident of mob justice after the February Revolution took place not in Petrograd, but in Moscow. Moscow's *Vechernyia novosti* reported on mob violence against a thief in Solianka on May 5, and another more brutal case against four thieves caught by the crowd on May 12. *VN,* 5 / 5 / 17, 5 / 12 / 17.

6 *PL,* 5 / 13 / 17.

7   *GK*, 6 / 20 / 17.

8   Ereshchenko, "Prestupnost'," 171. My data indicate the following: nine in May, seven in June, eighteen in July, twenty-two in August, eighteen in September, and seventeen in October. The differences may be the result of how we count instances of mob justice. I included not only the cases where victims were actually beaten or killed, but also the cases where the crowd attempted mob justice. Since Ereshchenko did not cite newspaper dates, there is no way to compare my data with his, but since he used newspapers and archival materials I did not use, the numbers may be much bigger than the ninety-one cases I have collected.

9   Based on my data, the comparable figure for May to July was 0.37 per day, and from August to October 24, 0.67 per day. This means two every five days from May to July, and two every three days from August to October.

10   *MG*, 5 / 28 / 17. This is the only time that the newspaper quoted one of the crowd using the word "comrades."

11   *PL*, 7 / 9 / 17.

12   *PL*, 8 / 20 / 17.

13   *PL*, 10 / 15 / 17; *GK*, 10 / 15 / 17.

14   *PL*, 10 / 17 / 17.

15   *PL*, 7 / 6 / 17.

16   *PL*, 8 / 3 / 17; *GK*, 8 / 3 / 17. The newspapers did not mention what happened to the young Jewish boy tied to the cart.

17   There was also a food riot in the Kolomenskii district in August, in which a pogrom against the Jewish merchants took place. See *PL*, 8 / 22 / 17; *GK*, 8 / 22 / 17.

18   *GK*, 9 / 8 / 17.

19   *PL*, 9 / 14 / 17, 9 / 17 / 17.

20   *PL*, 9 / 21 / 17.

21   *PL*, 9 / 21 / 17.

22   *GK*, 7 / 7 / 17.

23   *PL*, 8 / 15 / 17.

24   *PL*, 9 / 15 / 17.

25   *VGS*, 10 / 12 / 17.

26   It is known that soldiers' wives engaged in violence during the war and the revolution. See the Khar'kov case described in Baker, "Rampaging *Soldatki*," 137–155. For Odessa, see Penter, *Odessa 1917*, 251–252. Their grievances focused on the lack of financial support and the hardship of life, especially the food supply. In Odessa, *soldatki* (soldiers' wives) formed their own union in May. Penter, *Odessa 1917*, 249–252.

27   Kel'son, "Militsiia fevral'skoi revoliutsii," Pt 1: 174; Wade, *Red Guards and Workers' Militias*, 60.

28   Golder, *War, Revolution, and Peace in Russia*, 49–50.

29   For the change in the language in addressing people, see Kolonitskii, *Simvoly vlasti*, 275–276.

30   Figes and Kolonitskii, *Interpreting the Russian Revolution*, 110.

31   Penter, *Odessa 1917*, 220–252.

32   At the end of July, when Dubrovin, a member of the Petrograd Soviet Executive Committee, attempted to stop mob justice against merchants on Vasilievskii Island, the crowd shouted at him, "You *burzhui,* we will teach you a lesson," and started beating him, too. *PL,* 7 / 29 / 17; *GK,* 7 / 29 / 17. On the other hand, however, the man who shot a shoplifter wore an officer's uniform. Whether or not he was an officer is difficult to say.

33   See Kolonitskii, "Antibourgeois Propaganda and Anti-*'Burzhui'* Consciousness in 1917," 183–196.

34   *Petrograd po perepisi 15 dekabria 1910 goda* (Petrograd, 1914), Part 2, Raspledelenia gruppami zaniatii, Issue 1, 39.

35   See Orlovsky, "Lower Middle Strata in Revolutionary Russia," 248–268.

36   In the Narvskii District, 22 out of the total of 110 factories (20 percent) in January 1917 employed fewer than twenty workers, out of which four factories, which might be better called "workshops," employed fewer than ten workers. By the end of March of the following year, 37 out of a total of 109 factories in this district employed fewer than 20 workers, which is 34 percent of the total, and 23 workshops (21 percent) had fewer than 10 workers. In the Aleksandro-Nevskii District, 15 percent of all factories in January 1917 employed fewer than 20 workers, and this number increased to 43 percent by the end of March 1918, while the number of factories employing fewer than 10 workers increased from 3 percent to 17 percent by the end of March. In the Moskovskii District, 28 percent of all factories in the district employed fewer than 20 workers, and only 5 percent had fewer than 10 workers in January 1917, but these numbers increased to 46 percent (factories with fewer than 20 workers) and 17 percent with fewer than 10 workers. Statistical analysis based on *Spisok fabrichno-zavodskikh predpriiattii Petrograda* (Petrograd, 1918). See also Sovet narodnogo khoziaistvo Severnogo raiona, Statisticheskii otdel, *Spisok fabrichno-zavodskikh predpriatii Petrograda: Po dannym na aprel' 1918 g.* (Petrograd, 1918).

37   The breakdown of incidents of mob justice where locations are known shows the following numbers: Spasskii (20), Narvskii (10), Aleksandro-Nevskii (9), Moskovskii (8), Liteinyi (6), Vasilievskii (5), Petrogradskii (5), Kolomenskii (5), Rozhdestvenskii (4), Vyborgskii (4), Kazanskii (3), Poliustrovskii (2), Okhtenskii (1), and Petergofskii (1). Three cases in the Liteinyi District were pickpockets caught on the tram. They could have been anywhere along Nevskii and Liteinyi Prospects—Kazanskii, Spasskii, Liteinyi, and Rozhdestvenskii Districts. For the divisions in Petrograd, see map 2, p. 22.

38   Three cases were reported in the Vyborgskii District. One case involved mob violence against a Chinese criminal in the courtyard of the Second Vyborg District Commissariat. It may indicate that the residents were angered by Chinese criminal acts spreading beyond Chinese gang members. *PL,* 5 / 30 / 17. Two other cases of mob justice in the Vyborgskii District involved a gang of hooligans against a militiaman. *BV,* 8 / 11 / 17; *PL,* 10 / 19 / 17; *GK,* 10 / 19 / 17. The only exception that resembled mob justice in the center and the southern districts was a case in which the residents chased the robbers towards Nevka. But despite the crowd's demand for mob justice, the militia and the Grenadier Regiment soldiers stopped it. In other words, that was an abortive mob justice case. *PL,* 6 / 17 / 17.

One example in the Petergofskii District was a case of mob justice attempted by the Putilov Factory workers against a worker in the same factory stealing from his coworker. This was another case where mob justice was aborted. The workers' militia intervened and punished the offending worker.

39 *GK*, 7 / 9 / 17.

40 *VV*, 8 / 15 / 17.

41 *PL*, 10 / 11 / 17.

42 *VV*, 10 / 20 / 17.

43 M. Gor'kii, *Nesvoevremennye mysli: Zametki o revoliutsii i kur'ture* (Moscow: MSP Interkontakt, 1990), 148, quoted in Aksenov, "Povsednevnaia zhizn'," 58.

44 See "The Killinng of Farkhunda," International Times Documentaries, https://www.nytimes.com/video/world/asia/100000004108808/the-killing-of -farkhunda.html (accessed May 25, 2017).

45 A useful approach to mob justice is the application of methodology from psychological and historical studies of crowds developed by Gustav Le Bon, Georges Lefebvre, George Rudé, Charles Tilly, and others. For this, see Holton, "Crowd in History," 219–233. I only note that my focus is rather on what Rudé and other crowd historians exclude: "the crowds that are casually drawn together" in streets, squares, and marketplaces.

46 See Durkheim, *Division of Labor*, Book 1; Clinard, "Theoretical Implications of Anomie and Deviant Behavior," 3–9.

47 Lewin, "Civil War," 416. Lewin situates primitization during the Civil War, but one can argue that this process began during the Russian Revolution.

48 Durkheim, *Division of Labor in Society*, 75–76.

49 Durkheim, *Division of Labor in Society*, 68.

50 Durkheim, *Division of Labor in Society*, 77.

51 Le Bon has been maligned and dismissed by many historians, political scientists, and sociologists as a conservative political thinker, a misogynist and racist theoretician, and a vulgar popularizer who plagiarized the theories of others. He was a staunch defender of the old order that was threatened by emerging social movements in the Third Republic, and he threw all social and political movements into his crowd analysis. And yet *The Crowd* was an enormously popular and influential book, and even those who criticize him grudgingly acknowledge his influence on the study of crowd psychology. For Le Bon, see Nye, *Origins of Crowd Psychology*; Barrows, *Distorting Mirrors*; Moscovici, *Age of the Crowd*; Ginneken, *Crowds, Psychology, and Politics*. Barrows, though highly critical of Le Bon, notes his influence on Sigmund Freud, Georges Lefebvre, and George Rudé. Susanna Barrows, *Distorting Mirrors*, 168. Jaap van Ginneken also acknowledges Le Bon's influence on Georges Sorel, Vilfredo Pareto, and Robert Michels, and later on Theodore Roosevelt, Theodor Herzl, Benito Mussolini, and Adolf Hitler. Ginneken, *Crowds, Psychology, and Politics*, 183–186. For historical background on the emergence of crowd psychology, see Nye, *Origins of Crowd Psychology*, 72–78.

52 Le Bon, *Crowd*, 4. A similar observation was made by Gabriel Tarde. In his *Penal Philosophy*, he states about a mob: "It is a gathering of heterogeneous elements, unknown to one another, but as soon as a spurt of passion, having flashed out

from one of these elements, electrifies this confused mass, there takes place a sort of sudden organization, a spontaneous generation. This incoherence becomes cohesion, this noise becomes a voice, and these thousands of men crowded together soon form but a single animal, a wild beast without a name, which marches to its goal with an irresistible finality." Gabiel Tarde, *Penal Philosophy* (Boston: Little Brown, 1912), 232, quoted in Barrows, *Distorting Mirrors,* 141.

53 Le Bon, *Crowd,* 6.

54 Le Bon, *Crowd,* 6–7.

55 Le Bon, *Crowd,* 8.

56 Le Bon, *Crowd,* 22.

57 Graphic details of such punishments are given in Chalidze, *Criminal Russia,* 11–16. Also see Fierson, "Crime and Punishment in the Russian Village," 55–69.

58 Kanishchev, *Russkii bunt,* 100–103. The role of the Bolsheviks in preventing pogroms was noted by their opponents in the local soviets in Bendery, Moldova, and in Samara. Kanishchev, *Russkii bunt,* 102.

59 V. I. Lenin, *Polnoe Sobranie sochinenii* (Moscow: Izdatel'stvo politicheskoi literatury, 1974), 34:217.

60 Aksenov, "Povsednevnaia zhizn'," 56–59.

61 Reed, *Ten Days That Shook the World,* 110.

6. Crime after the Bolshevik Takeover

1 For instance, there is no reference to alcohol pogroms in two important books representing the two poles of American historiography on the early days of the Bolshevik regime: Richard Pipes, *The Russian Revolution,* and Alexander Rabinowitch, *The Bolsheviks in Power.* Nor is there any entry on "alcohol pogroms" or "wine pogroms" in Acton, Cherniaev, and Rosenberg, *Critical Companion to the Russian Revolution.*

2 There is vast literature on the government structure that the Bolsheviks created immediately after their assumption of power. For a concise summary, see Wade, *Russian Revolution,* 255–282. For the two opposing interpretations, see Rabinowitch, *Bolsheviks in Power,* 17–53, and Pipes, *Russian Revolution,* 506–565.

3 The results of the elections cannot be determined precisely because many parties in various localities formed coalitions, and some parties ran as nationalist tickets. I used Pipes for the number of votes and Wade for the number of seats. Pipes, *Russian Revolution,* 542; Wade, *Russian Revolution,* 279.

4 Wade, *Russian Revolution,* 279.

5 For the Constituent Assembly election returns in Petrograd, see *VGS,* 11 / 17 / 17; G. Karant, "Posle vybory," *VGS,* 11 / 17 / 17. See O. N. Znamenskii, *Vserossiikoe Uchreditel'noe Sobranie* (Leningrad: Nauka, 1976), Appendix, Table 1. According to Znamenskii, of 945,000 residents, 75 percent voted. Znamenskii, *Vserossiiskoe Uchreditel'noe Sobranie,* 262.

6 Rabinowitch argues that the Bolsheviks, who gained 45.2 percent, were clear winners, predominating the city's eighteen electoral districts and completely dominating Petrograd's working-class areas. This is a rather one-sided conclu-

sion. First, the Bolsheviks did not win the majority. Second, since the breakdown of the election was not known, how different layers of the population voted is also not known, especially the voting patterns of the urban poor. Rabinowitch, *Bolsheviks in Power,* 69.

7 Pipes, *Russian Revolution,* 544–545. The two arrested delegates to the Constituent Assembly were Pavel D. Dolgorukov and Fedor F. Kokoshkin.

8 See Wade, *Russian Revolution,* 279–282; Pipes, *Russian Revolution,* 545–555.

9 The Committee of the Public Safety, created on October 24, before the Bolshevik seizure of power, should be distinguished from the Committee for the Salvation of the Fatherland and the Revolution, created on October 26. For the formation of the Committee of Public Safety, see Kruchkovskaia, *Tsentral'naia gorodskaia duma,* 81–97; TsGA SPb, f. 3217, op. 1, d. 1, ll. 3–3ob, ll. 9–10. Both Alexander Rabinowitch and Richard Pipes, who represent opposite schools of interpretation on the Russian Revolution, ignore the existence and the role played by the Committee of Public Safety, and conflate the two organizations. See Rabinowitch, *Bolsheviks in Power,* 23; Pipes, *Russian Revolution,* 526.

10 Buchanan, *Petrograd,* 235.

11 *IZ,* 10/27/17; Fraiman, *Forpost,* 140. The commissars of the Second Lesnoi District, the Third Spasskii Subdistrict, the Malo-Okhtinskii Subdistrict, and the First Vyborgskii District reported that between October 25 and November 1, there were no criminal acts involving the use of weapons, no shootings, and no illegal searches in the subdistrict. TsGA SPb, f. 1312, op. 1, d. 7, ll. 3–3ob, 5, 6, 7, 10, 12–12ob, 48–48ob; Fraiman, *Forpost,* 140–141. Even in crime-prone subdistricts such as the First Narvskii Subdistrict and the Third Aleksandro-Nevskii Subdistrict, no serious crime was reported. TsGA SPb, f. 131, op. 1, d. 7, l. 7; TsGA SPb, f. 131, op. 1, d. 7, ll. 12–12ob.

12 Williams, *Through the Russian Revolution,* 117.

13 *PG,* 11/7/17, 11/8/17, 11/9/17, 11/10/17, 11/14/17. Three of these thefts took place on the tram.

14 After the October Revolution, it became more difficult than in the period between March and October to have accurate crime statistics, but it is possible to piece together a general picture of what crimes were committed and where by diligently following various newspapers that disappeared and reappeared from October 1917 to March 1918 by sneaking through the Bolshevik censorship. These numbers are grossly understated, however, since there are a number of days when I did not have access to newspapers. From November 7 through November 30, I did not have access to eleven days; eight days for December 1917; four days for January 1918; six days for March. Also I excluded a number of robberies that accompanied the alcohol pogroms mentioned below. Gabriel Domergue, a French journalist who was widely connected with political figures, including some Bolshevik high officials, published the number of robberies for a little over one month from December 2 through January 7: 15,600 apartment robberies (an average of 445 per day), 9,370 shop robberies (267 per day), and 203,801 pickpocketing incidents (5,822 per day). These numbers seem to be exaggerated. Domergue, *La Russie rouge,* 184–185.

15 N. Shebuev, "Dnevnik," *PGol,* 2/4 (17)/18. *Petrogradskii golos* is the successor of *Petrogradskii listok,* which, after being suppressed by the Bolshevik censor, reappeared briefly as *Petrogradskii vestnik* and then as *Petrogradskii golos.*

16 M. R—g, "Prestupnyi Petrograd," *VO,* 3/10 (23)/18.

17 *GDV,* 1/17/18. *Gazeta-Kopeika* reappeared as *Gazeta-Privennik, Gazeta-Drug,* and *Gazeta dlia vsekh* after each was closed by censors.

18 *PV,* 11/22/17. A similar raid was reported in *PG,* 11/30/17; *VCh,* 12/16/17; *PVP,* 1/27/18; *PGol,* 1/15 (28)/18; *KG,* 3/3/18; *GD,* 11/30/17. See also Musaev, *Prestupnost',* 77.

19 *VCh,* 12/14/17.

20 Already on November 24, 1917, the VRK issued an order to close all clubs and dens where gambling was conducted. *PVRK,* 3:318. On January 31, the Sovnarkom issued a decree completely banning gambling, including popular card games called Preference and Vint. But as soon as the authorities closed down a gambling den, another popped up somewhere else, as happened before the October Revolution. *PVP,* 2/1 (14)/18.

21 *GDV,* 1/14/18; *PGol,* 1/13 (26)/18. It is interesting to note that this murder was solved by none other than V. G. Botsvadze, who had played a crucial role in the formation of the workers' militia in the Vyborgskii District immediately after the February Revolution and later served as a commissar in the Liteinyi District Commissariat.

22 *GDV,* 1/18/18.

23 *PGol,* 2/1 (14)/18; Domergue, *La Russie rouge,* 183–184. Meriel Buchanan had a similar experience. Her British embassy car was stopped by the Red Guards, but thanks to the quick wit of her chauffeur, she escaped being mugged. Buchanan, *Petrograd,* 228–229.

24 Domergue, *La Russie rouge,* 183.

25 Musaev, *Prestupnost',* 79.

26 *NVek,* 2/9/28; *PVP,* 2/8 (21)/18. Fraiman, *Forpost,* 191. The Kadet paper, *Rech',* was banned on October 26. It briefly reappeared as *Nash rech', Svobodnyi rech', Vek, Novaia rech',* and from February 10 (23) to October 19 was published as *Nash vek.*

27 Fraiman, *Forpost,* 191; Musaev, *Prestupnost',* 75.

28 TsGA SPb, f. 143, op. 1, d. 181, l. 14, quoted by Musaev, *Prestupnost',* 76.

29 *VS,* 3/23 (4/13)/18. *Vechernee slovo* was the successor of *Vechernee vremia,* the evening edition of *Novoe vremia.*

30 Musaev, *Prestupnost',* 75; Fraiman, *Forpost,* 191.

31 *PVP,* 1/29/18; *PGol,* 1/28/18.

32 *NVek,* 2/19/18; Musaev, *Prestupnost',* 79.

33 The *Journal of Events* for December recorded armed robberies on December 1, 3, 4, 5, 9, and 19: TsGA SPb, f. 131, op. 1, d. 11, ll. 1, 2, 5, 9, 13, 21. None of these robberies, with the exception of the one on December 19, were reported in newspapers. This indicates the incidence of robberies was much higher than the data I collected from newspapers.

34 See *PGol,* 2/6 (19)/18 for a shootout at a department store on Suvorov Prospect; *KG,* 4/2/18 for the robbery near the Moscow Gate and the subsequent

shootout at the funeral procession; and Musaev, *Prestupnost'*, 87, for a shootout in which eight people died at the Sevastopol' restaurant in the First Aleksandro-Nevskii Subdistrict.

35 *PGol*, 2 / 6 (19) / 18.

36 Musaev, *Prestupnost'*, 87.

37 For the murders before October, see Chapter 2. Domergue gave 135 murders from December 15 through January 20 (January 2 to February 7). Perhaps the discrepancies result from the counting method: the number of murder cases and the number killed in each murder case. I count murder cases, not murder victims.

38 *NV*, 1 / 18 / 18; Musaev, *Prestupnost'*, 86.

39 *PGol*, 3 / 21 / 18; Musaev, *Prestupnost'*, 76.

40 Musaev, *Prestupnost'*, 87–89. See also Steinberg [Shteinberg], *In the Workshop of the Revolution*, 74–83. Shteinberg (SR), the Commissar of Justice, often fought with Dzerzhinskii and Lenin to curb the injustices without due process meted out against those the Bolsheviks considered to be class enemies.

41 Gorky, *Untimely Thoughts*, 143.

42 *PG*, 11 / 10 / 17, 11 / 14 / 17, 11 / 17 / 17, 12 / 24 / 17,, 12 / 29 / 17, 12 / 31 / 17; *PZh* 11 / 21 / 17, 11 / 22 / 17; *GD*, 11 / 30 / 17; *GDV*, 12 / 10 / 17, 12 / 21 / 17, 1 / 3 / 18, 1 / 12 / 18, 1 / 17 / 18, 1 / 19 / 18; *VCh*, 12 / 12 / 17, 12 / 13 / 17, 12 / 14 / 17; *VZvon*, 12 / 22 / 17; *PGol*, 1 / 3 / 18; *NPG*, 1 / 3 / 18, 2 / 2 / 18, 2 / 3 / 18; *NV*, 1 / 12 / 18; 1 / 17 / 18; 1 / 27 / 18; *KG*, 2 / 19 / 18, 2 / 21 / 18, 2 / 23 / 18, 2 / 28 / 18; *PVP*, 1 / 12 / 18, 1 / 26 / 18, 1 / 26 / 18.

43 *GD*, 11 / 30 / 17.

44 *GDV*, 12 / 10 / 17.

45 *GDV*, 12 / 21 / 17; *VCh*, 12 / 10 / 17.

46 *GDV*, 1 / 4 / 18; *NPG*, 1 / 4 / 18; *VV*, 1 / 2 / 18; *PGol*, 1 / 3 / 18. Each newspaper had a slightly different version. The reference to the Revolutionary People's Court is puzzling. People's courts did not have jurisdiction over murder cases.

47 *GDV*, 1 / 17 / 18.

48 O. Tomskii, "Petrograd v eti dni: Krovozhadnaia publika," *VCh*, 12 / 14 / 17.

49 *NPG*, 2 / 3 (16) / 18.

50 "Petrograd—razboiniche gnezdo," *PVP*, 1 / 19 / 18; "Okhrana Petrograda," *PVP*, 1 / 30 / 18.

51 Gorky, *Untimely Thoughts*, 111.

52 *IZ*, 1 / 9 / 18, quoted in Musaev, "Byt gorozhan," 84.

53 *KG*, 3 / 15 / 18.

54 *PEkho*, 2 / 16 / 18.

55 Cherniaev, "Anarchists," 224–225.

56 Quoted in Cherniaev, "Anarchists," 224.

57 Vlad. Bonch-Bruevich, "Strashnoe v revoliutsii," 286–327.

58 *IZ*, 2 / 17 / 18, quoted in Fraiman, *Forpost*, 191.

59 Fraiman, *Forpost*, 192.

60 *Prv*, 2 / 18 / 18, quoted in Fraiman, *Forpost*, 192. For another case, see *KG*, 2 / 29 / 18.

61 Fraiman, *Forpost*, 192.

62 On February 11 (24), 1918, fifteen anarchists raided the city pawnshop on Vasilievskii Island and robbed the warehouse of valuables worth six to seven hundred thousand rubles. *KG*, 2 / 25 / 18; Musaev, *Prestupnost'*, 77.

63 *Prv*, 2 / 16 / 18, quoted in Fraiman, *Forpost*, 192.

64 *IZ*, 2 / 17 / 18, quoted in Fraiman, *Forpost*, 193.

65 Prv, 1 / 30 / 18, quoted in Fraiman, *Forpost*, 192.

66 For the Bolsheviks' expropriations of houses, see TsGA SPb, f. 3217, op. 1, d. 5b, ll. 11–11b, 13, 15–15ob, 16.

67 The term "wine pogroms" (*vinnye pogromy*) is often used. But it is more accurate to use the term "alcohol pogroms," since the looters attacked not only wine and cognac, but also vodka, spirits, and beer; in other words, anything connected with alcohol.

68 Quoted in Fraiman, *Forpost*, 184. According to *Pravda*, there were more than seven hundred wine and vodka cellars and storages. *Prv*, 12 / 2 / 17.

69 Narsky and Khmelevskaya, "Alcohol in Russia," 398–399.

70 See Chapter 1.

71 Narsky and Khmelevskaya, "Alcohol in Russia," 402.

72 Musaev, *Prestupnost'*, 59.

73 TsGA SPb, f. 3217, op. 1, d. 1, l. 4.

74 TsGA SPb, f. 3217, op. 1, d. 1, ll. 18–18ob.

75 *PL*, 11 / 8 / 17; *PG*, 11 / 8 / 17; TsGA SPb, f. 131, op. 1, d. 14, l. 32, quoted in Musaev, *Prestupnost'*, 60.

76 The Kronstadt sailors themselves had already revolted. Their radicalism and anarchist tendencies were well known. Therefore Lunacharstkii's proposal had no realistic possibility of protecting the wines. The fact is that there was no safe place in the vicinity of Petrograd to transport these precious wines.

77 TsGA SPb, f. 3217, op. 1, d. 1, l. 78.

78 The first storming of the Winter Palace on the night of October 24–25 was accompanied by the systematic destruction of cultural treasures. Domergue values the damage at 500 million rubles. Domergue, *La Russie rouge*, 185. It was Lunacharskii and Lenin's wife, Nadezhda Krupskaia, who played an important role in preserving the city's cultural treasures.

79 Musaev, *Prestupnost'*, 60.

80 Musaev, *Prestupnost'*, 60–61; Buchanan, *Petrograd*, 230–231; Sorokin, *Leaves from a Russian Diary*, 102–103. See also the report by Commissar Ovshchinkov on November 20 at the Admiralteiskii District Soviet, *RSP*, 1:54.

81 The collection of VRK's decisions on November 29 does not include its resolution to liquidate the alcohol reserves systematically, but there are some specific orders for searches and arrests. See *PVRK*, 1:466–467. See also Musaev, *Prestupnost'*, 61–62. *GD*, 11 / 30 / 17. The following were listed as targets of destruction: Bauer, Denker (Kirochnyi Lane), the cellar of Bektov (Panteleimon Lane), the cellars of Princes Makeev and Romanov, wine trader Petrov (Panteleimon Street), and the cellar on Galernaia Street. *PGol*, 11 / 30 / 17.

82 *PGol*, 12 / 1 / 17; Buchanan, *Petrograd*, 235.

83 Buchanan, *Petrograd*, 233.

84 *GDV*, 12 / 1 / 17.

85 *GDV,* 12 / 3 / 17.
86 *GDV,* 12 / 3 / 17.
87 *GDV,* 12 / 3 / 17; *PGol,* 12 / 3 / 17.
88 *PGol,* 12 / 3 / 17.
89 *PGol,* 12 / 3 / 17.
90 Bonch-Bruevich, "Komitet po bor'be s pogromami," 191.
91 *GDV,* 12 / 6 / 17; *PGol,* 12 / 6 / 17; *VCh,* 12 / 4 / 17, 12 / 6 / 17.
92 O. Tomskii, "Petrograd v eti dni," *VCh,* 12 / 8 / 17.
93 Tomskii, "Petrograd v eti dni," *VCh,* 12/8/17.
94 *VCh,* 12 / 4 / 17, 12 / 5 / 17, 12 / 6 / 17; *GDV,* 12 / 5 / 17.
95 *VCh,* 12 / 6 / 17.
96 *GDV,* 12 / 6 / 17; *PGol,* 12 / 6 / 17. According to the daily reports of the Second
    Vasilievskii Subdistrict, only eleven people were detained for public drunken-
    ness from December 2 to December 5. Given the magnitude of the alcohol po-
    groms, this figure indicates that the city militia was not involved in the suppression
    of the alcohol pogroms. See TsGA SPb, f. 131, op. 1, d. 50, ll. 1–3ob.
97 *GDV,* 12 / 7 / 17.
98 Buchanan, *Petrograd,* 234.
99 *Bor'ba za ustanovlenie i uprochenie Sovetskoi vlasti,* 402; *GD,* 12 / 7 / 17. The VRK
    was abolished on this day.
100 Bonch-Bruevich, "Komitet po bor'be s pogromami," 191.
101 *PGol,* 12 / 6 / 17. The strike also meant that the dvorniks refused to carry fire-
    wood into the buildings. Residents were left in their freezing apartments. For
    the strike of the dvorniks and doormen, see "Noch' pri otkrytykh dveriakh," in
    VCh, 12 / 5 / 17.
102 *GDV,* 12 / 12 / 17.
103 Domergue, *La Russie rouge,* 188.
104 The following wine / vodka cellars were attacked: Savva Petrov, Panteleimon
    Street (First Liteinyi Subdistrict); Mel'gunov, No. 10, Zhukovskaia Street (Second
    Liteinyi Subdistrict); House 23, Millionnaia (First Admiralteiskii Subdistrict);
    Corner of 4th Rozhdestvennaia and Suvorovskii Prospect (First Rozhdestven-
    skii Subdistrict); Hotel Balabanskaia, Novgorodskaia 4 (Second Rozhdestvenskii
    Subdistrict); Nobility Assembly, Italianskaia (First Spasskii Subdistrict); Corner
    of Gorokhovaia and Sadovaia (Third Spasskii Subdistrict); Count Shremet'ev
    (First Liteinyi Subdistrict); Merchant Firm Keller, Obvodnyi Canal 92 (Third
    Aleksandro-Nevskii Subdistrict). These places cover almost all districts in the
    center of the city. *GDV,* 12 / 7 / 17. On the following day, the pogroms also spread
    to the Nevskii District, which had been relatively quiet until then. *GDV,* 12 / 8 / 17.
105 *GDV,* 12 / 7 / 17.
106 *PGol,* 12 / 9 / 17.
107 *GDV,* 12 / 9 / 17.
108 *PGol,* 12 / 9 / 17.
109 *GDV,* 12 / 10 / 17.
110 *GDV,* 12 / 12 / 17.
111 *Pt,* 12 / 13 / 17.
112 *GDV,* 12 / 24 / 17, 12 / 28 / 17; *PGol* 12 / 24 / 17, 12 / 29 / 17.

113 *PGol,* 12 / 24 / 17.

114 *Prv,* 12 / 24 / 17, quoted in Musaev, *Prestupnost',* 67.

115 Musaev, *Prestupnost',* 67.

116 On January 9, two attacks took place on the wine cellars in the hotels. On this day, around seventy armed soldiers attacked the wine cellar of Balabinskaia Hotel in the First Aleksandro-Nevskii Subdistrict. The Red Guards and the militia detachment that rushed to the hotel exchanged gunfire with the looters, killing two and wounding four invaders. Musaev, *Prestupnost',* 67. The wine cellar of the Hotel Frantrsuzkaia (location unknown) was raided by a band of armed soldiers. The looters and the Red Guards engaged in a shootout for two hours. *NVek,* 1 / 12 / 18.

117 *GDV,* 1 / 21 / 18.

118 *NVek,* 1 / 23 / 18; Musaev, *Prestupnost',* 67.

119 *NVek,* 1 / 24 / 18; Musaev, *Prestupnost',* 68.

120 *GDV,* 1 / 24 / 18, 1 / 25 / 18.

121 *PVP,* 1 / 30 / 18; *PGol,* 1 / 31 / 18.

122 Fraiman, *Forpost,* 185; Kann, "Bor'ba rabochikh Petrograda," 134.

123 Tomskii, "Petrograd v eti dni"; Homo Novus, "P'ianym delom," *VZ,* 12 / 7 / 17; F. Sologub, "Ozorstvo," *VZ,* 12 / 9 / 17.

7. The Bolsheviks and the Militia

1   McAuley, *Bread and Justice,* 48.

2   Pomeranz, "Law and Revolution"; Burbank, "Lenin and the Law," 23–44.

3   Lenin, "Letter from Afar, Concerning a Proletarian Militia," Lenin, *Polnoe sobranie sochineniia* (Moscow: Izdatel'stvo politichmeskoi literatury, 1974), 33:39–40; Leggett, *Cheka,* xxix; Collins, "Russian Red Guard," 4.

4   TsGA SPb, f. 3217, op. 1, d. 1, ll. 11ob, 16, 23–23ob, 50; *VGS,* 10 / 28 / 17, 10 / 29 / 17, 11 / 4 / 17; Kruchkovskaia, *Tsentral'naia gorodskaia duma,* 98.

5   *PVRK,* 1:109; TsGA SPb, f. 131, op. 1, d. 5, l. 17; TsGA SPb, f. 73, op. 1, d. 1, l. 9.

6   Gorodetskii, *Rozhdenie Sovetskogo gosudarstva,* 183; Musaev, "Byt gorozhan," 77. Rykov resigned from the post on November 4 and was replaced by Grigorii I. Petrovskii

7   *PVRK,* 1:206. Note the caveat added at the end, "unless physical force was exercised." From the very beginning the city militia had no intention to use force to resist the Bolsheviks' attempt to take over the militia.

8   Such was the case in the First and Third Liteinyi, Second, Third, and Fourth Spasskii, First Moskovskii, and Second Kazanskii Subdistricts. For the case of the Third Spasskii Subdistrict, see Hasegawa, "Crime and Police in Revolutionary Petrograd," 31–32; TsGA SPb, f. 131, op. 1, d. 5, ll. 24, 24ob, 25; TsGA SPb, f. 131, op. 1, d. 8, l. 25. For other subdistricts, see Musaev, *Prestupnost',* 50.

9   This took place at least in the following subdistricts: the Third Vyborgskii, First and Second Okhtenskii, and First Lesnoi. TsGA SPb, f. 131, op. 1, d. 8, ll. 37, 37ob.

10 TsGA SPb, f. 131, op. 1, d. 8, l. 37ob.

11 Second Vyborgski, Second Okhtenskii, and First Liteinyi Subdistricts; Musaev, *Prestupnost'*, 51.
12 TsGA SPb, f. 131, op. 1, d. 8, ll. 14, 14ob; also see Musaev, *Prestupnost'*, 50–51.
13 TsGA SPb, f. 131, op. 1, d. 8, l. 53.
14 *RSP,* 1:63.
15 Lenin, *Polnoe sobranie sochinenii*, 35:75.
16 *PVRK*, 1:497. For the VRK's Investigation Commission as the forerunner of Cheka, see Leggett, *Cheka,* 7–8.
17 *PL*, 11 / 18 / 17, 11 / 19 / 17; Fraiman, *Forpost,* 143; Musaev, *Prestupnost'*, 49.
18 *Dekrety sovetskoi vlasti*, 1:92; Kruchkovskaia, *Tsentral'naia goroskaia duma*, 112; Fraiman, *Forpost,* 130.
19 *Dekrety sovetskoi vlasti*, 1:91–92; Kruchkovskaia, *Tsentral'naia goroskaia duma*, 112. For the dissolution of the city duma, see also Mil'chik,"Petrogradskaia tsentral'naia gordoskaia duma," 208–218.
20 Not only the moderate socialists, but also the Menshevik-Internationalists and some Left SRs also jointed the protest. Famous Left SR, Maria A. Spiridovna, delivered an impassioned speech at the All-Russian Executive Committee of the Soviets denouncing the Bolshevik dissolution of the city duma. Fraiman, *Forpost,* 132–133. Ironically, when the Red Guards and sailors closed the city duma, it was in the middle of discussions on the measures to deal with the unemployment issue that would directly affect the workers and soldiers. See Mil'chik, "Petrogradskaia Tsentral'naia gorodskaia duma," 208–218.
21 Fraiman, *Forpost,* 130–132; Musaev, *Prestupnost'*, 49.
22 For the results of the election for the city duma see *IZ,* 12 / 1 / 18, 12 / 2 / 18. Altogether 395,844 voted; the Bolheviks received 358,684 votes for 188 seats, and Left-SRs received 19,190 votes for 10 seats. For the breakdown of votes by district, see "Novaia gorodskaia duma," *IZ,* 12/2/17. See also Kruchkovskaia, *Tsenral'naia gorodskaia duma,* 122. One Right SR and one deputy representing the housing committees, which ran under the name of the "Union of Property and Labor Equality," were elected. It is not clear why these anti-Bolshevik candidates were allowed to be included on the list. It appears that since the selection of candidates was entrusted to district soviets, they may have slipped some onto the list.
23 *IZ,* 12/2/17; Fraiman, *Forpost,* 135. Nevertheless, the city workers continued to pledge allegiance to the old city duma. Kalinin had to find a small number of city workers willing to work for the Soviet regime to continue the essential functions of the city.
24 Gorodetskii, *Rozhdenie Sovetskogo gosudarstva*, 184–185; *PVRK*, 3:168–169.
25 Gorodetskii, *Rozhdenie Sovetskogo gosudarstva*, 184.
26 The commission was composed of I. P. Bakaev (the representative from the Petrograd Soviet), F. E. Dzerzhinskii (from the commissariat of internal affairs), E. A. Trifonov (from the Central Staff of the Red Guards), I. S. Unshlikht (VRK), and Sergeev and Sozman (two representatives from the bureau on the liquidation of the militia). TsGA SPb, f. 73, op. 1, d. 1, ll. 3–5, 25–25ob, 60.
27 According to this proposal, each factory and industrial enterprise was to provide workers for militia duty, from whom the Red Guards squads (*desiatki*), platoons (*vzvody*), company (*druzhiny*), and battalions would be formed. The Red

Guards battalions would provide posting and patrol duties in the district under the control of the district Red Guards command and the district soviet of workers' and soldiers' deputies. The training and arming of the militia units would be conducted by the district Red Guards staff. The militia duty would last for one week, and the Red Guards militiamen who served one week would be replaced by other units. TsGA SPb, f. 73, op. 1, d. 1, ll. 5-5ob; *PVRK*, 3:286-287. There is no evidence to indicate that this proposal was implemented.

28 TsGA SPb, f. 131, op. 1, d. 7, l. 1; TsGA SPb, f. 73, op. 1, d. 1, ll. 1, 9, 10, 48-48ob; Gorodetskii, *Rozhdenie Sovetskogo gosudarstva,* 186.

29 Musaev, *Prestupnost',* 53. For the closing of the Narva District Duma and the Rozhdestvenskii District Duma, see *GDV,* 12/12/17.

30 TsGA SPb, f. 73, op. 1, d. 2, ll. 3-5; Musaev, "Byt gorozhan," 77. Also see Skili-agin, Lesov, Pimenov, *Dela i liudi Lenigradskoi militsii,* 23, 25, 26; Fraiman, *Forpost,* 194.

31 *PVRK,* 3:376. Bydzan is a Latvian Left SR.

32 *PVRK,* 3:400-401. The Military Revolutionary Court, which was created by the Provisional Government and inherited by the Bolshevik power, was different from the Revolutionary Tribunal set up after the decree on the courts intended to try counterrevolutionaries and saboteurs.

33 *PVRK,* 3:409.

34 *PVRK,* 3:469-470. Helsingfors is Helsinki in Swedish and was widely used at the time.

35 *PVRK,* 3:458, 507.

36 *IZ,* 12/3/17, quoted in Fraiman, *Forpost,* 187.

37 *Bor'ba za ustanovlenii i uprochenie Sovetskoi vlasti,* 402; *GDV,* 12/7/17.

38 Bonch-Bruevich, "Komitet po bor'be s pogromami," 191.

39 *GDV,* 12/12/17.

40 Quoted in Musaev, *Prestupnost',* 65.

41 *GDV,* 12/5/17, 12/7/17.

42 *GDV,* 1/28/18; *NPG,* 1/28/18; *PVP,* 1/30/18.

43 *PVP,* 2/9 (22)/18.

44 *VZvez,* 2/9 (22)/18, 2/13 (26)/18, 2/23/18 (3/8/18).

45 *VZvez,* 2/22/18 (3/7/18).

46 See the meetings of the city administration under the Bolshevik rule, TsGA SPb, f. 3117, op. 1, d. 1a, ll. 25, 27; TsGA SPb, f. 3217, op. 1, d. 5b, ll. 1ob, 2-2ob, 3-4, 5-5b, 7, 8-8ob, 11-11ob, 15-15ob, 29-29ob. The city did attempt to raise taxes: it imposed special luxury taxes on property owners' use of servants, bathrooms, and even pianos. Brown, *Doomsday 1917,* 168. For taxes on owning dogs, see note 52.

47 Musaev, "Byt gorozhan," 63-64. For a biting commentary on darkness in the streets and lack of heating, see Obyvatel', "Sovremennye monologii na dvesti let nazad," *VCh,* 1/4/18. For the dvornik strike and the resulting lack of service for staffing the night watch, clearing snow, and bringing firewood, see "Noch' pri otkrytykh dveriakh," *VCh,* 12/5/17.

48 Musaev, "Byt gorozhan," 61-63.

49 Musaev, "Byt gorozhan," 64-65; also see "Noch' pri otkrytykh dveriakh."

50 Musaev, "Byt gorozhan," 65. See also Marabini, *La vie quotidienne,* 166.

51 Musaev, "Byt gorozhan," 65–66. See Ivan Vladimirov's painting depicting residents taking meat from a dead horse while demonstrators are marching on the other side of the river, https://www.wikiart.org/en/ivan-vladimirov/famine.

52 "Massovyia otravlenii sobak," *NVCh,* 2 / 6 (19) / 18.

53 Musaev, "Byt gorozhan," 68–69.

54 Musaev, "Byt gorozhan," 70.

55 On November 22, 1917, the Central Medical-Sanitary Council and the Board of the Pirogov Society passed a resolution appealing to all doctors to resist all measures taken by the Bolshevik government. B. M. Khromov and A. V. Sveshnikov, *Zdravookhranenie Leningrada* (Leningrad: Lenizdat, 1969), 22, quoted in Musaev, "Byt gorozhan," 119. For graphic descriptions of how doctors worked in the difficult conditions, see "Uzhasy Petrogradskikh bol'nits," *PVP,* 1 / 27 / 18, 1 / 29 / 18.

56 *PVP,* 2 / 1 (14) / 18; *KG,* 4 / 21 / 18; Musaev, "Byt gorozhan," 120.

57 *KG,* 7 / 10 / 18, quoted in Musaev, "Byt gorozhan," 131.

58 *VS,* 3 / 23 / 18 (4 / 6 / 18).

59 *Bor'ba za ustanovleini i uprochenie Sovetskoi vlasti,* 411. For direct relations between the abolition of the VRK and the creation of Dzerzhinskii's All-Russian Cheka, see Leggett, *Cheka,* 20.

60 *GDV,* 12 / 18 / 17. See Leggett, *Cheka,* 10–27; Pipes, *Russian Revolution,* 789–802.

61 For this development, see Leggett, *Cheka,* 45–49; and McAuley, *Bread and Justice,* 375–393.

62 *RSP,* 1:271; Fraiman, *Forpost,* 194–195.

63 *PVRK,* 2:432.

64 Fraiman, *Forpost,* 195.

65 TsGA SPb, f. 74, op. 1, d. 6, ll. 11–11b.

66 *PGol,* 1 / 12 (25) / 18.

67 It was only after 1921, after the end of the civil war, that the independent Criminal Militia was created and its jurisdiction transferred to the commissariat of internal affairs.

68 For the Bolsheviks' policy toward law, see Berman, *Justice in Russia,* 7–24; Hazard, "Soviet Law," 235–255; Huskey, "From Legal Nihilism to *Pravovoe Gosudarstvo,*" 23–42.

69 Nikolai Maklakov was a notorious right-wing minister of internal affairs and a brother of a Kadet member, Vasilii Maklakov.

70 Lenin, *Polnoe sobranie sochinenii,* 25:155, quoted in Hazard, *Settling Disputes in Soviet Society,* 3.

71 Lenin, *Polnoe sobranie sochinenii,* 36:162–163.

72 *RSP,* 1:154; Fraiman, *Forpost,* 150; McAuley, *Bread and Justice,* 118.

73 *PVRK,* 2:60; Fraiman, *Forpost,* 150.

74 Musaev, *Prestupnost',* 120.

75 Fraiman, *Forpost,* 154–155; McAuley, *Bread and Justice,* 118–119. See the vivid and critical account of a journalist's visit to the people's court in Vyborg District, "V novom sude," *VCh,* 12 / 1 / 17. See also L. I. Antonova, "Velikaia Oktiabr'skaia revoliutsiia i sozdanie narodnykh sudov, 1917–1918," http://law.edu.ru/doc /document.asp?docID=1133185 (accessed April 10, 2017).

76 McAuley, *Bread and Justice,* 123.
77 For the entire text of this decree, see "Dekret o sude, No. 1," www.hist.msu.ru /ER/Etext/DECRET/o-sude1,htm (accessed September 9, 2016). Also see Kozhevnikov, *Istoriia sovetskogo suda,* 19–25.
78 "Dekret o sude," http://ru.wikipedia.org/wiki/Dekrety_o-sude (accessed December 3, 2013); Pomeranz, "Law and Revolution," 9; Huskey, "From Legal Nihlism to *Pravovoe Gosudarstvo,*" 24–25; Antonova, "Velikaia Oktiabr'skaia revoliutsiia i sozdanie narodnykh sudov."
79 The new law code was not established until 1922.
80 Quoted in Pipes, *Russian Revolution,* 797.
81 Quoted in Gertsenzon et al., *Istoriia Sovetskogo ugolovnogo prava;* also, "Dekret o sude." Richard Pipes takes this caveat as proof that Lenin intended to create a court system subservient to the whims of the regime. But Mary McAuley has a different interpretation. She argues that, by emphasizing "revolutionary conscience" and "revolutionary legality," the decree accepted the spontaneous initiative embodied in instituting courts from below. On this reading, the decree reflects a compromise between the early Bolshevik regime's two contradictory tendencies: spontaneity (accepting and encouraging local initiatives) and consciousness (an instinctive desire for centralized control). McAuley, *Bread and Justice,* 119.
82 Musaev, *Prestupnost',* 120–121. The District People's Court had three divisions: criminal, civil, and special. The criminal division was not opened until September 9, 1918.
83 Quoted in Pipes, *Russian Revolution,* 798. For the Revolutionary Tribunal, see Fraiman, *Forpost,* 220–228; Rendle, "Revolutionary Tribunals." See also *PGol,* 11/30/17.
84 *PGol,* 12/6/17.
85 McAuley, *Bread and Justice,* 59–61; Rendle, "Revolutionary Tribunals," 695, 696, 698–699, 704, 708–709.
86 Leon Trotsky, *Lenin: Notes for a Biographer* (New York: Putnam's Sons, 1971), 120.
87 Leggett, *Cheka,* 62–63.
88 Pipes, *Russian Revolution,* 798.
89 Startsev, *Ocherki,* 206.
90 See Wade, *Red Guards and Workers' Militias,* 315–330.
91 Fraiman, *Forpost,* 195–196.
92 Wade, *Red Guards and Workers' Militias,* 311–312; *RSP,* 2:306–307; Fraiman, *Forpost,* 196.
93 Musaev, "Byt gorozhan," 85. Petrograd region was reorganized into the Petrograd Labor Communes by absorbing the neighboring areas around the city.
94 Skliagin, Lesov, Pimenov, *Dela i liudi Leningradskoi militsii,* 29; Musaev, "Byt gorozhan," 85; Musaev, *Prestupnost',* 94–95; Leggett, *Cheka,* 121–123.
95 TsGA SPb, f. 142, op. 1, d. 8, l. 113; Musaev, *Prestupnost',* 95–96.
96 Musaev, "Byt gorozhan," 86; Musaev, *Prestupnost',* 97. It was published as "instructions" on October 20, 1918, signed by Grigorii Petrovskii (commissar of internal affairs) and Dmitrii Kurskii (commissar of justice), and contained in the collection of laws; Leggett, *Cheka,* 121. The "instructions" of October 20, introduced in detail by Murray Frame, appear to be identical with the Law (*Polozhenie*)

of the Soviet Militia described by Musaev. Frame, "Militsiia vo vremia Russkoi revoliutsii 1917 goda," 117-119.

97   Quoted in Collins, "Russian Red Guard," 8.

98   Musaev, *Prestupnost'*, 93-114.

99   Leggett, *Cheka*, 56-57; Steinberg, *In the Workshop*, 145; Pipes, *Russian Revolution*, 794; McAuley, *Bread and Justice*, 387.

100 Pipes, *Russian Revolution*, 794, 802.

101 Quoted in Pipes, *Russian Revolution*, 802. Emphasis added.

102 Hagenloh, *Stalin's Police*, 27-28.

103 McAuley, *Bread and Justice*, 389-390; Leggett, *Cheka*, 58.

104 For forced labor camps, see Leggett, *Cheka*, 175-181. For Dzerzhinskii's attempt to incorporate the militia into the Cheka, see Hagenloh, *Stalin's Police*, 29.

105 The classification of common criminals as "socially dangerous" developed into "socially harmful" during the Stalin period. In April 1935, Iagoda declared that "hooligans, bandits, and robbers were 'genuine' counterrevolutionaries" and subject to extrajudicial repression. During the mass operations of 1937-1938, they were to be eliminated "once and for all." See Hagenloh, *Stalin's Police*, 114, 175-180, 240, 287.

Conclusion

1   Fedor Sologub, "Ozorstvo," *VZvon*, 12 / 9 / 17.

2   Gramsci, *Prison Notebooks*, 276. Paul Vinogradov made a similar observation about revolution. He wrote: "[The Revolution] means the overthrow of all accepted creeds, morals and habits of the people, a confusion of their entire nature, in which, for a time, nothing could be relied upon—neither duty, nor humanity, nor affection." Paul Vinogradov, *Encyclopedia Britanica*, 12th edition, vol. 33 (1922), quoted in Brown, *Doomsday 1917*, 319.

3   Lukes, Introduction to *The Division of Labor in Society*, xxxii, xxxiv.

4   Lukes, Introduction to *The Division of Labor in Society*, xxxii, xxxiv.

5   De Grazia, *The Political Community*, xii-ix, quoted in Clinard, *Anomie and Deviant Behavior*, 9.

6   Lukes, Introduction to *The Division of Labor in Society*, xxxi.

7   Durkheim, *Division of Labor in Society*, 66.

8   Merton, *Social Theory and Social Structure*, 186-193.

9   Merton, *Social Theory and Social Structure*, 188, 189.

10 Brown writes: "Everyone who had been accustomed to exercise authority, whether as administrator, employer, manager or even head of a well-staffed household, now felt himself to be under the surveillance of those beneath him. A hierarchy that a few days before had been absolute had become conditional." Brown, *Doomsday 1917*, 70-71.

11 Durkheim, *Division of Labor in Society*, 77.

12 Durkheim, *Division of Labor in Society*, 68-69.

13 Gros, "Failed States," 536. For a brief history of the theories of the failed states, see Charles T. Call, "Beyond the 'Failed State': Toward Conceptual Alternatives," *European Journal of International Relations* 17, no. 2 (2010): 305-306. For the

relationship between classical revolutions and the state, see Skocpol, *States and Social Revolutions*.

14 Max Weber, *Economy and Society*, ed. G. Roth and C. Wittich (Berkeley and Los Angeles: University of California Press, 1978), quoted in Gros, "Failed States," 537.

15 Anter, *Max Weber's Theory of the Modern State*, 26, 33.

16 Anter, *Max Weber's Theory of the Modern State*, 58. Italics in original.

17 Weber, *Economy and Society*, quoted in Gros, "Failed States," 538–539.

18 Rotberg, "Failed States, Collapsed States, Weak States," 3. Charles T. Call refines the concepts of the failed states as manifested in three gaps: capacity gaps, security gaps, and legitimacy gaps. Capacity gap is when state institutions lack the ability to effectively deliver basic goods and services to its population. Security gap is when the state is unable to provide security to its population under the threat of armed groups. Legitimacy gap is when a significant portion of a state's political elites and society rejects the rules regulating the exercise of power and the accumulation and distribution of wealth. Call, "Beyond the 'Failed State'," 307–309.

19 Rotberg, "Failed States, Collapsed States, Weak States," 3. As for the nature of the state during the Russian Revolution, two important concepts should be noted. The first is the concept proposed by William Rosenberg of the state as "a social process" and "a site of negotiations and an arena of conflict." The second is the concept of the state as corporatism, developed by Daniel Orlovsky. See Rosenberg, "Social Mediation and State Construction(s)"; Orlovsky, "Corporatism or Democracy." My skepticism about these concepts derives from their neglect of the monopoly of coercion as one of the fundamental attitudes of the state.

20 Rotberg, *When States Fail*, 6.

21 Steinberg, "Blood in the Air," 109, 110.

22 Sanborn, *Drafting the Russian Nation*, 166.

23 Stepun, *Iz pisem praporshchika artrillerista*, 19–20, quoted in Sanborn, *Drafting the Russian Nation*, 171.

24 Sanborn, *Drafting the Russian Nation*, 168–170.

25 Ostroumov, *Prestupnost'*, 79–80.

26 E. K. Krasnuchkin, "Kriminal'nye psikhopaty sovremennosti i bor'ba s nimi," in M. N. Gernet, ed., *Prestupnyi mir Moskvy: sbornik statei* (Moscow: Izdatel'stvo "Pravo i zhizn'," 1924), 192, quoted in Kowalsky, "Transforming Society," 350.

27 *MG*, 3/5/17.

28 Quoted in Hayek, *Fatal Conceit*, 3.

29 Emilie Durkheim, *Moral Education: A Study in the Theory and Application of the Sociology of Education* (New York: Free Press of Glencoe), 54, quoted in Lukes, Introduction to *The Division of Labor in Society*, xxvii.

30 Emilie Durkheim, "Deux lois de l'évoution pénale," *L'Année sociologique*, 4, in Steven Lukes and Andrew Scull, eds., *Durkheim and the Law* (Basingstoke: Palgrave Macmillan, 2013), 80, quoted in Lukes, Introduction to *The Division of Labor in Society*, xxxiii.

31 Holoquist, *Making War, Forging Revolution*, 203, 285.

32 Gros, "Failed States," 537.

BIBLIOGRAPHY

Archival Sources

GARF (Gosudarstvennyi Arkhiv Rossiiskoi Federatsii)

f. 398   MVD Vremennogo pravitel'stva
f. 406   Glavnoe upravlenie po delam militsii MVD Vremennogo Pravitel'stva
f. 1503   Departament obshchikh del MVD Vremennogo Pravitel'stva
f. 1790   Ministerstvo Iustitsii Vremennogo Pravitel'stva
f. 1791   Glabnoe upravlenie po delam militsii
f. 5141   Upravlenie Petrogradski gorodskoi militsii

OR RNB (Otdel Rukopisei Rossiskoi Natsional'noi Biblioteki)

f. 581   Peshekhonov, A. V., Vospominaniia
f. 1052   Engel'gardt, Vospominaniia o Fevral'skoi revoliutsii

TsGA SPb (Tsentral'nyi Gosudarstvennyi Arkhiv Sankt-Peterburga)

f. 73   Petrogradskoe gorodskoe upravlenie raboche-krest'ianskoi militsii
f. 74   Petrogradskkii ugolovnyi rozysk
f. 131   Petrogradskaia gorodskaia militsiia

TsGIA SPb (Tsentral'nyi Gosudarstvennyi Istoricheskii Arkhiv Sankt-Peterburga)

f. 210   Petrogradskaia sanitarnaia komissiia
f. 225   Petrogradskii okuruzhnoi sud
f. 258   Petrogradskoe gubernskoe prisutsvie
f. 487   Prokuror Petrogradsogo okruzhnogo suda
f. 513   Petrogradskaia gorodskaia urpava
f. 520   Petrogradskii stolichnyi mirovoi s"ezd
f. 569   Kantseliaria Petrogradskogo gradonachal'nika
f. 573   Petrogradskaia gorodskaia uprava
f. 593   Petrogradskii vrachebno-politseikii komitet
f. 783   Revizionnaia komissiia gorodskogo obshchestvennogo upravleniia
f. 792   Petrogradskaia gorodskaia duma
f. 965   Petrogradskaia sysknaia politsiia
f. 1695   Prokuror Petrogradskoi sudebnoi palaty

Bakhmeteff Archives, Rare Book and Manuscript Library, Columbia University
E. V. Isaakova, Memoirs
K. I. Globachev, "Pravda o russkoi revoliutsii," byvshago nachal'nika Petrogradskogo Okhrannogo otdeleniia
N. N. Flige, Pervye dni revoliutsii v Petrograde i leto 1917 goda

Hoover Institution Archives
C. T. Swinnerton letter, 1917
Eugene A. Korvin-Kronkovsky diary
Ivan A. Vladimirov paintings
Izvestiia revoliutsionnoi nedeli article collection
Ksenia Aleksandrovna diaries
Leighton Rogers Memoirs
Leslie Urquart letters
Loehr (Mrs) Collection 1917
Madame Petouillet diary
Nadia L. Schapiro memoirs
Niva Vernadsky memoirs
Novaia zhizn' newspaper articles, 1917–1918
Ol'ga Valerianovna Palei typescript
Russian pictoral collection
Vera Cattell Collection

Newspapers

Birzhvyia vedomosti
Delo naroda
Ekho
Gazeta dlia vsekh
Gazeta drug
Gazeta-Kopeika
Izvestiia Komiteta Petrogradskikh zhurnalistov
Izvestiia Petrogradskogo Soveta rabochikh i soldatskikh deputatov
Krasnaia gazeta
Malen'kaia gazeta
Nash vek
Novaia Petrogradskaia gazeta
Novaia zhizn'
Novoe vremia
Novyi vechernyi chas
Petrogradskaia gazeta
Petrogradskaia vecherniaia pochta
Petrogradskaia zhizn'
Petrogradskii golos
Petrogradskii listok

Petrogradskii vestnik
Petrogradskoe ekho
Pieter
Pravda
Pravo
Rech'
Vecher
Vechernee slovo
Vechernee vremia
Vecherniaia pochta
Vecherniaia zvezda
Vechernie ogni
Vechernii chas
Vechernii zvon
Vechernyia novosti
Vestnik gorodskogo samoupravleniia

Contemporary Journals (published in 1917)

Gorodskoe delo
Niva
Novyi satirikon
Ogonek
Restorannoe delo
Sontse Rossii
Strekoza
Vestnik politsii
Zhurnal Ministerstva iustitsii

Census, Statistics, Address Books

Ezhenedel'nik statisticheskago otdeleniia Petrogradskoi gorodskoi upravy, nos. 1–42, January 1–7 to October 15–21, 1917. Petrograd: Petrogradskaia gorodskaia uprava, 1917.

Materialy po statistike Leningrada i Leningradskoi gubernii. Leningrad: Gubernskii otdel statistiki, 1925.

Materialy po statistike Petrograda, vols. 1–5. Petrograd: Petrogradskoe stolichnoe statisticheskoe biuro, 1920–1921.

Materialy po statistike truda, vols. 1–6. Petrograd: Tsentral'noe biuro statistiki truda, 1918.

Materialy po statistike truda severnoi oblasti, vol. 1. Petrograd: Petrogradskiii oblastnoi komissariat truda, Otdel statistiki 1918.

Petrograd po perepisi 15 dekabria 1910 goda. Petrograd: Petrogradskaia gorodskaia uprava, 1910.

Spisok fabrichno-zavodskikh predpriiatii Petrograda. Petrograd: Sovet narodnogo kho-
ziaistva Severnogo raĭona: Statisticheskiĭ otdel, 1918.

Statisticheskie dannye otnoshashcheisia k gorodu Petrograda. Petrograd: Petrogradskaia
gorodskaia uprava, 1916.

Statisticheskii sbornik po Petrogradu i petrogradskoi gubernii. Petrograd: Tsentral'noe
statisticheskoe upravlenie, Petrogradskiĭ gubernskii otdel statistiki, 1922.

Statisticheskii spravochnik po Petrogradu. Petrograd: S.F.S.R. Komissariat gorodskikh
khoziaistv, Statisticheskiĭ otdel, 1919.

Ves' Petrograd: adresnaia i spravochnaia kniga g. Petrograda. Petrograd: Tovarishchestvo
A. S. Suvorina, "Novoe vremia," 1917.

Encyclopledias

Entsiklopedicheskii slovar', vols. 1–81. St. Petersburg: F. A. Brokgaus, N. A. Efron,
1890–1904.

Novyi Entsiklopedicheskii slovar', vols. 1–29. St. Petersburg / Petrograd: F. A. Brokgaus,
N. A. Efron, 1911–1916.

Sankt-Peterburg, Petrograd, Leningrad: Entsiklopedicheskii spravochnik. Moscow:
Nauchnoe izdatel'stvo Bol'shaia Rossiiskaia Entsikolpediia, 1992.

Sankt-Peterburg: Entsikolpediia. http://www.encspb.ru/;jsessionid=A2E0D0AF3DAF
39720367BC9AB22A5B23?lc=ru.

Cited Primary Sources

Almedingen, E. M. *My St. Petersburg: A Reminiscence of Childhood.* New York: W. W.
Norton, 1970.

———. *Tomorrow Will Come.* Boston: Little, Brown, and Company, 1941.

Berman, Iak. "P'ianstvo i prestupnost'." *Pravo,* no. 37 (1914): 2578–2587.

Bonch-Bruevich, Vladimir. "Komitet po bor'be s pogromami v Petrograde." In *Na
boevykh postakh Fevral'skoi i Oktiabr'skoi revoliutsii.* Moscow: Izdatel'stvo Federatsiia, 1930.

———. "Strashnoe v revoliutsii." In *Na boevykh postakh Fevral'skoi i Oktiabr'skoi revoliutsii.* Moscow: Izdatel'stvo Federatsiia, 1930.

*Bor'ba za ustanovlenie i uprochenie Sovetskoi vlasti, 26 oktiabria 1917
g.-10 ianvaria 1918 g.* Moscow: Izdatel'stvo Akademii nauk SSSR, 1962.

Browder, Robert Paul, and Alexander F. Kerensky. *The Russian Provisional Government, 1917: Documents.* 3 vols. Stanford, CA: Stanford University Press, 1961.

Buchanan, Meriel. *Petrograd: The City of Trouble, 1914–1918.* London: W. Collins, 1918.

Dekrety Sovetskoi vlasti o Petgrograde, 25 oktiabria 1917 g.–29 dekabria 1918 g. Leningrad: Lenizdat, 1986.

Domergue, Gabriel. *La Russie rouge.* Paris: Perrin, 1918.

Fabrichno-zavodskie komitety Petrograda v 1917 godu: Protokoly. 2 vols. Moscow:
Nauka, 1979, 1982.

Gippius, Z. N. *Peterburgskie dnevniki, 1914–1918.* New York: Orfei, 1982.

Golder, Frank Alfred. *War, Revolution, and Peace in Russia: The Passage of Frank Golder, 1914–1927.* Stanford, CA: Hoover Institution Press, 1992.

Goldman, Emma. *My Disillusionment in Russia.* Garden City, NY: Double Day, 1923.

Gorky, Maxim. *Untimely Thoughts: Essays on Revolution, Culture, and the Bolsheviks, 1917–1918.* New York: P. S. Eriksson, 1968.

"Gorodskiia prestupleniia za 1915 god." *Vestnik politsii,* no. 39 (1916): 940–941.

"Gorodskiia prestupleniia za 1915 god—prodolzhenie." *Vestnik politsii,* no. 40 (1916): 957–958.

Grabbe, Paul. *Windows on the River Neva: A Memoir.* New York: Pomerica Press, 1977.

Iashinskii, I. I. *Roman moei zhizni.* Leningrad: Gosizdat, 1926.

Jones, Stinton. *Russia in Revolution: Being the Experiences of an Englishman in Petrograd during the Upheaval.* London: Herbert Jenkins, 1917.

Kaiurov, V. "Oktiabr'skie ocherki: Kornilov, krasnaia gvardiia, Vyborgskii narodnyi sud." *Proletarskaia revoliutsiia,* no. 7 (1925): 224–237.

Kanatchikov, Semen Ivanovich. *A Radical Worker in Tsarist Russia: The Autobiography of Semen Ivanovich Kanatchikov.* Edited and translated by Reginald E. Zelnik. Stanford, CA: Stanford University Press, 1986.

Kel'son, Z. "Militsiia fevral'skoi revoliutsii: Vospominaniia." Pts 1–3. Pt 1, *Byloe* 29, no. 1 (1925): 161–179; Pt 2, 30, no. 2 (1925): 151–175; Pt 3, 33, no. 5 (1925): 220–235.

———. "Padenie Vremennogo Pravitel'stva." *Byloe* 34, no. 6 (1925): 192–205.

"Khronika gorodkoi zhizni." *Gorodskoe delo,* no. 7 (1917): 280–297; no. 8 (1917): 330–340; nos. 9–10 (1917): 368–377; nos. 19–22 (1917): 433–440.

Kleinmikhel, Countess M. *Memories of a Shipwrecked World.* New York: Brentano's, 1923.

Kschessinska, Mathilde [Kshesinskaia, Matilda]. *Dancing in Petersburg: The Memoirs of Mathilde Kschessinska, H. S. H. The Princess Romanovsky-Krassinsky.* Translated by Arnold Haskell. Alton, Hampshire, UK: Dance Books, 2005.

Lansbury, G. *What I Saw in Russia.* London: W. Heinemann, 1920.

Lenskii, N. A. "Gorodskaia militsiia, ee organizatsiia i kompetentsiia." *Gorodskoe delo,* no. 7 (1917): 265–270.

Mantushkin, V. "Vremennye sudy v Petrograde." *Zhurnal Ministerstva iustitsii,* no. 4 (1917): 169–190.

Mil'chik, I. I. "Petrogradskaia tsentral'naia gorodskaia duma v fevrale-oktiabre 1917 g." *Krasnaia letopis'* 2, no. 23 (1927): 189–282.

Peshekhonov, A. V. "Pervyia nedeli (Iz vospominanii o revoliutsii)." *Na chuzhoi storone* 1 (1923): 255–319.

Pozner, S. M. *Dela i dni Petrograda, 1917–1921.* Berlin: Feichenfzld's Buchdruckerei, 1923.

Punin, Nikolai. *The Diaries of Nikolay Punin, 1904–1953,* edited by Sidney Monas and Jennifer Greene Krupala, translated by Jennifer Greene Krupala (Austin: University of Texas Press, 1999).

Raionnye sovety Petrograda v 1917 godu. 3 vols. Moscow, Leningrad: Nauka, 1964–1966.

Ransom, Arthur. *Russia in 1919.* New York: B. W. Huebsch, 1921.

Reed, John. *Ten Days That Shook the World.* New York: Vintage Books, 1960.

Sain-Wittgenstein, E. N. *Dnevnik, 1914–1918*. Paris: YMCA Press, 1986.

Schakovskoy, Zinaida. "The February Revolution as Seen by a Child." *Russian Review* 26, no. 1 (January 1967): 68–73.

Serge, Victor. *Memoires d'un revoliutionnaire*. Paris: Éditions du Seuil, 1951.

Shklovsky, V. B. *A Sentimental Journey*. Ithaca, NY: Cornell University Press, 1970.

Shliapnikov, A. *Semnadtsatyi god*. Vol. 1. Moscow: Gosudarstvennoe izdatel'stvo, 1923.

Snowden, E. *Through Bolshevik Russia*. London: Cassel, 1920.

Sorokin, Pitirim A. *Leaves from a Russian Diary—And Thirty Years After*. Boston: Beacon Press, 1950.

Stasova, E. D. *Stranitsy zhizni i bor'by*. Moscow: Izdatel'stvo politicheskoi literatury, 1957.

Steinberg [Shteinberg], I. N. *In the Workshop of the Revolution*. London: Victor Gollancz, 1955.

Stepun, Fedor. *Iz pisem praporshchika artillerista*. Prague: Plamia, n.d.

Storozhev, V. N. "Fevral'skaia revoliutsiia 1917 goda." *Nauchnye izvestiia: Sb. 1 (economika, istoriia, pravo)*. Moscow: Gosudarstvennoe izdatel'stvo, 1922.

Tagantsev, N. N. "Iz moikh vospominanii." In *1917 god v sud'bakh Rossii i mira: Fevral'skaia Revoliutsiia ot novykh istochnikov k novomu osmysleniiu*, edited by S. V. Tiutiukin. Moscow: Institut Rossiiskoi istorii RAN, 1997.

Timofeev, P. "What the Factory Worker Lives By." In *The Russian Worker: Life and Labor under the Tsarist Regime*, edited by Victoria E. Bonnell. Berkeley: University of California Press, 1983.

Tseretelli, I. G. *Vospominaniia o fevral'skoi revoliutsii*. 2 vols. Paris: Mouton, 1963.

Velikaia Oktiabr'skaia sotsialisticheskaia revoliutsiia: Dokumenty i materialy. 6 vols. Vol. 1, *Revoliutsionnoe dvizhenie v Rossii posle sverzheniia samoderzhaviia*. Moscow: Izdatel'stvo AN SSSR, 1957.

Vrangel', M. D. "Moia zhzn' v sovetskoi raiu." *Arkhiv russkoi revoliutsii* 4 (1990): 198–213.

Vrangel', N. E. *Vospominaniia: ot krepostnogo prava do bol'shevikov*. Moscow: Novoe literaturnoe obozrenie, 2003.

Williams, Albert Rys. *Through the Russian Revolution*. New York: Boni and Liveright, 1921.

Williams, Harold Whitmore. *Russia of the Russians*. London: Sir Isaac Pitman and Sons, 1915.

Cited Secondary Sources

Abbott, Robert James. "Police Reform in Russia." PhD diss., Princeton University, 1971.

Acton, Edward, Vladimir Iu. Cherniaev, and William G. Rosenberg. *Critical Companion to the Russian Revolution, 1914–1921*. London: Arnold, 1997.

Aksenov, V. B. "Militsiia v gorodskie sloi v period revoliutsionnogo krizisa 1917 goda: Problemy legitimnosti." *Voprosy istorii*, no. 8 (2001): 36–50.

———. "Povsednevnaia zhizn' Petrograda i Moskvy." Candidate diss., Moscow Pedagogical State University, 2002.

Anter, Andreas. *Max Weber's Theory of the Modern State: Origins, Structure and Significance.* New York: Palgrave Macmillan, 2014.

Antonova, L. I. "Velikaia Oktiabr'skaia revoliutsiia i sozdanie narodnykh sudov, 1917–1918." http://law.edu.ru/doc/document.asp?docID=1133185. Accessed April 10, 2017.

Antoshkin, D. V. *Ocherk dvizheniia sluzhashchikh v Rossii.* Moscow: Moskva, 1921.

Antsiferov, N. P. *Dusha Peterburga.* Paris : YMCA Press, 1978..

Ascher, Abraham. *The Revolution of 1905: A Short History.* Stanford, CA: Stanford University Press, 2004.

Badcock, Sarah. *Politics and the People in Revolutionary Russia: A Provisional History.* Cambridge: Cambridge University Press, 2007.

Baker, Mark. "Rampaging *Soldatki,* Cowering Police, Bazaar Riots and Moral Economy." *Canadian American Slavic Studies* 35, nos. 2–3 (2001): 137–155.

Barrows, Susanna. *Distorting Mirrors: Visions of the Crowd in Late Nineteenth-Century France.* New Haven, CT: Yale University Press, 1981.

Bater, J. *St. Petersburg: Industrialization and Change.* London: Edward Arnold, 1976.

Berman, Harold J. *Justice in Russia: An Interpretation of Soviet Law.* Cambridge, MA: Harvard University Press, 1950.

Blackbourn, David. *The Long Nineteenth Century: A History of German, 1780–1918.* Oxford: Oxford University Press, 1998.

Boll, Michael M. *The Petrograd Armed Workers' Movement in the February Revolution.* Washington, DC: University Press of America, 1979.

Bonnell, Victoria E., ed. *The Russian Worker: Life and Labor under the Tsarist Regime.* Berkeley: University of California Press, 1983.

Brown, D. *Doomsday 1917: The Destruction of Russia's Ruling Class.* London: Sidgwick & Jackson, 1975.

Burbank, Jane. "Lenin and the Law." *Slavic Review* 54, no. 1 (1995): 23–44.

Burdzhalov, E. N. *Vtoraia russkaia revoliutsiia: Vosstanie v Petrograde.* Moscow: Nauka, 1967.

Chagadaeva, Ol'ga. "Sukhoi zakon i chernyi rynok v gody Pervoi mirovoi voiny." http://wg-lj.livejournal.com/894057.html. Accessed December 17, 2013. Also in Politiko, http://politiko.ua/blogpost75564. Accessed December 17, 2013.

Chalidze, Valerii. *Criminal Russia: Essays on Crime in the Soviet Union.* New York: Random House, 1977.

———. *Ugolovnaia Russiia.* New York: Khronika, 1977.

Cherniaev, Vladimir Iu. "Anarchists." In *Critical Companion to the Russian Revolution, 1914–1921,* edited by Edward Acton, Vladimir Iu. Cherniaev, and William G. Rosenberg. London: Arnold, 1997.

———. "Gibel' dumskoi monarkhii: Vremennoe pravitel'stvo i ego reformy." In *Vlast' i reformy: Ot samoderzhavnoi k sovetskoi Rossii,* edited by B. V. Anan'ich, R. Sh. Ganelin, and V. M. Paneiakh. Moscow: DB, 1996.

Clinard, Marshall B., ed. *Anomie and Deviant Behavior: A Discussion and Critique.* New York: Free Press, 1964.

———. "The Theoretical Implications of Anomie and Deviant Behavior." In *Anomie and Deviant Behavior,* edited by Marshall Clinard, 1–56. New York: Free Press, 19674.

Collins, David. "The Russian Red Guard of 1917 and Lenin's Utopia." *Journal of Russian Studies* 32 (1976): 3–12.

Davydov, A. Iu. *Nelegal'noe snabzhenie Rossiiskogo naseleniia i vlast' 1917–1921 gg.: Meshochniki.* St. Petersburg: Nauka, 2007.

De Grazia, Sebastian. *The Political Community: A Study of Anomie.* Chicago: University of Chicago Press, 1948.

Dobson, G. *St. Petersburg.* Paintings by F. De Haenen. London: Adam & Charles Black, 1910.

Durkheim, Emile. *The Division of Labor in Society.* Edited and with a new introduction by Steven Lukes. New York: Free Press, 2014.

Eisner, Manual. "Long-Term Historical Trends in Violent Crime." *Crime and Justice* 30 (2003): 83–142.

Ereshchenko, D. Iu. "Prestupnost' v Petrograde v 1914–1917 gg." Candidate diss., A. I. Gertsen Russian State Pedagogical University, 2003.

Fierson, Cathy. "Crime and Punishment in the Russian Village: Rural Concepts of Criminality at the End of the Nineteenth Century." *Slavic Review* 46, no. 1 (1987): 55–69.

Figes, Orlando. *A People's Tragedy: A History of the Russian Revolution.* New York: Viking, 1997.

Figes, Orlando, and B. I. Kolonitskii. *Interpreting the Russian Revolution: The Language and Symbols, 1917.* New Haven, CT: Yale University Press, 1999.

Fraiman, Anton L. *Forpost sotsialisticheskoi revoliutsii: Petrograd v pervye mesiatsy Sovetskoi vlasti.* Leningrad: Nauka, 1969.

Frame, Murray. "Militsiia vo vremia Russkoi revoliutsii 1917 goda: kontseptsii i sravneniia." International Colloquim, "Epokha voin i revoliutsii (1914–1922)." Unpublished paper, St. Petersburg, June 9–11, 2016.

Frenkel', Z. G. *Petrograd perioda voiny i revoliutsii: Sanitarnye usloviia i kommunal'noe blagoustroistvo.* Petrograd: Petrogybotkomkhoza, 1923.

Gatrell, Peter. *A Whole Empire Walking: Refugees in Russia during World War I.* Bloomington: Indiana University Press, 1999.

Gerasimov, Ilya V. "The Subalterns Speak Out." In *Spaces of the Poor: Perspectives of Cultural Sciences on Urban Slum Areas and Their Inhabitants,* edited by Hans-Christian Petersen. Bielefeld, Germany: Transcript—Verlag für Kommunikation, Kultur und soziale Praxis, 2013.

Gertsenzon, A. A., Sh. S. Gringauz, N. D. Durmanov, M. M. Isaev, and B. S. Utevskii. *Istoriia Sovetskogo ugolovnogo prava.* 1947. Allpravo.ru. 2003. http://allpravo.ru /library/doc101p0/instrum107/item486.html. Accessed April 3, 2017.

Ginneken, Jaap van. *Crowds, Psychology, and Politics, 1871–1899.* Cambridge: Cambridge University Press, 1992.

Gorodetskii, E. N. *Rozhdenie sovetskogo godusarstva, 1917–1918 gg.* Moscow: Nauka, 1965.

Gramsci, Antonio. *Prison Notebooks.* Edited by Quintin Hoare and Geoffrey Nowell Smith. New York: International Publishers, 1971.

Gros, Jean-Germain. "Failed States in Theoretical, Historical, and Policy Perspectives." In *Control of Violence,* edited by Wilhelm Heitmeyer, Heinz-Gerhard Haupt, Stefan Malthaner, and Andrea Kirshcher. New York: Springer Science & Business Media, 2011.

Hagenloh, Paul. *Stalin's Police: Public Order and Mass Repression in the USSR, 1926–1941*. Washington, DC: Woodrow Wilson Center Press; Baltimore: Johns Hopkins University Press, 2009.

Haimson, Leopold. "The Problem of Political and Social Stability in Urban Russia on the Eve of War and Revolution Revisited." *Slavic Review* 59, no. 4 (2000): 848–875.

———. "The Problem of Social Stability in Urban Russia, 1905–1917." Pts 1 and 2. *Slavic Review* 23, no. 4 (1964): 619–642; 24, no. 1 (1965): 1–22.

Hasegawa, Tsuyoshi. "Crime and Police in Revolutionary Petrograd, March 1917–March 1918: Social History of the Russian Revolution Revisited." *Acta Slavica Iaponica* 13 (1995): 1–41.

———. "Crime, Police, and Mob Justice in Petrograd during the Russian Revolution of 1917." In *Religious and Secular Forces in Late Tsarist Russia*, edited by Charles E. Timberlake, 241–271. Seattle: University of Washington Press, 1992.

———. "The Duma Committee, the Provisional Government, and the Birth of 'Triple Power' in the February Revolution." In *A Companion to the Russian Revolution*, edited by Daniel Orlovsky. Oxford: Wiley-Blackwell, forthcoming.

———. *The February Revolution: Petrograd, 1917*. Seattle: University of Washington Press, 1981.

———. *The February Revolution: The End of the Tsarist Regime and the Birth of Dual Power*. Leiden: Brill, forthcoming.

———. "The Formation of the Militia in the February Revolution: An Aspect of the Origins of Dual Power." *Slavic Review* 32, no. 2 (June 1973): 303–322.

———. "Gosudarstvennost', obshchestvennoist' and klassovost': Crime, the Police, and the State in the Russian Revolution in Petrograd." *Canadian-American Slavic Studies* 35, nos. 2–3 (2001): 157–188.

———. "Gosudarsevennost', obshchestvenost' i klassovost': Prestuplenie, politsiia i gosudarstvo vo vremia Russkoi revoliutsii v Petrograde." In *Novyi mir istorii Rossii: Forum Iaponskikh i Rossiskikh issledovatelei*, edited by Gennadii Bordiugov, Isii Norie, and Tomita Takeshi, 218–246. Moscow: Airo-XX, 2001.

———. "Hanzai, keisatsu, samosūdo: Roshia kakumeika no petorogurādo no shakaishi eno ichishiron" [Crime, police, *samosudy*: An attempt at social history of Petrograd during the Russian Revolution]. *Surabu kenkyū* 34 (1987): 27–55.

———. "Prestupnost' i sotsial'nyi krizis v Petrograde vo vremia russkoi revoliutsii: mart-oktiabr'." In *Rossiia v 1917 godu: novye podkhody i vzgliady: Sbornik nauchnykh stat'i: vypusk tretii*, edited by O. A. Polivanov and V. I. Startsev, 72–79. St. Petersburg: Kafedra istorii RGPU imeni Gertsena, 1994.

———. *Roshia kakumeika petorogurādo no shimin seikatsu* [Daily Life of Petrograd during the Russian Revolution]. Tokyo: Chūōkōronsha, 1989.

Hayek, F. A. *The Fatal Conceit: The Errors of Socialism*. Chicago: University of Chicago Press, 1988.

Hazard, John N. *Settling Disputes in Soviet Society: The Formative Years of Legal Institutions*. New York: Columbia University Press, 1960.

———. "Soviet Law: The Bridge Years, 1917–1920." In *Russian Law: Historical and Political Perspectives*, edited by William E. Butler. Leyden: A. W. Sijitoff, 1977.

Holoquist, Peter. *Making War, Forging Revolution.* Cambridge, MA: Harvard University Press, 2002.

Holton, Robert J. "The Crowd in History: Some Problems of Theory and Method." *Social History* 3, no. 2 (1978): 219–233.

Huskey, Eugene. "From Legal Nihilism to *Pravovoe Gosudarstvo:* Soviet Legal Development, 1917–1990." In *Toward the "Rule of Law" in Russia? Political and Legal Reform in the Transition Period,* edited by Donald. D. Barry. Armonk, NY: M. E. Sharpe, 1992.

Iukhneva, N. V. *Etnicheskii sostav i etnosotsial'naia struktura naseleniia Peterburga: Vtoraia polovina XIX-nachalo XX vek: Statisticheskii analiz.* Leningrad: Nauka, 1964.

———. *Staryi Petersburg: Istoriko-etnicheskie issledovaniia.* Leningrad: Nauka, 1982.

Jahn, H. G. "Housing Revolution in Petrograd, 1917–1920." *Jahrbücher für Geschichte Osteuropas* 38 (1990): 212–227.

Kanishchev, V. V. *Russkii bunt—bessmyslennyi i besposhchadnyi: Pogromnoe dvizhenie v gorodakh Rossii v 1917–1918 gg.* Tambov: Gosudrasrstvennyi komitet Rossisskoi federatsii po vysshemu obrazovaniiu Tambovskii Gosudrastvennyi universistet im. G. R. Derzhavina, 1995.

Kann, P. Ia. "Bor'ba rabochikh Petrograda s p'ianymi pogromami, noiabr'-dek, 1917 g." *Istoriia SSSR,* no. 3 (1962): 133–136.

Kitanina, T. M. *Voina, khleb i revoliutsiia: prodovol'stvennyi vopros v Rossii, 1914-oktiabr' 1917 g.* Leningrad: Nauka, 1985.

Klier, John D., and Shlomo Lambroza. *Pogroms: Anti-Jewish Violence in Modern Russian History.* Cambridge: Cambridge University Press, 1992.

Kochakov, B. M. "Petrograd v gody pervoi mirovoi voiny i fevral'skoi burzhuazno-demokraticheskoi revoliutsii." In *Ocherki istorii Leningrada.* Vol. 3. Moscow-Leningrad: Izd-vo Akademii Nauk, 1956.

Kolonitskii, B. I. "Antibourgeois Propaganda and Anti-'*Burzhui*' Consciousness in 1917." *Russian Review* 53, no. 2 (1994): 183–196.

———. *Simvoly vlasti i bor'ba za vlasti: k izucheniiu politicheskoi kul'tury Rossiiskoi revoliutsii 1917 goda.* St. Petersburg: Liki Rossii, 2012.

———. *Tragicheskaia erotica: obrazy imperatorskaoi sem'i v gody pervoi mirovoi voiny.* Moscow: Novo literaturnoe obozrenie, 2010.

Konstantinov, Andrei. *Banditskii Peterburg-98.* Moscow: Olma-Press, 1999.

Kostiukovskii, Iakov. "Istoriia rossiiskoi organizovannoi prestupnosti." http:www.narcom.ru/ideas/socio/13.html. Accessed July 3, 2016.

Kowalsky, Sharon A. "Transforming Society: Criminologists, Violence, and Family on War and Revolution." In *Russia's Home Front in War and Revolution, 1914–22.* Vol. 2: *The Experience of War and Revolution,* edited by Adele Lindenmeyer, Christopher Read, and Peter Waldron. Bloomington, IN: Slavica, 2016.

Kozhevnikov, M. V. *Istoriia sovetskogo suda 1917–1918 gg.* Moscow: Gosudarstvennoe izdatel'stvo iuridicheskoi literatury, 1957.

Kruchkovskaia, V. M. *Tsentral'naia gorodskaia duma Petrograda v 1917 g.* Leningrad: Nauka, 1986.

Kruze, E. E., and D. G. Kutsentov. "Naselenie Peterburga." In *Ocherki istorii Leningrada.* Vol. 3. Moscow-Leningrad: Izdatel'stvo Akademii Nauk, 1956.

Kulegin, Alekseii. *Delo ob osobniake: Kak bol'sheviki 'uplotniali' Matil'du Kshesinskuiu.* St. Petersburg: Izdatel'skaia gruppa ZAO, Poligrafichekoe predpriatie no. 3, 2006.

Lebedeva, V. M., ed. *Nastol'naia kniga mirovogo sud'i: Uchebno-metodicheskoe posobie.* Moscow: Izd-o BEK, 2002. www.mos-sud.ruk/courtsrf/. Accessed July 15, 2016.

Lebina, Natalia. "Belaia feia ili 'kak navodili Marafet' v Sovetskoi Rossii." *Rodina,* no. 9 (1996): 64–66.

Lebina, N. B. *Povsednevnaia zhizn' sovetskogo goroda: Normy i anomalii, 1920–1930-e gody.* St. Petersburg: Zhurnal Neva, 1999.

Lebina, N. B., and M. V. Shkarovskii. "Detal' nochnogo peizazha, koe-chto iz mira prostitutok Sankt-Peterburga i Leningrada." *Rodina,* no. 2 (1994): 61–66.

———. *Prostitutsiia v Peterburge (40'e gg XIXv.—40e gg. XX v.).* Moscow: Progress-Akademiia, 1994.

Le Bon, Gustave. *The Crowd: A Study of the Popular Mind.* Mineola, NY: Dover, 2002.

Leggett, George. *The Cheka: Lenin's Political Police.* Oxford: Clarendon Press, 1981.

Leiberov, I. P. "Nachalo Fevral'skoi revoliutsii (sobytiia 23 fevralia 1917 g. v Petrograde." In *Iz istorii Velikoi Oktiabr'skoi sotsialisticheskoi revoliutsii i sotsialisticheskogo stroitel'stva v SSSR: Sbornik statei.* Leningrad: Izdatel'stvo Leningradskogo universitata, 1967.

———. *Na shturm samoderzhaviia.* Moscow: Mysl', 1979.

———. "Vtoroi den' Fevral'skoi revoliutsii: Sobytiia 24 fevralia 1917 g. v Petrograde." In *Sverzhenie samoderzhaviia: Sbornik statei,* edited by I. I. Mints and L. M. Ivanov. Moscow: Nauka, 1970.

Leiberov, I. P., and O. I. Shkaratan. "K voprosu o sostave petrogradskikh promyshlennykh rabochikh v 1917 godu." *Voprosy istorii,* no. 1 (1961): 42–58.

Lewin, Moshe. "The Civil War: Dynamics and Legacy." In *Party, State, and Society in the Russian Civil War,* edited by Diane P. Koenker, William G. Rosenberg, and Ronald Grigor Suny. Bloomington: Indiana University Press, 1989.

Lih, Lars T. *Bread and Authority in Russia, 1914–1921.* Berkeley: University of California Press, 1990.

Lincoln, W. Bruce. *Sunlight at Midnight: St. Petersburg and the Rise of Modern Russia.* New York: Basic Books, 2000.

Lohr, Eric. *Nationalizing the Russian Empire: The Campaign against Enemy Aliens during World War I.* Cambridge, MA: Harvard University Press, 2003.

Lukes, Steven. Introduction to *The Division of Labor in Society,* by Emile Durkheim. Edited by Steven Lukes. New York: Free Press, 2014.

Malakhovskii, V. "Perekhod ot krasnoi gvardii k krasnoi armii." *Klasnaia letopis',* no. 3 (1928): 5–51.

Mandel, David. *The Petrograd Workers and the Soviet Seizure of Power: From the July Days, 1917 to July 1918.* London: Macmillan, 1984.

Marabini J. *La vie quotidienne en Russie sous la révolution d'Octobre.* Paris: Hachette, 1965.

Martynov, E. I. *Tsarskaia armiia v fevral'skom perevorote.* Leningrad: Izdatel'stvo voennoi tipografii, 1927.

McAuley, Mary. *Bread and Justice: State and Society in Petrograd, 1917–1922.* Oxford: Clarendon Press, 1991.

McKean, Robert B. *St. Petersburg between the Revolutions: Workers and Revolutionaries, June 1907–February 1917*. New Haven, CT: Yale University Press, 1990.
McReynolds, Louise. *Murder Most Russian: True Crime and Punishment in Late Imperial Russia*. Ithaca, NY: Cornell University Press, 2013.
——. *The News under Russia's Old Regime: The Development of a Mass-Circulation Press*. Princeton, NJ: Princeton University Press, 1991.
Merton, Robert K. *Social Theory and Social Structure*. New York: Free Press, 1968.
Moscovici, Serge. *The Age of the Crowd: A Historical Treatise on Mass Psychology*. Cambridge: Cambridge University Press, 1985.
Munro, George E. *The Most Intentional City: St. Petersburg in the Reign of Catherine the Great*. Madison, NJ: Fairleigh Dickinson University Press, 2009.
Musaev, V.I. "Byt gorozhan." In *Petrograd na perelome epokh: gorod i ero zhiteli v gody revoliutsii i grazhdanskoi voiny,* edited by V. A. Shishkin and E. M. Balashov. St. Petersburg: Dmitrii Bulanin, 2000.
——. *Prestupnost' v Petrograde v 1917–1921 gg. i bor'ba s nei*. St. Petersburg: Dmitrii Bulanin, 2001.
Narsky, Igor V., and Yulia Y. Khmelevskaya. "Alcohol in Russia as a Means of Social Integration, Cultural Communication, and Survival during World I and the Revolution." In *Russia's Home Front in War and Revolution, 1914–22*. Vol. 2: *The Experience of War and Revolution,* edited by Adele Lindenmeyer, Christopher Read, and Peter Waldron. Bloomington, IN: Slavica, 2016.
Nazarenko, A. M. "MVD: Sankt-Peterburgskaia stolichnaia politsiia (1906–1913 gody)." Candidate diss., St. Petersburg University, 2000.
Neuberger, Joan. *Hooliganism: Crime, Culture, and Power in St. Petersburg, 1900—1914.* Berkeley: University of California Press, 1993.
Nikitin, B. V. *Rokovye gody (Novye pokazaniia uchastnika)*. Part 1. http://www.dk1868.ru/history/nikitin.htm. Accessed December 17, 2013.
Nikolaev, A. B. "Domovladel'tsy pered Vremennym sudom (Petrograd, vesna-leto 1917g.)." In *Revoliutsiia 1917 goda v Rossii: Novye podkhody i vzgliady,* edited by A. B. Nikolaev. St. Petersburg: Kafedra Russkoi istorii fakul'tet sotsial'nykh nauk Rossiiskii Gosudarstvennyi pedagogicheskii universitet im A. I. Gertsena, 2015.
——. "Nastroeniia i politicheskie vzgliady petrogradskikh politseiskikh nakanune Fevral'skoi revoliutsii." *Journal of Modern Russian History and Historiography* 5 (2012): 1–39.
——. "'Pod krasnym flagom': Petrogradskaia politsiia v dni Fevral'skoi revoliutsii." Mezhvyzovskaia nauchnaia konferentsiia. In *Russkaia revoliutsiia 1917 goda: Problemy istorii i istoriografii: Sbornik dokladov,* 38–50. St. Petersburg: Izdatel'stvo SPbGETU «LETI», 2013.
——. *Revoliutsiia i vlast': IV Gosudarstvennaia duma 27 fevralia-3 marta 1917 goda.* St. Petersburg: Izdatel'stvo RGPU im. A. I. Gertsena, 2005.
——. "Vremennye sudy v Petrograde (Mart-Iul' 1917 g.)." Paper presented at the International Colloquium, "Epokha voin i revoliutsii (1914–1922)." St. Petersburg, June 9–11, 2016.
Nye, Robert A. *The Origins of Crowd Psychology: Gustave LeBon and the Crisis of Mass Democracy in the Third Republic*. London: Sage, 1975.

Ocherki istorii Leningrada. 6 vols. Moscow-Leningrad: Izdatel'stvo Akademii Nauk, 1955–1970.

Ol'ginskii, Oleg. "Prostitutsiia i zhilishchnyi vopros." *Rabochii sud,* nos. 5–6 (1925): 205–206.

Orlovsky, Daniel. "Corporatism or Democracy: The Russian Provisional Government of 1917." In *Landscaping the Human Garden: Twentieth-Century Population Management in a Comparative Framework,* edited by Amir Weiner. Stanford, CA: Stanford University Press, 2003.

———. "The Lower Middle Strata in 1917." In *Critical Companion to the Russian Revolution,* edited by Edward Acton, Vladimir Iu. Cherniaev, and William G. Rosenberg. London: Arnold, 1997.

———. "The Lower Middle Strata in Revolutionary Russia." In *Between Tsar and People: Educated Society and the Quest for Public Identity in Late Imperial Russia,* edited by Edith W. Clowes, Samuel D. Kassow, and James L. West. Princeton, NJ: Princeton University Press, 1991.

———, ed. *A Companion to the Russian Revolution.* Oxford: Wiley-Blackwell, forthcoming.

Ostroumov, S. S. *Prestupnost' i ee prichiny v dorevoliutsionnoi Rossii.* Moscow: Izdatel'stvo Moskovskogo universiteta, 1980.

Pashkov, E. V. "Antialkogol'naia kampaniia v Rossii v gody Pervoi mirovoi voiny." *Voprosy istorii,* no. 10 (2010): 80–93.

Penter, Tanja. *Odessa 1917: Revolution an der Peripherie.* Cologne: Böhlau Verlag, 2000.

Petersen, Hans-Christian. "'Not Intended for the Rich': Public Places as Points of Identification for the Urban Poor—St. Petersburg, 1850–1914." In *Spaces of the Poor: Perspectives of Cultural Sciences on Urban Slum Areas and Their Inhabitants,* edited by Hans-Christian Petersen. Bielefeld, Germany: Transcript—Verlag für Kommunikation, Kultur und soziale Praxis, 2013.

Pipes, Richard, ed. *Revolutionary Russia.* Cambridge, MA: Harvard University Press, 1968.

———. *The Russian Revolution.* New York: Vintage Books, 1991.

Pomeranz, William E. "The Provisional Government and the Law-Based State." In *A Companion to the Russian Revolution,* edited by Daniel Orlovsky. Oxford: Wiley-Blackwell, forthcoming .

Rabich, S. N. "Bor'ba s prostitutsiei v Petrograde." *Kommunistka,* no. 1 (1920): 21–23.

Rabinowitch, Alexander. *The Bolsheviks Come to Power: The Revolution of 1917 in Petrograd.* New York: Norton, 1976.

———. *The Bolsheviks in Power: The First Year of Soviet Rule in Petrograd.* Bloomington: Indiana University Press, 2007.

———. "The Evolution of Local Soviets in Petrograd, November 1917–June 1918: The Case of the First City District Soviet." *Slavic Review* 46 (1987): 20–37.

———. "The Petrograd First City District Soviet during the Civil War." In *Party, State, and Society in the Russian Civil War,* edited by Diane P. Koenker, William G. Rosenberg, and Ronald Grigor Suny. Bloomington: Indiana University Press, 1989.

———. *Prelude to Revolution: The Petrograd Bolsheviks and the July 1917 Uprising.* Bloomington: Indiana University Press, 1968.

Rashin, A. *Naselenie Rossii za 100 let*. Moscow: Statistichekoe izdatel'stvo, 1956.

Rendle, Matthew. *The Defenders of the Motherland: The Tsarist Elite in Revolutionary Russia*. Oxford: Oxford University Press, 2010.

———. "Revolutionary Tribunals and the Origins of Terror in Early Soviet Russia." *Historical Research* 84, no. 226 (2011): 694–721.

Rosenberg, William G. " 'Beyond the Great Story' of War and Revolution." Paper presented at the International Colloquium, "Epokha voin i revoliutsii (1914–1922)." St. Petersburg, June 9–11, 2016.

———. "Social Mediation and State Construction(s) in Revolutionary Russia." *Social History* 19, no. 2 (1994): 169–188.

Rotberg, Robert I. "Failed States, Collapsed States, Weak States: Causes and Indicators." In *When States Fail: Causes and Consequences*, edited by Robert I. Rotberg. Princeton, NJ: Princeton University Press, 2014.

Russia's Home Front in War and Revolution, 1914–22. Vol. 2: *The Experience of War and Revolution*, edited by Adele Lindenmeyer, Christopher Read, and Peter Waldron. Bloomington, IN: Slavica, 2016.

Sanborn, Joshua. *Drafting the Russian Nation: Military Conscription, Total War, and Mass Politics, 1905–1925*. DeKalb: Northern Illinois University Press, 2003.

———. "The Mobilization of 1914 and the Question of the Russian Nation: A Reexamination." *Slavic Review* 59, no. 2 (Summer 2000): 267–289.

Sanchov, V. "Prostitutsiia, kak ona est' (Po ankete sredi prostitutok v Moskve)." *Rabochii sud*, nos. 3–4 (1925): 122–127.

Schapiro, Leonard. "The Political Thought of the First Russian Provisional Government." In *Revolutionary Russia*, edited by Richard Pipes. Cambridge, MA: Harvard University Press, 1968.

Shishkin, V. A., ed. *Petrograd na perelome epokh: gorod i ero zhiteli v gody revoliutsii i grazhdanskoi voiny*. St. Petersburg: Dmitrii Bulanin, 2000.

Shkarovskii, M. V. "Sem' imen 'koshki': rastsvet narkomanii v 1917–1920-e gody." *Nevskii arkhiv*, no. 3 (1997): 467–477.

Shvidkovsky, Dmitri. *St. Petersburg: Architecture of the Tsars*. Translated by John Goodman. Photographs by Alexander Orloff. New York: Abbeville Press, 1996.

Sidorov, Aleksandr. "Voina pervaia: 'Zhigany' protiv 'urkaganov.'" In *Velikie bitvy ugolognogo mira*. http://survivie.kudin.org/prisnrec13.htm. Accessed July 17, 2013.

Siegelbaum, Lewis. "Another Yellow Peril? Chinese Migrants in the Russian Far East and the Russian Reaction before 1917." *Modern Asian Studies* 12 (1978): 307–330.

Skliagin, A., V. Lesov, and Iu. Pimenov. *Dela i liudi Leningradskoi militsii*. Leningrad: Lenizdat, 1967.

Skocpol, T. *States and Social Revolutions*. Cambridge: Cambridge University Press, 1979.

Smith, S. A. *Red Petrograd Revolution in the Factories, 1917–1918*. Cambridge: Cambridge University Press, 1983.

———. "Russian Workers and the Politics of Social Identity." *Russian Review* 56, no. 1 (1997): 1–7.

Startsev, V. I. *Ocherki po istorii Petrogradskoi Krasnoi gvardii i rabochei militsii*. Moscow: Nauka, 1965.

Steinberg, Mark D. "Blood in the Air: Everyday Violence in the Experience of the Petersburg Poor, 1905–1917." In *Spaces of the Poor: Perspectives of Cultural Sciences on Urban Slum Areas and Their Inhabitants,* edited by Hans-Christian Petersen. Bielefeld, Germany: Transcript—Verlag für Kommunikation, Kultur und soziale Praxis, 2013.

———. *Petersburg Fin de Siècle.* New Haven, CT: Yale University Press, 2011.

———. "The Violence of the Petersburg Street, 1905–1917: Experience, Interpretation, Theory." In *Rossiia i SShA: poznavaia drug druga. Sbornik pamiati akademika A. F. Fursenko / Russia and the United States: Perceiving Each Other,* edited by V. V. Noskov et al. St. Petersburg: Nestor-Istoriia, 2015.

Stepanov, Z. P. *Rabochie Petrograda v period podgotovki i provedeniia Oktiabr'skoi vooruzhennogo vosstaniia.* Moscow: Nauka, 1965.

Stites, Richard. "Prostitute and Society in Pre-revolutionary Russia." *Jahrbücher für Geschichte Ostreuropas,* 31, no. 3 (1983): 348–364.

Suny, Ronald Grigor. "Revision and Retreat in the Historiography of 1917: Social History and Its Critics." *The Russian Review* 53, no. 2 (1994): 165–182.

———. "Toward a Social History of the October Revolution." *American Historical Review* 88 (1983): 31–52.

Tokarev, Iu. S. "Dokumenty narodnykh sudov, 1917–1922 gg." In *Voprosy istoriografii i istochnikovedeniia istorii SSSR,* edited by S. N. Valk. Moscow: Izdatel'stvo Akademii nauk SSSR, 1963.

———. "Iz istorii narodnogo pravotvorchestva v period podgotovki i proveneniia Velikoi Oktiabri'skoi sotsialisticheskoi revoliutsii." *Istoricheskie zapiski* 52 (1955): 49–79.

———. *Narodnoe pravotvorchestvo nakanune Velikoi Oktiabr'skoi sotsialisticheskoi revoliutsii (Mart–Oktiabr') 1917 g.* Moscow: Nauka, 1965.

———. "Petrogradskie rabochie v bor'be za ustanovlenie i okhranu revoliutsionnogo poriadka." In *Rabochie Leningrada v bor'be za pobedu sotsializma,* edited by Z. V. Stepanov, Moscow: Izdatel'stvo Akademii nauk SSSR, 1963.

———, ed. *Problemy gosudarstvennogo stroitel'stva v pervye gody sovetskoi vlasti.* Leningrad: Akademiia nauk SSSR, Institut istorii SSSR, Leningradskoe otdelenie, Trudy, vyp. 14, 1973.

Vasilyev, Pavel. "War, Revolution and Drugs: The 'Democratization' of Drug Abuse and the Evolution of Drug Policy in Russia, 1914–24." In *Russia's Home Front in War and Revolution, 1914–22.* Vol. 2: *The Experience of War and Revolution,* edited by Adele Lindenmeyer, Christopher Read, and Peter Waldron. Bloomington, IN: Slavica, 2016.

Visloukh, S. "Prostitutsiia i alkogolizm." *Rabochii sud,* nos. 7–8 (1925): 322–323.

———. "Prostitutsiia i narkomaniia." *Rabochii sud,* nos. 7–8 (1925): 318–321.

Volkov, Solomon. *St. Petersburg: A Cultural History.* Translated by Antonina W. Bouis. New York: Free Press, 1955.

Volkov, Vadim. *Violent Entrepreneurs: The Use of Force in the Making of Russian Capitalism.* Ithaca, NY: Cornell University Press, 2002.

Volobuev, P. B. *Ekonomicheskaia politika Vremennogo pravitel'stva.* Moscow: Izdatel'stvo Akademii nauk 1962.

Wade, Rex. "The Rajonnye Sovety of Petrograd: The Role of Local Political Bodies in the Russian Revolution." *Jahrbücher für Geschichte Osteuropas* 20, no. 2 (1972): 226–240.

———. *Red Guards and Workers' Militias in the Russian Revolution.* Stanford, CA: Stanford University Press, 1984.

———. "The Revolution at One Hundred: Issues and Trends in the Anglo-American Historiography of the Russian Revolution of 1917." *Journal of Modern Russian History and Historiography* 9 (2016): 9–38.

———. *The Russian Revolution, 1917.* Cambridge: Cambridge University Press, 2000.

Weissman, Neil. "Regular Police in Tsarist Russia, 1900–1914." *Russian Review* 44 (1985): 45–68.

White, H. J. "Civil Rights and the Provisional Government." In *Civil Rights in Imperial Russia,* edited by Olga Crisp and Linda Edmondson. Oxford: Clarendon Press, 1989.

Wildman, Allan K. *The End of the Russian Imperial Army: The Old Army and the Soldiers' Revolt (March–April 1917).* Princeton, NJ: Princeton University Press, 1980.

Za 8 let: Materaly po istoriii sovetskoi Raboche-Kresti'ianskoi militsii i ugolovnogo rozyska 1917–1 noiabria-1925 gg. Leningrad: Izdanie zhurnala Na postu, 1925.

Zlokazov, G. I. *Petrogradskii Sovet rabochikh i soldatskikh deputatov v period mirnogo razvitiia revolutsii, fevral'-iun' 1917 g.* Moscow: Nauka, 1969.

Zviagintseva, A. P. "Kontrrevoliutsionnaia sushchnost' militsii Vremennogo pravitel'stva." *Pravovedenie,* no. 4 (1971): 111–115.

ACKNOWLEDGMENTS

I have worked on this project, off and on, for thirty years. Over this time, I received help, advice, and encouragement from many scholars and colleagues. Rex Wade, Ron Suny, and Mark Steinberg have steadfastly supported this project. I have profited a great deal from my constant discussions at conferences and through spirited email exchanges with Michael Hickey, Daniel Orlovsky, Sarah Badcock, Alistair Dickins, Rex Wade, and Semion Lyandres. Russian historians, especially Boris Kolonitskii, Vladimir Cherniaev, and Vladislav Aksenov, have been generous in their help. My friend and colleague Aleksei Kulegin of the Museum of Contemporary Political History also provided much assistance, and read the earlier version of the manuscript.

I also express my gratitude to two senior Russian scholars: the late Vitalii Ivanovich Startsev, who guided my work at its early stage and helped me obtain access to archives when Soviet archives were virtually closed to foreign scholars; and the late Rafail Sholomovich Ganelin, who also provided constant assistance and advice. I regret that they are no longer here to see the fruit of their advice and assistance.

I especially owe intellectual debts to my colleague and friend, Andrei Borisovich Nikolaev, whose pioneering works on numerous aspects of the Russian Revolution provided great inspiration for my work. More than anyone else, I owe a great debt to Ekaterina Gavroeva, who provided invaluable assistance in locating obscure materials, reproducing essential sources and illustrations, and checking missing information for materials unobtainable in the United States.

I thank the two anonymous Harvard University Press reviewers of the original manuscript. Thanks to their insightful comments, I substantially revised the original manuscript.

I also have had the privilege of having numerous discussions on various aspects of the book with my colleagues and friends. I only name some here: Mike Urban, Cynthia Kaplan, Jon Cruz, Ken Moure, Jack Talbott, Harold Marcuse, John Lee, Susan Goodman, and Michael and Margaret Herzen.

My original work was rooted in the Japanese scholarly tradition, and many Japanese colleagues have given me valuable advice, help, and suggestions along the way. Among them I would like to single out one scholar, Wada Haruki, who has been the scholar and public historian I have always aspired to emulate. My friend and colleague, Uemura Tadao, has always inspired me with his prolific works on Vico, Gramsi, Croce, and other thinkers. My friendship with Uemura and Ito Takayuki dating from our university days has been a treasure I cherish.

Many foundations assisted me with this project by extending generous grants and fellowships. The Rockefeller Foundation gave me the opportunity to work at its magnificent Bellagio Center. The Likhachev Foundation, under Elena Vitenberg's able guidance, provided the opportunity for me to resume archival and library work in St. Petersburg. Thanks to a Fulbright fellowship, I spent a valuable four months in St. Petersburg working in the archives and the libraries. It took me a long time to complete the project, but I am happy finally to express my gratitude to these organizations for their support.

I would like also thank the archivists and librarians at: TsGA SPb, TsGIA SPb, the National Library (formerly the Saltykov-Shchedrin Library, especially its newspaper branch in Fontanka), the Library of the Academy of Sciences, the Museum of Political History at St. Petersburg (formerly the Museum of Revolution), the Herzen Pedagogical University Library in St. Petersburg, GARF, the Contemporary History Museum in Moscow (formerly the Museum of Revolution), the Russian State Library (formerly the Lenin Library), and the State Public Historical Library (GPIB) in Moscow. Two archival collections in the United States, Columbia University's Bakhmeteff collection and the Hoover Institution's archives, were also important sources for my project, and I thank the archivists, especially Tanya Chebrotarev of Bakhmeteff Archives, for their assistance.

My students at the University of California at Santa Barbara—John Conchola, Maria Fedorova, Ilya Bobkov, and Anastasia Nevyakina—provided me with bibliographical, computer, and translation assistance.

Kathleen McDermott of Harvard University Press has given me her generous support from the beginning. Simon Waxman, my superb copy editor, went through the rough manuscript and helped me to present my arguments clearly. Isabelle Lewis made the two wonderful maps that appear in the book. Finally, I thank Judith Riotto and Deborah Masi of Westchester Publishing Services for editing the manuscript.

But above all, I would like to thank my wife, Debbie Steinhoff who has lived for thirty years with this project, which she calls "the samosudy project," who has read everything I have ever written, and who has given me valuable suggestions and advice. She is the happiest person to see the publication of this book and to finally say farewell to "samosudy." Thanks also to my son, Kenneth, who has lived with this project all his life, and gave me various computer-related assistance.

And it is to Debbie and Kenneth that I dedicate this book.

INDEX

Admiralteiskii District, 57, 180, 202; alcohol pogroms in, 215, 218, 224; city militia in, 142, 232; Constituent Assembly election in, 195; heterogeneity of population in, 23, 24

Aksenov, Vladislav, 10

alcohol pogroms, 3, 11, 16, 44, 110, 193, 212, 214, 275; anarchists and, 212; Bolshevik reaction to, 190, 192, 215–216, 222–224, 226–227, 237–242, 245, 264–265; deaths and damage of, 193; on December, 218–224; on Gutuevskii Island, 225–226; historians' treatment of, 192; in January, 224–225; in November, 215–218; Tomskii's comments on, 220–221; in Winter Palace, 215, 216, 217

Aleksandro-Nevskii District, 24, 59, 104, 180; alcohol pogroms in, 219, 224; city militia in, 142–143, 152; Constituent Assembly election in, 195; crime in, 98, 155; mob justice in, 207; urban poor in, 207

Alekseev, Iu. A., 123

All-Russian Congress of Soviets of Workers and Soldiers Deputies, 193, 253

All-Russian Executive Committee of the Soviets, 70, 245, 251–252, 255

All-Russian Extraordinary Commission to Combat Counterrevolution and Sabotage. See Cheka

alternative police force, 158–159, 159–161

anarchists, 69, 161, 201, 205, 255; criminal acts committed by, 98–102, 205, 211–213; Durnovo dacha and, 84–86, 139, 145

anomie, 12–15, 191, 260, 266–269, 273, 276. See also Durkheim, Emile; Merton, Robert; theory of anomie

Anter, Andreas, 270

anti-German riots, 30–31

Antonov-Ovseenko, Vladimir A., 236

Apraksin Market, 171, 175, 180

April crisis, 39, 70

Arkhipkin, G. V., 231

Artemiev, N. A., 160

Asnin, Sh. A., 85

Avanesov, V. A., 236

Balashev, Ivan. V., 238

Balk, Aleksandr P., 117

Bater, James, 20, 23, 24

Bermanskii, K. L., 130–131

black automobiles, 108

Blagonravov, Georgii I., 139, 224, 238

Bleikhman, Iosif S., 211

Bloody Sunday, 18, 21, 25

Bolsheviks, 1, 3, 4, 108, 155, 189; alcohol pogroms, 192, 214, 215, 227, 237–242, 264, 265; anarchists and, 211–213; Cheka and, 257–259; city duma and, 196, 233–235, 242–245; city militia and, 138, 149, 164, 196,

Bolsheviks *(continued)*
231, 233, 235–237, 253; Constituent
Assembly and, 194–195; courts and,
249–250, 251–253, 256; crime and,
192, 196, 201, 221, 229, 264,
267–277; Criminal Militia and,
247–248; failed state and, 272;
housing committees, 246–247; July
Days and, 64, 65, 81, 84, 96, 138,
148, 149, 176; Kornilov Affair and,
65–66, 96; Kshesinskaia villa and,
83–84, 85, 86, 175; mob justice and,
16, 189–191, 264; Petrograd Soviet
and, 66, 165; police and, 245–247,
255–258, 260, 264–265; Red Guards
and, 165, 230, 254–255; seizure of
power, 10, 18, 41, 193–194, 260, 264;
social breakdown and, 69, 70, 110,
260, 276; urban poor and, 11;
violence and, 276–277
Bonch-Bruevich, Vladimir G., 212, 220,
221, 222, 239–240, 245, 254, 255, 264
Botsvadze, V. G., 120, 121, 145
Buchanan, Meriel, 196, 218
burzhui, 5, 154, 178
Bydzan, I. F., 238

Central Executive Committee of Soviets,
162–163
centralization of police, 130, 165–166,
256–257, 261–262, 265
Central Komendatura, 256
centrifugal movement, 3, 15, 41, 193,
237, 252, 262, 265, 272. *See also*
decentralization
Cheka (All-Russian Extraordinary
Commission to Combat Counterrevolution and Sabotage), 3, 202,
203, 245–246, 248, 255, 257–259,
265, 272
Chernev, A. V., 127
Chinese, 33, 40, 53, 104
city administration, 72, 106, 160, 166
city duma, 8, 20, 108, 110, 127, 179, 235;
alcohol pogroms and, 214, 215, 216;
Bolshevik policy toward, 164, 196,

215, 229, 232–237, 242, 246, 249,
253, 264; city governor and, 47, 60,
61, 83, 110, 117, 128–133, 159, 261;
Committee of Public Safety and,
205–230; control of city militia,
137, 149, 196, 261, 262; creation of
city militia and, 15, 117–118, 119,
120, 122, 158, 166; Provisional
Government and, 128–133; review
commission's report on, 142, 146;
temporary courts and, 86, 90, 91
city militia *(gorodskaia militsiia)*, 8–9,
41, 119, 157, 166, 196, 261–262;
alcohol pogroms and, 215, 221, 230;
Bolsheviks and, 179, 230–232, 233,
234–237, 246, 247, 253, 254, 264;
centralization of, 65, 141, 149–152,
261; city duma and, 15, 117–118,
120, 122, 129, 149, 158, 166,
261–262; city governor and, 47, 60,
61, 83, 110, 117, 128–133, 159, 261;
crime reporting by, 48; erosion of
prestige of, 53–54, 58, 95, 134,
152–158, 158, 232, 262; infiltration
of criminals into, 134–135, 143; July
Days and, 147–149; mob justice and,
170, 171, 181, 207; Petrograd Soviet
and, 126–128; Provisional
Government and, 65, 141, 151–152;
recruitment and reappointment of,
117–118, 125, 133, 136–137, 140,
145; Red Guards and, 229, 254–255;
review commission's report on,
141–147; satirical criticism of,
100–101, 152, 155; weapons and
uniforms of, 134, 143, 144, 145,
155–157; workers' militia and, 16,
109, 120–123, 126–128, 138–140,
161–164, 230–232. *See also*
municipal police; police
class-based police, 117, 122, 262.
See also police; workers' militia
collective consciousness, 132, 185, 266.
See also Durkheim, Emile;
mechanical solidarity; theory of
anomie

Commission to Liquidate the Old Militia and Organize Security for the City of Petrograd, 236

Commission to review the city militia, 141–147. *See also* review commission's report

Committee of Public Safety, 196, 215, 229, 230, 232

Constituent Assembly, 70, 78, 194–195, 195, 196, 205, 211, 233, 234, 235

Council of People's Commissars. *See* Sovnarkom

courts, 2, 9, 68, 82, 97, 182, 260, 263, 268; Bolsheviks on, 258–259; Lenin on, 249. *See also* courts of justice; Decree on the Courts; District Court; Military Revolutionary Court; people's courts; Revolutionary Tribunal; temporary courts

courts of justice, 83, 86–87, 93, 115, 122, 136, 248–249, 251–253

crime, geographic distribution of, 98; under Bolsheviks, 10, 16, 96, 197, 245, 264; in tsarist Russia, 27–28, 28, 29, 32, 33. *See also* murders; robberies, thefts

Criminal Militia (*militsiia ugolovnogo rozyska*), 97, 136–137, 143, 157, 199, 200, 247–248

Criminal Police (*sysknaia politsiia*), 28, 110–111, 112–114, 115

criminal population, number of, 96, 261

criminals, 96–97, 99, 203–204, 263

crowd (*tolpa*), 11, 168, 170, 177, 187–189

cultural structure 13, 267–268. *See also* Merton, Robert; theory of anomie

death penalty, 80, 82, 209, 253–254

decentralization, 159; as characteristic of revolution, 8, 9, 41, 67, 69, 109, 259; city militia and, 132–133; effects of, 69, 72; housing committees and, 160–161, 246–247; reversal of, 163–166, 247; temporary courts and, 87

Decree on the Courts, 151, 251, 251–252

deserters: crime and, 54, 57, 62, 72, 154; as criminal population, 61, 75, 98–99, 261; number of, 99; violence and, 274

District Court, 29, 115, 248, 251. *See also* courts; Decree on the Courts

district duma, 120, 121, 131, 138, 139, 146, 195, 215; Bolsheviks and, 229, 234, 237; city duma and, 72, 125; Tseretelli's law and, 151–152

district soviets, 59, 64, 213; alcohol pogroms and, 238, 240; city duma elections and, 234; city militia and, 120, 121, 123, 124, 127–128, 138, 147, 163–164, 230–232, 236; decentralization and, 67, 72, 232; housing committees and, 246–247; interdistrict conference of, 162–164; Kornilov Affair and, 163–164; people's courts and, 249–250; Red Guards and, 255; temporary courts and, 88, 93

Domergue, Gabriel, 222

doormen, 74, 94, 113

Drozdov, V. V., 122, 123–124, 125

drunkeness, 9, 36, 58, 107, 145, 148, 152, 207; dry law and, 32; militiamen and, 136; as prevalent phenomenon of revolution, 58–59, 108; public disturbances and, 154, 155. *See also* alcohol pogroms; dry law

dry law, 32, 33, 59, 82, 275

dual power, 41, 69, 79, 87, 171

Duma Committee (Provisional Committee of the State Duma), 26, 27, 43, 45, 79, 117, 126

Durkheim, Emile, 12–13, 164, 168, 185–188, 264, 266–269, 271, 273, 275. *See also* theory of anomie

Durnovo dacha, 82, 84–86, 99, 139, 145, 213. *See also* anarchists

dvordnik, 20, 53, 77, 105, 159, 179, 222; security duty of, 35–36, 74, 94–95; strikes of, 76, 159, 222, 239, 243;

dvordnik *(continued)*
   tsarist police and, 111, 113; union of, 94–95
Dzerzhinskii, Felix, 206, 236, 245, 246, 258

economic crisis, 71–73
electricity, 9, 242–243
Engelgardt, Boris A., 43–44
epidemics, 9, 66, 105
Ereshchenko, Dmitrii Iu., 33, 42–43, 47, 48, 50, 81, 96
evacuees, 33, 36, 72
Executive Committee of Petrograd Soviet, 118, 119, 126, 148, 151
Extraordinary Commission to Combat Counterrevolution and Sabotage. *See* Cheka; Dzerzhinskii, Felix
Extraordinary Commission to Combat Pogroms, 212, 222, 238–239, 242, 255, 264. *See also* alcohol pogroms; Bonch-Bruevich, Vladimir G.

failed state, 12, 14–15, 168, 266, 270–272, 277. *See also* theory of failed state
February Revolution, 1, 2, 18, 21, 26, 61, 87, 191; destruction of tsarist police in, 8, 115; rise of crime and, 15, 41
Filippov, Vladimir G., 113
food riot, 66, 170, 175, 307n17
food shortage, 9, 69, 71–72, 242–243, 254, 263
Fraiman, Anton, 254
Frame, Murray, 116, 119, 254, 256
fuel shortage, 242–243
Fundamental Laws, 25, 78–79

gambling, 9–11, 41, 53, 55–58, 66, 97, 104, 145, 197, 261
garbage collection, 9, 105, 242
Gatrell, Peter, 7
Gernet, M. N., 35
Glebov, Iurii N., 91
Globachev, Konstantin I., 55, 81, 95–96
golden youths, 34, 97

Golodai, 119, 154
Gorky (Gor'kii), Maxim, 184, 206, 210
gosudarstvennost. See state consciousness
Governing Senate, 28, 248, 251
Gros, Jean-Germain, 270
Gutuevskii Island, 225–226, 254–255

Haimson, Leopold, 25, 268
Higher Investigating Commission, 79–80
Holoquist, Peter, 276
homeless shelters, 36, 74, 110
hooligans, 40, 41, 87, 108, 201, 257, 261; alcohol pogroms and, 219, 220, 225, 226, 239; crime and, 29, 34–35, 42, 43, 46, 103, 154, 155; mob justice and, 181–182
housing committees, 72, 93, 124, 159–160, 230, 234, 243, 246–247, 272
housing crisis, 73–76
housing disputes, 92, 93
housing laws, 75, 76

illegal searches, 44–45, 50, 199
inflation, 77–78
Interdistrict Conference of Soviets. *See* district soviets
interdistrict conference of workers' militia. *See* workers' militia
Iurevich, Vadim A., 94, 117, 123, 129, 132, 136, 222
Ivanov, N. V., Bolshevik commissar, 145–146
Ivanov, N. V., chief of city militia, 149, 158–159, 230, 233

Journal of Events, 48, 58, 148
July Days, 21, 49–50, 64–66, 70, 81, 84, 96, 103, 147–149, 170
June demonstration, 85
justice of the peace, 61, 86, 90, 248, 294n48

Kadets, 79, 194–195, 205, 234, 237, 239
Kalinin, Mikhail I., 235, 242

Kanatchikov, Semen, 114

Karaulov, Mikhail A., 45–46

Kazanskii District, 24, 57, 99–100, 142, 143, 234

Kelson, Zigfrid, 43, 118, 127, 128, 130, 132–133, 158

Kerenskii, Alexander F., 26, 44, 65, 80, 83, 86, 96, 164, 193; death penalty and, 80–81, 253; lenient treatment of criminals and, 80–81, 240; temporary court and, 88, 92

Kirpichnikov, Arkadii A., 99, 247

Kokoshkin, Fedor E., 205, 293n27

Kolomenskii District, 24, 59, 100, 143

Kolonitskii, Boris I., 43, 178

Komendatura (Red Guards). See Central Komendatura

komendatura (workers' militia), 163

Kornilof Affair, 65, 70, 96, 162–163

Kresty Prison. See prisons

Krylenko, N. V., 254

Kryzhanovskii, Dmitrii A., 118–119, 123–124, 128–129, 132, 137–138, 141, 149, 178, 237

Kshesinskaia villa, 82–84, 175

Kulero murder, 38

language, 5, 178, 263

law, 67, 68, 79, 80, 81, 263, 267

Le Bon, Gustave, 168, 185, 187–189, 309n51

legal statutes of 1864, 79, 80, 87, 248, 251

legitimacy, 14, 270

Lenin, Vladimir I., 66, 81–83, 189–191, 193, 211, 233, 239, 245–246, 257; alcohol pogroms and, 239; anarchists and, 211; Cheka and, 245, 246; on city duma, 233; on crime, 257; on death penalty, 253; failure of Utopian vision of, 256; July Days and, 65; on law, 229, 249; on militia, 256; on Revolutionary Tribunal, 253; Shingarev-Kokoshkin murder and, 205–206

Lesnoi District, 24, 53, 54, 143–144, 183, 249

Ligovka, 21, 180, 223,

Liteinyi District, 24, 142

Lower Investigating Commission, 47

lumpen proletariat, 11, 180

Lunacharskii, Anatolii, I, 216, 217, 221

Lvov, Georgii E., 80, 96, 240

Manushkin, V. V., 88

Maps: map 1, Petrograd 1917, 19; map 2, administrative districts of, 22

Marquis del Torreta, 202

McAuley, Mary, 228, 250

mechanical solidarity, 13, 185–186, 264, 266. See also Durkheim, Emile; theory of anomie

Mensheviks, 70, 121, 127, 150, 194, 234, 235

Merton, Robert, 13, 267–268. See also theory of anomie

meshchane, 18, 180

Military Commission of the Duma Committee, 43, 45

Military Revolutionary Court, 222, 238, 239

militia, 2, 41, 109, 116; attacks on, 152–154; formation of, 119, 120, 121, 122–123, 124–125; instructions of, 127; recruitment for, 256, weapons and, 143. See also city militia; militiamen; police; workers' militia

militia law, 82, 147, 149–150, 150–151, 256

militiamen, 9, 38, 41, 50; attacks on, 57, 99, 103, 153–155; attempts at centralization and, 131, 137–138, 140; under Bolsheviks, 196, 231, 232, 236, 237, 257, 259; July Days and, 149–150; mob justice and, 170, 171, 173, 174, 175, 176, 178, 181, 183; raid of narcotic rings of, 62–63; review commission's report on, 141, 142–147; trade union of, 151, 157, 158; transgressions of, 133–136, 152; uniform and weapons of, 155–156; in Vasilievskii District, 122–124;. See also city militia; militia

Miliukov, Pavel N., 39, 79, 124
minister of internal affairs, 80, 110,
     117, 150
ministry of internal affairs, 129, 131,
     136, 141
mobilization riots, 29–30, 168
mob justice (*samosudy*), 1, 11, 46;
     abolition of temporary courts and,
     93; Bolsheviks and, 3, 110, 189, 197,
     199–201, 206–208, 226, 241–242,
     245, 264; criticisms of, 182–183,
     208–211; empowerment of crowd
     by, 263, 269; geographic breakdown
     of, 98, 180–181, 308n37; motives of,
     170, 174, 175, 263; numbers of,
     169–170, 206; participants in,
     177–183, 263; as phenomenon of
     revolution, 2, 66, 161, 166, 167, 168,
     263, 275; psychology of, 9, 16,
     180–189, 269; targets of, 145, 153,
     170, 171, 172, 173–176, 177;
     ultimatum of criminals against,
     172–173; village communes and,
     189
moderate socialists, 66, 70, 83, 151, 162,
     164
Moskovskii District, 24, 63, 142
mounted militia, 135, 155, 159, 172,
     175
mounted police, 115, 303n97
municipal police, 116, 119, 122,
     132–133, 160, 232, 261. *See also* city
     militia; militia
murders, 29, 37, 38–39, 40, 52–54, 161,
     204, 205, 207
Musaev, Vadim I., 226, 257

narcotics, 9, 62–64, 104, 161
Narsky, N., and Yulia Y. Khmelevkaya,
     214
Narvskii District, 24, 93, 143, 144, 149,
     150, 153, 154–155
Nashatyr, M. G., 138
Nevskii District, 161
Nevskii Prospect, 20, 37, 40, 60, 64, 263
Nicholas II, 1, 18, 25, 26, 27, 82

night shelters, 61, 242
Nikoklaevskii Railway Station, 21, 49,
     62, 155, 180
Nikolaev, Andrei B., 93, 114
nizy. See poor
Novaia Derevnia, 104, 161, 249,

Okhta (Okhtenskii) District, 144
Olikhov, P., 160
ordinary people, 2, 9, 10, 66, 69, 86, 110
organic solidarity, 13, 185, 266. *See also*
     Durkheim, Emile; Merton, Robert;
     theory of anomie
Order No. 1, of Karaulov, 45
Order No. 1, of Petrograd Military
     District, 240–241
Order No. 25, Ivanov's, 149
Orlovsky, Daniel, 179
Ostroumov, S. S., 274

Penter, Tanja, 178
people's commissariat of internal affairs,
     245, 255, 256,
people's commissariat of justice, 255
people's court, 86, 207, 249–250, 252
Peshekhonov, Aleksei V., 119, 124–125
Peski, 63, 96–99, 104, 180
Petergofskii District, 150, 164, 250
Petersburg Committee, 82
Petrograd, 2, 15, 24; map 1, Petrograd
     1917, 19; map 2, administrative
     districts of, 22
Petrograd Military District, 149, 158,
     194
Petrograd Military Revolutionary
     Committee. *See* VRK
Petrogradskii District, 119, 144–145,
     155, 250
Petrograd Soviet of Workers' and Soldiers'
     Deputies, 26, 45, 46, 66, 67, 69;
     alcohol pogroms and, 224, 238–239,
     240; anarchists and, 84; city militia
     and, 118, 124, 126–128, 148, 237, 246;
     Red Guards and, 255; temporary
     courts and, 88; VRK and, 238
Petrov family murder, 53–54, 104

Piatiev, V. P., 127
pickpockets, 1, 29, 35, 49, 106
Pipes, Richard, 257–258
polarizations, 25, 268
police, 2, 8, 15; centralization, 256–227; three concepts of, 116–118
police, tsarist, 8, 28, 29, 64, 69–71, 110–115, 262; destruction of, 41; February Revolution and, 115–116; modernization of, 113. *See also* Criminal Police
Polkovnikov, Georgii P., 58, 159, 222
Pomeranz, William, 251
poor (*nizy*), 21, 25. *See also* polarizations
primitization, 185, 264
prisons, 9, 41, 42, 66, 42, 95–96
privileged (*verkhi*), 20, 25. *See also* polarizations
prostitutes, 9, 41, 60–61, 66
Provisional Government, 2, 4, 8, 9, 26, 67, 69, 193; city duma and, 128–133; crime and, 67, 137; death penalty and, 80, 81, 82; July Days and, 65; law and, 68, 251, 261, 293n27; legitimacy of, 78–79, 166, 260; police and, 15, 41, 81, 109, 117, 118, 131, 148, 149–152; State Duma and, 78; temporary courts and, 86, 92
public health, 9, 66, 105, 242, 244–245

ration system, 71
Ravich, M. S., 90
Red Guards, 8, 84, 104, 195, 229; alcohol pogroms and, 219, 223, 224, 225–226, 229, 238, 239, 256; anarchist tendencies in, 213, 256; city militia and, 230–231, 233, 234, 236, 237; consolidation of, 16, 140, 166; July Days and, 148, 161–162; Kornilov Affair and, 162–165; as law enforcement agents, 203–204; loyalty of, 254–255; maintenance of public order by, 155, 163, 262, 246, 272; mob justice and, 207–208; Order No. 1, of Petrograd Military District and, 240–241, 242; organization of, 162, 164; raid of courts of justice by, 252–253; reduced number of, 254; review commission report on, 144, 146; street muggings by, 202, 256
Re-Mi, 153
Remizov, Nikolai Vladimirovich, 153
review commission report, 141–147, 151
revolutionary conscience, 251, 252
Revolutionary Tribunal, 252, 253–254, 318n32
R—g, M., 198–199
robberies, 5, 34, 50–51, 161, 199, 200, 202–203
Rodin, D. P., 35
Rogovskii, E. F., 150
Rotberg, Robert, 272
Rozenbakh, Pavel Ia., 107, 202, 205
Rozhdestvenskii District, 24, 63, 144
Russian Revolution, 2, 4, 12, 18, 69, 140, 260, 262, 264; as case study for transition from authoritarianism, 11, 15; in comparative revolutions, 12; historiography of, 4–7; theory of anomie and, 266–269; theory of failed state and, 270–272; violence in, 276–277
Rykov, Aleksei I, 230

Sadovaia Street, 20, 21, 23, 60
samosudy. See mob justice
Sanborn, Joshua, 31, 273
sanitary conditions, 92, 93
Seitola murder, 53, 58
Senate. *See* Governing Senate
Sennaia Market, 21, 60, 173–174, 180, 206
servants, 74–75
Sharikov, deputy commissar, 173–174
Shatov, Vladimir S., 211
Shchepkin, Dmitrii M., 149
Shebuev, N., 198
Shingarev–Kokoshkin murder, 205–206
Shlosberg murder, 37
Shreider, G. I., 233, 234
Shrippen, Baron G. E. von, 34, 39

Shteinberg, Isaak Z., 211, 245, 248, 252, 253

sluzhashchie, 18, 179

snow removal, 242, 243

social breakdown, 66–67, 105, 275

Socialist Revolutionaries (SRs), 69, 121, 194, 234, 235, 245, 317n20, 317n22

social structure, 13, 267–268. *See also* Merton, Robert; theory of anomie

soldiers, 69, 84, 124, 125, 138, 139, 178, 263; alcohol pogroms and, 59, 216–220, 223–226, 275; brutalization of war and, 273; as criminals, 37, 40, 43–45, 51, 96–100, 108, 154, 201, 203, 205; in February Revolution, 26, 75, 79; as judges of temporary courts, 88, 90, 91, 93; militia duty and, 144, 158–159, 160, 204; mobilization riots and, 29–30; mob justice and, 172, 174–177, 181–182, 208; number of, 20; as prison wardens, 95

Sologub, Fedor, 227, 264

Sorokin, Pitirim, 217

Sovnarkom (Council of People's Commissars), 193, 195, 255; alcohol pogroms and, 222, 238, 239; city duma and, 233, 235; Cheka and, 245; Decree on the Court and, 251–254

Spasskii District, 24, 61, 142, 143, 155, 170, 171, 173, 174, 250

Startsev, V. I., 128

state, 9, 14, 25, 110, 270–271

state consciousness (*gosudarstvennost*), 141, 146, 149, 151

state-driven police, 15, 117, 118, 130, 132, 141, 149, 261; Bolsheviks and, 256–257, 265. *See also* police

Steinberg, Mark, 11, 272–273

Steklov, Iurii M., 126

Stepun, Fedor, 273

St. Petersburg, 17, 18, 20. *See also* Petrograd

street mugging, 201–203, 255

Stuchka, Petr I, 202, 253

subdistrict autonomy, 8, 41, 120, 122–123, 127, 132, 152, 165, 231–232; in Kolomenskii District, 122; people's courts and, 249–250; in Vasilievskii District, 122–123. *See also* decentralization

Suny, Ronald Grigor, 6

Sviatolovskii, Vladimir V., 129–130

syphilis, 61

temporary courts (*vremmenye sudy*), 86–92, 93, 249, 250, 263

thefts, 33–34, 38, 48, 49, 261

theory of anomie, 14, 185–187, 266–269, 275. *See also* Durkheim, Emile; Merton, Robert

theory of failed state, 12, 14, 270–272

Tomskii, O., 208–209, 220–221, 227

transition from authoritarianism to democracy, 265–266

transportation, 9, 105–106, 242, 243–244

Trifonov, Valentin, 161, 236–237

Trotsky, Leon, 65, 66, 253

Tsiretelli, Irakli, 70, 150. *See also* militia law

unions, 76

urban poor, 10, 11, 179–180, 226, 263, 275

Uritskii, Moisei S., 202

Urusov, Sergei D., 129

Valua murder, 201–202, 205

Vasilievskii District, 123–124, 145, 146, 154, 231–232

violence, 273–274, 276–277

VRK (Voenno-revoliutsionnyi komitet, Military Revolutionary Committee), 193–194, 200, 211, 238, 245, 246, 255; alcohol pogroms and, 216, 217, 218, 238; city militia and, 230, 233, 236; Investigating Commission of, 238, 247, 250

Vyborgskii District, 23, 26, 42, 120, 144, 145–146, 149, 231, 249

Wade, Rex, 4, 148, 162, 194
wages, 76–78
water supply, 9, 105, 242
weapons, 41, 43, 66, 148, 149, 261
Weber, Max, 14, 270
well-ordered police state, 116, 119
Williams, Albert Rys, 78, 197
workers' militia, 8, 9, 15, 109, 118–122,
    127–128, 137, 194, 272; city militia
    and, 123, 126, 127, 128, 150;
    interdistrict conference of, 119,
    138–139, 142, 146; July Days and,

148–149, 150, 161–162; Korniolov
Affair and, 162–165; Red Guards
and, 164–165; review commission's
report on, 144–145; weapons and,
148, 149
World War I, 5, 12, 18, 25, 26, 29,
273–274

Zhelezniakov, Anatolii G., 211
Zhivotovskii, Abram L, 34, 39
Zhizhilenko, Aleksandr A., 95
Zhuk, Iustin, 161, 211